AF726258

Oxford Studies in European Law

General Editors: Paul Craig and Graínne de Búrca

THE LEGAL EFFECTS OF EU AGREEMENTS

Oxford Studies in European Law

Series Editors: Paul Craig, Professor of English Law at St John's College, Oxford and Gráinne de Búrca, Professor of Law at New York University School of Law

---

The aim of this series is to publish important and original research on EU law. The focus is on scholarly monographs, with a particular emphasis on those which are interdisciplinary in nature. Edited collections of essays will also be included where they are appropriate. The series is wide in scope and aims to cover studies of particular areas of substantive and of institutional law, historical works, theoretical studies, and analyses of current debates, as well as questions of perennial interest such as the relationship between national and EU law and the novel forms of governance emerging in and beyond Europe. The fact that many of the works are interdisciplinary will make the series of interest to all those concerned with the governance and operation of the EU.

European Law and New Health Technologies
Edited by Mark L Flear, Anne-Maree Farrell, Tamara K Hervey, and Thérèse Murphy

The Enforcement of EU Law
The Role of the European Commission
Stine Andersen

European Agencies
Law and Practice of Accountability
Madalina Busuioc

The Foundations of European Union Competition Law
The Objective and Principles of Article 102
Renato Nazzini

The Emergence of EU Contract Law
Exploring Europeanization
Lucinda Miller

Participation in EU Rule-making
A Rights-Based Approach
Joana Mendes

Regulating Cartels in Europe
Second Edition
Christopher Harding, Julian Joshua

Religion and the Public Order of the European Union
Ronan McCrea

Governing Social Inclusion
Europeanization through Policy Coordination
Kenneth A. Armstrong

Judicial Control in the European Union
Reforming Jurisdiction in the Intergovernmental Pillars
Alicia Hinarejos

EU Counter-Terrorist Policies and Fundamental Rights
The Case of Individual Sanctions
Christina Eckes

From Dual to Cooperative Federalism
The Changing Structure of European Law
Robert Schütze

Conflicts of Rights in the European Union
A Theory of Supranational Adjudication
Aida Torres Pérez

The Legal Effects of EU Agreements

Maximalist Treaty Enforcement and Judicial Avoidance Techniques

MARIO MENDEZ

OXFORD
UNIVERSITY PRESS

OXFORD
UNIVERSITY PRESS

Great Clarendon Street, Oxford, OX2 6DP,
United Kingdom

Oxford University Press is a department of the University of Oxford.
It furthers the University's objective of excellence in research, scholarship,
and education by publishing worldwide. Oxford is a registered trade mark of
Oxford University Press in the UK and in certain other countries

© M. Mendez, 2013

The moral rights of the author have been asserted

First Edition published in 2013

All rights reserved. No part of this publication may be reproduced, stored in a retrieval system, or transmitted, in any form or by any means, without the prior permission in writing of Oxford University Press, or as expressly permitted by law, by licence or under terms agreed with the appropriate reprographics rights organization. Enquiries concerning reproduction outside the scope of the above should be sent to the Rights Department, Oxford University Press, at the address above

You must not circulate this work in any other form
and you must impose this same condition on any acquirer

Crown copyright material is reproduced under Class Licence
Number C01P0000148 with the permission of OPSI
and the Queen's Printer for Scotland

Published in the United States of America by Oxford University Press
198 Madison Avenue, New York, NY 10016, United States of America

British Library Cataloguing in Publication Data
Data available

Library of Congress Cataloging in Publication Data
Data available

ISBN 978–0–19–960661–0

Links to third party websites are provided by Oxford in good faith and for information only. Oxford disclaims any responsibility for the materials contained in any third party website referenced in this work.

Para mis padres

PREFACE

Mario Mendez has written an engaging and informative account of the legal effect accorded by the European Court of Justice to international agreements concluded by the EU.

Certain aspects of this subject have attracted a great deal of attention from both scholars and practitioners over the years, such as the legal effects of the GATT and WTO agreements in EU law. Mendez's book however tackles the broader subject of the legal effects accorded by the Court to all manner of EU-concluded agreements, and places the GATT/WTO case law in this wider context.

The book begins, after reflecting on the importance of treaties as a source of law today, with a context-setting discussion of the ways in which domestic courts have generally treated the legal effect of international agreements. Eschewing the familiar but often confusing terminology of monism and dualism, Mendez identifies two broad judicial approaches to international treaties which he terms automatic incorporation, and non-automatic incorporation. He then looks at the foundational cases in which the Court of Justice articulated its approach to the legal effect of international agreements.

He moves on in the core three chapters of the book to identify the approach which the Court has taken to international agreements in three broad fields: those of (a) association, cooperation, partnership, and trade agreements (b) the GATT/WTO agreements, and (c) other non-trade agreements. What emerges is a picture of a variegated set of strategies on the part of the Court: using an automatic incorporation (and 'maximal enforcement') approach in some circumstances, and techniques for judicial avoidance in others. The crucial distinction, it emerges, between the cases in which the Court adopts a maximalist enforcement approach, and those in which it uses techniques of judicial avoidance, is whether or not the case involves a challenge to Member State action as compared with EU action.

Mendez has written a valuable book, based on a substantial data set of European Court case law, which includes thorough discussion and appraisal of the case law of the Court of Justice in this important field. In additional to marshalling and analyzing this useful empirical body of case law, the book provides a deft and authoritative evaluation and critique of the Court's approach to international treaties over the years.

This book should be of interest to students, scholars, and practitioners of EU law alike, and to all of those interested in this aspect of the European Court's contribution to the EU's emergence as a global actor.

Paul Craig
Gráinne de Búrca

ACKNOWLEDGEMENTS

This book is a revised version of a PhD thesis defended at the European University Institute in 2009. I am immensely grateful to my doctoral supervisor, Gráinne de Búrca, for her considerable input into this project and her support over the years. I am also grateful, for offering valuable insights in relation to aspects of this work, to the following: Kenneth Armstrong, Marise Cremona, Bruno de Witte, Piet Eeckhout, Robert Howse, Christian Joerges, Pieter-Jan Kuijper, Marc Maresceau, Valsamis Mitsilegas, Ernst-Ulrich Petersmann, and the late Eric Stein (I will long remember being driven through snowy Ann Arbor by a man already into his tenth decade when going for a farewell drink as I finished a period as a visiting researcher at the Law School of the University of Michigan). In addition, a number of current and former officials of the various EU institutions gave generously of their time some years ago to discuss various aspects of this work. I am also grateful for the constructive feedback from the OUP reviewers and to OUP more generally for their professionalism as well as their patience—Natasha Flemming in particular—as changes to the manuscript took longer to implement than I had anticipated.

I am very grateful to my friends and colleagues at Queen Mary, University of London. The School of Law has been an excellent place to work and accorded me the space to complete the PhD and research leave to convert it into this book. My biggest debt of gratitude is owed to Virginie Barral who, as well as having read and commented on every chapter, has discussed issues pertaining to this book with me over more years than she or I would care to remember. Both she and our young son have also lived with this project for some time and will perhaps be nearly as pleased as I am that it has finally been completed.

CONTENTS

LIST OF ABBREVIATIONS

ACHR	American Convention on Human Rights
ACP	African, Caribbean, and Pacific
ADA	Anti-Dumping Agreement
ADC	Anti-Dumping Code
ADR	Anti-Dumping Regulation
BHA	Blair House Agreement
CBD	Convention on Biological Diversity
CEDAW	Convention on the Elimination of All Forms of Discrimination against Women
CESCR	Committee on Economic, Social and Cultural Rights
CFSP	Common Foreign and Security Policy
DSB	Dispute Settlement Body
DSU	Dispute Settlement Understanding
EA	Europe Agreement
EAEC	European Atomic Energy Community
ECHR	European Convention on Human Rights
ECSC	European Coal and Steel Community
ECtHR	European Court of Human Rights
EEAA	European Economic Area Agreement
EEC	European Economic Community
EFTA	European Free Trade Association
EIA	Environmental Impact Assessment
GATS	General Agreement on Trade in Services
GATT	General Agreement on Tariffs and Trade
GC	General Court
HRC	Human Rights Committee
IACtHR	Inter-American Court of Human Rights
ICC	International Criminal Court
ICCPR	International Covenant on Civil and Political Rights
ICERD	International Convention on the Elimination of All Forms of Racial Discrimination
ICESCR	International Covenant on Economic, Social and Cultural Rights
ICJ	International Court of Justice
IDA	International Dairy Arrangement
ILO	International Labour Organisation
IMO	International Maritime Organization

ITA	Information Technology Agreement
MARPOL	International Convention for the Prevention of Pollution from Ships
MEA	Multilateral environmental agreements
MEQR	measure having equivalent effect to quantitative restrictions
OHIM	Office for Harmonization in the Internal Market
PCA	Partnership and Cooperation Agreement
PCIJ	Permanent Court of International Justice
PNR	Passenger Name Records
QR	quantitative restriction
RPT	reasonable period of time
SPS Agreement	Agreement on the Application of Sanitary and Phytosanitary Measures
TBT Agreement	Agreement on Technical Barriers to Trade
TEU	Treaty on European Union
TFEU	Treaty on the Functioning of the European Union
TRIPs Agreement	Agreement on Trade-Related Aspects of Intellectual Property Rights
UNCLOS	UN Convention on the Law of the Sea
VCLT	Vienna Convention on the Law of Treaties
VER	voluntary export restraint
WTO	World Trade Organization

INTRODUCTION

The use of treaties as a mechanism for governing an increasingly interdependent world has grown exponentially in the last century. To give a sense of this explosion in treaty-making activity it is revealing to consider statistics published in France—a medium-sized country that is one of the founding Member States.[1] Since the 1990s France has been negotiating roughly 200 bilateral treaties a year which is equivalent to 2.5 times the annual number of treaties negotiated during the 1950s. The 1950's rate of 80 treaties a year constituted over five times the number being negotiated during the interwar years (roughly 14 treaties per year) and the interwar years themselves constituted a significant expansion on the four treaties a year that were being negotiated during the period dating from 1881–1918. And as of 2005, France was bound by over 7,400 treaties.[2] However, such crude statistics, in and of themselves, reveal very little as to the significance of the expanding remit of treaty law. At the turn of the century, treaty-making was dominated by very few areas, most prominently peace treaties, maritime boundary treaties, and friendship, commerce, and navigation treaties. Today treaties have come to regulate all manner of affairs that would previously have been left to the internal regulation of the State and, indeed, but for the rise of the multilateral treaty we would be unlikely to have witnessed the constraining effect of the law brought to bear in many important areas. Thus, today we can point to large numbers of treaties in areas as diverse as: banking and finance; consumer protection; criminal law; data exchange; environmental protection;[3] human rights; immigration; investment; nuclear proliferation; regulation of the internet; transport; taxation, etc. This profound transformation in the remit of international treaty law was given particularly eloquent expression by Philip Allott:

[1] Conseil d'État (2006).

[2] The fact that France is a member of the EU and that much of its interstate cooperation and regulation within the EU will take place employing the law-making output of the EU, results in a significantly reduced number of treaties than one would expect to take place for any EU Member State were the EU not to exist.

[3] A study published in 2006 noted that of the more than 500 extant environmental treaties, over 60 per cent had been concluded since the early 1970s: see Conseil d'État (2006).

the national executive branches of government come together to regulate collectively every area in which the function of government extends beyond national frontiers and where the activities of governments overlap. The acceleration and intensification of international inter-government, as we may call it, means that there are now, in effect, two forms of international law. Old international law is the modest self-limiting of the potentially conflictual behavior of governments in relation to each other, as they recognise the emergence of new 'states', settle the limits of each other's land and sea territory and the limits of their respective national legal systems, resolve disputes and disagreements which may arise in their everyday 'relations'. New international law is universal legislation.[4]

We can expect this trend of growing recourse to treaties to continue unabated and the legal effect of this immensely significant and growing body of law becomes increasingly important. It is primarily the executive and legislative branches that are best placed to ensure that the treaty commitments to which the State voluntarily commits are respected domestically. Courts, however, have an increasingly important role to play in giving effect to this form of 'universal legislation' (to use Allott's terminology). First and foremost because a substantial portion of this international law-making is likely to find itself transposed into domestic legal norms on which national courts are then called upon to adjudicate. But even where this is not so, courts in most legal systems will find themselves faced with litigants invoking treaty law in support of their claims. Indeed, the EU itself provides an important example. It is through such a process tied to the preliminary reference procedure that the European Court of Justice (ECJ) was able to pronounce on the legal effect of EU norms and that gave rise to the earliest manifestation of the constitutionalization of EU law, whereby EU measures were hardened into supreme, and frequently directly effective, law.[5] This book touches upon a different dimension of this 'constitutionalization' debate, that concerns the legal status accorded to EU Agreements as refracted through the lens of EU law, which is rarely given explicit consideration, but nonetheless deserves incorporation within the conventional account that Weiler and others were so instrumental in framing.

The EU was only born with express treaty-making powers for tariff agreements, trade agreements, and the so-called Association Agreements.[6] Those express powers were, however, quickly and increasingly put to

[4] Allott (2001). [5] Weiler (1991) esp at 2430.
[6] Respectively the old Arts 111(2), 113, and 238 EEC.

significant use. By the early 1960s the EU had already become a party to Association Agreements with Greece, Turkey, and a collection of 18 (recently independent) African and Malagasy States (Yaoundé I),[7] by the late 1960s the growing web of Association Agreements had expanded to include Tanzania, Uganda, and Kenya (via the Arusha Convention) and Morocco and Tunisia;[8] by the early 1970s it had become a party to a significant batch of largely identical bilateral trade agreements with seven of the European Free Trade Association States,[9] and by the mid-1970s a successor to a second Yaoundé Convention had 46 African, Caribbean, and Pacific States as parties (Lomé I).[10] Today few parts of the world remain unconnected to the EU by some form of bilateral or regional trade-related agreement.

Whilst the EU may have been born with the barest of express treaty-making powers, this was famously and radically supplemented by the creation of implied treaty-making powers that was articulated in the 1971 *ERTA* ruling.[11] The 'masters of the treaties', for their part, gradually expanded the express treaty-making competence at successive treaty reforms. In its more than half a century existence, the EU—and its predecessors[12]—has become a party, whether alone, or in unison with one or more of its Member States (mixed agreements),[13] to well over 1,000 treaties at a gradually accelerating

[7] For Yaoundé I, see [1964] OJ 93/1431, for the Greek and Turkish Agreements see respectively [1963] OJ L293/63 and [1964] 217 OJ 3687.

[8] For the Arusha Convention see [1970] OJ L282/55, for the Morocco and Tunisia Agreements see respectively [1969] OJ L197/3 and [1969] OJ L198/3.

[9] Austria ([1972] OJ L300/1), Sweden ([1972] OJ L300/96) Switzerland ([1972] OJ L300/188); Iceland ([1972] OJ L301/1); Portugal ([1972] OJ L301/164); Norway ([1973] OJ L171/1); Finland ([1973] OJ L328/1).

[10] [1976] OJ L25/1.

[11] 22/70 *Commission v Council* [1971] ECR 263.

[12] ie treaties concluded by the European Economic Community (EEC), European Community (EC), European Coal and Steel Community (ECSC), European Atomic Energy Community (EAEC), and the EU.

[13] Mixed agreements are agreements to which both the EU and one or more Member States is a Contracting Party. The original EC Treaty, unlike the Euratom Treaty (Art 102), did not expressly sanction mixity nevertheless mixed agreements quickly emerged as a substantial component of its treaty-making practice, and in fact the very first Association Agreement (with Greece) from the early 1960s was a mixed agreement. The legal justification for this practice, as Eeckhout (2011: 212–13) noted, 'is that parts of the agreement do not come within the EU's competence, and that conclusion of the agreement therefore requires joint action by the EU and its Member States, the latter complementing ... the otherwise insufficient powers of the EU.' The political reality is that Member States, and often other Contracting Parties, see considerable benefit in recourse to mixed agreements: see Rosas (2010), Lenaerts and Van Nuffel (2011: 1037).

rate in line with its expanding competences.[14] The European External Action Service treaties office database lists the following areas of treaty-making activity (a number of which break up into further sub-activities): Agriculture; Coal and Steel; Commercial Policy; Competition; Consumers; Culture; Customs; Development; Economic and Monetary Affairs; Education, Training, Youth; Energy; Enlargement; Enterprise; Environment; External Relations; Fisheries; Food Safety; Foreign and Security Policy; Fraud; Information Society; Internal Market; Justice, freedom and security; Public Health; Research and Innovation; Taxation; Trade; Transport. None of these categories can, however, comfortably house the EU's first human rights treaty, it having recently become a party to the UN Convention on the Rights of Persons with Disabilities.[15] In sum, the extent of the EU's external treaty-making competence (and practice) has come a strikingly long way.

As with a domestic legal system, a portion of the treaties (or at least parts thereof) to which the EU becomes party will be legislatively implemented. There is thus a large body of EU legislation seeking to implement EU—and indeed non-EU[16]—Agreements (or parts thereof). This is particularly apparent with respect to EU-concluded environmental agreements.[17] To give a recent example, parts of the agreement popularly known as the Aarhus Convention, to which the EU became a party in 2005, have been implemented via EU legislative measures.[18] The result is that the full EU

[14] The Treaties Office database figures at the beginning of 2012 had the EU as a party to over 900 treaties, with more than 100 additional treaties not yet in force: see <http://ec.europa.eu/world/agreements/default.home.do>.

[15] [2010] OJ L23/35 (27.1.2010). Following the ratification of the Lisbon Treaty with its provision stipulating that the EU shall accede to the European Convention on Human Rights (ECHR) (Art 6(2) Treaty on European Union (TEU)), negotiations have been proceeding to make this a reality.

[16] The sphere of maritime policy provides a good example for the EU is not, nor can it currently become, a member of the International Maritime Organization (IMO) nor, accordingly, can it become a party to the 30-plus IMO Conventions that regulate international maritime transport and safety. Nevertheless, there is EU secondary legislation that effectively implements IMO Conventions (including conventions that were not yet in force) and Resolutions (see generally Jenisch 2006).

[17] The EU has become a party to a host of multilateral environmental agreements such as the UN Convention on the Law of the Sea; the UN Framework Convention on Climate Change and the Kyoto Protocol to that Convention; the Vienna Convention for the Protection of the Ozone Layer.

[18] The full title is the Convention on Access to Information, Public Participation in Decision-Making and Access to Justice in Environmental Matters. The relevant EU measures are Directive 2003/4/EC (public access to environmental information) and Directive 2003/35/EC (public participation) and Regulation 1367/2006 (with respect to the application of the Aarhus Convention provisions to EU institutions and bodies).

law enforcement armoury can be invoked for ensuring compliance with these EU legislative measures. This has in fact been the case with the Aarhus implementation measures as a string of Commission infringement proceedings have been brought to ensure compliance.[19] This can be viewed as a constitutionalization of international norms through their transformation into EU law provisions that are then endowed with those special hallmarks of EU law, supremacy and direct effect. This is unquestionably a very important dimension of the enhanced effect that can be accorded international agreements, whether concluded by the EU or not, which is worthy of closer analysis.[20] But this dimension of direct EU Agreement implementation and enforcement of such legislation is not explored in the present study for it does not usually raise the issue of the legal effects of the EU Agreements *stricto sensu*.[21] Indeed, the substantive provisions of the legislative measures, as is often the case in domestic legal systems, frequently do not even refer to the international agreement with which they are seeking to ensure compliance. Thus, the two EU Directives that effectively transpose obligations under the 1979 Convention on the Conservation of European Habitats and Species, to which the EU became a party in 1982, do not refer to the Convention at all.[22] Both Directives have been the subject of litigation before the European Courts but this usually turns on the legal effect and meaning of the specific provisions of the EU measures with the ECJ having rarely engaged with the Convention itself. There are important questions that arise as to why the Member States sometimes do, and sometimes do not, see fit to use the EU legislative process to take up EU Agreement norms in binding EU measures that will in principle be directly effective and supreme domestically. Nevertheless, once they

[19] For two recent examples where Member States failed to fulfil their obligations under the EU implementing legislation, see C-50/09 *Commission v Ireland*, Judgment of 3 March 2011, C-378/09 *Commission v Czech Republic* [2010] ECR I-78.

[20] It has received precious little attention in the literature. There is a monograph touching upon certain developments pertaining to decisions of international organizations to which the EU is, and is not, a party: Lavranos (2004).

[21] It is not wholly excluded in that some WTO Agreements considered in Chapter IV have been directly implemented which has given rise to relevant case law considered in that chapter; in addition, a legislative implementation measure can also be the subject of an EU Agreement-based challenge and one such case is considered in Chapter V.

[22] Directive 79/409/EEC on conservation of wild birds (which was adopted nearly six month before the Bern Convention though it was negotiated simultaneously) and Directive 92/43/EEC on the conservation of natural habitats and of wild fauna and flora which came ten years after the EU became a party to the Bern Convention.

exercise the option to employ such legislative instruments, the case law that emerges focuses on the secondary legislative measures themselves rather than the international norms that may lie behind them. In addition, also falling outside the remit of this study is the complexity to which the *inter se* legal effects of EU Agreements give rise.[23]

This study focuses instead on how EU Agreements themselves, rather than the legislative instruments implementing such Agreements, have been treated by the EU Courts in three main settings: as the basis for challenging either action at the Member State or EU level, or where in effect it is either the substance of the agreement or the procedure by which it was concluded that is being challenged. To this end, a data-set was developed that attempts to bring together these core strands of EU Agreement case law. The data-set contains some 337 cases, attached as an appendix, and forms the basis of the core empirical work conducted in this book.[24] This recourse to use of a data-set is intended as a response to a shortcoming in extant literature. Whilst there has been a general explosion in valuable work exploring the role of domestic courts in giving effect to international law,[25] which is only likely to grow given the expansion and changing remit of international law combined with the rise in domestic litigation, work of a more empirical bent is largely absent,[26] and even in places where one would expect attention to judicial practice it is to be found wanting.[27] The EU has been no exception to this broader trend, and few have sought to offer treatment of this terrain in a manner attentive to the breadth of judicial practice.[28]

The book is structured as follows. A first chapter explores the broader issue of the legal effects of treaties in domestic legal orders and the role of domestic courts in treaty enforcement. This is an attempt to offer a

[23] This issue has generated the important *MOX Plant* ruling (C-459/03 *Commission v Ireland* [2006] ECR I-4635), but it essentially concerns Member State compliance with internal EU law rather than with the EU Agreement itself.

[24] The appendix explains how the data-set was constructed. The cut-off point is 3 October 2011. A significant case since that cut-off point (C-366/10 *Air Transport Association of America v Secretary of State for Energy and Climate Change*, Judgment of 21 December 2011) is mentioned in a footnote to the concluding chapter.

[25] Recent examples include Nollkaemper (2011), Sloss (2009a), Benvenisti and Downs (2009), Benvenisti (2008).

[26] For valuable examples to the contrary in the US, see Sloss (2009c) and Wu (2007).

[27] Thus, some country reports in a recent edited collection on international law in domestic legal systems (Shelton (2011)) leave us little if not none the wiser as to domestic judicial practice (most starkly the chapter on the one Latin American State—Venezuela).

[28] The coverage in chs 8 and 9 of Eeckhout (2011) constitutes the most comprehensive and recent treatment of which the present author is aware.

different point of departure, and ideally a more context-sensitive approach, than is provided in much of the existing literature pertaining to the legal effects of EU (and indeed non-EU) Agreements in EU law. By articulating the core distinctions in the domestic constitutional approach to the legal status of treaties, and drawing upon the example of certain EU Member States to this end, this first chapter also provides the basis for articulating the constitutional significance of the ECJ's treatment of EU Agreements for the constitutional orders of its Member States. This latter issue, which remains insufficiently articulated in the existing literature, is teased out in Chapter II whilst exploring how the ECJ has responded to several foundational questions pertaining to the constitutional status and legal effects of EU Agreements in EU law. Chapters III, IV, and V then provide an assessment of the case law in the data-set divided into three core strands:[29] first, case law that can be classified as pertaining to the EU's Association, Cooperation, Partnership and Trade Agreements (excluding the General Agreement on Tariffs and Trade (GATT) and the World Trade Organization (WTO)), which has generated the bulk of the rulings in the data-set; secondly, case law pertaining to GATT and WTO Agreements which, although trade agreements, merit separate attention not least given that they have been on the receiving end of different judicial treatment than the agreements considered in Chapter III; thirdly, cases which pertain to what is categorized as simply non-trade agreements, insofar as they cannot be classified as pertaining to the agreements in either of the two preceding chapters, and which has generated a small, but gradually increasing, number of rulings. A concluding chapter brings together the findings from the preceding chapters. The extant case law provides some support for the existence of the emergence of a twin-track approach. The first exhibits the unleashing of a maximalist approach to treaty enforcement where it is action at the Member State level that is being challenged using EU Agreements in a manner that resembles the bold purposive treatment long accorded to internal EU law. In contrast the case law suggests that the ECJ has been willing to shield EU-level action from meaningful review. This trajectory has been built in accordance with the defensive submissions of the EU's political institutions and raises important questions about the EU's much-professed commitment to international law.

[29] With the exception of certain cases pertaining to ex post review of EU Agreements considered in Chapter II.

This work is intended to serve as further illustration that its subject matter is not to be reserved solely for the attention of that growing body of experts in EU external relations law (or international law scholars).[30] The relationship between international law and domestic law, and how the latter treats the former, is a central constitutional question in any legal order. Indeed, how to think about this relationship has been rightly referred to as 'one of the most pressing questions of contemporary constitutional law'.[31] Drawing on such logic, and as this book will also make apparent, the constitutional status and legal effects of EU Agreements in EU law is a crucial constitutional question for the EU, all the more so because in the federal-like system that is the EU how these issues are determined cannot but impact on the constitutional systems of all the Member States. In this sense, this work also aspires to be viewed as contributing to EU constitutional law.

Two final comments are in order. The first is that, as the title of this book itself would suggest, the legal effects in the EU legal order of agreements to which the EU is not a party are in principle excluded.[32] Were this study concerned with the legal order of a State there would be little need to proffer a justification for excluding international agreements that were not

[30] It is hoped that it might contribute to drawing to the attention of a broader international audience the significance of what has been taking place in the EU. It is surprising that even well into the twenty-first century edited collections exploring the legal effects in domestic legal orders of international law in general, and treaties specifically, have emerged without chapters on the EU. This is so for Hollis (2005) which contains 19 country reports, for Sloss (2009a) which contains 11 country reports (though the editor (Sloss 2009b: 16) mentions the issue very briefly in light of the Netherlands country report), and perhaps even more surprisingly in Shelton (2011) given that it contains 28 chapters nearly half of which cover EU Member States, including tiny Luxembourg. The obvious justification for exclusion may well be that the EU is not a State. A co-edited collection by a distinguished EU law scholar nearly 25 years earlier did include a chapter on the EU: Jacobs and Roberts (1987).

[31] Kumm (2006: 256–7).

[32] The principal exception is the now defunct 1947 General Agreement on Tariffs and Trade which was not concluded by the EU. There are two core reasons for its inclusion: first, its exclusion would have been anomalous given that the EU concluded international agreements within the GATT framework and these agreements were in fact at issue, as Chapter IV illustrates, in a majority of the GATT era case law, and a number of those cases involved the GATT 1947 itself thus making it impossible to disentangle this line of case law given that the judicial treatment accorded the GATT 1947 by the ECJ loomed large in the case law which involved GATT-concluded agreements; secondly, when the GATT metamorphosed into the WTO, the 1947 Agreement being rechristened GATT 1994, the EU was indeed a party and the ECJ's approach to the legal effects of GATT 1947 is an important aid to understanding the current stance.

concluded by the relevant State.[33] However, the EU is no ordinary international actor, for it is made up of sovereign States that were already bound by existing treaties when the EU came into being (or by the time they acceded) and continued to conclude their own treaties. The increasing EU litigation and debate to which pre-EU, pre-EU accession, and post-EU accession Member State treaties have given rise are clearly of immense importance and essential for a fuller picture of the judicial treatment accorded to international law,[34] indeed, in that respect as is consideration of the place of customary international law.[35] The non-EU concluded Agreement that dominated debate was traditionally the ECHR,[36] but more recently it has been the status of the UN Charter following the *Kadi*, and related, litigation involving the legal effect of UN Security Council Resolutions in the EU legal order.[37] While *Kadi* itself will be briefly considered in the concluding chapter, a boundary call was essentially made to opt for greater depth, manifested in particular by an empirically oriented focus, at the expense of the greater breadth that could be offered by exploring the broader judicial treatment of international law.

The second point is that this book employs the terminology of Union and the new post-Lisbon Treaty numbering generally throughout.[38] The terminology of Union rather than Community was of course particularly significant in the context of agreements concluded by either the then European Community or under the pre-Lisbon second and third pillar Union.[39] But as none of the case law explored in this book actually concerns

[33] Though even in this setting there have been controversies pertaining to judicial engagement with human rights treaties not ratified by the relevant State: see in relation to the US, Waters (2007).

[34] For a recent valuable monograph to that specific area, see Klabbers (2009).

[35] Casolari's monograph (2008) explores the much broader terrain of incorporation of international law in EU law, thus covering the pre-EU and post-EU Member State treaties and customary international law.

[36] The trials and tribulations of the relationship between the ECHR and the EU legal order generated jurisprudence at the level of both domestic courts and the Luxembourg and Strasbourg Courts: see Craig and de Búrca (2011: ch 7).

[37] C-402/05 P and C-415/05 P *Kadi and Al Barakaat v Council and Commission* [2008] ECR I-6351.

[38] Including where provisions have been replaced with some alteration such as the old duty of cooperation in Art 10 TEC, now Art 4(3) TEU.

[39] The basic position was that as a result of the old Art 46 TEU, combined with Arts 24 and 38 TEU, the ECJ had no jurisdiction to rule on the validity or interpretation of second and third pillar agreements: see Lenaerts and Van Nuffel (2011: 943–4), though for tentative suggestions to the contrary vis-à-vis third pillar or the third-pillar aspect of cross-pillar agreements, see Hillion

one of the old second or third pillar agreements, and as all the old first pillar Community agreements, have since become European Union Agreements, it was decided to employ the language of Union agreements even where the cases predate the entry into force of the Lisbon Treaty, rather than move backwards and forwards between different labels depending on when a judgment was handed down.

and Wessel (2008: 112–14). In contrast to the post-Lisbon concluded Agreements on Police and Judicial Cooperation, post-Lisbon Common Foreign and Security Policy (CFSP) Agreements will essentially continue to remain outwith the ECJ's jurisdiction as a result of Art 24(1) TEU and Art 275 Treaty on the Functioning of the European Union (TFEU), see Lenaerts and Van Nuffel (2011: 531).

I

The Legal Effects of Treaties in Domestic Legal Orders and the Role of Domestic Courts

1. Introduction

This chapter explores the general stance of international law and domestic legal orders on the issue of the legal effects of treaties in the domestic legal arena. It seeks to provide the basis for adopting a more contextual and comparative approach to the approach adopted in EU law to questions pertaining to the legal effects of EU Agreements. This is particularly appropriate because the EU itself is composed of States which have adopted their own diverging domestic constitutional approaches to such issues. In this fashion the impact of the EU law construct on domestic constitutional orders can be more persuasively articulated. It is also intended as a corrective to many existing accounts of the legal effects of EU (and indeed non-EU) Agreements which are largely acontextual—either simply looking at the approach of the EU alone or, where a comparative dimension is brought into the frame, perhaps not providing a nuanced recap of extant practice.

The chapter is divided into three core sections. The first addresses the requirements imposed by international law as to the legal effects to be accorded to treaties in domestic legal orders. The second looks at the basic dichotomy in approach at the domestic constitutional level to giving legal effect to treaties. The final section briefly revisits two opposing theoretical constructs used to conceptualize the legal effects accorded to international law (particularly as employed in the treaty setting) before offering some more general reflections pertaining to the role of domestic courts in treaty enforcement.

2. The Dictates of International Law

2.1 The basic precept

The core precept of the law of treaties is the principle of *pacta sunt servanda* enshrined in Article 26 of the Vienna Convention on the Law of Treaties and which states that: 'Every treaty in force is binding upon the parties to it and must be performed by them in good faith.'[1] But whilst treaties are to be performed in good faith, it remains the case that they are in principle no exception to the basic precept of international law that States are free to determine how they meet their international obligations.[2]

It is, indeed, rather striking that treaties do not as a general rule impose specific requirements as to how the substantive obligations that they lay out should be realized in the domestic legal orders of the Contracting Parties. There are several interlinked factors that have been adduced for this seemingly curious state of affairs. The core issue relates to the traditionally central tenet of international law, that of State sovereignty. As one scholar put it:

> States consider that the translation of international commands into domestic legal standards is part and parcel of their sovereignty and are unwilling to surrender it to international control.[3]

Accordingly States, in principle, are said to be concerned with whether compliance with the treaty obligations takes place and not with how this does or does not come about.[4] Related to this, is the fact that States have developed different approaches to seeking to ensure compliance with their treaty obligations which renders it all the less likely that treaties will expressly address themselves to how the obligations should be given effect internally.[5] In short, international law leaves it to the domestic legal order to determine how it gives effect to its treaty obligations in the domestic legal arena. In this respect a recent detailed assessment concluded that there

[1] On *pacta sunt servanda*, see Aust (2007: 179–81).

[2] On the basic rule, see Cassese (2005: 219); Jennings and Watts (1992: 82–3); Tomuschat (1999: 360); Tomuschat (2008: 110–11); Daillier, Forteau, and Pellet (2009: 251–2); Henkin (1995: 631).

[3] Cassese (2005: 220).

[4] Buergenthal (1992: 320); Cassese (2005: 218); Murphy (2009a: 70–1).

[5] For the core distinctions in approach see below.

is no general obligation under general international treaty law, customary international law, or general principles of international law requiring States to open their courts for invocation of treaty norms by individuals.[6] It is clear that however effect is to be given domestically to treaty obligations, a State cannot invoke its internal law as justification for a failure to perform.[7]

There are, however, exceptions to the basic rule in that in the case of some treaties States have sought to constrain this freedom of manoeuvre by stipulating some requirements as to how treaties, or specific provisions, are to be given effect in the domestic legal order. Thus, for example, treaties, and specific treaty provisions, can be drafted expressly to require the Contracting Parties to enact internal implementing legislation. An example of a treaty containing an express requirement for legislation to give effect to its provisions is the Genocide Convention (1948) (Art 5). The Geneva Conventions (1949), for their part, constitute examples of treaties containing specific provisions calling for implementing legislation.[8] And, indeed, in the general sphere of international criminal law it is evident that treaties have become increasingly exigent.[9] The UN Convention against Torture (1984), for example, contains a provision requiring each party to 'take effective legislative, administrative, judicial or other measures to prevent acts of torture in any territory under its jurisdiction' as well as a provision requiring the criminalization of certain acts.[10] Various human rights treaties also contain provisions stipulating that the Contracting Parties undertake to adopt legislative or other measures to give effect to the relevant rights where this is not already provided for in existing legislative or other measures.[11] In addition to this, there are examples of treaties—notably in areas such as friendship, commerce, and navigation, bilateral investment

[6] Murphy (2009a).

[7] A rule which now finds express articulation in Art 27 of the Vienna Convention on the Law of Treaties, see Shaw (2008: 133–7); Jennings and Watts (1992: 84); Aust (2007: 180–1); Brownlie (2008: 34–5).

[8] The four 1949 Geneva Conventions specifically require the Contracting Parties to enact any legislation necessary to provide effective penal sanctions for persons committing or ordering to be committed any of a series of grave breaches (respectively Arts 49, 50, 129, and 146 of the First, Second, Third, and Fourth Geneva Conventions). Examples of similar provisions, outside the human rights and humanitarian sphere, include Arts 27–9 of the 1958 Geneva Convention on the High Seas, Art 3(1) of the Aarhus Convention, Art 4(4) of the 1989 Basel Convention.

[9] See Denza (2010: 416).

[10] Respectively Arts 2(1) and 4(1).

[11] See eg Art 2(2) of the International Covenant on Civil and Political Rights (1966); Art 2 of the American Convention on Human Rights (1969). Contrast Art 2(1) of the International Covenant on Economic, Social and Cultural Rights.

treaties, as well as treaties pertaining to patents, copyrights, and trademarks—that expressly require access to local courts.[12]

2.2 Pronouncements of the World Court: from *Danzig* to *Avena*

Whilst it is recognized in international law that a treaty can require that it be directly applicable in domestic courts,[13] whether a particular treaty could indeed be relied on by individuals in a domestic court has only once been addressed by the Permanent Court of International Justice (PCIJ). At issue in the *Danzig Advisory Opinion*[14] was an international agreement between Poland and the Free City of Danzig, which concerned the transfer of Danzig railway officials into the service of the Polish Railways Administration (PRA) and regulated their employment conditions. Various actions against the PRA for pecuniary claims by railway officials who had passed into its service were then brought in the Danzig courts based on the Agreement. The Polish Treasury raised objections on the ground that the Danzig courts had no jurisdiction and Poland informed the High Commissioner of the League of Nations at Danzig that it would not comply with judgments based on the Agreement. This ultimately led to the Council of the League of Nations seeking an Advisory Opinion.

The PCIJ commenced by identifying the point in dispute as being whether the Agreement formed part of the series of provisions (the contract of service) governing the legal relationship between the PRA and the Danzig officials. The answer to this question was considered to depend on the intention of the parties. The Court asserted 'It may be readily admitted that, according to a well-established principle of international law... an international agreement, cannot, as such, create direct rights and obligations for private individuals.' However, the Court added, 'it cannot be disputed that the very object of an international agreement, according to the intention of the contracting Parties, may be the adoption

[12] See for these and other examples: Murphy (2009a: 87–96).

[13] See Buergenthal (1992: 320, 324); McNair (1961: 322); Mosler (1957: 631). See also Murphy (2009a: 96–7).

[14] *Jurisdiction of the Courts of Danzig Advisory Opinion* [1928] PCIJ, Ser B, No 15.

by the Parties of some definite rules creating individual rights and obligations and enforceable by the national courts.'[15]

But the Court seemed to cast doubt on the aforementioned assertion when it went on to find that the wording and the general tenor of the Agreement 'show that its provisions are directly applicable as between the officials and the [PRA]' and that its object was the creation of 'a special legal regime governing relations between the [PRA] and the Danzig officials'.[16] The Court seemed to be overlooking its earlier statements of treaties not being able to create direct rights and obligations for private individuals and it being the adoption of definite rules by the parties that creates the individual rights enforceable in national courts. This confusion appeared to be further cemented when it concluded that the provisions of the Agreement formed part of the contract of service and that the Danzig officials had a right of action against the PRA based on the Agreement. The Danzig courts did not appear to have any domestic legal difficulties in giving effect to the Agreement,[17] and this may explain the apparent dissonance in the reasoning of the PCIJ.[18]

Despite the aforementioned ambiguity in the reasoning, the Advisory Opinion has been considered as authority for the proposition that States can conclude treaties containing undertakings as to their domestic application and that they will be under an international obligation to ensure that the treaty is enforceable in the domestic courts.[19] And the *Danzig* Opinion affirmed that this can be so even absent an express undertaking to that effect, providing it can be deduced from the intention of the parties as evinced by the content of the agreement. It seemed that this would be a rare occurrence, the Court having underlined the special legal regime that the Agreement had created. Indeed, that Agreement was certainly unique in nature, concerning as it did the conditions of the transfer of employees into the service of the PRA and regulating their employment conditions.

[15] Ibid, 17–18.

[16] Buergenthal (1992: 323–4).

[17] As noted by Buergenthal (1992: 324).

[18] Lauterpacht saw the decision in a revolutionary light (1958: 173–6) whilst the extra-judicial observations of the then Court president emphasized that the Opinion did not say that the treaty itself could create rights and obligations for individuals without requiring that the rules be incorporated into domestic law: Anzilotti (1929).

[19] Buergenthal (1992: 324–5, 327).

Whilst the interwar years had already seen the emergence of treaties that did have the protection of the individual as their objective,[20] States were in principle not drafting treaties which one could realistically say were intended to create individual rights and obligations enforceable by national courts. And yet few could then have anticipated the transformation that was to take place in the subject matter of treaty-making in the post-Second World War era, particularly via the explosion in legally binding international and regional human rights treaties which had the protection of the individual as their leitmotif.[21] This is not to suggest that such treaties were drafted expressly to impose an international law obligation that they should be domestically judicially enforceable, but it nonetheless raised the possibility that where judicial organs and supervisory organs existed they might well reach such a finding following the path that the *Danzig* Advisory Opinion had opened up. Before turning to the pronouncements of such bodies, it is important briefly to note two rulings concerning the 1963 Vienna Convention on Consular Relations that are the closest the PCIJ's successor, the International Court of Justice (ICJ), appears to have come to engaging with the issue that arose in *Danzig*.[22] Here the US failure to give timely notification to foreign nationals of their right to consular protection was held to violate individual rights created by Article 36 of the 1963 Convention. The application of a US federal rule essentially precluding state criminal defendants from raising an issue in a federal appeal, in this context that they had not been notified of their right to consular assistance, that had not been raised in state courts also breached Article 36 of that Convention.[23] The first judgment (*LaGrand*) left the choice of means for review and reconsideration of convictions where faced with an alleged

[20] eg the 1919 Treaty Concerning the Protection of Minorities and the conventions that were beginning to be drafted under the auspices of the International Labour Organization (ILO).

[21] Amongst the most prominent examples at the international level have been the 1948 Genocide Convention, the four 1949 Geneva Conventions, the two 1966 Covenants (the International Covenant on Civil and Political Rights—ICCPR—and the International Covenant on Economic, Social and Cultural Rights—ICESCR), the 1965 Convention on the Elimination of Racial Discrimination, the 1984 Convention against Torture, and the 1989 Convention on the Rights of the Child; whilst at the regional level particularly prominent examples have been the 1950 ECHR and the 1969 American Convention on Human Rights (ACHR), both of which were later endowed with their own judicial organs.

[22] *LaGrand (Germany v United States of America)*, 2001 ICJ Rep 466; *Avena and Other Mexican Nationals (Mexico v United States of America)*, Judgment, 2004 ICJ Rep 12.

[23] A provision expressly requiring full effect to be given to the purposes for which the Art 36 rights were granted.

Article 36 violation to the US, but the second (*Avena*) made it clear that the review and reconsideration needed to be conducted by the US courts.[24] In sum, both the acknowledgement of treaty-created individual rights and the attempt to speak directly to the role of domestic courts with respect to those rights were novel contributions from the ICJ; however, they arose in the context of a single specific treaty provision which expressly referred to rights and concerned cases involving the death penalty and, accordingly, caution has rightly been emphasized in reading the cases too broadly.[25]

2.3 Pronouncements of other international courts and supervisory bodies

This section explores pronouncements from other international courts and supervisory bodies as to the legal effects of treaties. The sample is limited to the pronouncements of a range of regional human rights courts and human rights treaty supervisory organs on the assumption that, as they involve the very treaties that have the protection of the individual as their leitmotif, *Danzig*-type conclusions might have been forthcoming. In addition, this section addresses the paradigm-shifting approach evinced by the manner in which the ECJ interprets the treaties of which it is the authoritative interpreter.

2.3.1 *Examples from the sphere of human rights*

Regional human rights courts

When we turn to the most prominent of regional human rights instruments, the 1950 ECHR, we find that it provides no express stipulation as to how its substantive obligations are to be discharged. The presence, however, of two provisions has led to much controversy: the first being its Article 1 which provided that 'The high Contracting Parties shall secure to everyone within their jurisdiction the rights and freedoms defined in Section I of the Convention...'; and, the second, its Article 13 which provides that 'Everyone whose rights and freedoms as set out in this Convention are violated shall have an effective remedy before a national

[24] Murphy (2009a: 99–103).
[25] Murphy (2009a: 101–3).

authority ... '. These two provisions, as well as the precision of the ECHR articles and to an extent its *travaux préparatoires*, led numerous scholars to argue, some invoking the *Danzig* Opinion in support,[26] that there was an international obligation to make the Treaty part of domestic law enforceable before the domestic courts; whilst others strongly contested this reading and emphasized the freedom of the parties to choose how they are to give effect to their obligations.[27] As the ECHR was endowed with a judicial organ, there was a body that could resolve the controversy as to the obligations undertaken. In 1976 the European Court of Human Rights (ECtHR) held that 'neither Article 13 ... nor the Convention in general lays down for the Contracting States any given manner for ensuring within their internal law the effective implementation of any of the provisions of the Convention.'[28] The Court has since repeated on several occasions that there is no obligation to incorporate the ECHR into domestic law and that Article 13 does not go as far as to guarantee a remedy allowing a contracting State's laws to be challenged before a national authority on the ground of being contrary to the ECHR.[29] Leading scholars, including a former president of the Court, note that this remains the prevailing view.[30]

The 1969 ACHR is also endowed with a judicial body, modelled on its European counterpart, which is in a position to determine whether the convention needs to be directly applied by domestic courts. The Inter-American Court of Human Rights (IACtHR) has not had to address this issue head on. There has, however, been some controversy in the context of interpreting a 1986 Advisory Opinion.[31] Scholars on one side, including one of the judges sitting on that very case, consider the decision to establish the direct applicability of a particular ACHR provision as a matter of international law.[32] Notwithstanding that only one provision was at issue, they suggest that many ACHR provisions are thus directly applicable as a matter of international law.[33] By contrast, a former judge who also sat in the

[26] Such as Teitgen cited in Drzemczewski (1983: 40).

[27] For an overview of the debate, see Drzemczewski (1983: 40–53).

[28] *Swedish Engine Drivers' Union v Sweden* (1976) 1 EHRR 617, para 50.

[29] See *James and others v UK* (1986) 8 EHRR 123, paras 84–5; *Observer and Guardian v UK* (1991) 14 EHRR 153, para 76; *Sunday Times v UK (No 2)* (1992) 14 EHRR 229, para 61.

[30] See Bernhardt (2004: 433); Tomuschat (2008: 112–13); Polakiewicz (2001: 33).

[31] Advisory Opinion OC-7/86 of 26 August 1986, Ser A No 7.

[32] Jiménez de Aréchaga (1989: 416–18); Gros Espiell (2004: 538).

[33] Expressly so by Jiménez de Aréchaga (1989: 418), and implicitly by Gros Espiell (2004: 538).

case suggests that the Court did not go as far but that it did not reject the proposition that the Convention or some of its provisions were directly applicable as a matter of international law and that it was free in the future to so conclude.[34] The Court has not had to address this issue again, but it did hand down a judgment in the highly controversial terrain of amnesty laws where it appeared to read the Convention as imposing an obligation on domestic courts not to give effect to domestic law inconsistent with the ACHR.[35]

UN committees

The core international human rights instruments adopted within the UN framework establish committees of independent experts that monitor implementation of their provisions. There are currently seven such committees. Amongst other things, they publish 'general comments' which are interpretations of the provisions of the relevant treaty. Although such general comments are non-binding,[36] they are instructive. The two most well-known committees (the Human Rights Committee (HRC) and the Committee on Economic, Social and Cultural Rights (CESCR)) are assigned the task of monitoring State compliance with, respectively, the ICCPR and the ICESCR.

With respect to the CESCR, its general comment of 1998 on the domestic application of the Covenant initially gave the impression that it might be about to reach a *Danzig*-type conclusion when it asserted that 'legally binding international human rights standards should operate directly and immediately within the domestic legal system of each State party, thereby enabling individuals to seek enforcement of their rights before national courts and tribunals.'[37] That it was not about to pursue a *Danzig*-like path was then made crystal clear when it proceeded in the following paragraph to acknowledge that the Covenant itself does not stipulate the specific means by which it is to be implemented domestically nor is there any 'provision obligating its comprehensive incorporation or requiring it to be accorded any type of status in national law'.

[34] Buergenthal (1992: 339–40).

[35] *Almonacid-Arellano et al v Chile*, Judgment of 26 September 2006, Ser C 154 (2006), para 124. See Burgorgue-Larsen and Úbeda de Torres (2011: 260).

[36] Boyle and Chinkin (2007: 156).

[37] CESCR General Comment 9: The Domestic Application of the Covenant, adopted 1.12.98, para 4.

Turning to the HRC, its general comment on implementation at the national level of 1981 seemed to make clear that States are free to choose how they implement their obligations.[38] Nonetheless, in 2001 one author was to assert, drawing on the *Danzig* Opinion, that 'The object of the ICCPR is "to create a special legal regime" governing the relations between individuals and States parties which requires immediate resort to its provisions.'[39] The author amassed evidence of recent practice of the HRC in support of the proposition that the 'States parties need to ensure that the Covenant itself can be applied directly by domestic courts' and that it 'needs its own formal place in the domestic legal system so that the Covenant provisions themselves become enforceable by domestic courts.'[40] But that no such sweeping conclusion would be reached was made plain in its general comment of 2004 where the HRC affirmed that the Covenant does not require that it be 'directly applicable in the courts, by incorporation of the Covenant into national law'.[41]

2.3.2 *The European Court of Justice and maximalist treaty enforcement*

The notable exception of a judicial body that adopts a fundamentally different approach to the obligations that flow from the treaty that it is charged to interpret is the ECJ. This is a story so well told that only a few of the more salient fundamentals need to be outlined here.[42] The starting point for what has come to be known as the constitutionalization of European law[43] are two seminal judgments delivered some 13 months apart in the early 1960s, where the ECJ outlined the two central planks of the then Community legal order: the principles of direct effect and supremacy.

The direct effect principle was enunciated in the *Van Gend en Loos* judgment which saw the Court looking to the spirit, general scheme, and the wording of the then EEC Treaty provisions to determine whether an individual could lay claim to individual rights which the national courts must protect.[44] The objective of the Treaty being to establish a common

[38] HRC, General Comment 3: Implementation at the National Level, adopted 29.07.81, para 1.

[39] Seibert-Fohr (2001: 428).

[40] Seibert-Fohr (2001: 435–6) (the argument is developed at 420–38).

[41] ICCPR, General Comment 31: The Nature of the General Legal Obligation Imposed on State Parties to the Covenant, adopted 29.3.04, para 13.

[42] A recent insightful account is provided by de Witte (2011).

[43] The iconic account is provided by Weiler (1991). See also Stein (1981) and Mancini (1989).

[44] 26/62 *Van Gend en Loos* [1963] ECR 1.

market of direct concern to interested parties was held to imply that it was more than an agreement merely creating obligations between the Contracting States. Various factors were invoked as confirmation of this proposition: the preamble's reference to peoples; the establishment of institutions endowed with sovereign rights affecting citizens; the role of nationals in the functioning of the Community via the European Parliament and the Economic and Social Committee; and the preliminary reference procedure which confirmed that EU law could be invoked before domestic courts. The famed conclusion that followed was that EU nationals were held to be subjects of this new legal order which, independently of Member State legislation, is also intended to confer rights upon them. And in the face of contrary submissions from the three intervening Member States, and the Advocate General, the Court held that the Treaty provision at issue produced direct effects and created individual rights which national courts must protect.

This judgment constituted a radical point of departure from that of traditional international law which, as we have seen, starts from the proposition that the domestic legal order determines the legal effect that treaties have therein. The international lawyer might well have been surprised, in light of the *Danzig* Opinion, at the largely non-existent role played by the intention of the parties,[45] which is perhaps just as well for most commentators struggle to find such intention in the Treaty of Rome.[46] Admittedly, there have long been attempts to draw parallels with the *Danzig* Opinion.[47] But this is unconvincing for the ECJ was expressly purporting to tell the domestic courts that their obligation under the Treaty was to apply the relevant Treaty provisions. One should not lose sight of the fact that in *Danzig* the PCIJ referred to the object of the Treaty being the adoption by the parties of definite rules creating rights that would be enforceable in the national courts, whilst here the ECJ was asserting that the Treaty *itself* created the rights and required *no adoption of domestic rules* for them to be enforceable in the domestic courts.[48]

[45] De Witte (2011: 327) points out that whilst the Court did not openly contradict that the self-executing nature of a treaty provision had to be deduced from the intention of the parties, the Court did not try to reconstruct the actual, subjective, intention of the drafters of the Treaty.

[46] One eminent international law scholar involved in the legal drafting committee of the Treaty has suggested otherwise, see Reuter (1968: 679).

[47] See eg Verhoeven (1980: 257); Wyatt (1982: 150–1, 154); Spiermann (1999: 787).

[48] See further Buergenthal (1992: 327).

Any lingering doubt as to whether the ECJ was indeed claiming that EU law itself determines the effect it has in the domestic legal order was dispensed with in the *Costa* judgment the following year when it asserted that, unlike ordinary international treaties, the EEC Treaty had created its own legal system which had become an integral part of the Member States' legal systems and which their courts were bound to apply.[49] The distinction with respect to the basic premise of international law in terms of the relationship between the international and domestic legal systems could not have been articulated any more starkly.

The *Costa* judgment is, however, best known for its enunciation of the supremacy principle, namely that because of the special and original nature of Community law it cannot be overridden by domestic legal provisions. The detailed reasoning need not be repeated here,[50] it is important simply to underline the obvious contrast with respect to international law. Here the ECJ was purporting to tell domestic courts that they were to give EU law primacy in the domestic legal arena and that this requirement flowed from the very nature of Community law.[51] General international law certainly states no rule to the effect that domestic courts are to give effect to international law notwithstanding contrary domestic law.

Conceptually, the bold assertion of the doctrines of direct effect and supremacy represented a veritable paradigm shift: for the first time we had a judicial organ created by treaty asserting that this treaty obliged domestic courts to treat its provisions as the superior law of the land. The developments that have taken place since have been no less striking and have further accentuated the divergence between EU law and international law. The magnitude has been of such nature that over time the language of constitutionalism, fuelled by pronouncements of the ECJ,[52] has come to be

[49] 6/64 *Costa v ENEL* [1964] ECR 585.

[50] For a brief account see Craig and de Búrca (2011: 256–8).

[51] Perhaps the earliest scholarly publication acknowledging its significance came from Stein (1965: 513) who commented: 'The judgment...may be interpreted as holding that Community law...is superior to national law...not only in the Community legal order but also in the national legal orders and that the supremacy rule is directly and immediately applicable by national courts.'

[52] In particular its references to the EC Treaty as a 'constitutional charter' in 294/83 *Les Verts* [1986] ECR 1339, para 23 and *Opinion 1/91* [1991] ECR I-6079, para 21. The German Federal Constitutional Court had already referred in 1967 to the Treaty as 'in some way the Constitution of this Community': see Pernice (2010: 53).

employed in order to capture the richness of these developments.[53] The supremacy doctrine was further teased out such that primacy was to obtain, as far as the ECJ was concerned,[54] over the Constitution itself.[55] And the criteria for direct effect, that the relevant provision be clear, unconditional, and not require any further implementing measures, proved not to be a great constraint as, to give but two of the better known examples, Treaty provisions were held directly effective even where further implementation by EU legislative organs was envisaged,[56] or where a principle was at stake that left important criteria undefined.[57]

The direct effect doctrine was extended to EU legislative measures,[58] which proved especially controversial with respect to unimplemented Directives given that they are addressed to the Member States and the need for domestic implementation is expressly envisaged (Art 288 TFEU). Whilst the direct effect of Directives was ruled out in the context of the horizontal relationship between individuals,[59] numerous judicial innovations have arisen to mitigate this limitation,[60] of which the most controversial was State liability in damages for breach of EU law.[61]

Crucially, the very doctrine of direct effect has undergone, and continues to undergo, evolution. Traditionally, it was equated with the creation of individual rights,[62] but gradually it became clear that direct effect was by no means confined to provisions that create individual rights.[63] That is, unless we resort to the proposition that the right accorded is simply the right of the individual to rely on a particular provision before domestic courts which

[53] See eg Weiler and Trachtman (1997: 372–4); Weiler (1997: 98); Claes (2006: 403 et seq). Stein (1965: 513) had already suggested on the basis of *Costa* that 'the Court could be said to have dealt with the Community treaty as if it were a constitution rather than a treaty'.

[54] The national court response has been a matter that has generated a rich literature: see Claes (2006) with relevant citations therein, and briefly and more recently: de Witte (2011: 348–57).

[55] 11/70 *Internationale Handelsgesellschaft* [1970] ECR 1125; 106/77 *Simmenthal* [1978] ECR 629. Some had thought this much already followed from the *Costa* decision: Stein (1965: 513).

[56] The most famous example is 2/74 *Reyners v Belgium* [1974] ECR 631. On the significance of this judgment, see Craig (1992: 463–7).

[57] The most famous example is 43/75 *Defrenne v Sabena* [1976] ECR 455.

[58] Direct effect was first accepted in respect of Decisions and Directives in 9/70 *Franz Grad* [1970] ECR 825 and Regulations in 43/71 *Politi* [1971] ECR 1039.

[59] 152/84 *Marshall* [1986] ECR 723; C-91/92 *Faccini Dori* [1994] ECR I-3325.

[60] See generally Craig and de Búrca (2011: 200–15).

[61] The principle that emerged in C-6 & 9/90 *Francovich v Italy* [1991] ECR I-5357, on which see generally Craig and de Búrca (2011: 241–53).

[62] See eg Winter (1972).

[63] See eg Prechal (2005: 99–106, 231); Dashwood et al (2011: 258–60).

would, on most accounts, encapsulate all conceivable manners in which EU law can be employed in domestic courts. The ECJ has certainly lacked consistency in how it employs the language of rights in this context. Accordingly, the doctrine of direct effect which has mutated over time to include legal effects that do not strictly involve individual rights has given rise to ever-increasing commentary as the scholarly community, as well as the Court itself, have struggled to provide an analytical framework that captures the complex jurisprudence.[64]

One distinction, considered to be reflected in the case law, is that between narrow direct effect, understood as the capacity of a provision to confer individual rights enforceable before national courts, and broad direct effect, understood as the capacity of a provision to be invoked before a national court.[65] Others have largely avoided conceptualization in terms of direct effect preferring instead to conceptualize matters in terms of the different ways in which EU law can be invoked and articulating the hurdles that need to be satisfied for such effects.[66] Another scholar called for abandoning the doctrine and for Community law to be applied in the domestic legal order without the need for a preliminary inquiry into whether it meets the traditional criteria for direct effect.[67]

There has also been a growing focus upon whether the supremacy principle can be divorced from direct effect, such that it is possible for individuals to rely on primacy to disapply contrary domestic law even absent direct effect. The pedigree of this debate appears to lie in French academic thinking where a distinction has long been proposed between 'invocabilité d'exclusion' and 'invocabilité de substitution'.[68] The former referring to the setting aside of domestic law that conflicts with Community law based on the supremacy principle without the direct effect criteria needing to be surmounted; the latter referring to the application of the Community rule instead of the conflicting national rule and requiring satisfaction of the direct effect criteria.[69] Strong support for the essence of

[64] Recent valuable contributions in English include Lenaerts and Corthaut (2006); Dougan (2007); Prechal (2007); de Witte (2011).

[65] Craig and de Búrca (2011: 181–2); Dashwood et al (2011: 259–60).

[66] Simon (2001: 437–47).

[67] See Prechal (2000; 2002; 2007), who has since become a member of the Court.

[68] Galmot and Bonichot (1988).

[69] See eg Simon (2001: 441–7). It received the support of two Advocates General in cases concerning Directives: see C-240–4/98 *Oceano Grupo* [2000] ECR I-4941 and C-287/98 *Linster* [2000] ECR I-6917. However, it has been argued that this would involve a radical departure from

this exclusion–substitution distinction was advanced by a member of the ECJ in a co-authored piece which sought to build a general theory of the invocability of the broader sphere of EU law around the primacy principle. On this account, the conventional direct effect criteria of clarity, precision, and unconditionality need to be met where the issue is one of enforcing rights, which would not otherwise exist in the domestic legal order, but not where the issue is one of setting aside incompatible domestic law.[70]

It is clear that the doctrine of direct effect and the broader issue of the invocability of EU law remains shrouded in complexity and, with the judicial stance still evolving, the academic debate is sure to continue unabated. What bears emphasizing is that there has been a powerful current in both the judicial practice of the ECJ and academic thinking that sought to ensure the greatest possible domestic effectiveness for Community—and even pre-Lisbon Union[71]—law.[72] This overriding concern with ensuring the greatest possible effectiveness of EU law in the domestic legal arena—what we can also label a maximalist approach to treaty enforcement—has been a characteristic trait of the jurisprudence with textual niceties rarely standing in the way of this objective. This would account for the core doctrines of direct effect and supremacy and much further innovation by the Court too. Indeed, the case law pertaining to remedies in national law for the enforcement of EU law is replete with references to the mantra of ensuring the full effectiveness of EU law, as EU law so interpreted has come to play an ever more intrusive role in national remedial and procedural law.[73] That on occasion the Court has appeared to show restraint, where an

many of the leading authorities on direct effect: Arnull (2006: 240–50). Cf Lenaerts and Corthaut (2006: 292).

[70] Lenaerts and Corthaut (2006: 288–9). A core problem they saw with continuing to conceptualize the invocability of EU law in terms of direct effect was that it limited the role of framework decisions which were then expressly stated not to entail direct effect (Art 34(2)(b) TEU). This approach, which Prechal (2007) also appeared to adopt, accorded little respect to the intentions of the Member States for it is certainly likely that they drafted that Treaty provision precisely to foreclose such use of framework decisions.

[71] See C-103/05 *Pupino* [2005] ECR I-5285. See also Lenaerts and Corthaut (2006).

[72] A then sitting ECJ judge famously contended, extra-judicially, that direct effect is the normal state of the law and that it boils down to a question of justiciability, with the ECJ's dominant preoccupation having been to ensure the operative character of EU law: see Pescatore (1983). The work of other scholars can be situated within a similar paradigm, eg Prechal (2000; 2002; 2007); Allott (2000).

[73] See generally Craig and de Búrca (2011: 218–54); Dougan (2005).

unrelenting focus on domestic or maximalist effectiveness would have suggested a different path, does little to dispel the more general trend.[74]

3. Domestic Legal Orders and the Legal Effects of Treaties

Whilst the preceding section explored the general requirements imposed by international law with respect to the legal effects of treaties in the domestic legal arena and the pronouncements of several international courts and supervisory organs, this section looks at the other side of the legal effects of treaties coin, namely the different domestic approaches to their internal legal effect. The legal effect of treaties in the domestic legal order is a domestic constitutional question of immense and growing significance and in a world of over 190 States there is inevitably great variation. It is submitted, however, that we can draw two core distinctions in approach: constitutional systems that automatically incorporate at least certain categories of treaty into the domestic legal order and those that do not. This basic dichotomy will be further elucidated through a brief overview of the approach in the EU's founding Member States and the first batch of entrants. The approach of the founding Member States has the greatest capacity to shed light on what the drafters may have intended with the relevant provisions of the Treaty of Rome concerning the legal effects of international agreements in the EU legal order, which will be considered in Chapter II. The first batch of entrants represented a constitutional approach falling on the opposite side of the twofold dichotomy

[74] The classic example of self-restraint is usually considered to be the refusal to reconsider the rejection of horizontal direct effect for Directives despite the promptings of several Advocates General (eg in C-316/93 *Vaneetveld* [1994] ECR I-763; C-271/91 *Marshall II* [1993] ECR I-4367; and C-91/92 *Faccini Dori* [1994] ECR I-3325), to say nothing of the hostile academic commentary. However, the attribution of direct effect to Directives was an audacious move given the Treaty text and it generated an adverse reaction by senior courts of two of the founding Member States, namely the French Conseil d'État and the German Federal Tax Court. Accordingly, on one reading the rejection of horizontal direct effect of Directives was an issue of expediency so as to ensure that at least vertical direct effect of Directives was accepted by national courts: see Hartley (2003: 215). In short, arguably what for some was a missed opportunity by the Court was for others testimony to its political shrewdness. Moreover, emphasis on self-restraint overlooks the mitigating tools, hardly examples of self-restraint, employed to circumvent the absence of horizontal direct effect.

to that of the founding Member States. This is also significant because the foundational jurisprudence of the ECJ pertaining to the legal effects of international agreements developed at a time when these countries had acceded; the Court was thus composed of judges steeped in these distinct domestic constitutional traditions and faced with submissions from their governments on these very issues. By elucidating the diverging approaches in this fashion, the chapter that follows is able to articulate more clearly the constitutional ramifications for domestic legal orders of the foundational jurisprudence of the ECJ pertaining to the constitutional status and legal effects of EU Agreements.

3.1 Automatic treaty incorporation

3.1.1 *Defining automatic treaty incorporation*

The terminology of automatic treaty incorporation refers to a domestic constitutional approach to treaties that in practice operates to ensure that treaties, or certain defined categories of treaty, become automatically incorporated into the domestic legal order. By incorporation what is meant here is that the treaty is considered to become a binding part of domestic law. The adjective 'automatic' is intended to capture the fact that this aforementioned status is usually acquired upon the entry into force of the treaty for the relevant State. So defined, this simple categorization of automatic treaty incorporation can accommodate within its remit a great deal of sub-variation. The fact that the treaty becomes part of domestic law, or a variant of such language, can be expressly employed in the Constitution itself;[75] or it can effectively be read into a less explicit constitutional

[75] Examples include: Albania (1998: Art 122(1)); Armenia (1995: Art 6); Bulgaria (1991: Art 5(4)); Cape Verde (1992: Art 11(2)); Czech Republic (1992: Art 10); Ethiopia (1994: Art 9); Greece (1975: Art 28(1)); Kenya (2010: Art 2(6)); Kyrgyzstan (2010: Art 6(3)); Lithuania (1992: Art 138); Poland (1997: Art 91(1)); Portugal (1976: Art 8(2)); Russia (1993: Art 15(4)); Serbia (2006: Arts 16(2) and 194); Spain (1978: Art 96(1)); Turkey (1982: Art 90(5)); Ukraine (1996: Art 9). In some constitutions the few words providing for automatic treaty incorporation also add the adjective that seeks to assert their hierarchical status, thus Art VI, cl 2 of the US Constitution 1787 states that treaties are 'the supreme Law of the Land', (see similarly the 1994 Argentine Constitution (Art 31), the 1917 Mexican Constitution (Art 133). The US Constitution is also noteworthy in expressly providing for a judicial role as Art III, sect 2 provides that 'The judicial power shall extend to . . . treaties made . . . '; see also the Serbian Constitution (Art 142(2)), the Czech Republic's Constitution (Art 95), the Swiss Constitution (1999: Arts 189(1)(b) and 190).

provision by the courts;[76] or the Constitution itself can be silent with the courts nonetheless concluding that treaties, or certain categories of treaty,[77] do indeed become part of domestic law.[78]

Such automatic status can, however, be subject to the requisite domestic constitutional procedures for expressing consent to be bound to a treaty having been satisfied[79] and/or that the treaty has been published,[80] or alternatively certain legal effects of a treaty in the judicial arena can only be produced where these requirements have been satisfied.[81] Crucially, however, the practice is usually for such domestic requirements to be satisfied prior to entry into force of the treaty for the State concerned so that upon its entry into force it is considered to become part of the domestic legal order.[82]

In others, the confirmation of a hierarchically superior status for treaties can be viewed as acknowledgement that treaties become part of the legal order; this has long existed in the French Constitution (1958: Art 55) which was replicated verbatim by nearly all the former French colonies in Africa (see Maluwa (1999: 39–41) identifying 19 such States), other examples include Cyprus (1960: Art 169(3)), Estonia (1992: Art 123), Georgia (1995: Art 6(2)), Moldova (1994: Art 4(2)).

[76] eg Art 98(2) of the Japanese Constitution (1947): see Iwasawa (1998: 28–30), Hae Bong (2011: 365, 368, 371).

[77] Germany and Italy with respect to those that have received parliamentary authorization (and also those that have an implementation order in Italy).

[78] Examples include: Austria, see Handl-Petz (2011: 79); Switzerland, see Dominicé and Voeffray (1996: 547–8), and Belgium and Luxembourg on which see further below. The Chinese Constitution (1982) is silent on the matter but whilst one recent country report emphasized that treaties become part of the Chinese legal order, the authors' own analysis appears incompatible with this proposition (see Li and Guo 2011) and is inconsistent with the account of other particularly well-placed commentators: Hanqin and Qian (2009).

[79] For Spain, see Bermejo Garcia et al (1996: 197–8, 203–4); for Portugal, see Moura Ramos (1996: 466–7, 470, 477–8); for Greece, see Rouconas (1996); for Japan, see Iwasawa (1998: 26).

[80] For Portugal, see Moura Ramos (1996: 475–6); for Chile, see Orrego Vicuña and Orrego Bauzá (2005: 136–8); for Greece, see Yokaris (2011: 252), for Poland, see Wyrozumska (2011: 481–2), Garlicki et al (2009a: 378). In some legal orders, problems have arisen due to treaty publication being delayed or not taking place: for Spain, see Campos et al (2005: 279); for Greece, see Rouconas (1996: 299); for Russia and the USSR, see Butler (2009a: 417, 434–8); for France and Belgium see below.

[81] eg Switzerland, see Dominicé and Voeffray (1996: 537, 547, 548); for the founding Member States, see below; for Greece, see Rouconas (1996: 302), Yokaris (2011: 257); for Spain, see Campos et al (2005: 277–80); for Russia, see Butler (2009a: 417, 434–6).

[82] For confirmation with respect to Spain, see Bermejo Garcia et al (1996: 207–8, 212–13); for Greece, see Rouconas (1996: 297, 298); for Portugal, see Moura Ramos (1996: 473–5); for Switzerland, see Dominicé and Voeffray (1996: 539, 547–8) and Wildhaber et al (2005: 645, 658–9); for the Czech Republic, see Belohlavek (2011: 198); for the founding Member States, see below.

The relevant domestic constitutional procedures can include a constitutionally enshrined, or judicially mandated, requirement that parliamentary consent be given to at least certain treaties,[83] and this consent may or may not need to be given in the form of a legislative measure.[84] Where such measures are required, they can simply authorize ratification or approval of the relevant treaty,[85] though in some legal orders the practice is for such measures to contain further wording to the effect that the treaty is to be given effect domestically or implemented or some variation thereof.[86]

In terms of the hierarchical status of automatically incorporated treaties, there is considerable variation. The Constitution itself can seek to accord treaties a certain hierarchical standing by providing, for example, that they are superior to (or have precedence over[87]) statutes,[88] or that they are the supreme law of the land or nation or union,[89] or some similarly worded variant,[90] or with less explicit phrasing such as that they are 'to be faithfully observed'.[91] But even with express constitutionally enshrined language there can still be a crucial role for the courts in deciding whether

[83] Many constitutions contain an express requirement for at least certain categories of treaty: for the Czech Republic, see Belohlavek (2011: 196–8); for Spain, see Bermejo Garcia (1996: 200), for Greece, see Roucounas (1996: 291–2); for Poland, see Wyrozumska (2011: 469–70) and Garlicki et al (2009a: 376–7); for Portugal, see Moura Ramos (1996: 468); for Switzerland, see Wildhaber et al (2005: 644–5); for France, Italy, and Germany, see below. Some constitutions enshrine such a requirement for, in principle, all treaties although this can be subject to certain exceptions: examples include the US Constitution (Art II, sect 2); for Belgium and Luxembourg, see below.

[84] For examples where legislative measures are required for consent: see Greece, Rouconas (1996: 291–2), and for Germany, Italy, Luxembourg, Belgium, see below; Spain provides an example where it can be by legislation depending on the type of treaty, see Bermejo Garcia et al (1996: 200–1); in Portugal it is via parliamentary resolution, see Moura Ramos (1996: 469).

[85] For France and Germany, see below; for Switzerland, see Dominicé and Voeffray (1996: 540).

[86] For Greece, see Rouconas (1996: 293); for Belgium and Italy, see below.

[87] Poland as far as certain ratified treaties are concerned (Art 91(2), see also Garlicki et al (2009a: 379, 381)).

[88] eg France, see below, and most of its former African colonies.

[89] Respectively the US, Argentina, and Mexico.

[90] eg Albania (1998: Art 122(2)); Bulgaria (Art 5(4)); Cape Verde (Art 11(4)); Greece (1975: Art 28(1)); Czech Republic (Art 10); Russia (Art 15(4)).

[91] Japan (Art 98(2)). The Swiss Constitution (Art 5(4)) appears less exigent in stating merely that 'The Confederation and the Cantons shall respect international law'.

they are superior to later-in-time statutes,[92] and potentially even the Constitution and constitutional values.[93]

Where the Constitution itself is silent as to hierarchy, the issue is left to the courts. In some legal orders they have accorded treaties the same status as that of legislation, which can be of varying rank,[94] authorizing approval or ratification of the treaty;[95] in others, the treaty is accorded superior status to ordinary legislation even where it is later in time[96] and can potentially, albeit this appears extremely rare, even be superior to the Constitution.[97] Finally, it is important to note that some constitutional systems that automatically incorporate treaties nonetheless allow for challenges to the constitutional validity internally of ratified treaties.[98]

[92] For France, see below. The US Supreme Court decided that treaties have the same status as federal statutes and that the later-in-time rule applies, see Henkin (1995: 69–71); Paust (2002: 637–40). In Argentina the later-in-time rule was applied by the Supreme Court, but has since been rejected: see Buergenthal (1992: 358). In Mexico a 1999 Supreme Court judgment rejected the later-in-time rule: Miguel Díaz (2005: 452–3). In Russia, despite the text providing for treaties to be applied instead of existing law (Art 15(4)), for the Supreme Court only treaties approved by a federal law have priority over laws of the federation: Butler (2009a: 421, 429–31, 445), Tikhomirov (2011: 521, 524). The Serbian Constitution (Art 194) provides that statutes and other general legal acts must not be contrary to ratified treaties which courts have used as authorization to give priority to treaties including over later-in-time legislation; however, a new Act now requires national courts to suspend cases concerning the compatibility of domestic legislation with treaties and initiate the constitutional court review procedure: see Djajic (2011: 543–4). In the Czech Republic it appears that the Constitutional Court must be consulted on the compatibility of treaty law and domestic law: Belohlavek (2011: 199). For Japan lower courts have recognized that treaties prevail over statutes but the Supreme Court is reported never to have clearly addressed the issue: Hae Bong (2011: 375).

[93] As has taken place recently in France, see below.

[94] As is the case in Austria, see Buergenthal (1992: 356), Handl-Petz (2011: 90); and Italy, see below.

[95] eg Germany and Italy, see below.

[96] As in Luxembourg and Belgium discussed below; for Spain, see Campos et al (2005: 285–91); arguably this is so in Switzerland, see Dominicé and Voeffray (1996: 552) but the situation is not free from controversy: Wildhaber et al (2005: 662–3); for Portugal, see Moura Ramos (1996: 476–7).

[97] As was the case in Austria, subject to an increased parliamentary approval threshold, until a constitutional amendment in 2008 (Handl-Petz (2011: 64–5, 90)) and as is still currently the case in the Netherlands.

[98] Examples include: Austria, see Handl-Petz (2011: 69–70); Poland, see Wyrozumska (2011: 471, 489) and Garlicki et al (2009a: 381–2); Japan, see Hae Bong (2011: 380–1); Serbia, see Djajic (2011: 543–6); Spain, see Castillo de la Torre (2001: 63–4). On Belgium, Italy, and Germany, see below. However, there appear to be few examples of such ex post review actually taking place, much less successful challenges.

Having briefly defined automatic treaty incorporation and noted some of the extant variations in this respect, we can now elucidate in slightly more detail the automatic treaty incorporation model in the EU's founding Member States.

3.1.2 *Automatic treaty incorporation in the founding Member States*

All six founding Member States have a constitutional system that operates in practice to ensure that at least certain treaties are automatically incorporated. For the purposes of this brief overview they can be divided into pairs that share particular traits.

Germany and Italy both have Constitutions drafted shortly after the Second World War that provide for constitutionally defined categories of treaty that require parliamentary approval by law.[99] The German Federal Constitutional Court held that this law of approval confers the force of internal German law on the content of the treaty.[100] The Italian practice is for the statute authorizing ratification to contain an 'implementation order' in a separate article that provides that 'full and complete implementation is given to the treaty'.[101] Parliamentary authorization via a law takes place, in principle, prior to consent to be bound to the treaty being expressed and it is considered to render the treaty part of domestic law once it enters into force for the State concerned.[102]

Both Constitutions are silent on the issue of hierarchical status,[103] but their constitutional courts have hitherto remained faithful to the proposition

[99] Germany (1949: Art 59(2)); Italy (1948: Arts 80 and 87(8)).

[100] See case cited in Waelbroeck (1969: 69). The German Government has made it clear that international treaties become part of German law as a result of ratification, see the German response (25.07.2011) to a complaint (reference no ACCC/C/2008/31) before the Aarhus Convention compliance committee. For an earlier example, see 29/84 *Commission v Germany* [1985] ECR 1661, para 34.

[101] Treves (2005: 689–90); Gaja (1987: 89); Cannizzaro (2011: 462–3). In Germany the practice, discontinued in 1955, had been for the law to state that the treaty had the force of law: see Waelbroeck (1969: 66); Wildhaber (1971: 216).

[102] For Germany, see Frowein and Oellers-Frahm (1996b: 80–1); Beemelmans and Treviranus (2005: 322); Paulus (2009a: 209). Italian scholars have tended not to consider the implementation order as making the treaty part of domestic law as such but, rather, as making the necessary changes to domestic law to give effect to the treaty, see eg Treves and Frigessi di Rattalma (1996: 377); Waelbroeck (1969: 85–7). Italian submissions to treaty bodies, however, have emphasized that the implementation order incorporates the treaty within the domestic legal order and makes it an integral part of the Italian legal system: see eg the Annual Report Pursuant to the Protocol on Environmental Protection to the Antarctic Treaty (May 1999 - IP011), paras 2–3.

[103] A 2001 amendment to the Italian Constitution (Art 117) led to an argument that Italian laws inconsistent with treaty obligations are unconstitutional and that this can be policed by the Constitutional Court: see Cannizzaro (2011: 464–7).

that in the internal legal order treaties have the same status as the law implementing them.[104] This is subject to a disclaimer with respect to EU law which has acquired a special status within both legal orders.[105] Although treaties retain the hierarchical status of the approval law, both legal orders have developed techniques that avoid the State being placed in breach of its treaty obligations. One judicial mechanism is to consider the treaty *lex specialis* in order to avoid application of the later-in-time rule.[106] Courts in both legal orders also apply a canon of construction to the effect that absent clear contrary intent they will assume that the legislature intended to comply with its international obligations.[107] And human rights treaties have acquired a form of indirect constitutional status in that the respective constitutional courts have emphasized that constitutional norms of fundamental rights protection are to be interpreted in line with human rights treaties.[108] Both constitutional courts are, however, willing to review the constitutionality of the Act incorporating the treaty domestically which can deprive the treaty of internal effect.[109]

The Belgian and Luxembourg Constitutions require parliamentary assent for all treaties.[110] This requirement stems from constitutional reforms in 1993 in the case of Belgium where parliamentary assent had previously only been required for certain categories of treaty under its 1831

[104] For Germany, see Paulus (2009a: 216). For Italy, see Treves (2005: 691). However, recent Constitutional Court rulings appear to have reserved constitutional control of legislation, even where earlier in time, vis-à-vis treaties to the Constitutional Court: Cataldi and Iovane (2010: 19–22); Cannizzaro (2010: 176–7).

[105] Both Constitutional Courts have had a rather turbulent relationship with EU law and the ECJ and do not accept the supremacy doctrine unconditionally: see Claes (2006: 188–99, 596–624); Craig and de Búrca (2011: 272–85).

[106] For Italy, see Treves and Frigessi di Rattalma (1996: 384); Treves (2005: 694–5); Cannizzaro (2011: 466–71). For Germany, see Frowein and Oellers-Frahm (1996b: 84); Simma et al (1997: 89); Zimmermann (2001: 339–40).

[107] For Germany, see Paulus (2009a: 228); Frowein and Oellers-Frahm (1996b: 84). For recent affirmation by the German Federal Constitutional Court that it will seek to interpret the Constitution consistently with Germany's international obligations (see para 33 of *Görgülü*, 14 October 2004, BVerfGE 111). For Italy, see Treves (2005: 695); Treves and Frigesi di Rattalma (1996: 384); Gaja (1987: 100).

[108] For Italy, see Treves (2005: 694). For discussion in the German context, see Paulus (2009a: 228–35); Simma et al (1997: 95); Zimmermann (2001: 339).

[109] For Italy, see Treves (2005: 695–8); Treves and Frigesi di Rattalma (1996: 385); Gaja (1987: 101–2). For Germany, see Beemelmans Treviranus (2005: 327–8); Frowein and Hahn (1992: 384–5).

[110] For Belgium (1831: Art 167 § 2), see Verhoeven (2000); for Luxembourg (1868: Art 37(1)), see Biever et al (1996), Kinsch (2011: 386). On exceptions in Luxembourg, see Biever et al (1996: 410–14).

Constitution,[111] and from 1919 in the case of Luxembourg where parliamentary assent under its 1868 Constitution was also only required for certain categories of treaty.[112] In both cases, the practice was for this assent to be given by a law and this was constitutionally enshrined via reforms in 1956 in Luxembourg and 1993 in Belgium.[113] In Belgium, the practice is for this assent law also to state that the relevant treaty 'will have its full and complete effect'.[114] In both legal orders the assent takes place, in principle, prior to consent to be bound being expressed and the treaties are considered to become part of the domestic legal order once they enter into force for the State concerned.[115]

Both Constitutions are silent with respect to the hierarchical status of treaties but in seminal judgments the Supreme Civil Courts have held that the later-in-time rule does not apply with respect to treaties. In Luxembourg, this took place several years prior to the birth of the EEC,[116] but not until 1971 with respect to Belgium.[117] In both cases the conclusion was essentially held to flow from the very nature of international treaties, which was perhaps unsurprising considering the absence of an express constitutional anchor. Although the jurisprudence dispensed with the later-in-time rule it did not address the issue of whether the Constitution itself was subordinate to treaties. In Belgium, the Supreme Administrative Court has appeared to accord primacy to EU law over the Constitution basing itself primarily on the constitutional provision that authorizes transfers of powers to international institutions.[118] Attempts to enshrine the superior status of treaties have been unsuccessful in both countries.[119] However, when Luxembourg's Constitutional Court was set up, in the late 1990s, its power to review the conformity of laws with respect to the Constitution expressly excluded the laws that approve treaties.[120] By contrast, its Belgian

[111] See Verhoeven (1996: 124–5; 2000: 461); Holloway (1967: 153).

[112] See Pescatore (1964: 10 et seq). Holloway (1967: 154) on the requirement for all treaties with the 1919 Constitution.

[113] Luxembourg (Art 37(1)), see Pescatore (1964: 56); Belgium (Arts 75 and 77), see Verhoeven (1996: 126; 2000: 461–2).

[114] Verhoeven (2000: 461–2); Waelbroeck (1969: 103); Wildhaber (1971: 36).

[115] For Luxembourg, see Biever et al (1996: 414); for Belgium, see Verhoeven (1996: 126, 130).

[116] See Pescatore (1964: 105–7); Biever et al (1996: 418–19); Spielmann (2001: 532).

[117] See Verhoeven (1996: 135–6; 2000: 476); Claes (2006: 202–20).

[118] See Claes (2006: 510–13, 640–1).

[119] For Luxembourg, see Kinsch (2011: 387); for Belgium, see Bribosia (1998: 11, 18).

[120] Article 95ter(2) (Constitution as amended in 1996). See Kinsch (2011: 404).

counterpart, dating from the early 1980s, is not subject to this exclusion and has indeed held that it has jurisdiction to assess the constitutionality of such laws.[121]

Finally, turning to the Dutch and French Constitutions, these are distinctive in enshrining what is effectively a system of automatic treaty incorporation and expressly providing for the hierarchical status of treaties. The 1946 French Constitution was the first to do so by providing that lawfully ratified and published treaties had the force of law, even where contrary to French legislation, without the need for any further legislative measures to ensure their application other than those necessary for ratification.[122] The 1958 Constitution did not retain the force of law vocabulary but clearly affirmed that treaties become part of French law by providing that once lawfully ratified or approved they have from the date of publication an authority superior to that of legislation.[123]

The Dutch Constitution as amended in 1953 and 1956 provided that, and the essence of this was maintained in the 1983 revisions, treaties shall not be ratified and shall not enter into force until, subject to certain exceptions, they have received parliamentary approval.[124] The 1953 revisions made it clear that published treaties were part of Dutch law which was essentially maintained in the 1956 and 1983 revisions.[125] That published treaties were considered part of the domestic legal order was also made explicit by the fact that the 1953 reform provided that Dutch legal provisions shall not apply if they are incompatible with published treaties, which was essentially maintained in the 1956 and 1983 revisions.[126]

The French and Dutch constitutional provisions appeared similar in entrenching a superior status for published treaties. But whilst the wording of the latter made it quite clear that it was directed at the courts,[127] in France it was argued that as constitutional review powers were reserved to

[121] Verhoeven (1996: 12; 2000: 475, 477); Claes (2006: 506–10, 641–5).

[122] Articles 26 and 27 See Daillier, Forteau, and Pellet (2009: 253); Decaux (2011: 211–12).

[123] Article 55. See Decaux (2011: 216); Daillier, Forteau, and Pellet (2009: 253–4); Eisemann and Rivier (2005: 268). The 1958 French Constitution conditioned this supremacy on reciprocal application by the other party, see on the reciprocity criterion Combacau and Sur (2010: 195–8); Eisemann and Rivier (2005: 269–70).

[124] Currently Art 91(1) (former Art 60). See Brouwer (2005: 489–93).

[125] Article 66 (1953) which became Art 65 (1956) and then Art 93 (1983). The 1956 amendment adjusted the provision by confining it to provisions binding on all persons by virtue of their content.

[126] Originally Art 65, currently Art 94.

[127] See Van Panhuys (1953: 555).

the Constitutional Council, courts were not empowered to review legislation for its compatibility with a treaty.[128] It was not until 1975 that the Supreme French Civil Court accepted that a later-in-time law could be trumped by a treaty,[129] and it infamously took a further 14 years for the Supreme Administrative Court to so hold.[130] Recently the French Supreme courts have also held that the treaty supremacy enshrined in the Constitution does not apply with respect to constitutional provisions and values.[131] In contrast, since the 1953 amendments the Dutch Constitution has expressly precluded the courts from reviewing the constitutionality of treaties,[132] which in effect placed treaties at the apex of the Dutch legal order.[133] The Dutch courts thus had little difficulty accommodating the primacy of EU law,[134] whilst matters have been very different for their French counterparts, which have reserved for themselves a—hitherto untested—power to review the compatibility of EU law vis-à-vis fundamental principles of the Constitution.[135]

Two final points are in order. First, all six legal orders stipulate a requirement, whether constitutionally enshrined or otherwise, that a treaty be published (albeit subject to limited exceptions in certain cases) and its absence either results in the treaty not being considered internally effective or will have consequences for its capacity to be relied upon by individuals in the courts.[136] Secondly, with the exception of the Netherlands, a failure to

[128] References in Daillier and Pellet (1980: 257); Combacau and Sur (2010: 190–1).

[129] In the specific context of the Treaty of Rome, *Jacques Vabre*, 24 May 1975, but this was affirmed in general terms the following year in the *Gleaser* decision (30 June 1976).

[130] Again in a case concerning EU law (*Nicolo*, CE Ass, 20 October 1989), but it was soon confirmed with respect to other treaties (*Confédération nationale des associations familiales catholiques*, CE Ass, 21 December 1990).

[131] See Dupuy and Kerbrat (2010: 469–77); Combacau and Sur (2010: 202); Daillier, Forteau, and Pellet (2009: 313–14).

[132] Currently Art 120.

[133] Treaties deviating from the Constitution were expressly permitted subject to a more exigent requirement for parliamentary assent: currently Art 91(3).

[134] Although not necessarily on the grounds enunciated by the ECJ: see Alkema (2011: 414–15).

[135] See Mehdi (2011) for the latest developments including the Conseil d'État's 2009 decision finally to accept the direct effect of Directives in a challenge to an administrative Act.

[136] The publication requirement has proven particularly problematic in Belgium and France where treaties have been published late or not at all and where established jurisprudence holds that non-published treaties cannot be relied upon in the courts: for Belgium, see Verhoeven (1996: 134–5; 2000: 470–4), de Wet (2008: 243); for France, see Combacau and Sur (2010: 194–5); Decaux (2011: 226); Eisemann and Rivier (2005: 265–7, 299–301); Dupuy and Kerbrat (2010: 467). For Germany, see Frowein and Oellers-Frahm (1996b: 83–4); for Italy, see Treves (2005: 680); for

obtain parliamentary authorization where this is required can result in the treaty not being valid internally.[137]

3.1.3 *The domestic judicial determination of the direct effect of treaty norms*

To have a better understanding of the legal effects that treaties have in domestic legal orders as a result of their automatic incorporation therein, it is essential to grasp the role played by the domestic determination of the 'direct effect' of treaties and treaty provisions.[138] For a treaty to be employed by a court[139] in a capacity other than as an interpretative aid, there will usually be a threshold test that needs to be satisfied. Courts, scholars, and practitioners use various labels, frequently interchangeably, to refer to this test whether it be that the treaty or treaty provision be directly effective, domestically applicable, directly applicable, or self-executing.[140]

The dominant label in Europe, undoubtedly influenced by the jurisprudence of the ECJ, is probably now that of direct effect and this section will accordingly employ that terminology. Direct effect as utilized here is not intended to be wholly coterminous with the manner in which it is employed in the field of EU law, not least because there is controversy as to its meaning therein. Nonetheless, as in EU law, direct effect as employed in this section does not encompass use of a treaty for the purpose of seeking to

Luxembourg, see Kinsch (2011: 390–1), Biever et al (1996: 417–18), Pescatore (1964: 86–8); for the Netherlands, see Alkema (2011: 413), Brouwer (2005: 501), Brolmann and Vierdag (1996: 446–7).

[137] For Belgium, see de Wet (2008: 243), Verhoeven (1996: 128); for France, see Dupuy and Kerbrat (2010: 465–7), Eisemann and Rivier (2005: 262–3, 267), Combacau and Sur (2010: 194); for Germany, see Frowein and Oellers-Frahm (1996b: 74, 79); for Italy, see Treves and Frigessi (1996: 369–70, 374); for Luxembourg, see Kinsch (2011: 390), Biever et al (1996: 412–13), Pescatore (1964: 86–8); for the Netherlands, see Brolmann and Vierdag (1996: 437, 441–2).

[138] With respect to EU law, matters are different as domestic courts can have recourse to a centralized interpretation from the ECJ.

[139] The focus herein is on the role of domestic courts, but clearly it is a determination that will also be engaged in by administrative authorities.

[140] For use of effect, see Velu (1981); Vandaele and Claes (2001); Nollkaemper (2011: 117–38). For direct applicability, see Verhoeven (1980) and Hae Bong (2011); for direct applicability and domestic applicability, see Iwasawa (1998: 44 et seq). The phrase 'self-executing' first emerged with the US Supreme Court in the nineteenth century: see Paust (1988: 766); Sloss (2002: 31); and it continues to be the terminology used by US courts and scholars: see eg Sloss (2012a); Hathaway et al (2012); Vazquez (2008); see also the national reports questionnaire employed in Shelton (2011: 665). Several European scholars also employ this terminology: Cassese (2005); Conforti (1993; 2001); Brouwer (2005).

interpret a national legal norm in a manner consistent with the treaty norm. In the field of EU law this is commonly known as the principle or doctrine of consistent interpretation,[141] and frequently as the principle of 'indirect effect'.[142] This is an aspect of a treaty's capacity to have a potentially crucial legal impact in the domestic legal arena, the significance of which should not be underestimated.[143]

Such impact, however, is to be distinguished from the direct effect of a treaty provision understood in a more technical sense, denoting legal effects other than the indirect one of a treaty provision being used to influence the interpretation accorded to a provision of national law. A non-exhaustive list would include: direct use of a treaty provision by a domestic court to confer rights on an individual; direct use of a treaty provision—even where the provision itself may not confer individual rights—such that it is applied in lieu of inconsistent domestic rules; direct use of a treaty provision to review and potentially set aside incompatible domestic rules.

It is for these types of 'direct legal effects' in legal orders where treaties have been automatically incorporated that domestic courts will usually engage in an analysis as to whether they consider the treaty or a relevant treaty provision to satisfy this threshold test.[144] Indeed, the need for treaties to satisfy such a test was initially a judicial creation,[145] although it has been written into a number of constitutional documents,[146] as well as having been articulated in at least one legislative text addressing the law of

[141] Dashwood et al (2011: ch 8).

[142] See eg Craig and de Búrca (2011: ch 7); Chalmers, Davies, and Monti (2010: 294–300); Betlem and Nollkaemper (2003: 571–2).

[143] On its significance see Nollkaemper (2011: 139–65), and the two recently edited collections with country reports: Sloss (2009a) and Shelton (2011). The doctrine can be expressly written into the constitution; Nollkaemper (2011: 147) identifies in this respect South Africa, Malawi, and Spain, and one could add Moldova (1994: Art 4(1)) and Romania (1991: Art 20(1)).

[144] Even in legal orders where such a test applies, we find examples where courts have applied treaties without expressly addressing themselves preliminarily to this threshold test. With respect to Belgium, see eg Vandaele and Claes (2001: 440), see also Velu (1981); for the US, see Wu (2007: 585); for Japan, see Iwasawa (1998: 45).

[145] It is usually traced to a nineteenth-century judgment of the US Supreme Court: Iwasawa (1986: 627).

[146] In the Netherlands, it was expressly written into the Constitution via the 1956 constitutional reforms although the government had already made it clear that the 1953 revision was intended to be confined to treaty provisions satisfying this threshold test: see Claes and de Witte (1998: 175, 177); see also Albania (1998: Art 122(1), and, viewed as reflecting the concept, Wyrozumska (2011: 482), Poland (1997: Art 91(1)).

treaties.[147] In some constitutional systems where automatic treaty incorporation operates, the legislator has in certain cases taken this determination away from the courts by providing in the approval Act that the treaty or treaty provisions are not to have direct effect,[148] as has the executive by attaching an interpretative declaration to a treaty stating that its provisions are not directly effective.[149]

Turning now to the content of this threshold test, it is here that the real complexity commences for although many constitutional systems have converged around a similar label to refer to the test, the criteria used in determining whether a treaty or treaty provision is directly effective not only diverge, but they have varied over time, and across courts, within the same legal orders.[150] Thus, not only do courts in different countries reach different conclusions with respect to the same treaties,[151] but even courts within the same country have reached different conclusions and tracked their own path in making this determination.[152]

Frequently the criteria employed are bracketed into two main categories, those of a subjective nature and those of an objective nature.[153] The subjective aspect is usually considered to revolve around the intent of the parties.[154] The intention that is being looked for is phrased diversely not

[147] For Russia, see Tikhomirov (2011: 522).

[148] This has occurred in Germany, see Frowein and Oellers-Frahm (1996b: 81); Frowein (1987: 71–2); Frowein and Hahn (1992: 375).

[149] This has happened on various occasions in the US with respect to human rights treaties: see Vazquez (2008: 37 et seq). There is some controversy as to whether the treaty remains part of domestic law and whether all judicial application of the relevant treaties is precluded, see Sloss (2002: 39–44). Germany has also adopted such declarations with respect to several human rights instruments: see Simma et al (1997: 79).

[150] On the test being applied differently even though similar terminology is used, see Buergenthal (1992: 394–5); on the evolution of the criteria over time with respect to Belgium: see Vandaele and Claes (2001: 419 et seq); see also Frowein and Oellers-Frahm (1996a: 18) asserting that the criteria are neither well defined nor uniform.

[151] The direct effect of the European Social Charter was rejected by the French Conseil d'État, see Decaux (2011: 230–2), but a different line has been taken in the Netherlands, see below. A treaty that many legal orders appear to deem not directly effective, the ICESCR, has been accorded direct effect in Serbia and employed by the Constitutional Court in 2004 to strike down provisions of an Act: see Djajic (2011: 536).

[152] See the example below concerning the Rights of the Child Convention in France.

[153] For the objective/subjective categorization, see Vandaele and Claes (2001: 416–17); Iwasawa (1986: 653–86). For the same categorization but not using the language of subjective/objective, see Buergenthal (1992: 383–4).

[154] Some courts have looked to the intention of their own government: see Buergenthal (1992: 383) identifying the US, Switzerland, and Austria as examples, see further on the US, Vazquez (1995: 705–8; 2008: 652–6).

only across courts in different countries but even within the same country. Courts are variously said to be looking for the intention that the treaty 'confer subjective rights or impose obligations on individuals',[155] or that it creates 'private rights' or 'judicially enforceable private rights' or 'private rights of action' or a 'cause of action'.[156]

However, the whole notion of searching for any form of intention has long been criticized because it is rare for a treaty, especially in the multilateral context, to address itself to the manner in which it is to be implemented and whether it is to be domestically judicially enforceable.[157] Accordingly, one scholar memorably referred to efforts to ascertain the intent of the parties to most multilateral treaties as having 'only marginally greater chances of success than medieval attempts to capture the unicorn'.[158] In short, reliance on this subjective element is inherently problematic absent greater efforts on the part of treaty drafters to articulate how treaties are to be given effect in the domestic legal order.[159]

Turning to the objective criteria, these are usually concerned with requiring that the treaty or treaty provisions are clear and precise and do not require further implementing measures. In one sense, this is part of a general test as to whether a treaty or specific provision is even capable of judicial application: there are treaties which have more of a programmatic nature and need fleshing out via legislative or administrative measures.[160] And there is therefore some measure of analogy to be drawn with domestic norms whether of a legislative or constitutional status that will also not be judicially enforceable but will require further implementing measures to bring them into effect.[161] It is essential, however, to recognize that despite the tendency to give these criteria the label of 'objective' they are, like the subjective criteria, inherently malleable and leave the judge great freedom

[155] As the Belgian Supreme Court put the matter in the early 1980s, see Vandaele and Claes (2001: 417).

[156] See Vazquez (1995: 710) (discussing US case law).

[157] For such criticism, see Iwasawa (1998: 47; 1986: 654–5); Lillich (1985: 372–3); Wu (2007: 578–9); Paust (1988: 770–1); Vandaele and Claes (2001: 447); Sloss (2012a).

[158] Lillich (1985: 373).

[159] Courts have been known to look to the terms of the treaty (the objective criteria) as testimony to the intentions of the parties: see eg Leary (1982: 382); Iwasawa (1986: 655, 671); Vandaele and Claes (2001: 418).

[160] See Buergenthal (1992: 382–3).

[161] See Buergenthal (1992: 318, 369); Prechal (2002: 33).

for manoeuvre.[162] What is clear and precise and does not require further implementing measures will not only vary from court to court but also, not least given different legal cultures, across legal orders.[163] Thus, a treaty provision might be considered sufficiently precise in a legal order where the judiciary have broader interpretative powers but not so in a legal order where their powers are more circumscribed.[164] Moreover, there may well be variation depending on how the particular area of law with which the treaty is concerned is regulated domestically, and thus as Buergenthal pointed out:

> A treaty provision that Austrian judges, for example, may find too vague to apply as such because the particular subject is in Austria usually regulated by very specific national legislation, may in Germany or Switzerland pose no such problems because there the judges are required to apply national standards that are equally general. Other provisions of the same treaty might, however, create vagueness problems for German or Swiss judges that do not arise for Austrian judges.[165]

In sum, the direct effect determination is not only multifaceted but also inherently malleable. As a result, it is not surprising that the jurisprudence on this point in legal orders with a system of automatic incorporation is extremely complex and frequently beset by inconsistency.[166] A few brief examples from some of the founding Member States will serve to elucidate the point.

In Belgium, the jurisprudence was generally considered to have moved away from the subjective part of the analysis, expressly underlined by the Supreme Civil Court in the early 1980s, to a test focused on the so-called objective criteria.[167] But a spate of civil and administrative Supreme Court cases saw a focus on subjective rights, as well as on whether the treaty is addressed to States,[168] leading to the negation of the direct effect of various provisions of numerous conventions on the basis that the obligations are

[162] See for criticism: Frowein and Oellers-Frahm (1996a: 18); Vandaele and Claes (2001: 447–9).

[163] See generally Iwasawa (1998: 48); Buergenthal (1992: 395).

[164] Iwasawa (1986: 672; 1998: 48).

[165] Buergenthal (1992: 395).

[166] The classic example in this respect is the US where the jurisprudence continues to grow and where the scholarly commentary attesting to the disarray is vast. A recent selection includes: Sloss (2012a); Hathaway et al (2012); Vazquez (2008).

[167] See Verhoeven (2000: 469–70); Verhoeven (1996: 131); Bribosia (1998: 7–9, 21, 29); Vandaele and Claes (2001: 416, 426–7).

[168] Vandaele and Claes (2001: 429).

only created for the Contracting Parties.[169] Furthermore, there are many cases in the human rights sphere where direct effect has been either accorded or not to provisions without any justification proffered.[170] In such circumstances, it is understandable that a detailed study had emphasized that Belgian courts use the direct effect instrument in a non-transparent manner.[171]

A good example of the complexity in France was provided by the contrasting jurisprudence of the Supreme Administrative and Civil Courts with respect to the Rights of the Child Convention.[172] The latter, commencing in 1993, had rejected the direct effect of the entire Convention on the basis that it only creates obligations for States and requires further implementing measures, only to reverse that stance in mid-2005. Whilst the former adopted a case-by-case strategy that recognized the direct effect of certain of the provisions, notwithstanding the then contrary jurisprudence of the Supreme Civil Court, including allowing it to prevail over a law in 2006.

In Germany, the courts are still considered to have recourse to the subjective and objective elements.[173] There are examples of entire treaties held not to be directly effective, such as: the European Social Charter on the ground that most of its provisions lay down obligations expressly for the Member States and their legislatures;[174] extradition treaties on the ground that they do not confer subjective rights;[175] the Convention on the Elimination of all forms of Discrimination Against Women (CEDAW) because it was considered only to create obligations between State Parties and the ICESCR because it is of a programmatic character requiring further State action for implementation.[176] Some decades ago the reluctance of German

[169] Cases cited in Vandaele and Claes (2001: 427–8).

[170] Vandaele and Claes (2001: 439–40).

[171] Vandaele and Claes (2001: 450); see also Verhoeven (1996: 131).

[172] See Decaux (2011: 233–4); Daillier, Forteau, and Pellet (2009: 254–5). The confused Conseil d'État European Social Charter case law, the rejection of direct effect for the ICESCR by the Conseil d'État as contrasted with the acceptance of direct effect of one provision by the Cour de Cassation is discussed by Decaux (2011: 230–3).

[173] For reference to a twin-pronged test: see Uerpmann-Wittzack (2003a: 99) and Simma et al (1997: 85). The test was put in somewhat different terms by Frowein and Oellers-Frahm (1996b).

[174] Frowein and Oellers-Frahm (1996b: 82).

[175] Id. Frowein and Hahn (1992: 385–6).

[176] See Simma et al (1997: 86); Uerpmann-Wittzack (2003a: 96). Paulus (2009a: 222), however, refers to a 2009 case in which a Federal Administrative Court appears to have assessed the compatibility of student fees with the ICESCR. The Dutch Supreme Court in contrast accepted the direct effect of a CEDAW provision in 2010: see Fleuren (2010: 258).

courts to recognize the direct effect of treaties was noted,[177] more recent studies in the human rights sphere are testimony to existing difficulties,[178] and most recently a commentator has boldly asserted that 'German courts . . . tend to consider most treaty provisions as non-self-executing'.[179]

With respect to Italy, its Supreme Ordinary Court through to at least the late 1980s had frequently ruled that the ECHR was of a programmatic nature.[180] A more receptive approach has since developed,[181] but emphasis on the programmatic nature of certain provisions of the ECHR by the Supreme Ordinary Court was still apparent into the late 1990s.[182]

Luxembourg commentators frequently pointed to the open attitude of their courts to treaty norms,[183] and it has been asserted that they operate a presumption in favour of direct effect.[184] However, the Supreme Civil Court did reject the direct effect of the ICCPR considering it solely to create obligations for the Contracting States,[185] and recent work suggests an increasing willingness to reject direct effect influenced by hesitation between either using the objective or subject criteria or, indeed, their cumulative application.[186]

With respect to the Netherlands, it has become common ground to emphasize the flexibility exhibited by Dutch courts in making this determination, especially in the wake of a well-known Supreme Court judgment of the mid-1980s which accorded direct effect to a provision of the European Social Charter and in doing so expressly moved away from the parties' intentions, unless expressly stated, to focus solely on the content of the specific treaty provision.[187] But the Dutch Supreme Court has also developed an abstaining doctrine that sees it decline to apply treaty provisions, even where they have previously been recognized as directly effective,

[177] Frowein and Hahn (1992: 385).

[178] See Uerpmann-Wittzack (2003b); Simma et al (1997).

[179] Folz (2011: 243), albeit citing no supporting case law.

[180] Scovazzi (1997: 61–2).

[181] See Cannizzaro (2010).

[182] See cases cited in the Italian Yearbook of International Law (1999: 166).

[183] eg Pescatore (1964: 95–6; 1984: 383).

[184] Biever et al (1996: 415).

[185] See cases cited in Biever et al (1996: 415–16). Kinsch notes that this proposition has been followed by some courts but implicitly not accepted by others (2011: 393).

[186] Kinsch (2011: 392–5).

[187] See Schermers (1987: 115–16); Brolmann and Vierdag (1996: 445); Brouwer (2005: 503–4). Contrast Van Dijk and Tahzib (1992: 421) asserting that there were no indications that the Dutch courts were particularly liberal or restrictive with respect to accepting the direct effect of treaties.

where it requires national law to be set aside and leaves gaps that in the court's view should be filled by the legislature.[188]

It would be futile to attempt to gloss over the complexity of the domestic direct effect determination or to pretend that it is possible within the confines of a short section to bring any semblance of order even to the developments within a single legal order. What is important for the purposes of this section is to underscore two key points: first, the opaqueness of this domestic judicial determination; and, secondly, the fact that in legal orders where treaties are automatically incorporated it is this determination which will be of critical importance to the fortunes of the individual litigant and to the domestic effectiveness of treaty norms.

The fact that a treaty is constitutionally declared to be the superior law of the land will be of little consolation to the individual litigant who, for example, seeks to have an inconsistent administrative measure set aside only for the domestic court to conclude that the treaty or a particular provision is not directly effective. And yet it is equally clear that faced with the same treaty provision a court, in a legal order where the later-in-time rule prevails, might come to the opposite conclusion on the direct effect analysis and set aside an inconsistent earlier-in-time statute. It is evident, therefore, that the formal hierarchical standing of treaties in the domestic legal order can be deceptive. Indeed, in some legal orders there has been debate as to whether treaties or treaty provisions that are not considered directly effective are in fact part of the legal order.[189] One response to this argument is that they are like domestic legal norms which cannot be judicially enforced, absent further implementation, but are nonetheless law for various other purposes.[190] Clearly, the mantra of a treaty becoming part of the domestic legal order is typically used indiscriminately but where the treaty or specific provisions are considered directly effective it will result in radically different legal effects in the domestic judicial arena.

188 See Fleuren (2010: 258–9); Alkema (2011: 418).

189 For the Dutch debate see Brolmann and Vierdag (1996: 443–4) (arguing that they are not part) but contrast Van Dijk and Tahzib (1992); Fleuren (2010: 251); Alkema (2011: 410). For the US, see Dalton (2005: 788); Vazquez (1999: 2185; 2008); Paust (2002: 624) (that they are part of the law). Contrast, Iwasawa (1986: 643–5). For Austria they are still considered to be part of the legal order, see Handl-Petz (2011: 79–80). For Italy, see the Supreme Civil Court judgment cited in the Italian Yearbook of International Law (2001: 314) (asserting that where further implementation is required the relevant norms do not become part of the law of the land automatically and directly).

190 See Buergenthal (1992: 318).

3.2 Non-automatic treaty incorporation

3.2.1 *Defining non-automatic treaty incorporation*

The terminology of non-automatic treaty incorporation as employed here refers to an approach to treaties whereby they do not automatically become part of the domestic legal order upon entry into force for the State concerned. Rather, they are viewed as only becoming part of the domestic legal order where the legislature so provides, and although on occasion the legislature does so provide, this takes place in principle in an ad hoc fashion. They can do so by, for example, attaching the treaty or parts or provisions of a treaty to the schedule of an Act which basically declares that the treaty is to have the force of law,[191] or effect as part of domestic law,[192] or to be part of the law of the land,[193] or some variation thereof.[194] But the text or parts of the treaty can also form part of the body of the text of the legislative measure, or even be reformulated, without there necessarily being any reference to the treaty.[195] Where a treaty is made part of domestic law, it retains the hierarchical status of the incorporating legislation.[196]

This non-automatic approach to treaty incorporation can have its basis in the common law;[197] it can effectively be enshrined in a constitutional document;[198] it can be considered to be presupposed by or be implicit in the

[191] For Canada, see Van Ert (2009a: 169); for Australia, see Crawford (1979). See below for Ireland and the UK.

[192] eg Denmark, see below.

[193] eg Finland according to Rosas (2001: 291).

[194] For Canada, see Beaulac and Currie (2011: 120–2, 128–9).

[195] For incorporation techniques in Canada, see Van Ert (2009a: 160–70); for Australia, see Crawford (1979), Rothwell (2009a: 138–45); for Sweden, see Cameron (2005: 443); for Antigua and Barbuda, see Anderson (2002); for Israel, see Kretzmer (2009a: 283–5). With respect to Denmark, Ireland, and the UK see below.

[196] For Sweden, see Cameron (2005: 444); for South Africa, see Dugard (2009a: 463); for Canada, see Beaulac and Currie (2011: 144–5). For Ireland, Denmark, and the UK see below.

[197] eg UK, see below. For New Zealand, see Hopkins (2011); for Canada, see Beaulac and Currie (2011). Maluwa (1999: 41) has noted that most of Anglophone Africa avoided the incorporation of international law and left the matter to be determined by the common law approaches developed in English case law. The new Kenyan Constitution (2010), cited earlier, has however moved to an automatic treaty incorporation model.

[198] eg Ireland, see below; Nigeria (1999: s 12) which in effect codified the practice under the 1960 Constitution.

Constitution even if not expressly stated;[199] it can be enshrined in a parliamentary Act.[200] The role of Parliament can vary considerably in such legal orders, ranging from legal orders where the basic rule is that treaties are concluded by the executive with parliamentary approval or authorization rarely needed,[201] to those where certain categories of treaty require parliamentary approval,[202] to there being a constitutional requirement for parliamentary approval or authorization that in practice encompasses most treaties.[203]

We will now briefly touch upon this approach to treaties in the Member States that joined the EU in its first wave of enlargement.

3.2.2 *Non-automatic treaty incorporation in Denmark, Ireland, and the UK*

In all three legal orders, in principle treaties or specific provisions of treaties are said only to become part of the domestic legal order where Parliament so provides.[204] In the case of Denmark, the Constitution is considered to be premised on this proposition even if it does not state so in express terms.[205] In the case of Ireland, this has been written into its 1937 Constitution.[206] Whilst in the UK it has its foundation in the common law.

Treaties are frequently adhered to in all three legal orders without incorporating legislation being passed and, indeed, without any changes being made in domestic law; the logic being that they will in any event only adhere once their domestic law has been brought into compliance with the relevant treaty obligations.[207] And in all three legal orders domestic law was considered adequately to protect the rights enshrined in the

[199] eg Sweden, see Cameron (2005: 441–2); for Denmark, see below.

[200] Antigua and Barbuda, Ratification of Treaties Act 1987, Sect 3(3). See Aust (2007: 194).

[201] As in the UK. For India, see Thakore (2005: 351, 355); for Canada, see Copithorne (2005).

[202] Antigua and Barbuda.

[203] Scandinavian countries in general according to Buergenthal (1992: 364).

[204] For Denmark, see Harhoff (1996: 159 et seq); for Ireland, see Symmons (1996: 330–1, 337–8); for the UK, see Fox et al (1996: 502, 505) (there is a limited exception whereby treaties can have the force of law by virtue of the prerogative alone).

[205] Section 19(1) Danish Constitution 1953. See Espersen (1970: 293); Gulmann (1987: 29).

[206] Article 29.6. See Kelly (2003: 5.3.116); Symmons (1996: 330).

[207] For the UK, see Sinclair et al (2005: 735, 742); Higgins (1997: 38); Jennings and Watts (1992: 61); Fox et al (1996: 503); for Denmark, see Harhoff (1996: 159–60), see also Denmark's core report HRI/CORE/1/Add.58 (29 June 1995) (para 103); first State report under the Council of Europe's Framework Convention for the Protection of National Minorities (ACFC/SR (99) 9); for Ireland, see Symmons (1996: 333) and Ireland's State Party submission (HRI/CORE/1/Add.15/Rev.1 (1 July 1998), para 33.

ECHR therefore none provided for any incorporating legislation when they became parties in the early 1950s, only succumbing to the increasing pressure for incorporation in 1992 (Denmark), 1998 (UK), and 2003 (Ireland).[208]

Where legislative incorporation is deemed necessary, there are similar means to achieve this.[209] A common approach in all three is to incorporate the treaty or parts or provisions thereof by attaching it to the schedule to an Act that basically provides that the treaty is to have the force of law or effect as part of domestic law. Other methods include enactment of the treaty provisions within the body of a legislative measure with the legislative measure potentially referring to the treaty.

The treaty or the incorporated part or provisions of the treaty, putting the special case of the EU to one side for a moment, retain the hierarchical status of the incorporating legislation.[210] But there is an important canon of construction in all these legal orders by which courts seek to read domestic law consistently with international law obligations and it operates to mitigate both the later-in-time rule and the rule that an unincorporated treaty is not part of the domestic legal order.[211]

Turning to EU law, all three had to provide for a means to accommodate membership, and in particular the principles of supremacy and direct effect, within their existing constitutional framework. Accordingly, in all three legal orders the respective Accession Acts provided for the incorporation of EU law and, although none of the Acts expressly provided for the primacy of EU law, Ireland passed a constitutional amendment which sought constitutionally to enshrine primacy.[212] Dicta in the Irish Supreme Court has, however, suggested that primacy over the Constitution is not unconditional;[213] whilst the Danish Supreme Court affirmed that Danish

[208] For Denmark, see Germer (2001); Espersen (1970: 298); for the UK, see Blackburn and Polakiewicz (2001); for Ireland, see Hogan (2006).

[209] For Denmark, see Harhoff (1996: 159–60); Gulmann (1987: 30–1); Esperson (1970: 294–5); for Ireland, see Symmons (1996: 331–2); for the UK, see Aust (2007: 189–92), Fox et al (1996: 499).

[210] For Denmark, see Harhoff (1996: 163), Gulmann (1987: 31); for Ireland, see Symmons (1996: 337–8); for the UK, see Fox et al (1996: 505).

[211] For the UK, see eg Jennings and Watts (1992: 61–3), Fox et al (1996: 502–4), Aust (2009a: 479–81); for Denmark, see Harhoff (1996: 160–1, 164), Germer (2001: 260), Gulmann (1987: 32); for Ireland, see Kelly (2003: 5.3.126) and Symmons (1996: 333–4, 339–40).

[212] For Denmark, see Harhoff (1996: 170–3); for Ireland, see Symmons (1996: 345–50); for the UK, see Craig (2011), Craig and de Búrca (2011: 285–93), Fox et al (1996: 513–17).

[213] See generally Phelan (2008).

courts still retain the power to review the constitutionality of measures of EU law;[214] and in the UK a seminal House of Lords decision in 1991 accepted EU law supremacy—based on the UK Accession Act—but it remains to be seen what the outcome would be were Parliament expressly to legislate contrary to EU law.[215]

4. Revisiting the Theory and the Role of Domestic Courts

This section commences with a critique of the conventionally employed language of monism and dualism vis-à-vis the domestic constitutional regulation of treaties before engaging with the growing emphasis on the role of national courts in treaty enforcement.

4.1 Misleading labels: monism and dualism in the treaty context

It has become conventional practice for most studies touching upon the relationship between international law and domestic law to devote some attention, cursory as it may be, to two contrasting theoretical constructs. This controversy between the dualist and the monist schools is one that has, over the years, taxed the minds of many a distinguished international lawyer. The seminal texts in dualist thinking emerged a little over a century ago.[216] The essence of this approach was based on the proposition that international law and domestic law are distinct legal orders that operate in discrete spheres and regulate different relations: international law regulates the behaviour of, and relations between, sovereign States whilst domestic law regulates the relations of individuals both *inter se* and in their relationship to the State. Being distinct legal orders, it followed that the conditions for the validity and duration of international rules depend exclusively on international law and those for domestic law depend exclusively on

[214] See Biering (2000: 928–32), Claes (2006: 514–17, 625–7).

[215] See Craig (2011).

[216] In the work of Triepel (1899) and Anzilotti (1905). Their theories were later refined, see Triepel (1923) and Anzilotti (1929).

domestic law. The dualist school is thus able to accept the supremacy of international law, at the international level, while maintaining the supremacy of domestic law, at the domestic level.[217] Another tenet that flows from holding domestic law and international law to be distinct legal orders is that international law cannot, by definition, operate directly within the domestic legal order.

The monist approach, in contrast, was premised on the unity of the international and domestic legal orders; they are part of one and the same legal order. In its dominant variant, this model posits the supremacy of international law.[218] That is to say, that international law sits at the apex of this hierarchy. This proposition is reached in a different manner by the various exponents of the monist view. Kelsen, its most celebrated exponent, reaches the conclusion based on the proposition that international law and domestic law have their ultimate reason of validity in the same basic norm which is 'the fundamental rule according to which the various norms of the order are to be created'.[219] And for Kelsen the basic norm of international law—that 'States ought to behave as they have customarily behaved'—is the ultimate reason of the validity of the national legal order.[220] Lauterpacht's monistic construction, in contrast, is of a natural law bent, with an emphasis on the individual as 'the ultimate unit of all law'[221] and the supremacy of international law being asserted based on its capacity to protect the individual.[222] For the monist scholars, international law could indeed be applied directly as international law in the domestic legal order. Whilst some monist scholars went as far as suggesting that domestic law contrary to international law was 'abrogated',[223] Kelsen was converted to the view that contrary domestic law is valid until domestically annulled for whilst it will remain illegal from an international law perspective, international law itself does not provide for any annulment procedure.[224]

[217] For recent affirmation by a prominent dualist scholar, see Arangio-Ruiz (2003: 972; 2007: 19).

[218] There is a discredited approach that posited the supremacy of domestic law: see further Cassese (2005: 213–14, 216); Ruda (1994: 116–17).

[219] (1961: 367).

[220] (1961: 368–9).

[221] (1946: 27).

[222] Shaw (2008: 131–2).

[223] Notably Georges Scelle (1933: 331), but it has been suggested that this was a figure of speech: Daillier, Forteau, and Pellet (2009: 109).

[224] (1961: 371–2; 1923: 315). Kelsen initially expressed the view that contrary domestic Acts were void within the domestic legal order, see Simma (1995: 45); Ruda (1994: 121).

Since the early seminal texts in dualist and monist thinking emerged, there has been a radical transformation in international law.[225] A transformation which was captured lucidly in Friedmann's much-cited emphasis on the emergence of an international law of cooperation in existence alongside the traditional law of coexistence.[226] Prominent among these changes has been the ever-increasing resort to treaties and international organizations as a means to regulate the problems of an increasingly interdependent world. Thus we have seen, for example, the birth and growth of a range of different types of treaty premised on domestic authorities giving effect to the substantive norms. The post-Second World War period has also seen a proliferation of international courts, tribunals, and dispute settlement bodies.[227] And, more generally, we have seen an increasingly prominent role for the individual in the international legal system.[228] Such prominent changes, amongst others, and the inexorably increasing interaction between international and national law, have led many to question the validity of the dualist account.[229] Others, however, have had no difficulty in accounting for such changes within the dualist paradigm.[230] Clearly, there will continue to be controversy as to how to conceptualize the evolution of international law and how it sits with the dualist and monist accounts.[231] Whether conceptualizing matters in such terms has any purchase, and whether the monism–dualism debate is of any significance, is a matter on which there is disagreement. In relatively recent times, distinguished international lawyers have referred to it as 'fairly illusory',[232]

225 Indeed, the status of international law as 'law' had yet to be cemented when the dualist and monist controversy was raging in the earlier part of the twentieth century. The Austinian tradition proved difficult to displace and Kelsen himself made crucial contributions in this respect: see eg Leben (1998). The monist account had clear ideological objectives in terms of cementing the status of international law as law and the dualist account was criticized as denying the juridical nature of international law: Kelsen (1926: 276), see also Starke (1936: 78).

226 Friedmann (1964).

227 The Project on International Courts and Tribunals has put together a chart (November 2004) with some 125 bodies making legal determinations: <http://www.pict-pcti.org/publications/synoptic_chart/Synop_C4.pdf>.

228 See eg McCorquodale (2010).

229 eg Cassese (2005: 216–17); Dupuy and Kerbrat (2010: 451); Henkin (1995: 66); Jennings (1996: 41); Nollkaemper (2011: 13); Paulus (2007: 228–34).

230 See Arangio-Ruiz (2003: esp at 970–81).

231 See most recently Nijman and Nollkaemper (2007).

232 Tomuschat (1999: 363).

'passé',[233] 'fruitless and anachronistic',[234] and as 'intellectual zombies of another time'.[235] Others do, however, consider it to be a debate with practical import.[236] It is certainly difficult to contend that the debate is of—or has had—no practical consequence. There are some indications that it has influenced the drafting of constitutions,[237] and it may have practical relevance simply by dint of its influence on the mindsets of scholars, practitioners, and judges.[238]

The analytical utility of the increasingly common usage of the terminology of monism and dualism as a means of classifying different domestic constitutional approaches to the relationship between treaties and domestic law is questionable.[239] In earlier times, there was much debate as to whether treaties became part of a domestic legal order via 'transformation', whereby the treaty was transformed into national law such that it applied as national law and not international law, or whether it applied by virtue of 'adoption' or 'incorporation', such that it retained its character as international law.[240]

[233] Frowein according to Pescatore (1987: 191).

[234] Conforti (1993: 26). For a more recent reference to 'fruitless debates' see Kumm (2006: 260).

[235] Von Bogdandy (2008: 400).

[236] eg Higgins (1995: 206 et seq).

[237] Notably through the influence of Georges Scelle in the context of the drafting of the French Constitution: see Leary (1982) and Daillier, Forteau, and Pellet (2009: 253). Contrast Henkin (1995: 67) and Denza (2010: 417) suggesting otherwise.

[238] The seminal Belgian case rejecting the later-in-time rule vis-à-vis treaties saw the Procureur General's submissions include the views of a Conseiller d'État who used language strikingly reminiscent of Kelsen. And a judge who served on the ECJ for 18 years, and was the judge-rapporteur in a seminal case asserting the supremacy of EU law (*Simmenthal*) has declared his adherence to the monistic account: Pescatore (2003).

[239] A few examples amongst prominent international law scholars, not all of whom clearly articulate which traits represent the monist and which the dualist approach, include: Jiménez de Aréchaga (1989: 410–11); Aust (2007); Buergenthal (1992); Dupuy and Kerbrat (2010: 452–4); Henkin (1995: 64–77); Higgins (1995: 205 et seq). The editor and most of the country reports in the two recent general surveys of domestic practice use the terminology to refer to the different domestic constitutional approaches to treaties (Sloss 2009a; Shelton 2011), as does Nollkaemper (2011: ch 4), and a recent study on reception of the ECHR (Keller and Stone Sweet 2008). States have also taken to referring to their legal orders as dualist or monist in the treaty context, eg the Norwegian submission to the Human Rights Council A/HRC/WG.6/6/NOR/1 (14/09/09), the Irish submission to the Committee on the Rights of the Child CRC/C/IRL/2 (9/12/05). The Irish Foreign Affairs website contrasts its own, and that of other common law countries, dualist approach to the monist approach of other countries: <http://www.dfa.ie/home/index.aspx?id=351>.

[240] The original dualist thinkers argued that international law could only ever apply by virtue of this transformation, see eg Anzilotti (1929: 62–3); Triepel (1923: esp at 91).

The tendency was to consider transformation as representing dualism, and adoption or incorporation as representing monism.[241] It was a debate, however, of doubtful value given that it left the door open to much disagreement as to what counts as transformation and what is instead merely adoption or incorporation.[242] Indeed, the terminological niceties of 'transformation' versus 'adoption' or 'incorporation', that had so troubled many a scholar, appear to have been wholly eschewed by one distinguished international lawyer who explored 'how some representative monist States *transform* treaties into domestic law'.[243]

If the confusion cemented between transformation versus adoption or incorporation were not problematic enough, for some the key in using the terminology of monism and dualism to describe the approach taken by a domestic legal order to treaties is whether the domestic legal order functions such that treaties become part of the domestic legal order once they enter into force for the State concerned.[244] Where they do so, that State is considered to adopt a monist approach to treaties and, where they do not, then it is viewed as taking a dualist approach, with these classifications applying regardless of the hierarchical status attributed to treaties in the domestic legal order. In this sense, the basic fault-line would clearly overlap with the distinction drawn between automatic and non-automatic incorporation in the preceding section. Others, however, who employ the terminology of monism and dualism in this fashion, insist that treaties must have a hierarchically superior status to ordinary law in order for a legal order to be

[241] See eg Morgenstern (1950). The terminology, however, was not always so used, eg Mosler (1957); Seidl-Hohenveldern (1963). And Jennings and Watts (1992: 54) used the terminology of adoption in the context of the dualist approach.

[242] As evinced by the debate in Germany concerning the supposed move from the transformation to adoption/incorporation model: see Mosler (1957); Seidl-Hohenveldern (1963); Waelbroeck (1969: 71–6); Simma et al (1997); Paulus (2009a: 217–18). But note Frowein (1987: 66) stating that 'the law transforms, adopts or incorporates the rules of the treaty into the German legal system'. For a similar debate in Italy, see Condorelli (1974). Note also the current usage of this terminology in various country chapters in Hollis (2005) and the confusion in this respect pointed to by the editor: Hollis (2005: 40–1). One practical consequence of the emphasis on transformation was whether it suggested that once international norms were transformed into domestic law, they were to be interpreted as domestic law rather than being subject to international treaty interpretation rules.

[243] Buergenthal (1992: 341). Emphasis added.

[244] Jiménez de Aréchaga (1989); Aust (2007: 181–95); Buergenthal (1992: 315–17, 341); Weiler (1991: 2415); Van Alstine (2009a: 569–70).

considered monist.[245] Clearly, this difference in stance results in different legal orders being referred to as dualist or monist depending on which side of the domestic hierarchical divide they fall.[246]

Further terminological confusion has emerged due to the various permutations in the use of the dualist and monist labels, with some legal orders in the treaty context being described, to use only a handful of the variations, as 'radically dualist',[247] 'formally dualistic with monistic characters',[248] 'mitigated dualism',[249] 'dualistic' but representing 'de facto monism',[250] 'moderately dualist',[251] 'moderately monistic',[252] 'quasi-monist',[253] 'hybrid monism',[254] or even 'stumbling towards a modified monism'.[255] To complicate matters further, these varying permutations often come with little if any attempt at explanation.

The analytical utility of the monist–dualist terminology as shorthand for different constitutional approaches to the relationship between treaties and the domestic legal order is further compromised by additional objections to its continued use in this fashion. First and foremost, a central tenet of the dualistic understanding was that it was for the domestic legal order to determine the legal effects that international law has in the domestic legal order. And it is clear that international law scholars generally acknowledge

[245] An example is Lillich (1985). For Uerpmann-Wittzack (2009: 135), 'A strictly monist conception would mean that international law automatically takes precedence over all norms of internal law, including constitutional law.' The Belgian approach to treaties was also considered by some to have moved from dualist to monist with the seminal judgment in *Le Ski* that dispensed with the later-in-time rule, and indeed some considered Belgium to have reverted to dualism with the creation of the Constitutional Court and its willingness to review the Act concerning the conclusion of treaties.

[246] Buergenthal (1992: 341) thus considers Italy, Germany, and the US to be monist. Aust (2007: 183–4) considers Germany to be monist, as do Sloss (2009b: 7) and Van Alstine (2009a: 570) (they use the label of hybrid monism).

[247] The UK according to Pescatore (1987: 191).

[248] Spain according to Bermejo Garcia et al (1996).

[249] Schermers (1979: 83–4) referring to Germany and Italy.

[250] Finland according to Karapuu and Rosas (1990: 201), see also Scheinin (1996: 258) referring to 'dualism in form but monism in practice'.

[251] Papier (2006) the then President of the German Federal Constitutional Court referring to the German system. Terminology which some also use with respect to Italy: Wildhaber (2007: 218).

[252] The Netherlands, see Alkema (2011: 408); Spain, see Candela Soriano (2008: 403).

[253] The US according to Weiler (1991: 2415).

[254] Van Alstine (2009) and Sloss (2009b) use this terminology in relation to Germany, the Netherlands, Poland, Russia, and the US.

[255] New Zealand according to Hopkins (2011: 447).

that international law does not determine the legal effects that treaties have in the domestic legal arena and that this is actually a domestic constitutional choice.[256] In one respect, it could thus be argued that the constitutional choice for what in common scholarly parlance is referred to as monism is but a modality of dualism.[257] Put most bluntly, being a domestic constitutional choice means that it is perfectly understandable in dualist terms. And, thus, as one international law scholar has emphasized this is no monism at all, for the domestic constitutional choice is made on a clearly dualistic premise, namely, that there exists more than one legal order and that any juridical impact of international law in the domestic legal arena is not the product of international law but rather of national law.[258] Accordingly, on this account the current commonly employed usage of the monist label is an oxymoron.

It should not be forgotten that the main architects of dualist thinking were fully aware of the US Constitution and its express provision stipulating that treaties are to be the supreme law of the land. Certainly, they may not have been able to predict that the post-Second World War period would lead to the emergence of many a constitution, commencing with the French (1946), that sought constitutionally to enshrine a status for treaties above at least ordinary law.[259] But this development, in and of itself, does not take away from their theoretical construct. As Triepel himself pointed out in commenting on the US Constitution, the binding domestic force of the treaty stems from a source of domestic law.[260] And this would even be so where the constitutional choice stems from court judgments rather than the constituent power; courts, after all, are organs of national law.[261] Put another way, if international law has no means of realizing its own impact in the domestic legal arena, then on one account we cannot but

[256] Arangio-Ruiz (2003; 2007); Jiménez de Aréchaga (1989: 410–11); Bernhardt (2004: 430); Combacau and Sur (2010: 180, 185); Dupuy and Kerbrat (2010: 451); Henkin (1989: 424); Higgins (1995: 210); Treves (2005: 658); Mosler (1957: 631); Jennings and Watts (1992: 82); Riesenfeld (1980); Von Bogdandy (2008: 402–3); Nollkaemper (2011: 68–73, 301). See also Paulus (2007: 218). Cf Conforti (2001: 24) who contests the proposition that it is for the law of each State rather than international law to determine how the former must conform to the latter.

[257] For this point, see Combacau and Sur (2010: 185).

[258] Arangio-Ruiz (2003: 922–4, 937–9).

[259] For a general overview see Cassese (1985), with respect to Africa (Maluwa 1999); for Central and East European States (Stein 1994) and CIS States (Danilenko 1999). See also a range of country reports in Shelton (2011), Sloss (2009a), and Hollis (2005).

[260] (1923: 91) (emphasizing that the dualist theory cannot be refuted by the US Constitution).

[261] See to this effect, Arangio-Ruiz (2003: 923–4, 930).

have dualism because it will always be a question of how a particular legal order regulates its relations vis-à-vis international law. Dualism thus understood essentially becomes irrefutable.

Given the existing terminological confusion with the usage of the monist label, as well as the more potent criticism premised on current usage amounting to an oxymoron, we would ultimately be better served by dispensing with this conventional terminology. Indeed, the increasing use of this label with respect to legal orders that have what this chapter has referred to as automatic treaty incorporation, with or without superiority over ordinary law enshrined, can be misconstrued as indicative of the monist explanation of the relationship between international and national law having greater credence, despite the fact that for a committed dualist no such conclusion follows. And retention of the dualist label itself is apt to mislead, not only because it is likely forever to be viewed as a binary opposite to a monistic account, but also because as it is currently often employed with respect to constitutional systems adhering to non-automatic treaty incorporation it suggests that treaties can only have a domestic legal effect where legislation so provides. It is, however, strikingly clear that unincorporated treaties can have significant legal effects. Most obviously they do so via a canon of construction employed in many legal orders whereby domestic norms, potentially even constitutional provisions, are interpreted where possible in conformity with international obligations.[262] And, for some, to this extent the treaty can be conceptualized as being part of the domestic legal order;[263] after all, if it is not to some extent part of the domestic legal order, how can it have such an impact on domestic norms? A related point concerns the use of unincorporated treaties in reviewing the exercise of statutory discretion and as the basis for the founding of a legitimate expectation in administrative law both of which can result in quashing administrative decision-making.[264] Thus, whilst the dualist label

[262] See the non-automatic treaty incorporation section. The growing tendency of courts in common law countries judicially to incorporate human rights treaty provisions has been referred to as 'creeping monism': Waters (2007).

[263] This position was once advanced by the Norwegian Government in ICJ litigation, see *Certain Norwegian Loans (France v Norway)* (1957), Separate Opinion of Judge Lauterpacht, at 40–1. A monograph on the use of human rights in English courts predating ECHR incorporation rightly underscored the shortcomings of looking at the status of international law domestically as an 'in–out' question of whether the norm has been made part of domestic law given the more nuanced reality pertaining to the judicial use of international norms: Hunt (1997, see eg at 41–3).

[264] Canada and Australia offer famous examples of this taking place: see, respectively, Van Ert (2009a: 193–7) and Rothwell (2009a: 147–50). New Zealand appears to be proceeding down a

tends to conjure up images of watertight separation between legal orders,[265] absent legislative intervention, the real world leaves no doubt that matters are considerably more nuanced. It is also worth underscoring that the dualist label is frequently employed for both Germany and Italy, resulting in these two States being grouped rather indiscriminately alongside States such as Ireland, Denmark, and the UK, despite the fact that the German and Italian constitutional systems function in a manner akin to, for example, the French system, usually labelled monist—for as in France and unlike in Ireland, Denmark, and the UK, duly ratified treaties do effectively become part of domestic law albeit the later-in-time rule applies unlike in France.[266] This classification problem cannot be solved by reclassifying Germany and Italy under the monist umbrella.[267] That would merely solidify the usage of this problematic terminology in a manner that clashes directly with the extant judicial and scholarly self-identification within those systems.[268] The automatic and non-automatic distinction outlined earlier can serve as a less contentious and descriptively more accurate label for the basic constitutional fault-line in approach.[269] Crucially, it is also more flexible in that it can accommodate considerable sub-variation within its remit, not least in terms of the hierarchical status of treaties.

What is, however, crucial in practical terms to the legal effect of treaties in domestic legal orders, is not merely the constitutional provisions proclaiming treaties as part of domestic law or comparable domestic judicial

similar route concerning review of executive discretion (Hopkins (2011: 439–42)), and perhaps in India to some extent: see Jayawickrama (2009a: 251–3). South Africa offers a recent example of subordinate legislation being struck down as unreasonable due to its incompatibility with an unincorporated WTO Agreement: de Wet (2011: 587–8).

[265] Not, however, that dualist scholars do indeed conceive of the relationship as in any sense a hard and fast separation: see Arangio-Ruiz (2003; 2007) on the interdependence of legal orders.

[266] One scholar with a particularly acute grasp of domestic practice has recently been willing to bracket Germany and Italy with the UK as an adherent to a transformation approach: Nollkaemper (2011: 77).

[267] As has become increasingly common, see Buergenthal (1992), Sloss (2009a), and Van Alstine (2009a), and also Aust (2007: 183–4) with respect to Germany.

[268] Only recently the German Federal Constitutional Court itself has insisted that the German Constitution 'is clearly based on the classic idea that the relationship of public international law and domestic law is a relationship between two different legal spheres' (*Görgülü*, 14 October 2004, BVerfGE 111).

[269] Various international law scholars have avoided the monist–dualist label when referring to the varying domestic constitutional approaches: eg Cassese (2005); Denza (2010: 417–24); Iwasawa (1998); Jennings and Watts (1992: 56–81); Hollis (2005) (but this was not followed in the relevant country studies, eg Switzerland is referred to as monist).

pronouncements; but, rather, how courts actually deal with such treaties when they are raised in domestic litigation. Too often distinguished scholars have been willing to invoke constitutional provisions without drawing attention to the role that domestic courts have in making them reality,[270] and whilst commendably some have emphasized the importance of assessing domestic judicial practice,[271] studies actually providing the empirical work appear conspicuously absent.[272] What is, therefore, needed is less face-value acceptance of generously phrased constitutional provisions and seminal judicial pronouncements as to the relationship between treaties and the domestic legal order, and greater empirical analysis of what actually takes place in judicial practice.[273] This needs to be combined with greater focus on the normative justifications underpinning the role to be played by domestic courts in treaty enforcement. The suggested rejection of the monist and dualist labels is thus in no sense intended as a plea to avoid engaging with the important normative questions to which the relationship between international law and domestic law give rise. The suggestion is rather that this dated and loaded vocabulary can actually serve to obscure the issues at stake and can even be employed as a rhetorical device that contributes to closing off necessary debate on important constitutional choices. In particular, they can be used as labels to criticize particular judicial rulings on the relationship between treaties and domestic law. Dualism is increasingly employed in a pejorative fashion to criticize specific rulings.[274] Thus, determinations that certain treaties or treaty provisions are not directly effective can be seen as a dualist stain for what is otherwise a monistic system. A judicial willingness to provide ex post constitutional

[270] Franck and Thiruvengadam (2003); Stein (1994).

[271] Examples include Buergenthal (1992: 393); Maluwa (1999: 51); Danilenko (1999); Dupuy and Kerbrat (2010: 451, 464–5); Nollkaemper (2011). See also Peters (2007: 270).

[272] Empirically grounded studies of US judicial practice have recently emerged: Sloss (2009c); Wu (2007). However, in two recent edited collections (Sloss (2009a), Shelton (2011)) a surprising number of country reports unfortunately provide little if any reference to actual judicial practice. Nollkaemper (2011) provides impressive engagement with domestic judicial practice in exploring the role of national courts in protecting the international rule of law but states (at 17) that contrary practice 'has been so pervasive and so often described that there is no need to document it in this book'.

[273] In some instances where actual practice is engaged with, commentators appear guilty of placing a positive spin on that practice; the Russia country report in Sloss (2009a) appears to be one such example as the editor appears to acknowledge: see Sloss (2009b: 39–43); see also concerning the application of the ECHR in Russia, Nußberger (2008).

[274] More rarely a so-called monistic judicial approach has been criticized, see eg Waters (2007), and Chapter VI.

review of treaties is a similar stain,[275] as would be an unwillingness to allow constitutional values to be trumped by treaty commitments.[276] Ultimately, one could always seek to castigate as dualistic any instances of apparent judicial unwillingness to cement the supremacy of treaty law in the domestic legal arena, at least in systems that in principle allow for automatic treaty incorporation. However, by dispensing with such labels we are likely to encourage a more balanced assessment of the issues at stake.

The emerging emphasis on a pluralistic approach to the relationship between domestic and international law may well offer us a more comprehensive toolkit with which to consider the issues at stake than recourse to the classic monist–dualist language.[277] In contrast to a monistic account, this perspective contests a formally hierarchical relationship between legal orders and emphasizes a hetararchical relationship between diverse legal orders with competing claims to authority. For Von Bogdandy such theories offer the way forward not least as they promote the insight that there is interaction among different legal orders and they also have far-reaching consequences for our understanding of constitutional law, for on this account 'any given constitution does not set up a normative *universum* anymore, but is, rather, an element in a normative *pluriversum*.'[278] Crucially, adherents to forms of legal pluralism are willing openly to embrace what constitutes a threat for a standard monistic account, namely limitations on the internal legal effect of international norms that conflict with internal constitutional principles.[279]

4.2 Reflections on the role of domestic courts in treaty enforcement

Despite the notoriously weak international mechanisms for ensuring compliance with international norms, there was a time when the well-known

[275] This can be so even when it is a constitutional creation, such as the ex post review powers that were attributed to the Belgian Constitutional Court. Though not, it would seem, in Germany and Italy that after all have long been labelled dualist.

[276] Concerning the latter in France, see Daillier, Forteau, and Pellet (2009: 314).

[277] eg Von Bogdandy (2008); Kumm (2009); Krisch (2010). For a brief overview of pluralist approaches, see de Búrca (2012: 127–30).

[278] (2008: 400–1).

[279] See Von Bogdandy (2008) and Kumm (2009). Nollkaemper (2011: 280–95) is also willing to accept domestic judicial restrictions on the supremacy of international norms, but only on the narrower ground that it furthers the rule of law both domestically and at the international level.

assertion by one distinguished international law scholar that 'almost all nations obey almost all principles of international law and almost all of their obligations almost all of the time' appeared to be accepted by legal scholars with little hesitation.[280] Today, there is a burgeoning literature, predominantly from US-based legal scholars, which does not take this optimistic assertion at face-value.[281] And with treaties being 'the all-purpose workhorse of international law',[282] compliance concerns in the treaty context have become especially paramount.[283]

The natural consequence of this turn to focus on issues of compliance has been an increase in attention attributed to the role that domestic courts can play in this respect.[284] It is self-evident that, other things being equal, the greater the willingness on the part of the domestic judiciary to apply and enforce treaty norms, including setting aside contrary domestic norms where necessary, the greater will be compliance with such norms. This has surely been one of the key lessons of the European integration project. And with the rapid growth in treaties that no longer have purely interstate relations as their focus but increasingly seek to regulate areas with direct consequence for individuals and their daily lives, one can envisage an incomparably broader role for domestic courts in treaty enforcement than has ever been possible before. Of least surprise, in this respect, has been the increasing emphasis on the role of national courts in securing compliance with international human rights norms, whether treaty-based or otherwise.[285] Human rights treaties are, after all, unique in that unlike other

[280] Henkin (1979: 47). It is questionable whether States themselves accepted this proposition given their increasing propensity, at least in certain areas, to draft treaties with mechanisms seeking to induce compliance (such as dispute settlement procedures, including the creation of international tribunals, and non-compliance procedures), see eg Ulfstein et al (2007). And, indeed, to bolster compliance mechanisms in existing treaties as was the case, eg, with changes to the ECtHR's judicial architecture and with the addition of a judicial organ to the African Charter.

[281] Examples include Goldsmith and Posner (2005); Scott and Stephan (2006); Victor et al (1998); Brown Weiss and Jacobson (1998); Hathaway (2002).

[282] See Berman (2005: 1–2) for this expression.

[283] Ulfstein et al (2007: 4).

[284] See eg Conforti (1993; 2001); Cassese (2005: 236); Knop (2000); Koh (1997: 2656–9); Henkin (1995: 63); Nollkaemper (2011); Shany (2012).

[285] eg the chapters in Conforti and Francioni (1997); Lillich (1985); Frowein (1997); Heyns and Viljoen (2001); Tomuschat (2008: ch 5), and, concerning the ECHR, Keller and Stone Sweet (2008). The relevant supervisory organs of the core UN human rights instruments have also over the years underscored the role to be played by domestic courts. Note also the Bangalore Principles (1998) and the Vienna Declaration on the Role of Judges in the Promotion and

areas of treaty law the obligations they provide for are owed by State Parties to individuals.[286] It is the treatment of individuals that constitutes the subject matter of human rights treaties and thus, for them to be effective, the rights need to be protected in the domestic legal arena, including via the courtroom. This emphasis on the enforcement role of domestic courts is bolstered by the fact that human rights treaties operate subject to the requirement that individuals exhaust local remedies—including via domestic court procedures—prior to bringing claims before international organs.[287]

In the context of international environmental law where multilateral environmental agreements (MEAs) have proliferated at a frenetic rate since the 1960s, attention has progressively turned towards issues of compliance and enforcement,[288] including through the use of domestic courts.[289] With regard to the emphasis of the domestic judicial role in giving effect to international criminal law,[290] it is worth noting that the Statute of the International Criminal Court (ICC) expressly articulated the role of the new Court as 'complementary to national criminal jurisdictions' and restricted the jurisdiction of the Court where cases were being prosecuted or investigated in a relevant State.[291]

Another area of treaty law that has seen a focus on the role of domestic courts is the trade sphere. A long-standing GATT official, Jan Tumlir, had argued in the 1980s for domestic judicial enforcement of the most-favoured-nation clause in the GATT.[292] This strain of argument, which seeks to co-opt individuals and domestic courts into advancing the objectives of a liberal trading regime, has been developed in the many writings of Tumlir's former colleague at the GATT, Ernst-Ulrich Petersmann.[293] It is

Protection of Human Rights and Fundamental Freedoms (2003). This emphasis on domestic courts is also apparent in the closely related field of labour rights and standards, as the ILO committee of experts, alongside the scholarly community, has long emphasized: see Thomas et al (2004).

286 Higgins (1995: 95).

287 See Amerasinghe (2004: 64–83, 303–65).

288 See generally Beyerlin et al (2006); Ulfstein et al (2007); UNEP (2006).

289 UNEP (2006); Johannesburg 'Principles on the Role of Law and Sustainable Development' 2002 (adopted at the Global Judges Symposium held in South Africa in August 2002). See Shelton and Kiss (2005); Anderson and Galizzi (2002); O'Connell (1995).

290 Ferdinandusse (2006).

291 Shaw (2008: 414–15).

292 Tumlir (1985: 61–70).

293 Representative examples include: (1983); (1986); (1992); (2000a); (2001); (2002); (2003); (2007).

an approach that goes considerably further than that of Tumlir, not least given that while Petersmann developed his own thesis the GATT mutated into the WTO and with the new areas brought within the remit of the world trading system (eg intellectual property, services), the subject matter for which the role for domestic judicial enforcement was envisaged has undergone considerable expansion. This account emphasizes the character of GATT and now WTO rules as rights for individuals—rather than simply obligations owed to other States. In more recent times Petersmann has emphasized that WTO law serves human rights functions,[294] and he has had no qualms in acknowledging the instrumentality of this approach, referring to human rights law as offering 'WTO rules moral, constitutional and democratic legitimacy that may be more important . . . than the traditional economic and utilitarian justifications.'[295] As well as seeking to draw support for the domestic judicial enforcement of WTO norms from a strongly contested human rights analogy,[296] this account also seeks to draw on the experience of the EU project where domestic judicial enforcement of EU norms has been central to the core goal of integrating markets.

Aside from this more sectoral focus on the role of domestic courts as a means to promote compliance with treaty norms—in the sense that it is a focus on specific sectors or areas of treaty law, whether it be human rights as has been by and large the case, MEAs as has become increasingly common, or GATT and now WTO law as represented most staunchly in the work of Petersmann—we have also seen an account of the role of domestic courts emerge that sees their application of international law 'as the keystone of international law'.[297] Domestic courts are viewed as providing the judicial and coercive enforcement procedures that are found wanting at the international level with judges being encouraged to use all means to ensure compliance with international law. It is an approach which can be referred to as a 'full domestic judicial enforcement model', for it does not seek to differentiate between different categories of treaty but, rather, can be seen as a rallying call for a domestic judicial role largely across the gamut of treaty-making.

However, there are problems with both the model that advocates sectoral enforcement and that which advocates the full domestic judicial

[294] (2000a: 1375; 2001: 30 et seq; 2002; 2003).
[295] (2000a: 1377; 2000b: 24).
[296] See Alston (2002); Cass (2005).
[297] Conforti (1993: 9; 2001).

enforcement of treaties. Perhaps, first and foremost, these approaches—which essentially envisage domestic courts as bringing to bear the enforcement arsenal found wanting at the international level for the policing of treaty obligations—fail to give due attention to the intent of State Parties. To the extent that they have not taken the opportunity to draft treaties with more potent mechanisms for ensuring compliance and, indeed, consciously avoid such mechanisms,[298] it is imperative that we ask in what circumstances it is appropriate for domestic courts to give such treaty norms a harder legal status in the domestic legal arena.[299] This criticism has greater purchase with respect to the full domestic judicial enforcement model because this question is simply not posed; it is taken for granted that domestic courts *should be* policing compliance with treaty obligations.[300] But we need to ask whether this one-size-fits-all logic clashes with the flexibility sought by States when they conclude treaties with varying levels of enforcement potential, not least given that they are concluding treaties against a backdrop of what is not slavish domestic judicial enforcement of treaties regardless of what constitutional provisions on treaty reception might seem to suggest. One commentator has underscored that other than 'parts of . . . human rights law and the protection of foreign nationals, states have generally had little interest in agreeing on empowerment of national courts in other areas of international law.'[301]

The full domestic judicial enforcement model, as well as to an extent the more sectoral models, starts from the premise that there is not enough enforcement of treaty law and that domestic courts and domestic litigants should be co-opted into securing maximum treaty enforcement. There has, however, been a growth of literature that seeks to contest the very premises of a maximum law enforcement approach in the international and treaty law context.[302] Maximum law enforcement is not viewed as an unqualified good, rather it can have both positive and negative consequences. Thus,

[298] An emerging literature seeks to explain why States do not draft treaties to include mechanisms that are more likely to generate compliance: see esp Guzman (2005); Raustiala (2005).

[299] One answer, discussed further below, is that it is certainly appropriate where the domestic legal order has opted for a system of auto-incorporation.

[300] This is apparent in both the approaches of Conforti (1993) and Frowein (1997).

[301] Nollkaemper (2011: 38).

[302] eg Scott and Stephan (2006); Pauwelyn (2008); Trachtman and Moremen (2003); Jackson (1992). Note also Koh (1997: 2641), 'Nor is securing greater compliance with treaties always good per se. Indeed, securing compliance may even be undesirable if the treaties are themselves unfair or enshrine disingenuous or coercive bargains.'

for example, in those States automatically incorporating treaties and especially when combined with a higher legal status for such norms, this will inevitably impact upon the willingness of those States to sign up to treaties in the first place.[303] This can be viewed as having negative repercussions, for example if it prevents otherwise beneficial treaty-making from transpiring, even if not policed by domestic judicial actors.[304] The full judicial enforcement camp might, on the other hand, view this differently and consider that States should only be signing up to the treaty in the first place if they are willing to allow their domestic courts to police their commitments.[305] This is tied to a broader fixation with maximum compliance and promoting the somewhat amorphous concept that is 'the international rule of law'.[306]

There are further concerns that are raised by seeing domestic courts as playing a principal enforcement role for the ever-expanding body of treaty law. A call for greater domestic judicial enforceability of treaty norms brings to the fore important questions as to the legitimacy of the norms that are, on this account, entitled to such a potent status in the domestic legal order.[307] One of the lessons to be learned from the European project, often used in analogy by those calling for a greater role for domestic courts,[308] is that the harder the legal status domestically of the treaty-based norms the more vociferous become the input and output legitimacy concerns with such norms. And it becomes fitting, if not indispensable, to ask how well the treaty-making process in international law holds up in this respect. There is certainly criticism that can be advanced concerning the absence of openness and transparency,[309] which becomes all the more significant in an era where treaty-making is no longer confined to matters of limited relevance to the daily lives of individuals but, to the contrary, have come and will continue to touch many aspects of their daily lives.

[303] See eg Jackson (1992: 325–6, 334); Iwasawa (1998: 2, 291).

[304] Note Jackson (1992: 325) (some breaches may be minor and therefore preferable to the alternative of refusing to join altogether).

[305] eg Frowein expressly (1997). Pescatore (2003: 330) sees in 'dualism' 'une régle de duplicité'.

[306] On the international rule of law in this context, see Kumm (2003: 21–2); Nollkaemper (2011).

[307] Such concerns are pressing independently of a strong domestic judicial enforcement role and there is growing literature addressing the legitimacy problems posed by international law: Wheatley (2010); Wolfrum and Roben (2008); Weiler (2004); Kumm (2004).

[308] See eg Nollkaemper (2011: 83), Slaughter and White (2007).

[309] eg Kälin (2000).

The standard response to many concerns with the treaty-making process is simply to underline that the outcome only becomes binding upon a State if it has consented. At least two points are worth noting in this respect. The first is the conflation of State with executive in the context of international law, which, as one scholar has suggested, is 'nothing more than a monstrous empowerment of the executive branch at the expense of other political estates or an empowerment of those internal special interests who have a better capture of the executive branch.'[310] Admittedly, in the context of certain treaties there may be a domestic constitutional requirement in many legal orders that parliamentary authorization be provided before a State expresses its consent to be bound, but this does little to dispel the basic criticism of the actual treaty-making process itself.[311] The second point is that in any event this consent is increasingly attenuated by virtue of the law-making activities of multilateral institutions including, in some cases, albeit currently very limited, binding decision-making by treaty bodies taking place via majority vote.[312]

Even in a domain with such powerful legitimacy claims as human rights treaties, there is debate to be had as to the role of domestic courts. Not all would concede that we should necessarily foresee a prominent role for domestic courts in treaty enforcement. Certainly, there continues to be some debate as to the very justiciability of economic, social, and cultural rights,[313] but even where we turn to the classic domain of civil and political rights—where justiciability concerns have generally been absent—there is contestation as to whether it is the place of domestic courts (much less a supranational court such as the ECtHR) rather than the legislature to have the final say on the meaning of rights which in many cases are inherently contested.[314]

Ultimately, it is essential to recognize that underlying the thinking of the role to be played by domestic courts in treaty enforcement are normative

[310] Weiler (2004: 558).

[311] Note also on the 'fiction of consent', Weiler (2004: 557–8).

[312] See Boyle and Chinkin (2007: 99); Kumm (2004: 914).

[313] See eg Steiner et al (2007: 313–58).

[314] See, eg, the mission statement in a collection of essays where a group of authors expressed concerns with the passage of the Human Rights Act in the UK, essentially incorporating the ECHR, and 'question whether the primary responsibility for the articulation of these rights ought to be taken away from the normal political processes of representative government': Tomkins (2001: 2). See also the recent important contributions from Waldron (2006) and Bellamy (2007) essentially arguing against judicial review of primary legislation vis-à-vis fundamental rights in functioning democracies.

considerations that are rarely openly addressed. Of course treaty law, given the growing recourse to it as a regulatory tool in an increasingly interdependent world, indeed as one manifestation of the turn to international law as governance,[315] needs to be routinely applied in the domestic legal arena by relevant authorities including courts. An effective international legal system serves important values,[316] and obviously cannot be effective if domestic authorities were not routinely adhering to and enforcing its norms. They can do so very much indirectly—in the sense of applying and enforcing the expressly enacted implementing legislation which may not even reference the international norms themselves—as is perhaps the primary mechanism for treaty application and enforcement in States adhering to non-automatic treaty incorporation albeit with judicial tools for giving a measure of effect to unimplemented treaties clearly growing in prominence. This form of direct legislative implementation is also not only commonly employed in States adhering to automatic incorporation,[317] but essential if such States are not routinely to flout their treaty commitments.

It is a mistake to assume that the automatic incorporation model necessarily ensures greater compliance with treaty obligations.[318] This is not simply because it is ultimately up to the courts to make a reality of the domestic constitutional choice for automatic incorporation, but also because treaties will often contain provisions that are not capable of being applied by domestic courts and will require implementing measures by the legislature. Indeed, the requirements of treaty law have become ever more complex and demanding and frequently treaty compliance will be a rolling process in which domestic legal orders will need, as is most notably the case in the fields of international human rights and international environmental law, to be continuously adapting to evolving international norms if treaty compliance is to be ensured. Where implementing measures and domestic adaptation does not take place, treaty compliance will be imperilled. It is for this reason that we have seen numerous treaty bodies express concern over the absence of implementing measures in States wedded to automatic

[315] See Kumm (2004); Weiler (2004); Wolfrum (2008).

[316] On which see briefly Kumm (2004: 918–20).

[317] See eg Nollkaemper (2009a: 335) (referring to the introduction of legislation transforming treaties into national law as the usual way in which the Netherlands performs its treaty obligations, with the result that the executive and courts then apply Dutch law rather than the international legal rules underlying that law).

[318] See also, though using terminology of monism and dualism, Sloss (2009b), Dugard (2009a), and Keller and Stone Sweet (2008: 686).

incorporation.[319] Thus, whilst in theory the automatic incorporation model appears to ensure greater compliance with international obligations, the reality is that this is only ever possible other things being equal, which they of course rarely are across constitutional systems.[320] Even if we draw on comparisons of economically advanced Western democratic nations we find that Denmark, wedded to the non-automatic incorporation model, ensured that it had passed amendments to its criminal code to comply with the obligation under the OECD Bribery Convention requiring each Contracting Party to take such measures as necessary to establish the liability of legal persons for the bribery of foreign public officials, whilst Luxembourg, wedded to the automatic incorporation model, did not.[321]

Substantive legislative change will thus often be essential to ensure adequate compliance with many treaty norms. And such substantive legislative change is, in principle, endowed with a more potent democratic seal of approval than the rather weak democratic legitimacy that flows from the wholly routine legislative approval of treaties in automatic treaty incorporation States that usually serves formally to incorporate such treaties. In this sense the non-automatic approach has in its favour that it at least ensures that to achieve the most potent legal effects internally for duly ratified

[319] eg the Aarhus Convention Compliance Committee, 2005 (Report to the Second Meeting of the Parties at <http://www.unece.org/env/documents/2005/pp/ece/ece.mp.pp.2005.13.e.pdf>) at para 36, see also Jendroska (2011: 108–11). See also the Espoo Convention Implementation Committee note: ECE/MP.EIA/IC/2011/INF.1, paras 7–8. For early discussion by the ILO committee see Leary (1982: 17, 24–5, 137–8, 142) and the committee continues to reiterate the need for the adoption of laws, regulations, and other measures to give full effect to ILO convention provisions. With respect to the WTO Secretariat see Kuijper and Bronckers (2005: 1315). Note also Hae Bong (2011: 366–7) decrying the absence of implementing measures in Japan for an ILO convention and for the International Convention on the Elimination of All Forms of Racial Discrimination (ICERD), and Sloss (2012b) calling for federal legislation in the US to give effect to human rights treaties.

[320] A rudimentary awareness of political events would rightly lead one to view with deep scepticism the practical value of some of the constitutional provisions on treaty reception identified in s 3.1.1 whilst, in contrast, the non-automatic treaty incorporation States include a number of long-standing democracies which one would expect to exhibit a strong commitment to ensuring treaty compliance.

[321] See the OECD working group on Bribery phase 1 reports on Denmark and Luxembourg available at <http://www.oecd.org/document/24/0,3343,fr_2649_34859_1933144_1_1_1_1,00.html#Phase_1>. To take another example from the international criminal law field, the UK legislated to implement provisions of the Statute of the ICC prior to ratification, while several years after ratification and entry into force Italy had failed to do so, calling into question its compliance with the Statute: on Italy and the absence of ICC implementing measures, see Roscini (2007).

treaties will generally require more than mere parliamentary approval of a treaty and in fact substantive debate as to why, and the extent to which, domestic courts should have a role with respect to particular treaties combined with use, usually, of the ordinary legislative process to provide for any such role.[322] It might be thought that this is all well and good for systems adhering to non-automatic incorporation but that where a constitutional system has in principle attached its flag to the automatic treaty incorporation mast, then the case for engaging with the costs and benefits of domestic judicial enforcement loses its purchase. There is, however, much evidence to suggest that domestic courts in automatic treaty incorporation States exhibit varying degrees of reluctance in enforcing treaty norms. The 'direct effect' test can operate as a 'judicial avoidance technique',[323] a flexible device employed by domestic courts to avoid enforcing treaties.[324] Where we are dealing with clashes between treaties and legislation this is perhaps not altogether surprising, given that judicial review of legislation is a power that ordinary courts simply do not have in many legal systems. Accordingly, the paradox is that in many automatic treaty incorporation States, the effect is that legislation can be 'disapplied' due to its incompatibility with a treaty despite the fact that were such an inconsistency to exist vis-à-vis a constitutional provision this power would either be confined to a constitutional court or may simply not even exist.[325] This can thus contribute to judicial reticence to enforce treaties at least where a contrary legislative measure is at issue. Whilst there are numerous factors that contribute

[322] This was, eg, the case with respect to the ECHR in Denmark, Ireland, and the UK, and debate continues with respect to the ICESCR in all three of these legal orders.

[323] Benvenisti (1993) employed the terminology of 'avoidance doctrines' in exploring the way national courts can limit the application of international law. Although he touched both the direct applicability of treaties as well as the narrow interpretation of a treaty in order to protect domestic law, neither of these were labelled avoidance doctrines in contrast to, eg, the act of State or political question doctrine.

[324] In general terms see Cannizzaro (2011: 483–4); Buergenthal (1992: 376 et seq); Cassese (2005: 227); Conforti (1993: 25–34); Jackson (1992: 327–8, 333–4). In the specific context of Japan, see Iwasawa (1998: 289); for the US, see Vazquez (1995: 710–18), Sloss (2009c); for Italy, see Francioni (1997: 29–30).

[325] In five of the founding Member States this power is confined to a Constitutional Court, in the Netherlands, however, the inviolability of the law is constitutionally enshrined. And where the power has been confined to a Constitutional Court as in France, a model copied by many of its former colonies, the power only existed prior to promulgation of law (until reforms in 2008). On the European model of centralized constitutional review, see Ferreres Comella (2009).

to explaining domestic judicial reticence in treaty enforcement,[326] domestic separation of powers concerns and the concern of courts with their appropriate role within the domestic constitutional set-up are significant. This inevitably becomes more pronounced with the exponential growth in treaty law that domestic courts can be called upon to apply. Consequently, one can simply chide any indicia of judicial reticence as exhibiting unfaithfulness to the constitutional text,[327] and the more explicit the constitutional text the more purchase such criticism might have. However, one can also seek to engage more critically with the factors contributing to reticence and ultimately whether the one-size-fits-all logic is appropriate even where this may appear to be a natural reading of the domestic constitutional text.

Judicial developments in the US are illuminating in this respect. Its Constitution contains the oldest known general treaty incorporation clause, and its Supreme Court is increasingly viewed as having moved from a presumption, particularly dominant pre-Second World War, in favour of domestic judicial enforceability of treaties at the behest of private parties to a recent presumption against such enforceability absent express legislative incorporation.[328] One might view this reversal in presumption as bordering on an informal constitutional amendment.[329] It is accordingly open to well-founded accusations of exhibiting disdain for the constitutional text. But one can also detect in this transformation in judicial stance a response, albeit not openly acknowledged, to broader concerns with the qualitative shift in the remit of treaty law and the perceived democratic shortcomings of the international law-making process. The US judicial reaction has been extreme and by giving inadequate consideration to countervailing considerations that seek to promote the rule of law in international affairs, it considerably jeopardizes US capacity to comply with its treaty commitments. However, similar concerns along with the proliferation in domestic

[326] See eg Higgins (1995: 206–7) and Dupuy and Kerbrat (2010: 457) pointing to, inter alia, lack of familiarity with international law.

[327] Much of the US debate has focused specifically on the constitutional text and what the Founding Fathers intended, see eg Paust (2003); Vazquez (1992; 1995; 1999; 2008); Yoo (1999a; 1999b).

[328] See Hathaway et al (2012) drawing in particular on lower court responses to the controversial Supreme Court *Medellín* ruling considered briefly in Chapter VI.

[329] The US Constitution is notoriously difficult to amend given the sacrosanct status it has acquired (see eg Levinson (2006)) but there were constitutional amendment attempts in the 1950s (the 'Bricker Amendments'), that had significant bi-partisan support, to move from the automatic to non-automatic approach to treaty incorporation as a response to discontent in some quarters with the emerging UN human rights regime: Hathaway et al (2012).

litigation involving treaties, and the complexity and political sensitivity of the issues involved, have rightly left political actors and courts reluctant to see the few words in the constitutional text where they exist, to the effect that treaties are law of the land and potentially supreme law of the land to boot, or similar phrasing by superior courts, as always dictating specific outcomes in judicial proceedings.[330] To pretend otherwise is largely to ignore considerable empirical evidence of domestic judicial practice to the contrary. Much of that domestic judicial practice may well be open to powerful and well-deserved critique (beyond any apparent tension with existing constitutional text). Nonetheless it must also be conceded that in a terrain that often pits the idealism of the international law scholar with the concerns of the domestic constitutional order, there can be legitimate grounds for political and judicial reticence to treating all treaties and their provisions as fully operative supreme domestic law notwithstanding sweepingly phrased constitutional provisions on treaty incorporation.

5. Conclusions

Strikingly, international law continues to have remarkably little to say on the issue of the domestic legal effects of treaties, with the basic rule remaining in place that States are free to determine how they meet their treaty obligations. And States clearly remain reluctant to draft treaties that restrict this free rein and that seek expressly to accord domestic courts a judicial enforcement role. The reality must surely be that this stance reflects a desire for flexibility in treaty implementation. It is true that the *Danzig* Advisory Opinion appeared to open the door to future findings by international courts and tribunals that certain treaties imposed an international law obligation that they be made domestically judicially enforceable, but such findings have not been forthcoming. The notable exception was provided by the ECJ which proceeded to push the boundaries much further than the PCIJ had in *Danzig*. But crucially there is a bi-dimensional character at play here, in that the stance adopted as to the claims made by EU

[330] Indeed, the US is not alone in generating calls for constitutional amendments to move away from the automatic incorporation of treaties; there have recently been such calls in Switzerland (see Swiss Federal Council (2011)) and in the Netherlands in order to preclude treaty supremacy applying in Dutch law where conflict exists with fundamental legal principles: see discussion in Fleuren (2010: 264).

law in the domestic legal order—and the paradigm shift this represented—could only become a reality once, and to the extent that, it was accepted by domestic courts.[331] Acknowledging this bi-dimensional character enables us to have a greater appreciation of why, since the *Danzig* Opinion, international tribunals and organs have hitherto abstained from reaching such conclusions much less assertions of the revolutionary *Van Gend en Loos* or *Costa* type.

It is one thing for such an organ to assert that a particular treaty or certain provisions are to be directly applicable in the domestic legal order, even asserting supremacy to boot, it is quite another for this to be accepted with equanimity within the domestic orders of the parties to that treaty.[332] *Van Gend en Loos* and *Costa* were decided when there were only six Member States and two of those—the Netherlands and France—had Constitutions which were ostensibly, if not yet in practice, favourable to the doctrines of direct effect and supremacy, and in a third—Luxembourg—supremacy of treaty law had already been given the seal of approval by the Supreme Court. In a sense, the ECJ took a calculated risk by anticipating that the necessary political backing for its decisions would be forthcoming.[333] The very political objectives of this project should not be lost sight of, and this made the circumstances as propitious as possible for the elaboration of the EU law doctrines of direct effect and supremacy. It is instructive to contrast the ECHR which was signed by some ten States and entered into force simultaneously for eight of those States in 1953. Amongst this group were several prominent representatives of the non-automatic approach to treaty incorporation, namely Denmark, Ireland, Norway, Sweden, and the UK, none of which initially provided for the ECHR to be legislatively incorporated. In these circumstances, it is unsurprising that a *Danzig*-type conclusion, much less findings with the import of *Van Gend en Loos* and *Costa*, were not forthcoming from the ECtHR. And when one considers that there

[331] The bi-dimensional character of supremacy was articulated by Weiler (1981).

[332] The US reaction to what struck most international law scholars as a logical interpretation of the Vienna Convention on Consular Relations in *Avena* illustrates the potential problems. The US withdrew from the optional protocol that accorded the ICJ jurisdiction over the Vienna Convention on Consular Relations in disputes initiated by or against the US and its Supreme Court proceeded to conclude, essentially in direct confrontation with the ICJ, that the Convention provided no basis for a judicial remedy (*Sanchez-Llamas v Oregon*, 548 US 331 (2006)) and then rejected the direct effect of the UN Charter provision requiring compliance with ICJ decisions in cases to which the State is party (*Medellín v Texas*, 552 US 491 (2008)).

[333] See eg Stein (1965: 516–17). Political backing which was, indeed, forthcoming, see Vauchez (2010).

are at least 160 parties to the ICCPR and ICESCR—and the concomitant domestic constitutional divergence vis-à-vis the legal effects of treaties that this entails—it is a chimera to expect the relevant UN committee to assert that these norms, or certain of them, are directly applicable as a matter of international law.

Undoubtedly, treaty norms will whether directly or indirectly, including via ad hoc legislative incorporation, be given effect as routine activity by domestic authorities and courts. However, it is important to question the notion that the constitutional choice for automatic treaty incorporation will or should actually resolve *all* the difficult questions to which the growing interaction between domestic law and treaty law gives rise. There is a clear need for greater empirical work on how domestic courts actually deal with treaties when they are invoked. In that respect, even a cursory overview attests to the domestic judicial direct effect determination being dogged by varying degrees of incoherence. More generally, it can function as one of a number of judicial avoidance techniques to restrict the impact of treaty law in the domestic legal arena. This need not always be viewed in a negative light. For it is perfectly appropriate to question the role that domestic courts should be playing in treaty enforcement and not uncritically to accept that they should always be seeking to enforce all treaties all of the time simply because they operate within constitutional systems that adhere to automatic treaty incorporation.

II

The Constitutional Status of EU Agreements: Revisiting the Foundational Questions

1. Introduction

This chapter revisits several of the foundational questions pertaining to the constitutional status and legal effects of EU Agreements. These questions are, first, whether EU Agreements upon their entry into force become in principle part of the EU legal order; that is, does the EU adhere to a model of automatic treaty incorporation. A sub-question that flows from an affirmative answer to that question is whether those external treaty commitments are then subject to the *lex posterior* rule. The second critical question is whether there is scope to constitutionally review the EU's actual treaty commitments. The third question concerns the test to which EU Agreements are subject in order to have their most potent legal effects, namely, forming a criterion for judicial review.

Constitutional systems may have a text which itself provides answers to some of these questions but it will ultimately fall upon domestic judicial actors to provide the authoritative response. The EU context is no exception and it has been the supreme judicial arbiter within this legal system that has had to answer these core questions. But in the federal-like system that is the EU, these questions acquire additional constitutional salience because as a supranational organization composed of formally sovereign States the answers to these questions have particularly marked constitutional ramifications for its component States. Accordingly, in addressing how the aforementioned questions have been answered in the three sections that follow, this chapter also seeks to articulate the ramifications of the choices adopted for the constitutional orders of the Member States

2. Opting for Automatic Treaty Incorporation: EU Agreements as Acts of the EU Institutions and an Integral Part of EU Law

The ECJ put in place a central plank of the EU's external relations constitution when it first expressly addressed itself to its jurisdiction over EU Agreements in its *Haegeman II* ruling that firmly established that the EU was attached to a model that automatically incorporates EU Agreements into its legal order.[1] In *Haegeman I* a Belgian importer sought to challenge EU measures that allegedly breached the Association Agreement with Greece.[2] The Court concluded that disputes concerning the levying of charges were to be brought domestically and national courts could then use the preliminary ruling procedure to ensure uniform application of EU law. That importer duly brought proceedings domestically and some 18 months later the Court responded to a Belgian court's questions as to the

[1] Several earlier cases saw EU Agreements invoked. The first involved infringement proceedings in which Belgium unsuccessfully sought to have the oral procedure reopened to invoke the recently ratified Association Agreement with Greece: 2–3/62 *Commission v Luxembourg and Belgium* [1962] ECR 445. In C-40/72 *Schroeder v Germany* [1973] ECR 125 the ECJ responded to a question as to the interpretation of the Greek Association Agreement by interpreting it in a manner preserving the validity of the EU measure at issue but did not engage with the issue of direct effect. The ECJ appeared to accept that EU Agreements could be used to challenge EU measures, however, the parent Regulation to the challenged measure required the Commission to have due regard to Agreements binding the EU. In 9/73 *Schlüter* [1973] ECR 1135 a preliminary reference challenged an EU measure imposing levies that resulted in duties provided for in a tariff Agreement negotiated with Switzerland being exceeded. The Court did not consider that agreements negotiated within the GATT could alter the nature of the obligations assumed in the GATT framework which did not confer on parties within the EU a right to invoke them in court. The ruling was shaped by the judicial treatment accorded to the GATT 1947 which is considered in Chapter IV. However, as the relevant duties were included in an EU Regulation, the ECJ reviewed the challenged measure. In a 1973 preliminary ruling, a reading of the Yaoundé Convention allowing a trader to take advantage of the exemption of customs duties for products originating from a State which was not a party to that Convention was rejected: 147/73 *Lenzing* [1973] ECR 1543.

[2] 96/71 *Haegeman v Commission* (*Haegeman I*) [1972] ECR 1005. It was both an annulment and damages action.

interpretation of that Agreement.[3] The response centred largely on finding that the relevant charge was a permitted levy under the Agreement and thus not caught by the interdiction on customs duties and charges having equivalent effect. The real significance of the case lay in the assertion of jurisdiction over EU Agreements and the constitutional ramifications to which this gave rise.

Jurisdiction in the preliminary ruling context was provided for in two main contexts, namely interpretation of the Treaty or the validity and interpretation of acts of the institutions. The judicial response to this textual hurdle commenced with an assertion of preliminary rulings jurisdiction concerning the interpretation of acts of the institutions, followed by the assertion that the Agreement was concluded by the Council under Articles 218 and 217 TFEU and was therefore 'an act of one of the institutions . . . within the meaning of . . . Article [267]'. Two more single-sentence paragraphs followed, the first ruling that 'The provisions of the Agreement, from the coming into force thereof, form an integral part of [EU] law', and the second affirming preliminary rulings jurisdiction within the framework of this law. The crucial proposition that EU Agreements are both acts of the institutions and form an integral part of EU law have been repeated to this day.[4] The implications of the stance first taken in *Haegeman II* for the EU's external relations constitution and the consequential implications for the external relations constitutions of the EU's Member States are outlined in the two subsections that follow.

2.1 Automatic treaty incorporation and the EU's external relations constitution

Haegeman II established that the EU was to be wedded to a model of automatic treaty incorporation. This is evident merely from the unreasoned assertion that once the Agreement comes into force its provisions form an integral part of EU law. The language of being part of domestic law is language expressly written into certain national constitutions in addressing

[3] 181/73 *Haegeman v Belgium* (*Haegeman II*) [1974] ECR 449.

[4] See most recently, C-160/09 *Katsivardas* [2010] ECR I-4591; C-386/08 *Brita* [2010] ECR I-1289.

the relationship between legal orders.[5] The ECJ itself had already used such language in such a context. In the seminal *Costa* judgment it asserted that the Treaty of Rome 'became an integral part of the legal systems of the member states ... which their courts are bound to apply'. And, thus, if one read *Haegeman II* alongside *Costa*, it would appear to follow that whatever is an integral part of EU law is also an integral part of the legal systems of the Member States which their courts are bound to apply. The conclusion flowing inexorably from this, is that such Agreements are in principle capable of possessing those two central distinguishing attributes of EU law: direct effect and supremacy. But the manner in which jurisdiction was established was contestable. The procedure for EU Agreements does require the Council to conclude them and the immediate practice used a Council act to this end. In this sense an act of one of the institutions is at issue. However, it was pointed out that there was a distinction between the EU Agreement and the internal EU act concluding it and that provisions in the former, rather than the latter, were being interpreted;[6] indeed, it is the Agreement itself that was asserted to be an act of the EU institutions. One response is that in EU practice the Agreement itself is actually included as an annex to the Council act concluding it and therefore part of the act.[7] Two related points are that EU Agreements are exactly that, Agreements to which the EU is a party and in this sense acts of the EU rather than of an institution and, moreover, they are not unilateral acts, which was arguably the natural remit of Article 267.[8]

There was, arguably, a textually more faithful way to have resolved *Haegeman II*. Express preliminary rulings jurisdiction exists with respect to the validity of acts of the institutions. *Haegeman II* was such a challenge,[9] and therefore jurisdiction could have been asserted simply on this basis. The grounds of validity review are not outlined in Article 267, but if one reads the grounds as coterminous with Article 263,[10] then infringement of

[5] See Chapter I. Language also used vis-à-vis customary international law: see art 25 of the German Basic Law. One of the *Haegeman II* judges, a member of the delegation drafting the Treaty of Rome, previously argued that EU Agreements form part of EU law: Pescatore (1961: 124, 133).

[6] See Hartley (1983: 390–1).

[7] On annexes being a part of the act, see Wainwright (1996: 13).

[8] So ran the argument of Hartley (1983: 390–1).

[9] The national court having asked both questions as to interpretation and as to the validity of a regulation.

[10] There has never been any indication to the contrary from the Court, see Hartley (2003: 411–12).

the Treaty offers a suitable review ground given that a Treaty provision (Art 216(2) TFEU) expressly provides that EU Agreements bind the institutions.[11] Moreover, it had recently been established that non-EU concluded Agreements could be used to challenge EU measures rendering it unsustainable to argue that this would not be possible where EU Agreements were at issue.[12]

The Advocate General had clearly felt more constrained by the text of the preliminary ruling procedure, for he argued that vis-à-vis EU Agreements this jurisdiction only obtained where interpretation was relevant to the validity or interpretation of an act of an EU institution. Had the ECJ followed those promptings it would have generated a very different EU Agreements enforcement model. That approach would have countenanced challenges to EU acts via the preliminary ruling procedure, whilst rejecting cases seeking interpretations where national measures were challenged.[13] On this account, individuals would have a limited role as enforcers of EU Agreements. The conclusion that the Agreement was an act of one of the institutions assured jurisdiction whenever a national court sought interpretation of an EU Agreement.[14] That reading co-opted individuals and national courts into ensuring compliance with EU Agreements by the Member States rather than just by the EU institutions.[15] It was in embryonic form the external relations counterpart of *Van Gend en Loos*, for, just as that ruling co-opted individuals and national courts into the enforcement game with respect to Treaty provisions, later extended to secondary measures, so *Haegeman II* co-opted them with respect to EU Agreements.[16] These constitutional ramifications were somewhat camouflaged because *Haegeman II* revolved fundamentally around the validity of an EU, rather than national, measure.

[11] The French delegation's report to the ECSC Treaty (Rapport de la Délégation Française 1951), which contained textually identical grounds of review for an annulment action (Art 33 ECSC), considered that 'any rule of law relating to its application' would include international agreements.

[12] 21–4/72 *International Fruit* [1972] ECR 1219. See further Chapter IV.

[13] Subject, one assumes, to the exception where the national measure merely implements an EU measure.

[14] Subject to the peculiarities of mixed agreements, considered further in Chapters III–VI.

[15] Individuals, as contrasted with national courts, could even under the Advocate General reading have had a role in challenging a national measure through their input into the infringement procedure.

[16] Both *Van Gend en Loos* and *Haegeman II* allowed for perfectly sustainable, indeed textually stronger, alternative readings.

It requires little reflection to understand why this construct was pursued, textually contestable though the rationale employed may have been. The EU was beginning to assert itself on the international stage, but was finding resistance in some quarters to its international role,[17] and the judicial reading offered a crucial mechanism for assuring to Contracting Parties that international obligations would be complied with in the EU. Even if this enforcement avenue had not been established, infringement proceedings would still comfortably have accommodated non-compliance with EU Agreements for Article 216(2) TFEU clearly stipulates that the Agreements bind the Member States, thus providing the necessary EU Treaty obligation to police.[18] Challenging EU action via the annulment procedure would also have posed little textual difficulty given the infringement of the Treaty ground of review and that Article 216(2) TFEU asserts that EU Agreements bind the institutions.[19] Thus, for most proceedings jurisdiction over EU Agreements was assured with little textual difficulty, but the role for individuals and national courts that *Haegeman II* generated was no textual inevitability as the alternative largely-forgotten reading by the Advocate General illustrated. The 'catch-all' assertion that provisions of EU Agreements form an integral part of EU law made it crystal clear that all the EU enforcement machinery was available for policing their compliance, even if it was to be some time before this was put into practice. The constitutional significance of *Haegeman II* should therefore not be underestimated. By assimilating EU Agreements to 'EU law proper'[20] it also ensured that as EU law develops and the remedial tools at its disposal are bolstered, as with the judicial creation of State liability,[21] they become equally available for the EU Agreements setting.

Article 216(2) TFEU clearly offered a strong textual lynchpin for running arguments for jurisdiction over EU Agreements in most settings. The ECJ, however, made no reference to it despite the presence of precious little

[17] See eg Bourgeois (1984: 1273).

[18] Subject to the complications resulting from mixed agreements considered further in Chapters III–VI.

[19] This also applies with the plea of illegality (Art 277 TFEU) which cross-refers to the grounds of review in Art 263 TFEU.

[20] The phrasing is borrowed from the earlier use of 'Community law proper' by Bourgeois (1984: 1260).

[21] C-6 & 9/90 *Francovich v Italy* [1991] ECR I-5357. Other judicial-led developments from which Agreements could theoretically have benefited included the addition of the European Parliament to the list of potential challengers, later to be incorporated within the text: see Craig and de Búrca (2011: 490).

constitutional text to rely upon. Arguably, it could have provided a free-standing constitutional anchor for automatic treaty incorporation in the EU legal order.[22] The Court was faced with either rejecting decentralized enforcement of EU Agreements vis-à-vis Member States or reconciling that with the text, but it is debatable whether its attempt to do so did less violence to the text than simply basing itself on Article 216(2) TFEU.[23] This could also have been supplemented by Article 19 TEU which required the Court to ensure that in the interpretation and application of the Treaty the law is observed.[24]

As it turned out, the Court referred to Article 216(2) as rendering EU Agreements binding on the EU and Member States in its very next ruling on an EU Agreement (a case involving domestic action).[25] And whilst this axiomatic point was soon repeated,[26] it was not until the *Kupferberg* judgment in 1982 that greater principled consideration was accorded to Article 216(2) and the logic of *Haegeman II*.[27] In *Kupferberg* Article 216(2) was reiterated with the Court asserting that it was incumbent on both EU institutions and Member States to ensure compliance with EU Agreement obligations. The ECJ then proceeded to reveal why EU Agreements form an integral part of EU law. It was not simply because Agreements were considered to be acts of the institutions as one may have suspected given that this holding directly preceded the single-sentence paragraph in *Haegeman II* asserting that their provisions were an integral part of EU law,[28] rather it was because in ensuring respect for commitments arising from EU Agreements the Member States were fulfilling an obligation above all in relation to the EU which has assumed responsibility for due performance. This ex post justification for *Haegeman II* was indicating that the reasoning

[22] See Gaja (2002: 119) suggesting that Art 216(2) implies that EU Agreements are part of the sources of EU law. A textual argument for Art 267 purposes could have been constructed by viewing the ECJ as effectively interpreting an EU Treaty provision, namely Art 216(2) and what it means for an agreement to be binding on the Member States or the EU institutions as the case may be. A related point was made by Waelbroeck and Waelbroeck (1993: 215).

[23] Reservations were soon voiced as to the jurisdictional argument employed: see the Advocate General's Opinion in 87/75 *Bresciani*. For early praise, see Jacot-Guillarmod (1979: 232–5).

[24] For Rideau (1990: 342), Art 19 TEU alone sufficed to establish jurisdiction.

[25] 87/75 *Bresciani* [1976] ECR 129, para 18.

[26] 270/80 *Polydor v Harlequin* [1982] ECR 329, para 9.

[27] 104/81 *Hauptzollamt Mainz v CA Kupferberg* [1982] ECR 3641.

[28] That jurisdictional argument was not acknowledged, however, it was repeated in the earlier *Opinion 1/76* [1977] ECR 741, and significant later rulings such as 12/86 *Demirel* [1987] ECR 3719, C-192/89 *Sevince* [1990] ECR I-3461, and *Opinion 1/91* [1993] ECR I-6079, as well as most recently in C-386/08 *Brita* [2010] ECR I-1289 and C-160/09 *Katsivardas* [2010] ECR I-4591.

was shaped by the EU's international responsibility.[29] The EU by definition is always a party to EU Agreements, and thus in principle internationally responsible for performance of the obligations assumed thereunder,[30] accordingly it would seem logical to underscore the EU law obligation of the Member States.[31]

In federal systems, the centre will usually be equipped with tools to ensure that the sub-units comply with the State's treaty obligations.[32] This, one suspects, did not escape the Treaty drafters given the ease with which a combined reading of Article 258 and Article 216(2) yields such a tool. But *Kupferberg* involved the preliminary ruling procedure and, accordingly, the international responsibility rationale might be viewed as an additional functional argument in support of general Article 267 jurisdiction. It was curious, however, that the assertion that EU Agreements are an integral part of EU law was first made in a case revolving around an EU measure's validity and yet eight years later a differently composed bench proffered the ex post rationalization, in a case challenging a domestic measure, that this was so because the Member States have an obligation to the EU. Being an integral part of EU law must surely also relate, to use the federal language, to the centre, rather than just the sub-units, being obliged to comply with its treaty commitments? The judicial explanation could arguably be read more charitably, with the focus being on the EU's international responsibility and Article 216(2) TFEU rather than merely the obligations of the Member States to the EU flowing from the latter's international responsibility.

In any event, another critical point drawing on the assimilation of EU Agreements with EU law proper was made:

> It follows from the [EU] nature of such provisions that their effect in the [EU] may not be allowed to vary according to whether their application is in practice the responsibility of the [EU] institutions or of the Member States and, in the latter

[29] For emphasis on international responsibility for jurisdictional purposes see Holdgaard (2008a: ch 10).

[30] This is subject to the particularities of mixed agreements explored further in Chapters III–VI.

[31] The Court also referred to the Member States having an obligation in relation to the non-member countries. There is clearly no international law obligation on the part of Member States with respect to pure EU Agreements and in future cases that reference was appropriately dropped, see eg 12/86 *Demirel*, para 11.

[32] Indeed, the absence of centre versus sub-unit treaty enforcement contributed to the move from Confederation to Federation in the US: Burgess (2006: 57).

case, according to the effects in the internal legal order of each Member State which the law of that State assigns to international agreements.

The Court then asserted its responsibility via its interpretative jurisdiction for ensuring the uniform application of such provisions throughout the EU. In short, what had been implicit in *Haegeman II* was confirmed: within the EU legal order the ECJ was to be the authoritative interpreter of EU Agreements.[33]

Chapter I noted that while the controversy between the monist and dualist schools was particularly pronounced in the earlier parts of the twentieth century, even into the twenty-first century pieces from prominent scholars have contributed directly to this debate.[34] Moreover, within the founding Member States international lawyers had been engaging in heated debate as to how best to conceptualize the legal status and potential domestic effects of treaties.[35] Unsurprisingly the monist and dualist conceptual lenses and the debates to which they gave rise were directly transposed to the debate on the internal effect of the EU's external commitments. As early as 1960, the use of Regulations for concluding EU Agreements had been called for to ensure their internal legal effect.[36] Two factors pertaining to Regulations are particularly noteworthy in this respect. The Treaty text states that they are directly applicable and expressly required their publication.[37] In contrast, no such publication requirement was imposed for EU Agreements.[38] This was no small issue for, as noted in Chapter I, States wedded to a model of automatic treaty incorporation usually stipulate a publication requirement for treaties which if not met has repercussions for their internal legal effects. The Council did not (at least initially) follow the promptings of some commentators in that it opted to use Decisions for the concluding act. However, it would also publish that Decision with the annexed Agreement in the Official Journal thus neutering a potential

[33] As a matter of international law, the authoritative interpreter is a different matter.

[34] Notably contributions by Arangio-Ruiz (2003; 2007).

[35] For the debates in the founding Member States through to the late 1960s, see Waelbroeck (1969).

[36] By Wohlfarth according to Pescatore (1961: 118).

[37] Current Arts 288 and 297 TFEU.

[38] Indeed, it was some years before this requirement was stipulated in the Treaty for Council Decisions.

publication-based objection to the internal effect of an Agreement.[39] By the late 1960s the Council appeared to have a change of heart for it commenced with increasing frequency to use Regulations.[40] One well-placed observer suggested this was out of caution to prevent even inveterate dualists from objecting that the Agreements were not capable of application within the EU.[41] This alteration in practice only fuelled debate as to whether this internal EU measure could be seen as 'transforming' the EU Agreements.[42] This seemingly arcane debate was not devoid of considerable practical consequence. As noted in Chapter I, in Germany and Italy such reasoning had a prominent hold resulting in treaties obtaining the internal rank of the law of approval and therefore the *lex posterior* rule applied.

The Greek Association Agreement at issue in *Haegeman II* was concluded via a Decision and the fact that no express significance was attributed to the type of concluding act appeared to resolve any debate as to the need for Regulations to ensure particular internal effects for EU Agreements. Put simply, the assertion that EU Agreements were acts of the institutions and an integral part of EU law owed nothing to the type of internal concluding EU measure. To this day, any attempt to gain purchase out of the type of concluding measure has failed.[43] In this sense, the stance first employed in *Haegeman II* favoured the growing chorus of voices rejecting any notion of the EU concluding act 'transforming' EU Agreements.[44] The apparent need for a concluding act was, however, viewed by some as evidence of dualism insofar as it suggested that the internal EU measure made the Agreement operative within the EU,[45] but generally *Haegeman II* has

[39] See currently Art 17.1(d) of Council Decision 2009/937/EU (OJ L325, 11.12.2009, p 35). Pescatore (1961: 118) had called for publication of Agreements as non-publication would deprive them of internal effect.

[40] The first examples being the Association Agreements with Morocco and Tunisia in 1969: see Louis and Bruckner (1980: 38).

[41] Bebr as cited by Everling (1986: 96). See relatedly Pescatore (1973: 151–2).

[42] For contributions prior to the move to Regulations, see Megret (1965) and Pescatore (1961: 118 et seq), for commentary following that move and prior to *Haegeman II*, see Pescatore (1973: 151–2), Kovar (1974: 351–4); Constantinesco and Simon (1975: 441–3). Many commentators post-*Haegeman II* have touched on the transformation issue: eg Bebr (1983: 39); Joliet (1983: 244–5); Boulouis (1992: 74–5); Everling (1986: 95–6); Louis (1977: 136–7); Kapteyn (1999: 276); Waelbroeck (1984: 582); Rideau (1990: 308–12, 371–2). An interesting take on that debate was offered by Peters (1997: 23–35).

[43] See most recently, C-160/09 *Katsivardas* [2010] ECR I-4591.

[44] See in addition to the earlier citations, Schermers (1975: 84); Louis and Brückner (1980: 191); Boulouis (1978: 385).

[45] See discussion by Everling (1986: 96) and Klabbers (2002: 277, 293–4).

been viewed as monistic by those inclined to use such terminology.[46] The language of being part of the legal order is associated with legal systems usually characterized as monist in that treaties are automatically incorporated without ad hoc domestic implementation being necessary. Furthermore, *Haegeman II* could be viewed as implicitly rejecting the *lex posterior* rule,[47] in effect the most practical manifestation of the transformation debate at the heart of the monist–dualist controversy. The interpretative engagement with an EU Agreement invoked in a challenge to a later-in-time EU measure unsurprisingly led some to cite *Haegeman II* as authority for the primacy of EU Agreements over EU secondary legislation.[48] In any event, many viewed the question as having been answered vis-à-vis international law in general in the *International Fruit* ruling,[49] which rendered an alternative outcome concerning EU Agreements untenable, for they, unlike other forms of international law, benefit from a potential constitutional anchor for primacy provided by Article 216(2). Many a commentator has seen in this provision a rejection of the *lex posterior* rule.[50] But one can also understand the view of those who do not see it as answering the question.[51] A textually more explicit provision was certainly possible.[52] This might explain why it was not invoked when the primacy of EU Agreements over secondary legislation was first expressly stated judicially in 1996.[53] Indeed,

[46] Examples include: Pescatore (2003); Bourgeois (2000: 93); Timmermans (1999: 189); Thym (2009: 321); Rodriguez Iglesias (2003: 396); Adam (2011: 34); Kuilwijk (1996: 82–4).

[47] *Haegeman I* had already been viewed in this fashion: Kovar (1974: 355); Constantinesco and Simon (1975: 441). A position advanced long before any judicial pronouncements: Pescatore (1961: 125–6); Megret (1965: 25).

[48] Groux and Manin (1985: 117); Meesen (1976: 498); Hoffmeister (2008: 59). *Haegeman II* was unlike C-40/72 *Schroeder* which could be read as a review of an implementing measure vis-à-vis an EU Agreement as required by its parent Regulation.

[49] 21–4/72 *International Fruit.* See Constantinesco and Simon (1975: 456–7); Louis (1977: 139); Louis and Brückner (1980: 182); Joliet (1983: 253–4, 272); Stein (2000: 168–9); Ehlermann (1986: 131).

[50] Examples include Maresceau (2006: 236); Boulouis (1992: 75); Uerpmann-Wittzack (2009: 138, 147).

[51] Pescatore (1973: 150–1); Constantinesco and Simon (1975); Louis and Brückner (1980: 183).

[52] Chapter I illustrates that many a constitutional text is considerably more explicit. However, the US Constitution which appears to read as a rejection of the *lex posterior* rule has, in fact, been interpreted as enshrining that rule.

[53] C-61/94 *Commission v Germany* [1996] ECR I-3989, para 52. The commentary had long coalesced around that view: Constantinesco and Simon (1975: 455–6); Ehlermann (1986: 131); Macleod et al (1996: 134); Louis and Brückner (1980: 181–2, 192); Rideau (1990: 402–4); Boulouis (1978: 388); Meesen (1976: 500); Schermers and Waelbroeck (1992: 217).

no judicial justification has been forthcoming. One early argument was that it would be inappropriate to apply different reasoning depending on whether it was the relationship between EU law and domestic legal systems or that between EU law and international law.[54] But as one commentator astutely remarked, if this were so no federal State which stipulates federal law's primacy over state law would be entitled to apply the *lex posterior* rule in relation to treaty law.[55] Moreover, followed through to its logical conclusion, application of equivalent reasoning should require the EU's international obligations to trump its own constitutional text, precisely the outcome the ECJ demands of the domestic legal order, and precisely the outcome, as Section 3 illustrates, that the ECJ has been unwilling to countenance.

When *International Fruit* was decided, the Member States adhering to the *lex posterior* rule were outnumbered by four to two, but by the *Haegeman II* ruling this had become five to four the other way. By the time of the first express acknowledgement of the hierarchically superior status vis-à-vis secondary EU law in 1996, three more States had joined each group and thus eight of 15 States were domestic adherents to the *lex posterior* rule.[56] This divergence in domestic approach offers a strong argument in favour of rejecting the *lex posterior* rule to the benefit of all EU Member States. To have adopted the *lex posterior* rule would have resulted in four of the founding States being able to achieve collective outcomes through their EU treaty-making power combined with their EU legislative output that would not be possible with respect to their non-EU treaty-making and law-making capacities; later-in-time EU secondary legislation could trump EU Agreements but later-in-time Member State legislation could not trump that Member State's own treaty commitments. The corollary to this is that rejection of the *lex posterior* rule results in an outcome not ordinarily possible (outside the field of EU law) for adherents to the *lex posterior* rule; their collective exercise of the EU treaty-making power could not be trumped via their collective exercise of the EU legislative process, but precisely this outcome could be achieved where the domestic treaty and law-making processes were employed. The logic for the *lex posterior* rule is usually traced back to this being a later expression of the democratic will, but if the German or Italian model were transposed to the EU level this

[54] Megret (1965: 25–6), AG Mayras in 21–4/72 *International Fruit*.

[55] Meesen (1976: 499). Though many would baulk at the federal analogy.

[56] With regard to EU law proper, the *lex posterior* rule was no longer possible.

would not result in the Italian or German legislative will being able to trump such Agreements. Rather, the EU's legislative output would theoretically be capable of trumping such Agreements.[57] As qualified majority voting applies, that would mean that States such as Germany or Italy could find EU Agreements being trumped by EU legislative output for which they were outvoted in the Council. In sum, from the perspective of both the Member States adhering to the *lex posterior* rule and those that did not, the case for EU Agreements to have a hierarchically superior status internally than EU legislative output is compelling.

2.2 Automatic treaty incorporation and the external relations constitutions of the Member States

The ramifications of the *Haegeman II* ruling, as further articulated in *Kupferberg*, were substantial for the external relations constitutions of the Member States. This was palpably so for those States attached to non-automatic treaty incorporation. For the three Member States wedded to such an approach at the time of these early judgments (Denmark, Ireland, and the UK) the effect was to convert them into automatic treaty incorporation States for a category of treaty law. One category of treaties, to which they may or may not themselves be parties, would through the conduit of EU law become automatically incorporated into their domestic legal orders,[58] sitting alongside the other categories of treaty to which they are a party but that do not, in principle, subject to ad hoc domestic implementation, become part of the domestic legal order. This accordingly qualifies the classification in Chapter I of Denmark, Ireland, and the UK as non-automatic incorporation States, for the constitutional effect of EU membership is that there is a growing category of treaties for which their orthodox constitutional model no longer applies. In such States, the domestic legislature no longer determines the role, if any, that domestic courts play with respect to this particular category of treaties. Rather, the ECJ assumed that role as *Haegeman II* intimated and as *Kupferberg* made explicit. This is unquestionably of momentous constitutional import for those States

[57] EU Agreements themselves could, of course, also be the product of majority voting.

[58] The status of mixed agreements is a complex matter given further consideration in Chapters III–VI.

and any other State wedded to the non-automatic incorporation model that has since contemplated EU accession (such as the Nordic group that joined in 1995).

Whilst the impact of automatic treaty incorporation for EU Agreements was thus most profound for the non-automatic treaty incorporation States, one should not underestimate the impact that the emerging construct would have on the States already familiar with automatic treaty incorporation.[59] Most obviously, it would no longer be for their courts alone to determine the legal effect and interpretation of this category of treaty, rather this became a role in which they were supervised by the higher authority of the ECJ; this meant that the direct effect determination, the traditional preserve of the national court when dealing with treaties,[60] would not be their authoritative prerogative for EU Agreements. This is of critical significance for whilst national courts have on occasion been guilty of shielding their domestic legal order from the impact of treaties, there would be an important category of Agreements for which they would no longer have free rein. And endowing EU Agreements with the general attributes of EU law logically included a hierarchically superior status to domestic law. The later-in-time rule which remains the default rule in Germany and Italy gives way not only to EU law proper but would also, in principle, now do so with respect to EU Agreements. Indeed, the logical implication of this assimilation to EU law proper is that their status became superior to that of the domestic constitution itself and only one of the founders—the Netherlands—accorded treaties a supra-constitutional status.[61]

Furthermore, whilst legislatures in automatic treaty incorporation States would have a constitutionally entrenched role in assenting to at least certain types of treaty they would no longer have such a role for pure EU

[59] That the six founders all knew of automatic treaty incorporation no doubt aided the ECJ in advancing the construct it did. Whilst judges from Denmark, Ireland, and the UK sat in the *Haegeman II* ruling, including the judge-rapporteur, they were outnumbered by two to one given the judges from the six founding Member States. Indeed, to have permitted the founding six to use a Treaty creation, the Treaty of Rome, collectively to sign up to treaties not then automatically incorporated in EU law, would have amounted to bypassing the applicability of their domestic constitutional strictures for treaty-making and the legal consequences of that output.

[60] Although in some legal orders they had been known to defer to the executive, most notably France, even on this question. On the French judicial move away from accepting as binding the Ministry of Foreign Affairs determinations on treaty interpretation, see Daillier, Forteau, and Pellet (2009: 260–1).

[61] And that is subject to an increased parliamentary approval threshold.

Agreements.[62] Indeed, here the initial EU parallel with domestic automatic treaty incorporation models broke down: the European Parliament's input into the treaty-making process was astonishingly meagre until the Maastricht Treaty gave it an assent requirement for some categories of significant Agreements,[63] but it was not until the Lisbon Treaty that an assent requirement became the norm (Art 218(6) TFEU). The EU model, therefore, vastly empowered the domestic executive in external relations via its control of the EU's treaty-making powers, the significance of which was accentuated by the exalted legal status of this output. EU Agreements thus exacerbated the impact of EU membership on the domestic separation of powers: it increased the empowerment of domestic executives via their new collective treaty-making role, with a concomitant disempowerment of the domestic legislature, and an empowerment of the domestic and supranational judiciary for whom another category of EU law emerged.

The constitutional ramifications of adherence to a fully-fledged automatic treaty incorporation model signified by *Haegeman II* can be further illustrated when viewed alongside the substantial expansion of the EU's limited express treaty-making competence via the implied treaty-making powers doctrine. The effect of the seminal *ERTA* jurisprudence was that over time as internal EU legislative output expanded, there was a greater corpus of law capable of being affected by an independent treaty-making power of the Member States and for which the EU instead would accordingly acquire the treaty-making power in the affected sphere. This reduction in the Member States' independent treaty-making power was replaced by the capacity to assume contractual obligations with third parties via the EU framework, only now the internal legal effect of such norms was not to

[62] As Member States would be parties to mixed agreements this requires satisfaction of their domestic constitutional requirements prior to expressing their consent to be bound (EU practice, following what was expressly required for Euratom Agreements (Art 102 Euratom Treaty), is in principle not to conclude a mixed agreement until all the Member States have ratified (Eeckhout (2011: 259), though this is not always followed with multilateral agreements (see Rosas (2010: 373)). For the most part Member State ratification appears to be something of a formality, see, however, Rosas (2010: 367–70) for an instance with a bilateral agreement where this proved especially arduous. For a brief overview of ratification practice vis-à-vis mixed agreements in Finland, France, Germany, and the UK, see Heliskoski (2001: 89–92).

[63] The assent requirement was first introduced for Association Agreements by the Single European Act.

be authoritatively determined by their domestic constitutional order but rather by a supranational court.[64] Nor could the EU legislative process itself be used domestically to trump these external obligations;[65] appropriate as this outcome may be, as suggested above, it does nothing to detract from the domestic constitutional ramifications for Member States as compared to the position that would exist in the EU's absence.

The constitutionally powerful repercussions for the Member States of the EU Agreements model to which the Treaty text combined with judicial rulings gave rise, was accentuated by two predictable developments. First, the emergence of qualified majority voting for the treaty-making process, which post-Lisbon has become the norm, such that the constitutional impact of EU Agreements for any specific domestic legal order can apply even though that State's Council representative voted against its conclusion. Secondly, the rapid expansion of the EU's treaty-making activity thus forming an increasingly significant component of the treaty obligations to which Member States are bound.[66] The fact that much of this is then also implemented via EU legislative output is a further illustration of the constitutional ramifications, for that form of EU law proper, of course, acquires supra-constitutional status in the domestic legal arena (with a supranational court entrusted with compliance control).

3. Constitutional Review of EU Agreements: Constitutionalism Running Wild?

Since at least 1960 there has been debate as to whether ex post constitutional review of the EU's treaty commitments was possible.[67] Indeed, the

[64] Two qualifiers are in order: first, mixed agreements are a more complicated matter as considered in Chapters III–VI; secondly, *Kupferberg* acknowledged the unrealistic possibility of the Contracting Parties determining the legal status in the Agreement itself.

[65] Arguably, it can where the relevant EU Agreement is not a review criterion for EU action: see Chapter VI.

[66] For pure EU Agreements they would be bound as a matter of EU law.

[67] Wohlfarth (1960) cited by Pescatore (1961); Pescatore (1961: 126–9); Bebr (1962: 54–6, 187); Catalano (1964: 72–3); Megret (1965: 26); Kovar (1974: 356–9); Constantinesco and Simon (1975: 451–4). The language of constitutional review of Agreements had already been used by Kovar in 1974.

jurisdictional rationale employed in *Haegeman II* fuelled this,[68] and may even have owed something to the need to contemplate how to establish a jurisdictional basis for ex post constitutional review. For if such Agreements are indeed acts of the institutions for the purposes of reviewing the validity of EU or domestic measures, must they not also be acts of the institutions should they be the object of the challenge? Such logic was bolstered when in *Opinion 1/75* the ECJ offered as a rationale for the ex ante review procedure that it would forestall complications resulting from legal disputes as to the compatibility with the Treaty of binding EU Agreements.[69] The ECJ added that a ruling that a binding EU Agreement was incompatible with the EU Treaty, either because of its content or the procedure adopted for its conclusion, could not fail to provoke serious difficulties and might give rise to adverse consequences for all interested parties, including third countries. For good measure, it explicitly stated that the EU Treaty compatibility of the exercise of the treaty-making power could be submitted to the ECJ in infringement proceedings, annulment actions, and preliminary references. This obiter dictum came from a Full Court pronouncing after having heard from four Advocates General, four Member States, and the Commission and Council; many unsurprisingly saw it as having clearly answered this fundamental question.[70]

It took over a decade for the first ex post constitutional challenge; a plea that has arisen in 18 additional cases in which the EU courts have ruled. This line of jurisprudence and its constitutional significance are explored in the two subsections that follow. The first outlines the authorities, thus providing the basis for critical engagement in a second subsection with the debate to which this form of constitutional review gives rise.

3.1 The authorities

The 19 challenges have dealt with some of the core questions generated by ex post review. The most important question is whether such review is even

[68] See Boulouis (1978); Waelbroeck (1978; 1984); Jacot-Guillarmod (1979: 241–2). A particularly expansive approach to reviewable acts had been taken in an earlier ruling: 22/70 *Commission v Council* [1971] ECR 263.

[69] *Opinion 1/75* [1975] ECR 1355.

[70] Examples include Joliet (1983: 251–2); Manin (1984: 296–7); Waelbroeck (1984: 582); Groux and Manin (1985: 124–5).

possible and, relatedly, if so, what is the justificatory rationale. The first challenge left little doubt as to the answer to the first question but provided no clarification as to the second. In 1987 the Commission brought annulment proceedings against a Council act concluding an agreement on the ground that the common commercial policy legal basis alone should have been used.[71] That argument was rejected on the merits but without any explanation supporting ex post review. The judicial parsimony did not detract from the significance of the case given that, first, and most importantly, an 11-judge Court reviewed the legality of the concluding act and, secondly, the guardian of the treaties (the Commission) had made its position clear, ex post review should be possible, while the Member States' representative (the Council) focused its defence on the substantive legal basis argument advanced rather than contesting the issue of principle.

The next challenge offered some express justification for ex post constitutional review. In 1991 France brought annulment proceedings against a competition agreement concluded by the Commission and the US.[72] The Commission raised the question of whether France should have challenged the decision by which the Commission's Vice-President was authorized to sign the Agreement. The ECJ responded that as the Agreement was intended to produce legal effects, the Commission act seeking to conclude it must be susceptible to an annulment action and the French challenge was to be understood as a challenge against that act. The only additional argument advanced was that exercise of the powers delegated to the EU institutions in international matters could not escape judicial review under Article 263 of the legality of the acts adopted. France's plea that the Commission had no competence to conclude such an agreement was upheld and the concluding act was declared void.

None of the additional 17 cases have provided any additional general support for this form of review.[73] Indeed, the ECJ did not even seize the

[71] 165/87 *Commission v Council* [1988] ECR 5545.

[72] C-327/91 *France v Commission* [1994] ECR I-3641.

[73] Ten of those cases have either included or exclusively concerned challenges to the chosen legal basis for the concluded Agreement: C-360/93 *Parliament v Council* [1996] ECR I-1195; C-268/94 *Portugal v Council* [1996] ECR I-6177; C-189/97 *Parliament v Council* [1999] ECR I-4741; C-36/98 *Spain v Council* [2001] ECR I-779; C-281/01 *Commission v Council* [2002] ECR I-12049; C-211/01 *Commission v Council* [2003] ECR I-8913; C-94/03 *Commission v Council* [2006] ECR I-1; C-347/03 *ERSA* [2005] ECR I-3785; C-231/04 *Confcooperative* [2006] ECR I-61; C-317/04 & C-318/04 *Parliament v Council* [2006] ECR I-4721. Eight of those cases repeated the conventional point when the choice of legal basis of an EU measure is challenged, namely that the choice must be based on objective factors, including as to aim and content,

occasion to expand its justification where the Council raised the inadmissibility objection that a Member State could not challenge a binding EU Agreement via annulment proceedings against the concluding act.[74] It simply reiterated that an annulment action against the concluding act was possible as it had already asserted in dispensing with Germany's attempted ex ante control of the relevant Agreement because it had become devoid of purpose once it had been concluded.[75]

In terms of routes to ex post challenges, the preliminary rulings procedure has generated two unsuccessful challenges to the concluding act of the same agreement. That Agreement was concluded ten years before the first ruling was sought but the relevance, if any, of this was not addressed and the relevant pleas were rejected on the merits.[76] The General Court (GC) also rejected as inadmissible two incidental pleas, pursuant to Article 277 TFEU, to the same bilateral fisheries agreement on the basis that the challenge to the relevant contested Regulation was inadmissible as the applicants did not satisfy the standing requirements.[77] That led to an unsuccessful damages action before the GC in which it dismissed a range of pleas pertaining to unlawful action by the Commission and Council in concluding that bilateral fisheries agreement.[78] The GC has also rejected on the facts two damages actions directed at EU institutions for the conclusion of EU Agreements.[79]

amenable to judicial review. The two exceptions were C-231/04, where the ECJ responded by order with the same response given in C-347/03; and Joined Cases C-317/04 & C-318/04 (the sole case where the appropriate legal base was arguably to be found in the then TEU).

[74] C-122/95 *Germany v Council* [1998] ECR I-973. The Council emphasized that Germany could have voted against the unanimously adopted concluding act.

[75] *Opinion 3/94* [1995] ECR I-4577.

[76] The cases involved a Wine Agreement between the EU and Hungary with the first ruling (C-347/03) simply reiterated in the order that dispensed with C-231/04.

[77] T-194/95 *Area Cova v Council* [1999] II-2271 (upheld on appeal: C-300 & 388/99 P [2001] ECR I-983) and T-12/96 *Area Cova v Council* [1999] II-2301 (upheld on appeal C-301/99 P [2001] ECR I-1005).

[78] T-196/99 *Area Cova v Council* [2001] ECR II-3597.

[79] In T-572/93 *Odigitria v Council and Commission* [1995] ECR II-2025 (upheld on appeal: C-293/95 P *Odigitria* [1996] ECR I-6129) the applicant unsuccessfully alleged breach of several general principles in the conclusion of protocols to EU Fisheries Agreements with Senegal and Guinea-Bissau respectively. In T-212/02 *Commune de Champagne v Commission* [2007] ECR II-2017, concerning an Agricultural Agreement with Switzerland, the damages action was rejected because of absence of causation. In a discontinued case where the compatibility of the Sixth International Tin Agreement with the EU Treaty was at issue, the Advocate General appeared to have little reservation about the use of damages actions (C-241/87 *Maclaine Watson v Council and Commission* [1990] ECR I-1797).

When it comes to the grounds of challenge, in 11 of the 19 cases the exclusive plea or one of the pleas concerned the appropriate legal basis.[80] Of those 11 cases, four were brought by the Commission, three by the European Parliament, two by Member States, and two via domestic disputes. Five of those challenges, brought by either the Parliament or Commission, were successful.[81] Cases have included an array of different pleas including alleged breaches of EU treaty provisions,[82] other EU Agreements,[83] and non-EU concluded treaties,[84] as well as general principles of EU law.[85] These pleas have generally only been rejected on the facts or as not necessary for consideration because the challenge was upheld on other grounds.[86] The only successful plea other than the no legal competence to conclude the agreement plea, and the inappropriate legal basis plea in five cases, has been a general principles plea advanced in the previously mentioned case rejecting the Council inadmissibility objection. In that case, Germany sought annulment of the Council Decision concluding the WTO Agreements. A Bananas Framework Agreement with several Latin American countries was included in the EU's WTO tariff schedule and thus formed an integral part of the WTO Agreements. That Framework Agreement breached the general principle of non-discrimination by unjustifiably exempting a category of banana importers from the Agreement's export licence system. The Council Decision was accordingly annulled to the extent that it approved the conclusion of the Bananas Framework

[80] The exceptions are C-327/91; C-122/95; C-149/96 *Portugal v Council* [1999] ECR I-8395 (a challenge to use of a qualified majority legal basis was, however, smuggled into a general principles plea and rejected); C-327/91; T-572/93; T-196/99; T-212/02. Two cases do not actually disclose the specific pleas (T-194/95 and T-12/96).

[81] C-360/93 (Parliament); C-211/01 (Commission); C-281/01 (Commission); C-94/03 (Commission); C-317/04 & C-318/04 (Parliament).

[82] eg the duty of cooperation currently in Art 4(3) TEU in C-149/96 and C-317/04 & C-318/04.

[83] WTO Agreements as was the case in C-149/96; C-347/03; C-231/04. One might see this as therefore constituting a breach of EU primary law itself, namely Art 216(2) TFEU.

[84] The ECHR in C-347/03, C-231/04.

[85] C-327/91; T-572/93; C-122/95; C-149/96; T-196/99; T-212/02; C-317/04 & C-318/04. To the extent that the ECHR is relied upon, as in C-347/03 and C-231/04, this could be viewed simply as a general principles plea given that the latter currently functions as the conduit for ECHR-based challenges.

[86] In C-149/96 the plea pertaining to a breach of an EU Agreement was rejected because the WTO did not form a review criterion for EU action (see Chapter IV). It also rejected a plea pertaining to breach of a principle of economic and social cohesion set out according to Portugal in EU treaty provisions as the provisions merely laid down a programme.

Agreement and insofar as the Agreement exempted a category of importers from the export licence system.

Two further significant points emerge from this line of authorities. First, the ex ante procedure does not have suspensory effect as the Bananas Agreement case illustrated. In fact, the ex ante procedure was only invoked in two out of the possible ten institutional or Member State ex post challenges.[87] Clearly, institutions and Member States can challenge Agreements even where they have not sought to avail themselves of the ex ante review possibility.[88] Indeed, even a Member State voting in favour of approval of an agreement can bring an ex post challenge.[89]

The second point relates to the consequences of annulment. The seven successful annulment cases have involved eight Agreements.[90] In two of those rulings, both successful legal basis challenges, the ECJ limited the effects of its judgment with respect to the annulled concluding act. On the first occasion the Agreement had already expired and it was underscored that the effects of the annulled decision were being preserved for reasons of legal certainty and in order not to affect the rights that had arisen under the Agreement adversely.[91] In the second, the avoidance of legal uncertainty justification was specifically referred to with respect to the Agreement's applicability within the EU legal order.[92] The other five successful annulment cases all have their own stories to tell which require awareness of institutional activity in the wake of the rulings. New Decisions approving the Agreements were adopted with retroactive effect in two instances.[93] In a

[87] C-122/95 and C-317/04 & C-318/04 in both of which the Council proceeded to conclude the Agreement. Two of the Parliament's ex post challenges predated the Treaty of Nice which accorded it the power to seek an Opinion: C-360/93 and C-189/97.

[88] In some of those eight challenges, availing oneself of the ex ante procedure would not have been easily achieved. The Council opted for its preferred legal basis at the point of adopting the concluding act itself in C-165/87; C-211/01; C-94/03; and in C-327/91, it appears France was initially unaware of the Agreement.

[89] C-122/95.

[90] C-211/01 concerned two Agreements.

[91] C-360/93.

[92] C-211/01.

[93] C-327/91 (see Art 2 of Council and Commission Decision 95/145/EC) and C-94/03 (see Art 3 of Council Decision 2006/730/EC). Concerning the latter judgment on the Rotterdam Convention, the ECJ on the same day annulled, on inappropriate legal basis grounds, the Regulation (304/2003/EC) implementing the Convention in EU law whilst maintaining its effects in force until adoption within a reasonable period of a new Regulation (see now Regulation 689/2008/EC): C-178/03 *Commission v Council* [2006] ECR I-107.

third, the new decision was adopted without a retroactive effect provision.[94] However, to the extent that that Agreement imposed obligations these arguably would have been fulfilled via the EU implementing legislation that had not been challenged.[95] In the Bananas Framework Agreement case the Commission was able to eliminate the discrimination with which the Court had taken issue via a Regulation without challenging the validity of the Agreement.[96] Finally and, most recently, while annulling the concluding Decision of a passenger data transfer agreement, the ECJ preserved in force for four months a Data Protection Directive adequacy decision necessary for permitting the data processing under the Agreement.[97] The Grand Chamber ordered the EU institutions to terminate the Agreement.[98] Crucially, it justified preserving the effects of the adequacy decision on the basis of legal certainty and the fact that the EU could not rely on its own law as justification for not fulfilling the Agreement which remained applicable during the 90-day termination period.

3.2 *Pacta sunt servanda* versus constitutionalism

The debate pertaining to ex post constitutional review initially pitted those against any such form of review versus those in favour in at least certain circumstances. The two much-cited initial contributions were diametrically opposed.[99] For Catalano, the presence of the ex ante review procedure ruled out ex post review. For Pescatore, where the ex ante review procedure had not been invoked the Member States and institutions, at least, were not precluded from an ex post challenge for otherwise Agreements could be used to achieve treaty revision by abstention from use of the ex ante review procedure.[100]

94 C-281/01. Decision 2003/269/EC.

95 Regulation 2422/2001/EC.

96 Regulation 1087/98/EC. See further Castillo de la Torre (2001: 195).

97 For details, see Mendez (2007).

98 Which they duly did: see OJ C219/1 (12/09/06).

99 They came from two former members of the legal drafting team of the Treaty of Rome who both became judges at the Court. Pescatore (1961: 126–9) was writing prior to becoming a judge (while on the bench his published views appeared to support ex post review (1973: 156)), the other once he was no longer a judge: Catalano (1964: 73).

100 That procedure expressly provides that an Agreement for which a negative Opinion is given cannot enter into force without treaty revision.

Simply put, on one side there was an argument against ex post review, tied to the presence of the ex ante procedure, grounded in notions of international legal certainty; on the other, an argument grounded in what might now appropriately be referred to as notions of constitutionalism.[101] It was essentially the tension between these two strands of thinking that was to varying degrees to be played out in the doctrinal debate. Some contributions predating *Haegeman II* and *Opinion 1/75* advanced a staunchly anti ex post review line grounded primarily in concerns with legal certainty and the consequences for third parties.[102] Despite the ECJ essentially committing itself to ex post review in *Opinion 1/75*, some continued to treat this question as largely unresolved and adopted a markedly hostile stance to acceptance of ex post review. Thus Jacot-Guillarmod emphasized that the arguments in favour were ultimately of a constitutional nature, which for him was precisely their weakness.[103] He joined the growing chorus of voices emphasizing the impossibility of annulling an Agreement binding in international law. Like others, he explored annulling the concluding act, but saw this as leading to a catastrophic result with grave international consequences and underscored that to pretend that annulling that act would not impact on the Agreement was a misplaced dualist understanding because the two were indissociable.

Rideau, writing after the very first ex post challenge, also exhibited considerable difficulty in accepting that review would or should be possible.[104] He was one of the first explicitly to suggest that the Court's concern in this context was with the autonomy of the EU legal order. For him, this explained why the ECJ was seeking to adopt one model for the relationship between EU law and domestic law whilst seeking to opt for the primacy of the EU Treaty vis-à-vis EU Agreements. Indeed, for Rideau the most fundamental line of criticism one could advance of this jurisprudential turn would be grounded in integral monism.[105] In effect, and this seemed to be an undercurrent to much of the earlier criticism, ex post review was symptomatic of a dualistic construction that was inappropriate

[101] Pescatore's contribution came well before the express language of constitutionalism in the EU context began to take hold.

[102] Kovar (1974); Constantinesco and Simon (1975).

[103] Jacot-Guillarmod (1979: 237–42); Kovar (1981: 368–9) expressed doubts as to whether ex post review had actually been accepted.

[104] Rideau (1990: 305–8, 380–402). As did Waelbroeck and Waelbroeck (1993: 103–4, 214–15) who surprisingly made no mention of C-165/87.

[105] See also Waelbroeck and Waelbroeck (1993: 214).

for a judicial actor viewed as imposing a monistic construction of EU law upon Member States. The academic debate following the first successful annulment action has generally been shaped by the aforementioned tension between constitutionalism on the one side and international legal certainty or *pacta sunt servanda* on the other, but in principle no longer with a view to employing arguments stemming from the latter in support of wholesale rejection of ex post review.[106] Rather, such concerns were usually invoked as a means to minimize the impact on international law and international legal certainty notably through suggestions for constraining the circumstances in which ex post review could be used,[107] and expanding the potency of the ex ante procedure,[108] as well as by calls for the ECJ to limit the effects of its judgments,[109] or for EU institutions where possible to apply the new concluding act retroactively.[110]

Few engaging with the ex post review debate have been able to resist employing the language of monism and dualism.[111] And many, including judges in extra-judicial comments, have attached the label of dualist, or a rejection of monism, to this line of jurisprudence.[112] The dualist label has been employed in a somewhat descriptive and non-judgemental fashion

[106] Examples include Charpentier (1997); Leray and Potteau (1998); Kapteyn (1999); de Walsche (2005: 164–6); Monjal (2004); Castillo de la Torre (2001); Adam (2011). For the exception, see the critical comment on acceptance of ex post review by Kaddous (1996).

[107] By, eg, precluding Member States from ex post challenges where they had not invoked the ex ante procedure: Charpentier (1997: 419–21); Cebada Romero (2002: 318); De Walsche (2005: 165–6), see also for nuanced discussion Castillo de la Torre (2001: 50–3). Others have simply called for greater use of the ex ante procedure where compatibility doubts arose: see Lenaerts and de Smijter (2000: 137).

[108] By, eg, imposing an obligation on the Commission to invoke the ex ante procedure, Kaddous (1996: 631); Charpentier (1997: 420–1) (favouring judicial acceptance of parliamentary recourse to the ex ante procedure); Kovar (1981: 363) (arguing for suspensory effect so that the Council cannot conclude the Agreement while the Opinion is pending). A particularly compelling case for according a more central role to the ex ante procedure is articulated by Adam (2011).

[109] Lenaerts and Van Nuffel (2011: 873) suggest annulments should invariably be accompanied by a declaration that the legal effects of the Agreement remain unaffected. The Lisbon Treaty expanded the Treaty text expressly to accommodate judicial use of Art 231 TEC to measures other than Regulations (Art 264 TFEU).

[110] See Kapteyn (1999: 284).

[111] Examples of those referring to monism or dualism when engaging with this debate include: Bourgeois (2000); Kapteyn (1999); Kaddous (1996); Lenaerts and de Smijter (2000: 98–106); Peters (1997); Rideau (1990: 308, 380 et seq); Jacot-Guillarmod (1979); Waelbroeck and Waelbroeck (1993: 214–15).

[112] Examples from judges include Kapteyn (1999) and Rodriguez Iglesias (2003: 397–8). The jurisprudence led Judge Lenaerts and his co-author to conclude that 'The Court thereby applies a somewhat limited version of the monistic approach' (Lenaerts and de Smijter (2000: 105–6)).

that does not attack ex post review,[113] in contrast to the pejorative usage often prevalent in earlier work arguing against ex post review.[114] Broadly, the logic would appear to be that countenancing ex post review constitutes a direct threat to the domestic primacy of binding treaty law and is therefore in tension with a central tenet of the monistic account.[115]

But the acceptance of some (limited) form of ex post review need not be viewed as in tension with monism to the extent that monism is understood as requiring domestic primacy for binding treaty commitments. The rule that domestic law cannot be invoked as justification for failure to perform treaty obligations is currently enshrined in the 1969 and 1986 Vienna Conventions on the Law of Treaties (VCLT).[116] However, States and international organizations can rely on their own law as invalidating their consent to be bound where that consent was expressed in manifest violation of a provision of their internal law (or organizational rules) of fundamental importance regarding the competence to conclude treaties.[117] On this basis, those inclined to use the language of monism could well argue that where a domestic legal order seeks to condition ex post review on satisfaction of the exacting standards required for an invalidation of consent to be bound under the Vienna Convention, no incompatibility with the monistic account need arise. After all, this would be to attempt to use international law itself as the benchmark for the validity of treaty commitments.

It is not surprising, then, that one of the early critics of ex post review appeared willing to countenance review where firmly attached to the Vienna Convention test.[118] In the EU context it has long been emphasized how difficult it would be to square any challenges with the Vienna Convention test.[119] One might intuitively assume that the Competition Agreement scenario was capable of meeting that test. It obviously violated internal law of fundamental importance regarding who is empowered to conclude

[113] As was the case for the then Judge Kapteyn (1999) who expressly defended ex post review; the brief coverage by Thym (2009: 327) and Rodriguez Iglesias (2003: 397–8) was not expressly critical.

[114] Prominent examples are Jacot-Guillarmod (1979) and Kaddous (1996).

[115] Ex post review prevailed in the two founding Member States (Germany and Italy) long referred to in scholarly literature as dualist.

[116] Article 27. The EU is not a party to the Vienna Conventions, although their provisions are increasingly referred to.

[117] Article 46 VCLT.

[118] See Kovar (1974: 358). Kaddous (1996) appeared to adopt the same stance.

[119] See eg Rideau (1990: 397–8); Leray and Potteau (555–70); Aust (2007: 314); Macleod et al (1996: 131).

treaties; indeed, the ECJ expressly referred to the constitutional nature of the EU's general treaty-making clause.[120] However, the Vienna Convention 1986 (Art 46(3)) expressly provides that for a violation to be manifest it would have to be objectively evident to any State or international organization conducting itself in accordance with the normal practice of States and, where appropriate, of international organizations and in good faith; a threshold leading to the near unanimous view that this violation was not manifest.[121] A then GC judge, now at the ECJ, asserted in a co-authored paper that the formal compatibility control employed in the Competition Agreement case did not call into question the ECJ's own monistic approach to the status of international agreements in the EU legal order nor, because of Article 46 VCLT, did it necessarily breach *pacta sunt servanda*.[122] And yet the closest the Court has ever come to express engagement with the Vienna Convention test is the assertion in the Passenger Name Records (PNR) ruling (C-317/04 & C-318/04) that the EU 'cannot rely on its own law as justification for not fulfilling the Agreement'.[123] This could be read as affirmation of Article 27 VCLT, but also as implicit rejection of the applicability of its Article 46 to the PNR Agreement.

The end result is that ex post constitutional review is conducted even in circumstances where the necessary internal rule of fundamental importance would never have attested to manifest incompetence for Vienna Convention purposes. This line of authority implicitly accepts the possible inapplicability of an EU Agreement within the EU legal order whilst it remains binding internationally. And precisely this premise, often disparagingly referred to as dualist[124] and even duplicity,[125] was derided in earlier literature. If the only way to acquire or retain what for some appears to be the much-prized monist label is by either rejecting ex post review or confining it to the narrow Vienna Convention grounds, then the Court

[120] For the suggestion that the ECJ's formulation can be explained by the Vienna Convention test: see Lenaerts and de Smijter (2000: 101) and Azoulai (2005: 215). The constitutional adjective, though included in the headnote, is missing from para 28 of the ruling in English.

[121] Examples include Kaddous (1996: 627–8, 632); Leray and Potteau (1998: 560); Cebada Romero (2002: 320). A Commission Communication expressly asserted that it had not been manifestly incompetent and that the EU remained internationally bound by the Agreement (COM(94) 430 final, 12.10.94). For the express suggestion that it was a manifest violation vitiating consent, see Azoulai (2005: 215).

[122] Lenaerts and de Smijter (2000: 100–1). See also Bourgeois (2000: 78–80).

[123] See, however, the Advocates General Opinions in 165/87 and C-122/95.

[124] Kovar (1981: 369); Kaddous (1996: 628–9); Jacot-Guillarmod (1979: 240).

[125] Kaddous (1996: 628–9).

was right to renounce that path. Monist and dualist language can close off appropriate engagement with the issues at stake. Undoubtedly, monist and dualist labels need not simply be used as rhetorical devices, for in this debate they are usually simply another means to advance wholly legitimate concerns with due respect for *pacta sunt servanda*, international legal certainty, and the rights of third parties. But we should also weigh fully legitimate concerns with the values of constitutionalism on the other side of the scale, concerns given insufficient consideration by those rejecting ex post review per se or willing only to countenance it where Article 46 VCLT might be satisfied.[126] After all, that test settles the tension between *pacta sunt servanda* and constitutionalism in a way that concedes very little to the latter.

There are several particularly good examples in the extant case law attesting to the constitutional importance of ex post review. The Competition Agreement case illustrated a surreptitious[127] attempt by the Commission to expand its treaty-making competence. The Advocate General was scarcely able to conceal his contempt for the Commission's attempts to justify a general power consolidated by practice to conclude international agreements of an administrative nature. Constitutionalist values were clearly being articulated in the Advocate General's Opinion, for whom the argument pertaining to repeated practice was tantamount to acknowledging that an infringement of the Treaty rules acquired legitimacy because of its repetition and who also rightly emphasized:

- that institutions are to act within the limits of the powers conferred on them by the Treaty;
- the constitutional significance of the general treaty-making clause which would have required consultation of the European Parliament were the Agreement at issue to have been concluded by the Council;[128]

[126] Admittedly, those arguing against ex post review did so for a system with ex ante review and thus a mechanism (which many would have expanded) to give legitimate expression to concerns with constitutionalism. However, they effectively rejected any balancing post conclusion of an Agreement between the dictates of international law and those of constitutionalism; the former simply took precedence, for even those who would concede review on Vienna Convention grounds were still effectively giving precedence to international law.

[127] The Advocate General explained, inter alia, that the Agreement was not published, the Commission's approval and the decision authorizing the Vice President to sign and conclude it was recorded in the minutes of the meeting which were not communicated to the Member States.

[128] A Council-concluded Agreement would also have required it to issue the negotiating Directives.

- that the EU is governed by the rule of law based on the principle of legality and conferred powers.

It is difficult to see how these core values pertaining to constitutionalism in the EU-specific context could have been upheld in the absence of ex post review, particularly as France was unable to use the ex ante procedure against an agreement of which it was apparently unaware. Similar logic applies to the Bananas Framework Agreement which was concluded while an Opinion was pending. The German challenge was based exclusively on several general principles of EU law, specifically a combination of fundamental rights and other constitutional values, none of which could be said to pertain to an EU rule of fundamental importance regarding the competence to conclude treaties. And even if these unwritten rules relevant to the substantive compatibility of an EU Agreement with EU law of primary rank could be so construed,[129] this was never an example of manifest incompetence.

The 2004 EU–US PNR Agreement offered a more egregious example of substantive EU compatibility concerns. Essentially, that Agreement legalized the transfer of a wide range of passenger-related data held by airlines to US authorities. The Opinion sought by the Parliament expressly queried its compatibility with Article 8 ECHR.[130] An astonishing array of data protection shortcomings existed making compliance most unlikely.[131] That plea was evaded by the ECJ, but the Agreement offers a powerful illustration of the acute tension that can arise between treaties and core components of constitutionalism. This is precisely why mere recourse to notions of monism or, more persuasively, *pacta sunt servanda*, international legal certainty, and the rights of third parties should not as of right, and subject only to Article 46 VCLT, trump wholly legitimate concerns with constitutionalism. Arguably, there was all the more justification for this proposition in what was the curious external relations set-up to which the EU was until recently wedded. Until the Treaty of Nice, the Parliament was not even able to seek an Opinion on an envisaged Agreement and it was not until

[129] Lenaerts and de Smijter (2000: 102–4) did not rule out the possibility.

[130] Registered as *Opinion 1/04*.

[131] As attested to by an Opinion from the Data Protection Working Party (*Opinion 2/2004*), as well as the European Data Protection Supervisor's intervention in support of the Parliament. See generally, and also on the Advocate General's unconvincing attempt to reconcile the Agreement with the ECHR, Mendez (2007) and de Hert and Gutwirth (2009: 37–9).

Lisbon that its approval became the norm for most EU Agreements.[132] To have rejected ex post review would have sanctioned a system empowering executive actors to create binding Agreements without, in most instances, any direct democratic approval and with the only directly elected body (post-1979) being unable to contest the constitutionality of an Agreement either ex ante or ex post.[133] That would have further exacerbated the democratic deficit to which the EU gave rise through its empowerment of insufficiently accountable executive actors. The Parliament's improved status within the external relations set-up does not warrant a different outcome. The controversial SWIFT Agreement with the US on the processing and transfer of financial messaging data, first voted down by the Parliament before an amended version was approved in 2010, raises a myriad of fundamental rights concerns and should certainly not be immune to an ex post challenge.[134] That Agreement, like the 2004 US PNR Agreement and its successor, is further testament to why domestic constitutionalism concerns should weigh increasingly heavily in any such balancing exercise. The remit of international treaty-making has significantly changed in recent times and the post-9/11 fixation with terrorist threats has increasingly given rise to treaties raising significant concerns with fundamental rights standards and other constitutional values. And this treaty-making, as with treaty-making per se, is a process dominated by executive actors in which Parliaments, even where their assent is generally required as now applies in the post-Lisbon EU context, have limited influence.

An additional justification for ex post review emerges from consideration of the constitutional ramifications for the Member States of its absence. Section 2.2 underscored the constitutional impact of the EU's *Haegeman II* line of jurisprudence, read in the light of *ERTA*, for the Member States: vast swathes of their independent treaty-making powers had been replaced by the capacity to assume international obligations in the EU setting, even against their will if they were outvoted in the Council, and these international obligations would have a supra-constitutional status in the Member States which their domestic courts and the ECJ could police.

[132] For the changing parliamentary role pertaining to EU Agreements, see Corbett et al (2011: 251–6).

[133] Unless the ECJ had filled in the ex ante textual lacuna as some had called for: Charpentier (1997). Mixed agreements would also have required domestic ratification.

[134] Recent revelations concerning its implementation have also been disconcerting: see 'EU hands personal data to US authorities on daily basis' (22.06.12) at <http://euobserver.com/justice/116719>.

Outright rejection of ex post review would have been viewed with considerable trepidation in those Member States where ordinarily treaties acquire no such supra-constitutional status. In Germany ex post review exists and the tension between no such possibility for EU Agreements and the *Rechtsstaat*[135] would seem self-evident. The ex ante review possibility alone would hardly have solved that tension for as it originally existed its use was confined to the Council, the Commission, and the Member States. Exclusively ex ante challenges would prevent later challenges based on the operational impact of a particular Agreement and, unless the ex ante procedure were accorded suspensory effect, would not preclude the Council from concluding Agreements in any event. But even for those States in which treaties can obtain a supra-constitutional status, this status would result for Agreements on which they had been outvoted in the Council. In short, the EU constitutional set-up offers additional explanation for why ex post review is constitutionally fitting. To the extent that a Member State's constitutional standards are reflected in EU primary law, those standards could form a review criterion for EU Agreements. It is also likely that the Court was concerned that insulating EU Agreements from review would have made unconditional acceptance of EU law supremacy an even harder pill to swallow in certain quarters than it had already proved to be.[136]

The defence and justification for review offered here is not intended to suggest that the tension between the values of constitutionalism and those of *pacta sunt servanda*, international legal certainty, and the like should be resolved wholly in favour of the former. The latter concerns can still be given a considerable measure of legitimate expression even in a system with ex post review. Many have asserted that successful annulment challenges result in the inapplicability of the relevant Agreement within the EU legal order,[137] a view often expressed without even acknowledging the use, or possible use, of the limitation of the effects of a judgment power or

[135] On this German constitutional concept, see Heun (2011: 35–44).

[136] A judge who sat in the first successful annulment action (C-327/91) and the Bananas Framework Agreement case (C-122/95) later revealingly and rhetorically asked whether the Member States where constitutional review of treaties exists and where respect for EU law supremacy rests upon the ECJ ensuring that the EU and its institutions do not exceed their competences and exercise them with respect for fundamental rights would still have that faith if the ECJ renounced ex post review of EU Agreements: Kapteyn (1999: 281).

[137] Díez-Hochleitner (1998: 120); de Walsche (2005: 163–4); Monjal (2004: 418); Kapteyn (1999: 281–3); Rideau (1990: 398–400); Leray and Potteau (1998: 546–9). This view predated the case law: Louis and Bruckner (1980: 185); Bebr (1981: 37); Joliet (1983: 250–1).

retroactive Council concluding acts.[138] In contrast, a senior Commission legal official asserted that it was incorrect to take the view that a treaty the conclusion of which has been declared void could no longer have effects under internal EU law and that 'Insofar as acts under national or [EU] law are necessary in order to carry out the international obligations under the treaty, such acts and the laws or regulations on which they are based... continue to have legal effect under internal law.'[139] Further clarification drawn from judicial and institutional practice is required but it is certainly clear that preserving the effects of annulled measures and retroactively-applied Council concluding acts have been employed in a manner that protects *pacta sunt servanda*, and international and domestic legal certainty. This seems fully appropriate for the mainly inter-institutional legal basis disputes that account for most of the successful ex post review cases. But it is doubtful whether such devices would be appropriate for an annulment on substantive grounds such as rights violations. It would be incongruous for the ECJ or the political institutions via secondary measures to employ such devices in a manner that effectively condones continuing breaches of human rights or, indeed, other fundamental constitutional values. One might view the PNR ruling in such terms given the limitation on the effects of the judgment, but the ECJ actually evaded the fundamental rights challenge.[140] If we take two of the currently especially constitutionally controversial Agreements, ACTA (2011)[141] and SWIFT (2010),[142] they both have

[138] Examples include Azoulai (2005: 216); Neframi (2007: 486); Peters (1997: 16–17, 40); Thym (2009: 327); Rodriguez Iglesias (2003: 398). Lenaerts and de Smijter (2000: 103, 105–6) noted that a new Agreement was concluded eight months after the C-327/91 ruling but mentioned neither the retroactive concluding decision nor the Commission Communication ((COM (94) 430 final); the Advocate General's Opinion in C-402/05 P and C-415/05 P *Kadi* [2008] ECR I-6351(para 21) referred to 'cases in which the Court barred an international agreement from having effect within the EU legal order on the ground that it was concluded on the wrong legal basis' and pointed to the PNR ruling (C-317/04 & C-318/04) as a recent example and also drew attention to the Competition Agreement case. The PNR case actually illustrates the contrary as the Court sought to maintain the Agreement's internal and external legal applicability pending its internationally lawful denunciation.

[139] Kuijper (1998: 13).

[140] For which the Court could be criticized, given that its ruling sanctioned the continued (for several months) internal effect of an Agreement of doubtful compatibility with fundamental rights.

[141] The compatibility of the Anti-Counterfeiting Trade Agreement with fundamental rights was strongly contested in an expert opinion prepared for the Parliament's Green/European Free Alliance Group: Korff and Brown (2011).

[142] OJ L195 (27.07.2010), p 3.

withdrawals that take effect 180 days after written notification.[143] One needs to query whether in the event of a successful ex post challenge on rights grounds,[144] it would be compatible with the rule of law in the EU to limit the effects of such a judgment for at least six months, or more depending on what a particular Agreement provides, to enable the EU to denounce the Agreement.[145] Put another way, where substantive compatibility concerns are at stake, a judicial order to denounce an Agreement while its legal effects continue in the EU will not always constitute an appropriate reconciliation between the interests of constitutionalism and those of *pacta sunt servanda*, international legal certainty, and the like. Indeed, it concedes everything to the latter for the only concession to the former is wholly consistent with international law. To deprive, in certain limited instances, a specific Agreement, or at least certain of its provisions,[146] of its legal effects within the EU, and thus likely trigger the EU's international responsibility, can be a price worth paying. The potential impact on the international legal order should not be overstated. Only eight concluding acts have been annulled: retroactive concluding acts and limiting the effects of judgments have curtailed the legal consequences within the EU of a number of these annulments, and only one successful challenge was directly because of the actual content of the Agreement (Bananas Framework Agreement).

Furthermore, the inter-institutional legal basis disputes may well become less likely given the considerable expansion in qualified majority voting and parliamentary assent for the conclusion of EU Agreements thus reducing the incentive for ex post challenges by the Commission and Parliament. But precisely the changing remit of EU treaty-making, suggests that ex post constitutional value-based challenges may become more frequent. The EU's political institutions would accordingly do well to heed such concerns

[143] See Art 41 of ACTA and Art 21(2) of the SWIFT Agreement. The EU–US PNR Agreement (2011) has a 120-day termination clause (see Art 25(2)).

[144] Assuming ACTA is actually approved, at the time of writing the Commission had agreed to use the ex ante review procedure.

[145] In *Kadi* the effect of the annulled Regulation was preserved for three months during which the EU institutions sought to address the procedural shortcomings and duly re-enacted the substantive measure: de Búrca (2010: 26).

[146] In the Bananas Framework Agreement case (C-122/95) the ECJ concluded that the concluding Decision was annulled to the extent that it approved the Agreement and insofar as the Agreement exempted a category of importers from the export licence system. This suggests, as Casolari (2008: 311) has noted, that an Agreement could continue to be internally effective in EU law with the exception of the part held incompatible with the EU Treaty.

where possible in the treaty-making process itself—indeed, this is a likely salutary effect of acceptance of ex post review—as well as by contemplating both more frequent recourse to the ex ante procedure and a more collaborative and respectful approach to its use. The ECJ for its part could still ensure more potent effect for the ex ante procedure by providing for an expedited procedure[147] or, perhaps less realistically, by affirming that a violation of the duty of cooperation can result where an Agreement is concluded while the ex ante procedure is pending.[148]

The aforementioned suggestions to reduce the likelihood of ex post challenges arising and to limit the consequences of clashes between the competing values at stake, would sit well with the new Treaty provision providing that 'the Union . . . shall contribute to . . . the strict observance . . . of international law'.[149] This section has not attempted to ground the arguments for ex post review in the Treaty text. Many have engaged with such arguments illustrating how the provisions can often be read in opposed fashions.[150] But there is certainly no convincing EU Treaty textual argument against review and, if anything, the fact that an EU concluding act is clearly at play makes the case against the reviewability of that act hard to sustain. The ECJ has not troubled itself with the textual debates other than to reach the textually artificial conclusion that an Agreement is an act of the institutions for interpretative jurisdiction purposes under Article 267 (*Haegeman II*) but not so for ex post challenges (Competition Agreement case).[151] That does not lead to an absence of judicial protection as the concluding act itself is reviewable, even where in effect the actual review is as to the substantive content of the Agreement (as in the Bananas Agreement case).

[147] See also Adam (2011: 220–7). The Court's proposed new rules of procedure (2011) would replace the need for all Advocates General to be heard with one Advocate General.

[148] An argument advanced by the Parliament that was not addressed by the ECJ and was rejected by the Advocate General in the PNR ruling. See further Adam (2011: 214–17).

[149] Article 3(5) TEU. Some might, however, see in this a constitutional anchor for rejecting ex post review.

[150] Bebr (1981: 34–9, 355–6, 467–9); Díez-Hochleitner (1998: 114–16); Charpentier (1997: 415–21); Jacot-Guillarmod (1979: 237–42); Kovar (1974: 356–9); Kaddous (1996: 615–17, 620 et seq); Kapteyn (1999: 281); Manin (1984: 295–7); Rideau (1990: 381 et seq); Peters (1997: 39–40); Casolari (2008: 191–201).

[151] See Eeckhout (2011: 289) for criticism of this conclusion.

4. The Judicial Application of EU Agreements and Direct Effect

Having opened the gateway for national courts and individuals via the jurisdictional rationale employed in *Haegeman II*, consolidated further in *Kupferberg*, the crucial question was how the Court would respond to its newly assumed interpretative task. After all, there is no scarcity of generous language, whether expressly provided for in constitutional text or judicial pronouncements, as to the status of treaties in the domestic legal arena; whether the logical implications can then be found in judicial practice remains an altogether different matter.

4.1 Engaging and avoiding the direct effect question

In *Haegeman II* an interpretation of the Greek Association Agreement was provided that preserved the EU measure and with no discussion of direct effect.[152] But the very next EU Agreement case stemmed from a court expressly framing its question in the language of *Van Gend en Loos*, namely, did the particular provision confer an individual right which the national courts must protect.[153] The dispute in *Bresciani* concerned charges imposed under national law on both French and Senegalese imports. With respect to the former, this was alleged to breach the EU provision on the abolition of customs duties and charges having an equivalent effect and, with respect to the latter, the equivalent Yaoundé Convention provision (an Association Agreement to which Senegal was a party). Both the Commission and the Advocate General argued that like its EU law counterpart it too was directly effective.

The Court did not deal sequentially with the Italian court's questions, preferring, as would seem logical, to commence with whether the provision conferred the right to rely on it, before addressing the specific interpretation to be accorded to the provision. In order to determine this, it held that 'regard must be simultaneously paid to the spirit, the general scheme and the wording of the Convention and of the provision concerned'. This

[152] The questions put to the Court were not framed in terms of direct effect and rights.

[153] 87/75 *Bresciani* [1976] ECR 129.

language was strikingly reminiscent of that employed in *Van Gend en Loos* when the direct effect of the Treaty itself was first dealt with. The Court emphasized the origins of the Yaoundé Convention, stemming as it did from the EU seeking to retain an association with certain dependent overseas countries and territories—now independent and hence the need for the Agreement—that had been provided for in the Treaty with the objective of furthering their interests and prosperity.

With respect to the customs duties and charges having equivalent effect provision, it was correctly concluded that there was an imbalance in the obligations, in that whilst the EU had committed to abolishing charges having an equivalent effect, the Associated States were expressly accorded flexibility. The Agreement was concluded to promote their development and this imbalance, it was held, did not prevent recognition that some provisions have direct effect. A particular quirk of the Yaoundé Convention provision was that it actually referred to its EU law counterpart and for the ECJ this express reference meant that the EU undertook precisely the same obligation to Associated States as the Member States had assumed towards each other and being a specific obligation, not subject to any implied or express reservation, it conferred rights that national courts must protect.

Thus, less than two years after the seminal *Haegeman II* ruling, its implications were clearly laid bare. EU Agreements, like the Treaty and secondary measures, could be used by domestic courts in challenges to national rules. They would, it seemed, have to satisfy the direct effect hurdle in the same way that EU law proper must. Strikingly, the very first case explicitly accepting that EU Agreements could be so used gave rise to neither Member State nor Council interventions. When the direct effect of the Treaty first arose in *Van Gend en Loos*, three of the then six Member States had intervened, two contested jurisdiction, and all three contested the direct effect of the relevant provision. And yet here, 13 years to the day later, direct effect was accorded to a very similar provision in an EU Agreement without any argument to the contrary from the Member States.

It is worth briefly reiterating the argumentation first employed in support of direct effect and supremacy. The groundbreaking conclusion of *Van Gend en Loos* was reached with reliance on particular attributes of the Treaty of Rome: the preamble's reference to peoples; the establishment of institutions endowed with sovereign rights affecting citizens; the role of nationals in the functioning of the EU via the European Parliament and the Economic and Social Committee; the preliminary ruling procedure. In *Costa* the contrast with ordinary international treaties had been underscored: the EU created its own legal system; it was of unlimited duration; it has its own institutions and personality; its own legal capacity and representation on the international plane and real powers stemming from Member States that have created a body of law binding both their nationals and themselves. All this is inevitably lacking on the part of your average international treaty, of which substantively Yaoundé was no exception, which could well have led one to doubt whether EU Agreements could be held directly effective. But the potential hurdle that the *Van Gend en Loos* and *Costa* logic posed, with their sharp and exaggerated differentiation between the Treaty of Rome and ordinary international treaties, is simply bypassed because the Treaty of Rome became the conduit for 'ordinary international treaties' in the internal EU legal arena which can acquire the central hallmarks of the former.

It is important to underscore the idiosyncratic aspect of the particular provision, and indeed Agreement, at issue. Not only was there a directly effective EU law counterpart, but it was expressly referred to by the Yaoundé Convention provision,[154] and the contracting partners were a large number of predominantly former colonies of various Member States. Arguing against the invocability of that Agreement, which ultimately had important developmental objectives, is unlikely to have been a position with which any Member State would then have been keen to associate itself.[155]

In the wake of *Bresciani* one might have expected that the legal effects of EU Agreements would immediately become firmly nailed to the direct effect mast, with the Court compelled to look to whether particular Agreements conferred rights on individuals. In fact, the next five preliminary rulings provided interpretations of several EU Agreements without direct effect being addressed.[156] The first saw the Court rule that the Lomé Convention[157] non-discrimination provision concerning establishment and services did not require either African, Caribbean, Pacific (ACP) States

[154] Although the first Yaoundé Agreement was signed in July 1963 it was likely to have been drafted before the *Van Gend en Loos* judgment of February 1963 had even accepted that provisions of the Treaty of Rome could be directly effective.

[155] The seminal Declaration for the Establishment of a New International Economic Order pushed by the developing world had been adopted by the UN General Assembly only two years before the *Bresciani* ruling (UN Doc A/RES/S-6/3201).

[156] In chronological order: 65/77 *Razanatsimba* [1977] ECR 2229; 52/77 *Cayrol v Rivoira* [1977] ECR 2261; 225/78 *Bouhelier* [1979] ECR 3151; 65/79 *Chatain* [1980] ECR 1345; 270/80 *Polydor v Harlequin* [1982] ECR 329.

[157] The 1975 successor to the second Yaoundé Agreement (1969).

or EU States to accord identical treatment to that reserved to their own nationals. The other four rulings involved provisions in various bilateral trade agreements with Austria, Spain, Switzerland, and Portugal concerned mainly with quantitative restrictions on imports and exports as well as a non-fiscal discrimination provision in the Greek Association Agreement. In the first three cases, the national courts asked for interpretations without explicitly asking whether the provisions were directly effective and conferred individual rights. The Commission and Advocates General proffered interpretations without engaging in such an analysis, and the ECJ followed suit. The fourth case was a rather different affair.

The *Polydor* ruling arose out of a copyright dispute between two private parties involving the Portugal Agreement's provisions pertaining to the abolition of quantitative restrictions and equivalent measures on imports. The referring court expressly asked whether the relevant provision was 'directly enforceable by individuals' and had indicated that it felt that it was both directly effective and to be given the same meaning as its EU law counterpart.[158] Such a ruling would be controversial indeed, as the ECJ had already determined that in intra-EU trade it would breach Article 34 TFEU for intellectual property rights to be relied upon to restrict imports from another Member State where the product had been placed on the market by the intellectual property right holder or with the right holder's consent.[159] Precisely this interpretation, known as the exhaustion doctrine, was being sought of the Portugal Agreement to challenge enforcement of domestic copyright law. However, this reading of identical provisions in the Agreements with Switzerland and Austria had already been rejected by their respective Supreme Courts.[160]

The direct effect issue, therefore, loomed particularly large in *Polydor* and, in contrast to the backdrop of relative calm surrounding the preceding EU Agreements cases, there were now five Member States intervening; that is, more than half the then members, including three of the then big four (France, Germany, UK). The significance of the constitutional choices at stake had by this stage clearly impressed itself upon the Member States and they were eager to ensure their input into the emerging judicial construct.

[158] See the judgment of Templeman LJ, who was especially influenced by the fact that the Agreement had been concluded by a Council Regulation, with whom Ormrod LJ agreed [1980] 2 CMLR 347.

[159] See, eg, in the copyright context 78/70 *Deutsche Grammophon v Metro* [1971] ECR 487.

[160] Cited by the Advocate General at 354.

They argued that the structure of the Agreement and the intention of its authors was that any infringements would give rise to consultations between the EU and Portugal, or possibly the adoption of safeguard measures, and that this precluded direct effect. One might say, to use the language of *Van Gend en Loos* and *Costa*, they were arguing that the Portugal Agreement (unlike the Treaty of Rome) was an ordinary international treaty which merely creates mutual obligations between the Contracting States. They also argued that whatever the conclusion on direct effect, the exhaustion doctrine should not be applied. The Commission expressed some doubts as to direct effect and strongly supported the Member States' rejection of the applicability of the exhaustion doctrine. The Advocate General managed to skirt around the issue of direct effect, whilst nonetheless concluding that the exhaustion doctrine was inapplicable to the Portugal Agreement.

The ECJ found it necessary to analyse the provisions in light of the Agreement's object, purpose, and wording; language which suggested that a direct effect analysis was to commence, but no such analysis was forthcoming. The purpose of the Agreement, as the Court noted, was to consolidate and extend economic relations with Portugal and in pursuance of this objective it sought to liberalize trade in goods. But the similarity of several of its provisions with those on the abolition of restrictions on intra-EU trade was not a sufficient reason to transpose the exhaustion of rights case law. That case law developed in the context of the EU's objectives and activities which sought, unlike the Portugal Agreement, 'to unite national markets into a single market having the characteristics of a domestic market'.[161] Trade restrictions could accordingly be justified for protecting industrial and commercial property in the EU–Portugal context where this would not be possible in the intra-EU context. Put simply, the exhaustion doctrine did not apply to the Portugal Agreement.

One might surmise that the Court viewed the provisions as directly effective given its willingness to proffer an interpretation. However, it was striking that it did not respond directly to this express question from a domestic court, especially given the strong views advanced by the Member States. A further factor that may account for this judicial reticence was that *Polydor* raised the issue of an EU Agreement's horizontal direct effect—the

[161] That provisions of EU Agreements would not necessarily be given the same meaning as their internal EU law counterparts had already been established in 225/78 *Bouhelier*.

case concerned an action between individuals rather than an individual and the State.[162]

Following the seminal *Bresciani* ruling, we had witnessed a marked judicial aversion to formulating matters in terms of rights and direct effect. One likely explanation was a judicial reluctance to follow the implications of the automatic treaty incorporation model through to its logical conclusion unless the particular case left no alternative. After all, it was one thing to accept such implications in *Bresciani* where no Member States intervened and the significance of what had taken place was somewhat concealed by the particularities of the Agreement at stake; it was another matter altogether to do so with the broader category of trade agreements. The Court had already been put on notice prior to *Polydor* that transposing its internal EU law direct effect test to EU Agreements was unlikely to be well received by the Member States.[163] And the Court was still in the process of building and consolidating central aspects of the EU legal order, with seminal judgments being handed down on a regular basis across diverse areas of EU law. Central pillars of this new legal order such as supremacy, and the direct effect of Directives, were meeting resistance in senior courts of several Member States. In these circumstances, when offered a straightforward opportunity to evade the direct effect framework and the attendant controversy it might generate, it is not altogether surprising that it was seized with vigour.

4.2 Embracing direct effect

The contentious direct effect question could only be avoided for so long and, as it turned out, two months on from the *Polydor* judgment, and just over six years since *Bresciani*, saw the Court finally answer whether it would extend direct effect to Agreements that did not share the favourable traits of

[162] This was at the same time as the horizontal direct effect of Directives was becoming especially controversial: see 8/81 *Becker* [1982] ECR 53. An early suggestion in favour of horizontal direct effect of EU Agreements was offered by Tagaras (1984: 53), a UK parliamentary committee expressed marked concerns: House of Lords (1985).

[163] See the Opinion of Advocate General Trabucchi in *Bresciani*. The Advocate General, who had sat as the Italian judge in *Van Gend en Loos* and *Costa*, was acutely aware of Member State sensibilities coming from a State whose senior courts have exhibited a marked reluctance to accept certain central tenets of EU law.

the Yaoundé Agreement. In *Pabst* a clear question was referred from a German court on the Greek Association Agreement in a challenge to a German compensatory tax: was the provision prohibiting discriminatory import taxes, alongside its directly effective EU counterpart, applicable and, if so, did it confer a legal right on importers to demand that imported spirits be treated equally to domestic spirits.[164] The Commission and Advocate General both argued that the provision was directly effective but curiously no Member State intervened. The direct effect question was dealt with in a surprisingly curt manner by the Court. It found that as the non-discriminatory taxation provision was worded similarly to its EU law counterpart, it fulfilled the same function within the framework of the Association between the EU and Greece. The ECJ underscored that it formed part of a group of provisions the purpose of which was to prepare for Greece's EU entry and then simply concluded that it followed from the wording of the provision, and the objective and nature of the Agreement, that it precluded discriminatory tax compensation with respect to Greek imports. Without any further attempt at justification, it ruled that the provision 'contains a clear and precise obligation which is not subject, in its implementation or effects, to the adoption of any subsequent measure' and is accordingly directly effective. And the result, in contrast to *Polydor*, was to give the provision the same meaning as its directly effective EU counterpart.[165]

The *Pabst* ruling constituted only the second occasion on which an EU Agreement provision had been held directly effective. The ECJ has been no stranger to handing down significant judgments with little by way of reasoned justification, and *Pabst* is a prominent example. Moreover, the ECJ did itself little credit by giving this significant ruling via a three-judge chamber when its difficulty and importance seemed to render this inconsistent with its own rules of procedure.[166] Although not the first case on the Greek Agreement, it was the first time that direct effect was expressly addressed. And, unlike in *Bresciani*, this was not an Agreement with non-reciprocal provisions nor a specific provision that referred to a directly effective EU counterpart. It was, however, an Association Agreement preparing a country for accession which had become a Member State by the time of the judgment. Whether the accession dimension was essential was

[164] 17/81 *Pabst & Richarz* [1982] ECR 1331.

[165] A provision considered to preclude the discriminatory tax compensation in intra-EU trade.

[166] See on this point, Bebr (1983: 59).

resolved six months later when the Court was faced with the equivalent provision in the Portugal Agreement.

In *Kupferberg* (104/81), as in *Pabst*, a German court dealing with a challenge to national charges framed a question expressly in the language of direct effect and rights. The Member States came out in force, with four of them rehashing similar arguments to those invoked in *Polydor*. Thus, not only were arguments being run against the direct effect of the provision prohibiting fiscal discrimination on imports but, more broadly, the very capacity of the Portugal Agreement, and a host of largely identical free trade agreements, to be directly effective in domestic legal orders.

The logic of the Member States was simple and cogent. Despite the judicial assimilation of EU Agreements with EU law proper, there were crucial differences which warranted differential treatment. The Portugal Agreement, as with the other European Free Trade Association (EFTA) Agreements and in stark contrast to the EU Treaty, contained no mechanism for ensuring uniform interpretation and the Contracting Parties had built in a particular mechanism for resolving disputes and difficulties arising from the application of its provisions: a joint committee structure composed of representatives of the Contracting Parties; procedures which could not function if courts were allowed to determine the content of the obligations.

Furthermore, in articulating the absence of uniform interpretation, Member States drew attention to case law from certain Contracting Parties to the trade agreements with the EFTA countries that suggested that the Agreements were not directly effective therein. This implicitly struck at the very heart of a critical distinction between EU law proper and EU Agreements: the ECJ is the authoritative interpreter of the former but at most it can only be the authoritative interpreter of the latter within the EU legal order. Direct effect and supremacy were eventually accepted, even if not unconditionally, within a community of States in which the central enforcement role was delegated to the national judiciary with the ECJ as the overseer keeping the construct together. Accepting a similarly exalted status for EU Agreements, where equivalent enforcement assurances from the other Contracting Parties were absent, would be a much harder pill to swallow.

The Advocate General drew on the reasoning advanced by the Member States in giving her opinion against direct effect. The Commission, however, raised its own equally principled objections to the principled arguments of the Member States. Thus, it argued that the relative weakness of the structure of an Agreement is not a sufficient reason to deny a priori direct effect to all its provisions, alluding also to the fact that looking for similar structures to those of the Treaty of Rome was unrealistic. Crucially, it emphasized the normative underpinnings of its own emerging vision: recognizing direct effect gives the Agreements greater weight and strengthens the effectiveness of the international legal order and as a subject of international law particularly dependent on its proper functioning the EU had no interest in impeding that process by an a priori restrictive attitude.[167]

The ECJ, influenced no doubt by the penetrating Member State submissions, commenced its judgment, as discussed above, with a strong and bolstered reassertion of its jurisdiction over EU Agreements. It also ruled that the effects of an EU Agreement's provisions cannot be determined without taking into account their international origins. EU institutions are free, the Court held, to agree with Contracting Parties what effect the provisions will have in their internal legal orders and it was only if that question had not been settled that it would be for the relevant courts, and the ECJ within the framework of its jurisdiction, to resolve. This offers the EU institutions and the Member States a potential way out of ECJ judicial determinations, as rightly noted,[168] but it requires an unrealistic alteration in the practice of treaty negotiations. There are many reasons why the Member States, in all but the most exceptional circumstances, would consider it counter-intuitive to seek, even if they could,[169] to insert provisions into EU Agreements rejecting domestic judicial application not least of which would be fears that such provisions would consequently limit the impact in the legal orders of the Contracting Parties with which the Agreement was being negotiated.

With regard to the absence of direct effect reciprocity, the Court pointed to the international law obligation of bona fide performance of every agreement and stated that although each party is responsible for fully executing its commitments it was free to determine the legal means, unless specified in the Agreement, for attaining this end in its legal system. Subject

[167] It thus does not appear accurate to state as Pescatore did (1986) that the Commission was systematically against the direct effect of all types of international obligations from the GATT to free trade agreements.

[168] Koutrakos (2006: 226).

[169] The EU is an increasingly powerful international actor but clearly even in bilateral agreements with powerful contracting partners, much less wide-ranging multilateral treaties, it is unlikely to be able to insist on provisions for or against domestic judicial enforceability.

to that reservation, the absence of judicial reciprocity was held not in itself to be 'such as to constitute a lack of reciprocity in the implementation of the agreement'.

Short shrift was equally given to the relevance of the Agreement's special institutional framework, this being held not in itself sufficient to exclude all judicial application: 'the fact that a court . . . applies . . . a provision . . . involving an unconditional and precise obligation . . . not requiring any prior intervention on the part of the joint committee does not adversely affect the powers that the agreement confers on that committee.'[170] Finally, the ECJ dispensed with the Member States' argument against direct effect that relied on the Agreement's safeguard clause by ruling that this was only possible in specific circumstances which generally required consultation within the joint committee. The clauses were held not sufficient in themselves to affect the direct effect of certain provisions of the Agreement.[171]

Concluding on the basis of the aforementioned reasoning that neither the nature nor structure of the Portugal Agreement prevented traders from relying on its provisions before a court in the EU, the Court was left to address whether the provision invoked was unconditional and sufficiently precise. This required it to be considered 'in the light of both the object and purpose of the Agreement and of its context'. This purpose was 'to create a system of free trade' and the function of the provision invoked was to prevent the prohibitions of quantitative restrictions and customs duties from being rendered nugatory by fiscal practices. It was held to be an unconditional rule against fiscal discrimination dependent only on a like product finding and which was thus directly effective.

Less than 20 years earlier in *Van Gend en Loos*, the Court boldly constructed its own vision of the nascent EU legal order in the face of contrary submissions from a large proportion of the then existing Member States; in *Kupferberg* it had done the same with respect to its emerging vision of the place of EU Agreements within that legal order. The direct effect test that had emerged as the key conceptual frame for the legal effect of EU law proper in the domestic legal order had likewise established itself with EU Agreements. Indications that direct effect might be limited to Agreements

[170] As Eeckhout (2011: 336) pointed out this was classic direct effect reasoning, for with EU law proper the absence of certain implementing measures has been irrelevant if the provision is sufficiently clear, precise, and unconditional.

[171] It was suggested that the derogation being subject to a merely political procedure called into question the unconditional character of the relevant obligations: Bebr (1983: 63, 70).

creating particularly special and close relationships, fostered by the Court itself in the *Bresciani* and *Pabst* rulings, were dispelled in *Kupferberg* to the consternation of the intervening Member States. But, more importantly, the manner and the boldness with which the weighty objections of the intervening Member States were dispensed with, suggested a willingness to transpose to the EU Agreement context the increasingly flexible attitude to the direct effect determination that had characterized the ECJ's approach to EU law proper.

The seven EU Agreement cases that followed *Haegeman II*, up to and including *Kupferberg*, were all preliminary rulings in which the challenge was to Member State-level action. It was thus expected that direct effect would cement its place as the hurdle for such Agreements to have their fullest possible domestic legal effect in such a context. This has remained the case to this day even if the nature of the test, as in EU law proper, has evolved over time. A question that troubled many following the inclusion of what was in all but name a direct effect hurdle where preliminary reference validity challenges to EU action vis-à-vis binding international rules occurred,[172] and thus applicable by analogy to EU Agreements, was whether this hurdle would apply in annulment actions.[173] It took until 1994 for confirmation that this was so.[174]

5. Conclusions

In revisiting several foundational questions concerning the constitutional status and legal effects of EU Agreements, this chapter has shown how key aspects of the EU's external relations constitution was put in place by a small number of rulings between the early 1970s and the early 1980s that either expressly answered the core question of principle or left little doubt

[172] The test for review laid out in 21–4/72 *International Fruit* [1972] ECR 1219 is considered in Chapter IV.

[173] Kovar (1974: 359–60); Jacot-Guillarmod (1979: 223–30); Rideau (1990: 358–62, 404); Ehlermann (1986: 137–40); Pescatore (1973: 240).

[174] C-280/93 *Germany v Council* [1994] ECR1-4973, on which see further Chapter IV. Long predicted by some commentators: Rideau (1973: 481); Waelbroeck (1974: 621–2); Joliet (1983: 256–7).

as to the appropriate answer.[175] Most significantly of all, *Haegeman II* constituted clear attachment to the automatic treaty incorporation model and provided the seed of acknowledgement that the full armoury of EU enforcement tools was applicable. These powerful enforcement tools strengthen the effectiveness of international treaty law within the EU.[176] Seemingly ordinary international treaties would now be refracted through the lens of EU law resulting in a supra-constitutional status within the Member States' legal orders. This was not merely a question of the domestic constitutional orders having to adjust to an additional source of EU law, that is simply a further, though largely ignored, manifestation of the 'constitutionalization' debate to which Weiler gave particularly eloquent expression.[177] For this additional category of 'EU law' was, unlike the other sources with the exception of the Treaty articles themselves, made in a markedly distinct manner. It raises additional and distinct questions as to the role of domestic courts as the decentralized enforcers of treaty law given, in particular, the evident shortcomings of the international law-making process itself, accentuated in the EU Agreement context by the traditionally inconsequential role afforded to the European Parliament. That the emerging construct raised grave concerns for certain Member States was accordingly inevitable. This was first strongly evinced by the interventions in *Polydor* and *Kupferberg*.[178] Those cases attested to an issue of central importance in the 30 years of case law that has followed, namely, the threshold test for EU Agreements to be used as review criteria for EU or domestic level action. As Chapter I illustrated, the crucial issue is how that test, regardless of its label, is actually applied in practice. It can be used to shield the domestic legal order from the full implications of the much-employed mantra of treaties becoming part of the legal order, precisely the outcome sought by the Member States intervening in *Polydor* and *Kupferberg*. The judicial response was famously emphatic in *Kupferberg*. However, whether that would be sustained as the breadth of the EU's treaty-making

[175] It was not until 1987 (12/86 *Demirel* [1987] ECR 3719) that the Court began to address itself expressly to certain specificities pertaining to mixed agreements, which continues to be a work in progress.

[176] Indeed, with potential knock-on effects for the Member States' approach to their own international treaty commitments. See for a related point Buergenthal (1992: 385, 391).

[177] Weiler (1991).

[178] Significant concerns had previously been raised by the UK's Joint Committee on Statutory Instruments (1976–1977) cited in Maresceau (1979: 253–4), with a House of Lords committee later following suit: House of Lords (1985).

activity increased alongside the complexity and sensitivity of the disputes, including crucially via challenges to EU action, constitutes the core concern of the chapters that follow.

This chapter also illustrated that the clear indication of an infra-constitutional status for EU Agreements in *Opinion 1/75* was confirmed in a line of authorities that have generated critical comment that has often exhibited insufficient accommodation of legitimate concerns with constitutionalism.[179] The constitutional ramifications for the Member States of the EU's treaty-making in a system where qualified majority voting applies and the output has supra-constitutional status internally, with a supranational court capable of policing compliance to boot, are such that the absence of ex post constitutional review would have been problematic to say the least. Allowing the EU's primary law, which ultimately can constitute a mechanism for channelling the Member States' constitutional values, in limited instances to preclude the internal applicability of an EU Agreement, may have a salutary effect in this new age where recourse is had to treaties to enshrine constitutionally suspect provisions which can otherwise hide behind the protective veil that *pacta sunt servanda* and the Vienna Convention on the Law of Treaties offer.

[179] Arguably the infra-constitutional status can in actual practice be devoid of real meaning where despite a successful challenge the Agreement continues to be legally operative within the EU and where retroactive Council concluding acts and limiting the effects of a judgment are employed.

III

The Association, Cooperation, Partnership, and Trade Agreements Before the EU Courts: Embracing Maximalist Treaty Enforcement?

1. Introduction

This chapter assesses the EU Courts' case law in what has been the vast bulk of their activity concerning EU Agreements, namely, the Association, Cooperation, Partnership, and Trade Agreements (henceforth, for ease of reference, Trade Agreements). This body of case law, a total of 184 cases,[1] developed at a remarkable rate following the early batch of cases that culminated with the bold *Kupferberg* ruling. This chapter aims to redress an existing gap in the literature whereby particular EU Trade Agreement judgments are singled out for praise or criticism without situating them within the broader framework of the case law. This accordingly also creates a key pillar for the empirically grounded overall assessment of the judicial treatment accorded EU Agreements which constitutes a core objective of this book. It is only in this fashion that one can assess whether the lofty judicial language commencing with *Haegeman II*, and for many the promise that the full enforcement arsenal of EU law would be unleashed for policing this additional category of EU law, has been adhered to in judicial practice.

The chapter is divided into two main sections. The first assesses preliminary rulings, where the bulk of EU Court activity has occurred (131 cases),

[1] Excluding cases pertaining to the review of the act concerning conclusion.

and the second direct actions, that is, actions commencing and terminating before the EU Courts in Luxembourg (53 cases).

2. Preliminary Rulings

The preliminary rulings jurisprudence in the EU Trade Agreement context can be divided into two core categories involving, respectively, challenges to domestic action or to EU action.

2.1 Challenges to domestic action

The Trade Agreement case law challenging domestic measures can be divided into three categories concerning, respectively, provisions pertaining, first, to trade in goods, where the EU Trade Agreement jurisprudence commenced, secondly, to movement of persons which rapidly became the dominant sources of litigation activity, and, thirdly, to a small generic category concerning neither of the aforementioned provisions.

2.1.1 *Provisions pertaining to goods*

The case law concerning provisions pertaining to goods has given rise to 35 rulings, 27 of which have come since *Kupferberg*. The number of rulings by decade is represented in Figure III.1, with only six having arisen since 1997.

Through to the emphatic *Kupferberg* ruling in 1982 only two specific EU Agreement provisions had been expressly found directly effective: the customs duty prohibition in the Yaound Convention (*Bresciani*), and the fiscal discrimination prohibition in both the Greek Association Agreement and the Portugal Trade Agreement (*Pabst* and *Kupferberg*). These types of provision have given rise to a further six preliminary rulings, two pertaining to the customs duty prohibition,[2] and four for the fiscal discrimination prohibition.[3] In none were the questions framed in terms of direct effect

[2] C-163/90 *Legros* [1992] ECR I-4625 and C-125/94 *Aprile SRL* [1995] ECR I-2919.

[3] 253/83 *Kupferberg II* [1985] ECR 157; C-312/91 *Metalsa SRL* [1993] ECR I-3751; C-114/95 & C-115/95 *Texaco A/S* [1997] ECR I-4263; C-102/09 *Camar* [2010] ECR I-4045.

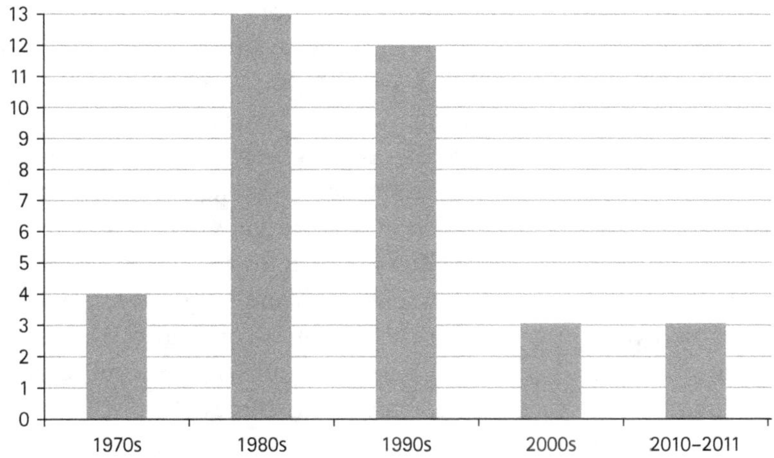

Figure III.1 Preliminary rulings challenging domestic action and concerning goods-related provisions in EU Trade Agreements (35 cases, 1970–2011 (03/10/11))

and in all six the ECJ provided interpretations without expressly conceptualizing matters in such terms.

As far as the non-fiscal discrimination provision is concerned, in the first two cases the Court's reading preserved the national measure at issue.[4] The second of the cases, *Metalsa*, is the more significant for current purposes. It concerned whether an interpretation accorded to Article 110 TFEU applied to its counterpart in the Austria Trade Agreement.[5] The Commission and the Member State whose legislation was at stake successfully argued, invoking *Polydor*, against such an interpretative transposition. The ECJ concluded that the interpretation accorded the EU provision was based on the aims of the Treaty including the establishment of a common market which were not part of the Austria Agreement and was accordingly unwilling to countenance the same interpretation.[6] The third case, the *Texaco* ruling, saw the ECJ asked effectively whether a certain charge was

[4] In *Kupferberg II* this concerned the Portugal and Spain Agreements. And the validity of the taxation reduction at issue would be preserved providing that the rate applied to imported products did not exceed that levied on corresponding domestic products.

[5] The interpretation rendered national legislation incompatible with Art 110 TFEU where it penalized certain tax offences disproportionately more severely where they concerned imported rather than domestic goods.

[6] Such reticence was unsurprising given that the alternative would have constrained Member State competence with regard to criminal penalties in the Trade Agreement sphere.

consistent with the customs duty prohibition (Art 6) and the fiscal discrimination prohibition (Art 18) in the Sweden Agreement and Agreements containing corresponding provisions. Little attention was given to the customs duty prohibition, but the ECJ invoked *Kupferberg* and the identical fiscal discrimination prohibition at issue in that case in concluding that the charge was contrary to Agreements containing provisions similar to the fiscal discrimination prohibition in the Sweden Agreement. The fourth was a recent domestic damages action in which the ECJ curiously expressly asserted that it only needed to engage with the scope of the non-fiscal discrimination provision of the first Yaoundé Convention (Art 14) and not its direct effect.[7] A reading of that provision was proffered preserving the validity of the relevant domestic tax in this context.[8]

In both the customs duty prohibition cases the interpretations given made it clear that domestic measures breached EU Agreements. The first, *Legros*, established that certain 'dock dues' constituted a charge having an equivalent effect to a customs duty in breach of the EU Treaty. France argued, invoking *Polydor*, that it did not follow that this also rendered it a prohibited charge under the Sweden Agreement. The Court underscored that the Agreement would be deprived of much of its *effet utile* if the term were interpreted as having a more limited scope than its EU law counterpart. The second case made it clear that this interpretative transposition of the term 'charge' applied to all EU Trade Agreements containing such a prohibition.[9]

On several occasions prior to *Kupferberg*, the ECJ interpreted provisions in EU Trade Agreements on quantitative restrictions (QRs) and measures having equivalent effect to quantitative restrictions (MEQRs) without first asking whether they were directly effective or conferred rights.[10] The five additional preliminary rulings continued in this vein[11] but one is worthy of

[7] C-102/09 *Camar*.

[8] The Court was unwilling to bring within its scope discriminatory taxation of unlike products which are in competition with each other.

[9] C-125/94 *Aprile*.

[10] Even where the referring court expressly framed its question in the language of direct effect.

[11] 314–16/81 & 83/82 *Waterkeyn* [1982] ECR 4337 was an unsuccessful attempt to have an infringement ruling holding French legislation to breach Art 34 TFEU interpreted as also breaching the equivalent Portugal Agreement provision. In 125/88 *HFM Nijman* [1989] ECR 3533 the ECJ reinterpreted the questions referred as also concerning the Sweden Agreement and having upheld the compatibility of the national legislation as a result of the derogation (Art 36 TFEU) to the Art 34 TFEU prohibition, the ECJ did likewise vis-à-vis the counterpart (Art 20) to the equivalent Sweden Agreement proscription (Art 13). In C-143/06 *Ludwigs-Apotheke* [2007]

additional comment. In *Bulk Oil* a UK court asked several questions concerning the Cooperation Agreement with Israel.[12] At issue was the then UK policy precluding exports of crude oil to certain countries, a policy to which a contract between two firms had linked a sale and which led to litigation and the reference for a preliminary ruling. The relevance of the Cooperation Agreement to this sensitive dispute was easily dispensed with. The ECJ, following the UK and Commission submissions, concluded that it did not contain provisions expressly prohibiting export QRs/MEQRs.[13] The case shares a clear parallel with the *Polydor* judgment in that a judicial interpretation preserving the national measure at issue was proffered while sidestepping the express direct effect question, including its particularly controversial horizontal manifestation.[14]

Nine cases have concerned rules of origin provisions, in none of which did the domestic court frame its question in terms of direct effect, instead seeking only interpretations of provisions in disputes in which disgruntled traders challenged decisions of, inter alia, customs authorities.[15] In one, the

ECR I-9623 no EU Agreement question was referred but the Court found a national provision caught by Art 34 TFEU and not legitimized by Art 36 TFEU, with the EEA Agreement rules held to be essentially identical (Arts 11 and 13) and also prohibited the national measure insofar as it applied to goods from non-Member State EEA Agreement signatories. In C-207/91 *Eurim-Pharm GmbH* [1993] I-3723 a German court sought a ruling as to whether the QR/MEQR prohibition in the Austria Trade Agreement was to be interpreted in accordance with its EU counterpart. Two Member States and the Commission intervened to defend the German legislation, arguing against such interpretative parallelism because, unlike EU law proper, the Austria Agreement made no provision for legislative harmonization or administrative cooperation in the relevant sector. The Court held that even on the assumption that this reading could not be applied to the Austria Agreement, the German authority had the necessary information such that their securing cooperation from the Austrian authorities was unnecessary. To hold that the provisions did not preclude the rules at issue would deprive them of much of their *effet utile*.

[12] 174/84 *Bulk Oil* [1986] ECR 559.

[13] As QRs on exports were held to be outside the scope of the Agreement, the ECJ rejected arguments as to the compatibility of measures imposing QRs on exports with other provisions of the Agreement.

[14] The famous 152/84 *Marshall* [1986] ECR 723 ruling on the absence of horizontal direct effect for Directives arrived barely a week after *Bulk Oil*.

[15] In chronological order: 218/83 *Les Rapides Savoyards* [1984] ECR 3105 (Swiss); 156/85 *Perles Eurotool* [1986] ECR 1595 (interim Yugoslavia Agreement); C-292/91 *Weis* [1993] ECR I-2219 (Yugoslavia Cooperation Agreement); C-12/92 *Huygen* [1993] ECR I-638 (Austria); C-432/92 *Anastasiou* [1994] ECR I-3087 (Cyprus); C-334/93 *Bonapharma* [1995] ECR I-319 (Austria); C-56/06 *Euro Tex* [2007] ECR I-4859 (Poland); C-23–5/04 *Sfakianakis* [2006] ECR I-1265 (Hungary); C-386/08 *Brita* [2010] ECR I-1289 (Israel Association Agreement and PLO Association Agreement). The Austria Agreement's rules of origin provisions were also interpreted in C-207/91 *Eurim-Pharm*.

ruling made clear that the domestic customs authority decision was invalid but without addressing the relevant Agreement.[16] Of the remaining eight, in seven the Court interpreted the relevant provisions without, like the Advocate General before it, framing matters in terms of direct effect.[17] The remaining case, where direct effect was explored, merits additional comment.

The 1994 *Anastasiou* judgment saw the ECJ and the Advocate General expressly respond to the UK and Commission submissions that the provisions invoked were not directly effective concerning, as they did, administrative cooperation between customs authorities; a rather counter-intuitive argument given that the Court had already proffered interpretations of similar provisions in Agreements with Switzerland, Yugoslavia, and Austria[18] that effectively proscribed domestic customs authorities decisions. The explanation for such argumentation lies in the controversial nature of the dispute. It concerned a judicial challenge based on the Cyprus Association Agreement—which Greece supported before the ECJ—to the UK practice of permitting certain imports from the Turkish Republic of Northern Cyprus[19] to benefit from the Agreement's preferential tariffs.

The judgment commenced with invocation of the direct effect test for EU Agreements which provides that a provision 'must be regarded as having direct effect when, regard being had to its wording and the purpose and nature of the agreement itself, the provision contains a clear and precise

[16] C-292/91 *Weis*.

[17] The interpretation proffered effectively proscribed the relevant customs authority decision in five instances (218/83 *Les Rapides Savoyards*; 156/85 *Perles Eurotool*; C-12/92 *Huygen* (the national court was given the green light to invalidate the customs decision); C-334/93 *Bonapharma*; C-23–5/04 *Sfakianakis*) and preserved the validity of the relevant customs authority decision in two instances (C-56/06 *Euro Tex* and more controversially in C-386/08 *Brita* where the Court relied on a general principle of international law (*pacta tertiis nec nocent nec prosunt*) which finds expression in Art 34 VCLT in holding that the Israel Association Agreement (Art 83) precluded products originating in the West Bank from falling within its territorial scope. The Court also interpreted both protocols to the Israel and Palestine Liberation Organisation Agreements in rejecting the notion that importing customs authorities can make an elective determination that leaves open the question of which of the two Agreements applies and whether proof of origin is to be issued by Israeli or Palestinian authorities. Finally, it held that an inconclusive reply from the Israeli authorities was not binding under the administrative cooperation provisions of the Israel Agreement, nor was there an obligation by the customs authorities of the importing State to refer to the Customs Cooperation Council a territorial scope dispute).

[18] Respectively 218/83 *Les Rapides*; 156/85 *Perles Eurotool*; C-12/92 *Huygen*.

[19] Not, however, where the movement certificate had been issued in the name of the Turkish Republic of Northern Cyprus.

obligation which is not subject, in its implementation or effects, to the adoption of any subsequent measure.'[20] Applying the test, the Court pointed to the aim of the Agreement, which was the progressive elimination of obstacles to trade, and the rules of origin play an essential role in determining which products benefit from preferential treatment. The rules were asserted, without explanation, to lay down clear, precise, and unconditional obligations. Two of the earlier EU Agreement rules of origin cases were cited, with the ECJ noting that this by implication showed that similar provisions could be applied by national courts. It was accordingly concluded that the provisions had direct effect.

Anastasiou shed important light on the ECJ's then emerging approach to EU Agreements. The judicial approach to EU law provisions has been characterized (in Chapter I) as a maximalist model in which, amongst other things, the link between individual rights *stricto sensu* and direct effect was gradually discarded. *Anastasiou* sat comfortably within that evolving framework. The provisions concerned administrative cooperation between importing and exporting customs authorities rather than, as the UK and Commission's logic would have it, individual rights for traders and producers of Republic of Cyprus goods enforceable before domestic courts. Expressly rejecting this argument indicated that the judicial approach to EU Agreements was developing in line with the approach to EU law proper. As Judge Pescatore once argued, direct effect is the normal state of the law and ultimately it is a question of whether a rule is capable of judicial adjudication.[21] This presumption of justiciability equally appeared to be taking hold in certain dimensions of the Trade Agreement jurisprudence.

Four further cases involving the finer points of customs law have also arisen, in none of which were the questions or the responses framed in terms of direct effect.[22] One, *Deutsche Shell*,[23] was notable in that a German

[20] The classic formulation stems from C-12/86 *Demirel* which employed the language of direct applicability.

[21] See Pescatore (1983). He was the judge-rapporteur for the first of the rules of origin cases (218/83 *Les Rapides Savoyards*) which did not employ a direct effect analysis.

[22] In 170/82 *Ramel* [1983] ECR 1319 the ECJ interpreted the interim Algeria Trade Agreement which was not expressly referred to in the national court questions. In 266/81 *SIOT* [1983] ECR 731 the ECJ responded to an Italian court question on the compatibility of an Italian charge with a Transit Agreement with Austria by holding that it did not contain a specific commitment in relation to tax treatment of goods in transit. In 99/83 *Fioravanti* [1984] ECR 3939 the judicial response to an Italian court's requested interpretation of a Transit Agreement with Switzerland left little doubt as to the invalidity of the domestic duties.

[23] C-188/91 *Deutsche Shell AG* [1993] ECR I-363.

court asked several questions pertaining, inter alia, to a Transit Agreement with EFTA States and a recommendation of the Joint Committee established to administer it. The Court first asserted its interpretative jurisdiction over non-mandatory measures of bodies established by EU Agreements, considering them to be directly linked to the Agreement itself and thus forming part of the EU legal order.[24] The ECJ ruled that it was not precluded from ruling on the interpretation of a non-binding measure in Article 267 proceedings,[25] and whilst acknowledging that Joint Committee recommendations do not confer domestically enforceable individual rights, national courts were obliged to take them into consideration.[26]

An Italian consumption tax on bananas from non-member countries generated litigation in Italian courts which sought preliminary rulings on the compatibility of the legislation mainly with the common commercial policy.[27] The Italian magistrates had not put forth any question as to the compatibility with EU Trade Agreements, but both the Commission and traders invoked EU Agreements. The ECJ gave a strong signal that the legislation breached the Lomé Convention (Art 139(2)), and that domestic courts should disregard national law incompatible with EU provisions contained in Agreements conferring rights on individuals. The manner in which the ruling was framed would inevitably invite further rulings and a different Italian court asked whether the Lomé Conventions confer domestically enforceable rights and whether the consumption tax was incompatible therewith.[28] Italy argued that the Lomé Conventions did not contain provisions conferring domestically enforceable individual rights.[29] But the other intervening Member State, the Commission, and the Advocate General, all appropriately pointed to the *Bresciani* judgment on a predecessor Agreement. The ECJ predictably reiterated *Bresciani* in holding that the Lomé Convention at issue may contain provisions conferring domestically enforceable individual rights. The relevant standstill clause was then held to

[24] In line with the earlier ruling in C-192/89 *Sevince* [1990] ECR I-3461, considered below, as to decisions adopted by such bodies.

[25] The Commission argued that there was no jurisdiction over non-binding measures.

[26] The substantive interpretations of the recommendation and the Transit Convention clearly left the domestic customs decision, which was based on the recommendation, intact.

[27] C-228/90–234/90, 339/90 & 353/90 *Simba* [1992] ECR I-3713. Its applicability to bananas in free circulation in the Member States breached the EU Treaty: 184/85 *Commission v Italy* [1987] ECR 2013 and 193/85 *Cooperativa Co-Frutta Srl* [1987] ECR 2085.

[28] C-469/93 *Chiquita Italia SpA* [1995] ECR I-4533.

[29] Italy pointed to the dispute settlement provisions of the Fourth ACP–EEC Convention as a factor negating the direct effect of any of its provisions.

be worded in clear, precise, and unconditional terms upon which individuals could rely and which precluded tax increases on banana imports from ACP States.[30]

Finally, in *Katsivardas* a Greek court asked whether an individual trader could plead the incompatibility of a national law with the most-favoured-nation clause in a Cooperation Agreement with several Latin American countries.[31] The ECJ predictably reiterated an earlier ruling rejecting the direct effect of the equivalent provision in the successor Agreement;[32] a decision considered equally valid for the most-favoured-nation clause of the predecessor Agreement.

2.1.2 *Provisions pertaining to the movement of persons*

Provisions pertaining to the movement of third country nationals in EU Trade Agreements have given rise to 77 rulings with only one prior to 1987

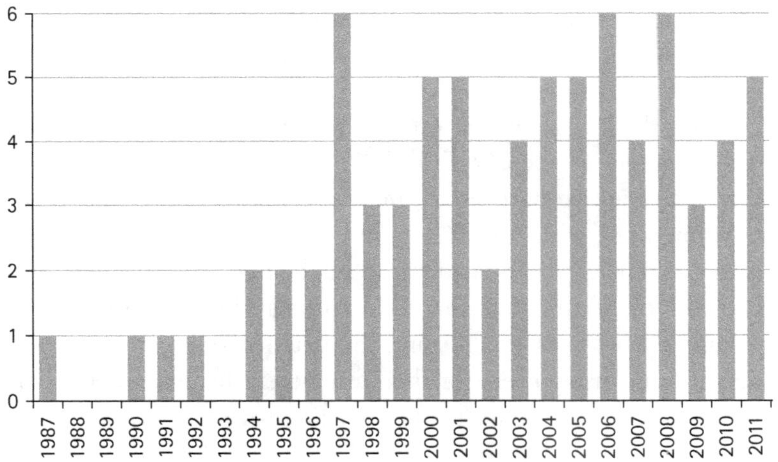

Figure III.2 Preliminary rulings challenging domestic action and concerning persons-related provisions in EU Trade Agreements (76 cases, 1987–2011 (03/10/11))

[30] Article 1 of Protocol No 5. Italy argued that the tax predated the entry into force of the first Lomé Convention. C-102/09 *Camar* involved the same provision, however the domestic court did not frame its question in the language of direct effect and the Court simply put forth its interpretation of the provision.

[31] C-160/09 *Katsivardas* [2010] ECR I-4591. The Court rejected the Italian argument that individuals could not rely on Cooperation Agreements, an argument which flew in the face of long-standing jurisprudence, most obviously C-18/90 *Kziber* considered below.

[32] C-377/02 *Van Parys*, considered below.

(*Razanatsimba*). The activity since the second of these rulings in 1987—a trickle of cases in the early 1990s and growing substantially since then—is represented in Figure III.2:

This case law can be broken down into four core categories that will each be taken in turn.

2.1.2.1 *Provisions specific to the Turkey Agreement*

Revisiting *Demirel* and *Sevince* Provisions pertaining to the movement of Turkish nationals first arose in the *Demirel* judgment.[33] A Turkish woman who entered Germany on a short visitation visa and lived with her husband, a lawfully employed Turkish worker, challenged an expulsion order. The German court asked whether certain Turkey Agreement provisions prohibited these new restrictions affecting resident Turkish workers. The UK and Germany argued that the free movement of workers provisions of this mixed agreement were commitments entered into by the Member States exercising their own powers and which the ECJ was not competent to interpret. The ECJ responded by holding that Article 217 TFEU empowered the EU to guarantee commitments in all fields, of which free movement of workers was one, covered by the Treaty of Rome. It in effect viewed the EU as having exercised that competence in concluding this Agreement via Article 217 TFEU.[34]

The now classic two-part direct effect test was articulated and its application commenced with the ECJ pointing to the various stages of the Agreement. Looking to its structure and content, it was found to be characterized by setting out the Association's aims and guidelines for their attainment without establishing the detailed rules for doing so and with decision-making powers for their attainment being conferred on the Association Council. Turning to the specific provisions invoked, the first (Art 12) provided that the Contracting Parties agreed to be guided by the EU Treaty provisions on free movement of workers for the purposes of progressively securing freedom of movement of workers, while the second, in a Protocol to the Agreement (Art 36), provided that this was to be secured in progressive stages and that the Association Council was to decide on the necessary rules.[35] The conclusion that followed was that these provisions set out a programme and were not sufficiently precise and unconditional.

[33] 12/86 *Demirel* [1987] ECR 3719. [34] See Dashwood (2000).

[35] The Court added that this constituted an exclusive rule-making power and that no Decision in the family reunification sphere had been adopted.

Four Member States and the Commission had intervened against direct effect, and the Advocate General reached the same conclusion, in a textually irreproachable argument. Implementing decisions for the said rules had simply not been forthcoming. And a *Reyners*-type conclusion where, in the internal EU law context, the Court was unwilling to let the absence of explicitly textually envisaged implementation measures impede 'one of the [EU's] fundamental legal provisions' was never a likely eventuality.[36] Implementation of the free movement of workers objectives of the Agreement had been thrown wildly off track as a result of the global economic shocks of the 1970s and their consequences for the labour requirements of West European industry, combined with the 1980 coup in Turkey and Greece's EU accession.

Nevertheless, the Association Council adopted Decision 2/76 pertaining mainly to the access to employment of Turkish workers and their family members which was superseded in 1980 by Decision 1/80 which expressly sought to revitalize the Association. These two Decisions were the subject of litigation shortly after *Demirel*. The *Sevince* ruling concerned a Turkish national challenging a residence permit refusal, invoking the two Association Council Decisions, in a Dutch court which referred questions as to their interpretation.[37] The two intervening Member States, the Netherlands and Germany, were split on jurisdiction; the former siding with the Commission in arguing that Association Council Decisions were acts of the institutions for which there was preliminary ruling jurisdiction, and the latter contesting this by arguing that the Association Council is an autonomous institution with a different identity to that of the EU institutions. This was a powerful textual objection to jurisdiction, however, less than a year earlier in a direct action in which Germany had not intervened, it was held that a particular Turkey Association Council Decision, being directly connected with the Agreement, formed from its entry into force an integral part of the EU legal system.[38] The ECJ invoked that ruling and further held, citing *Haegeman II*, that since it has jurisdiction to give preliminary rulings insofar as Agreements are acts adopted by the institutions it likewise has jurisdiction over the interpretation of decisions adopted by authorities established by Agreements and with responsibility for their implementation. That the latter proposition does not in itself follow from the former,

[36] 2/74 *Reyners v Belgium* [1974] ECR 63.
[37] C-192/89 *Sevince* [1990] ECR I-3461.
[38] 30/88 *Greece v Commission* [1989] ECR 3711, para 13.

obviously did not trouble the Court. And Germany would take little consolation that the textually indefensible argument that such Decisions are indeed acts of the EU institutions was not adopted,[39] given that the practical consequences are indistinguishable.[40]

The Court then turned to the specific provisions which both Germany and the Netherlands, in contrast to the Commission, argued were not directly effective. The provisions at stake provided Turkish workers with certain rights depending on the length of their employment in the relevant Member State (Art 2(1)(b) of Decision 2/76 and Art 6(1) of Decision 1/80) and prohibited the introduction of new employment access restrictions (Art 7 of Decision 2/76 and Art 13 of Decision 1/80). It was held that Association Council Decision provisions would have to satisfy the same direct effect conditions as those applicable to the Agreement itself. The ECJ merely paraphrased the first batch while referring to them as upholding 'in clear, precise and unconditional terms, the right of a Turkish worker...', whilst the second batch were referred to as 'contain[ing] an unequivocal standstill clause'. Direct application was held to be confirmed by the purpose and nature of the Association Council Decisions and the Turkey Agreement. The fact that the Decisions were intended to implement the Turkey Agreement provisions recognized as programmatic in *Demirel* was also noted, the logic seemingly being that they serve to concretize the programmatic norms. Following the Advocate General, several arguments against direct effect were then rejected: first, provisions in the Decisions providing that the procedure for applying the relevant provisions are to be established under national law did not empower Member States to restrict the application of precise and unconditional rights granted to Turkish workers by the Decisions; secondly, provisions in the Decisions providing that the Contracting Parties are to take any measures required for implementation merely emphasizes the obligation to implement in good faith; thirdly, the non-publication of the Decisions may prevent their application to a private individual but not their enforcement by a private individual vis-à-vis a public authority; fourthly, the safeguard

[39] Contrast McGoldrick (1997: 117).

[40] It added in support of jurisdiction the functional argument that Art 267 TFEU serves to ensure uniform application of all EU provisions. The argumentation employed for jurisdiction in *Sevince* was one of the cases employed to illustrate judicial activism at the Court in a much-cited critique: Neill (1995: 29–31).

provisions only apply to specific situations. Direct effect of the relevant provisions was then confirmed.[41]

The self-interest of the two States putting forward the direct effect objections is not difficult to discern: of the Turkish citizens residing in the EU some 90 or so per cent did so in Germany (in the mid-1980s),[42] with the largest percentage of the remainder residing in the Netherlands. But such self-interest should not detract from the cogency of some of the arguments advanced. Provisions clearly calling for both EU and domestic implementing measures had not been pursued; the safeguards clause was of a unilateral nature and did not require any authorization from the Association Council; and the EU institutions had not published the two Decisions at issue which could be seen as indicative of the non-judicially applicable status intended.[43] Given these factors, it would be difficult to conclude that the Contracting Parties (in reality the Member States) intended Association Council Decisions to be directly effective.[44] The judgment evoked a similar dynamic to the maximalist enforcement model characterizing internal EU law, a model which, as in *Sevince* and *Kupferberg*, has frequently developed in the face of powerful contrary submissions from Member States. For precisely this reason, it has been criticized as a manifestation of judicial activism employing dubious reasoning.[45]

Post-*Sevince* case law on Articles 6 and 7 of Decision 1/80 The Court has addressed direct questions from national courts pertaining to the Association Council Decision provision (Art 6(1)) first held directly effective in

[41] Mr Sevince was left no better for it. The interpretation of legal employment was such that the period for which he worked did not count for Association Council Decision purposes: O'Leary (1998: 739) referred to the definition as not generous. This might be viewed as sweetening the pill of a bold and far-reaching judgment on jurisdiction and direct effect.

[42] Figures cited in Nolte (1988: 403–4).

[43] Gilsdorf (1992: 332) asserted that non-publication served exactly this objective. In contrast, the practice was for EU Agreements, despite no EU Treaty requirement, to be published. And as noted in Chapter I, in the domestic legal orders of the founding Member States and many other automatic incorporation States, non-publication will impede direct judicial application of a Treaty. Decision 1/80 was never published in the Official Journal, however shortly after *Sevince* it did appear in a Council Publication (1992).

[44] Indeed, Commission counsel in *Sevince* noted that the Council and the Commission clearly considered the applicability of Association Council Decisions to require adoption of a legal act to produce their effects: Gilsdorf (1992: 331). See also Hailbronner and Polakiewicz (1992: 57).

[45] Hailbronner and Polakiewicz (1992: 56–9).

Sevince on 21 occasions,[46] and in addition offered a detailed interpretation of that provision in responding to a question on a different provision.[47] Of these 22 cases, six included national court questions regarding Article 7 of Decision 1/80.[48] The first paragraph of Article 7 concerns certain employment entitlements for family members of Turkish workers conditional on the length of their legal residence, and the second concerns employment entitlements for Turkish workers' children conditional on their completion of vocational training in the Member State and one of their parents having completed a three-year period of legal employment there. It is useful at this point to digress momentarily with respect to the conceptually and substantively similar Article 7 line of case law. Aside from the aforementioned six judgments that also saw questions raised regarding Article 7, there have been an additional 11 cases in which national courts have raised Article 7.[49] Thus, together this Article 6 and Article 7 jurisprudence has yielded a further 33 post-*Sevince* judgments. Both paragraphs of Article 7 were held directly effective in two cases in which the national courts did not frame their questions in such terms but appeared to assume they were directly effective; the Court's reasoned justification amounted to an assertion that, like Article 6(1), the relevant provisions clearly, precisely, and unconditionally embodied the rights of Turkish workers' children and conferred rights on their family members and were directly effective like Article 6(1).[50] This was perhaps a foregone conclusion given the previous direct effect finding in *Sevince* on the related Article 6 question, but it

[46] C-237/91 *Kus* [1992] ECR I-6781; C-355/93 *Eroglu* [1994] ECR I-5113; C-434/93 *Bozkurt* [1995] ECR I-1475; C-171/95 *Tetik* [1997] ECR I-329; C-386/95 *Eker* [1997] ECR I-2679; C-285/95 *Kol* [1997] ECR I-3069; C-36/96 *Gunaydin* [1997] ECR I-5143; C-98/96 *Ertanir* [1997] ECR I-5179; C-210/97 *Akman* [1998] ECR I-7519; C-1/97 *Birden* [1998] ECR I-7747; C-340/97 *Nazli* [2000] ECR I-957; C-65/98 *Eyup* [2000] ECR I-4747; C-188/00 *Kurz* [2002] ECR I-10691; C-467/02 *Cetinkaya* [2004] ECR I-895; C-136/03 *Dörr* [2005] ECR I-4759; C-373/03 *Aydinli* [2005] ECR I-6181; C-383/03 *Dogan* [2005] ECR I-6237; C-230/03 *Sedef* [2006] ECR I-157; C-294/06 *Payir* [2008] ECR I-203; C-14/09 *Genc* [2010] I-931; C-187/10 *Unal*, Judgment of 29 September 2011.

[47] C-4/05 *Güzeli* [2006] ECR I-10279.

[48] C-355/93 *Eroglu*; C-65/98 *Eyup*; C-188/00 *Kurz*; C-467/02 *Cetinkaya*; C-373/03 *Aydinli*; C-136/03 *Dörr*.

[49] C-351/95 *Kadiman* [1997] ECR I-2133; C-329/97 *Ergat* [2000] ECR I-1487; C-275/02 *Ayaz* [2004] ECR I-8765; C-502/04 *Torun* [2006] I-1563; C-325/05 *Derin* [2007] ECR I-6495; C-349/06 *Polat* [2007] I-8167; C-337/07 *Altun* [2008] ECR I-10323; C-453/07 *Er* [2008] ECR I-7299; C-303/08 *Bozkurt* [2010] ECR I-13445; C-462/08 *Bekleyen* [2010] ECR I-563; C-484/07 *Pehlivan*, Judgment of 16 June 2011.

[50] C-355/93 *Eroglu* (on Art 7(2)); C-351/95 *Kadiman* (where *Eroglu* was invoked in support of the same finding for Art 7(1)).

remains noteworthy that direct effect was so casually established (and via Chamber rulings).

Certain key traits emerge from this batch of 33 judgments on Articles 6 and 7. First, in none were the questions expressly framed in terms of direct effect and yet in 26 rulings the ECJ has either asserted or expressly reiterated its direct effect holding, and in the remaining seven, whilst the language of direct effect was not expressly employed, reference to the conferral of rights by the relevant provisions was.[51] Secondly, in 26 cases the domestic action challenged came from Germany.[52] Germany has intervened in all bar two of the cases,[53] usually seeking, mostly unsuccessfully, a restrictive reading.[54] Thus, in the first post-*Sevince* case, the *Kus* case concerning Article 6(1), as well as seeking unsuccessfully to reiterate the argument against jurisdiction over Association Council Decisions employed in *Sevince*, Germany contested any inherent correlation between a right of access to employment and a residence permit.[55] The ECJ, however, relied on the 1964 Free Movement of Workers Directive (64/221/EEC), and a judgment on the EU free movement provisions,[56] in holding that a right of residence is indispensable to access to paid employment and concluded that a Turkish worker who fulfilled the Article 6(1) requirements could rely on it to obtain both a work permit and residence permit renewal. The judgment was equally notable for finding that the reason a Turkish worker is legally resident is irrelevant to the renewal of a work permit.[57]

Sharpston appropriately underscored the significance of this ruling:

> Traditionally Member States retain the right to determine, not only access to their territory, but also the right to stay and reside there. That right has already

[51] The seven being C-434/93 *Bozkurt*; C-285/95 *Kol*; C-294/06 *Payir*; C-275/02 *Ayaz*; C-349/06 *Polat*; C-14/09 *Genc*; C-187/10 *Unal*.

[52] Of the data-set rulings, only courts in three other countries have sought rulings on these provisions: the Netherlands three times since C-192/89 *Sevince* (C-434/93 *Bozkurt*; C-484/07 *Pehlivan*; C-187/10 *Unal*); Austria (C-136/03 *Dörr*; C-383/03 *Dogan*; C-65/98 *Eyup*); the UK (C-294/06 *Payir*).

[53] C-187/10 *Unal* and surprisingly C-462/08 *Bekleyen* which emanated from Germany.

[54] To use a recent example, Germany, joined by Denmark and the *Land* Baden-Württemberg, argued unsuccessfully that, unless the status of family member is retained, those rights are lost: C-303/08 *Bozkurt*.

[55] C-237/91 *Kus* [1992] ECR I-6781. A correlation articulated in *Sevince* to the chagrin of some commentators: Hailbronner and Polakiewicz (1992: 56–7).

[56] C-292/89 *Ex parte Antonissen* [1991] ECR I-745.

[57] In *Kus* a worker who obtained a residence permit to marry a German national was entitled to a work permit renewal even though the marriage had been dissolved.

disappeared in relation to [EU] nationals exercising rights of free movement. Now... third country nationals claiming rights under an association agreement may also acquire entrenched rights, which defeat the ordinary immigration policy of the Member State concerned.[58]

The *Kus* reading expressly linking the work permit and residence permit was transposed in the very next judgment to Article 7(2) concerning the rights of the children of Turkish workers, as was the finding, contrary to German submissions, that the right to respond to employment offers was not conditioned upon the grounds on which entry was originally granted.[59]

Of the remaining Article 6 and Article 7 cases, many involved transposing internal EU law principles and/or the Court responding with bold interpretations frequently in the face of contrary Member State submissions. The 1995 *Bozkurt* ruling was particularly significant, for here the ECJ first emphasized that it was essential to transpose as far as possible the principles enshrined in the Treaty provisions on free movement of workers to Turkish workers enjoying rights conferred by Decision 1/80. It is true that Article 12 of the Agreement expressly refers to the Contracting Parties agreeing to be guided by the EU Treaty free movement of workers provisions for progressively securing freedom of movement for workers,[60] but it is contestable whether this provides a sufficient anchor for the extent of judicially created interpretative borrowing.[61] In *Bozkurt* itself, in line with the Commission and contrary to the four intervening Member States, the internal EU law meaning of legal employment was transposed to Article 6(1) of Decision 1/80,[62] later followed by the EU meaning of a 'worker' and a 'family member' being transposed, respectively, to Article 6(1) and Article 7 of Decision 1/80.[63] In *Tetik* it was concluded, in line with Commission

[58] (2003: 239). Footnote omitted.

[59] C-355/93 *Eroglu*. The residence permit logic was duly transposed to Art 7(1) in C-351/95 *Kadiman*.

[60] Articles 13 and 14 of the Agreement make the same point with respect to establishment and services.

[61] Even when read alongside the expressly articulated accession dimension to the Agreement (Art 28).

[62] C-434/93 *Bozkurt*. It has been considered restrictively to interpret the right to remain as the Court held, in line with the intervening Member States and the Advocate General but contrary to the Commission view, that it is lost as a result of permanent incapacity to work; O'Leary (1998: 747–50) offers an alternative reading situating it within the context of the free movement of EU nationals jurisprudence, whilst Peers (1996b: 109–10) provided a brief textual defence.

[63] In respectively C-188/00 *Kurz* (a case notable for rejecting the submissions of Germany, and the Commission to the effect that a trainee is not duly registered as belonging to the labour

submissions but in opposition to the Advocate General and the submissions from the three intervening Member States (Germany, the UK, and France) and the *Land* Berlin, that a Turkish worker who fulfilled the four-year legal employment period in Article 6(1) did not forfeit rights by leaving employment on personal grounds and searching for new employment for a reasonable period;[64] strikingly, the analogy with internal EU law concerned a case outlining that EU nationals should be given a reasonable time to apprise themselves of offers of employment but without acknowledging or explicating how this was relevant when dealing with someone entering the host State for the first time as opposed to someone already employed in the relevant State.[65] Nor are these rights forfeited through temporary interruptions resulting from both suspended and non-suspended prison sentences, the Court having sought to interpret the public policy, public security, or public health exception in Decision 1/80 (Art 14(1)) analogously with the almost identically phrased Article 45(3) TFEU exception.[66]

In addition, important judgments have established that the rights for family members and children are not forfeited because of the attainment of adulthood and independent living. This conclusion was initially reached contrary to German submissions.[67] Crucially, it was reiterated against strong opposition from several Member States and a national court contesting such reasoning as incompatible with Article 59 of the Additional Protocol providing for Turkey not to receive more favourable treatment than that granted under EU law between Member States.[68] That ruling arguably deprived Article 59 of its natural meaning and was further consolidated when it later held that the child of Turkish workers who had returned with her parents to Turkey and returned alone to Germany ten years later, when over 21, to continue with and duly complete a vocational higher

force for Art 6(1) purposes), and C-275/02 *Ayaz* (which resulted in a step-child being included). C-14/09 *Genc*, offered a more generous interpretation of 'worker' than has hitherto been employed for EU workers, by accepting that it could include someone working 5.5 hours a week (see further, Martin (2012: 90)).

[64] C-171/95 *Tetik*.

[65] C-292/89 *Antonissen*. See further Martin (2000: 439–40).

[66] Case law commencing with C-340/97 *Nazli* and including C-467/02 *Cetinkaya*; C-136/03 *Dörr*; C-383/03 *Dogan*; C-373/03 *Aydinli*; C-502/04 *Torun*; C-325/05 *Derin*; C-349/06 *Polat*; in which Germany was usually unsuccessfully arguing for a restrictive interpretation and the Commission the contrary.

[67] C-329/97 *Ergat*.

[68] C-325/05 *Derin*; reiterated in C-349/06 *Polat*. EU nationals only have the right to install themselves with family members where they are under 21 years of age or dependants.

education course, was entitled to rely on the right of access to the employment market and a residence permit.[69]

A final case worthy of particular mention saw the Court faced with four Member States arguing that Turkish nationals who had not entered the host State as workers could not rely on Article 6(1).[70] The strenuous Member State objections, including that an adverse judgment would lead them to restrict their policy of admitting Turkish students and au pairs, were to no avail for in *Payir* the ECJ held, in line with the Commission submissions but contrary to the Advocate General as concerned students, that being granted leave to enter as an au pair or student cannot deprive them of the status of worker and being duly registered as belonging to the labour force under Article 6(1).

Cases on the standstill clauses in Decision 1/80 and the Additional Protocol The employment restrictions standstill clause (Art 13) held directly effective in *Sevince* has led to three further preliminary rulings. The first was in *Abatay & Sahin* where the Court engaged with both that provision and the services and establishment standstill clause in the Additional Protocol (Art 41(1)).[71] It held that the former standstill clause was not applicable to the facts,[72] while rejecting a textually viable argument that it only operated with respect to those already in lawful employment.[73] The services and establishment clause had been held directly effective in the earlier *Savas* judgment where a UK court put forth questions as to its direct effect and that of Article 13 of the Agreement (the freedom of establishment

[69] C-462/08 *Bekleyen*. A reading contrary to the arguments advanced by two Member States. See for criticism of both rulings: Martin (2012: 86–90).

[70] C-294/06 *Payir*. At issue was the status of Turkish citizens permitted entry to the UK for studying, albeit with permission to work for a limited period during term-time and full time outside term-time, and as au pairs.

[71] C-317/01 & 369/01 *Abatay & Sahin* [2003] ECR I-12301. Although the German court's questions were not framed in terms of direct effect, the ruling commenced with reiterating the direct effect of both standstill clauses.

[72] The international haulage workers were not, nor did they have the intention of becoming, integrated in the German employment market.

[73] The argument advanced by Germany, two additional intervening Member States, and the Commission, and accepted by the Advocate General. The Court also rejected a Dutch argument, followed by the Advocate General, that the services and establishment standstill clause did not apply to the transport sector and proffered an interpretation drawing expressly on internal EU law principles pertaining to the right of establishment and freedom to provide services. Little doubt was left that if the German work permit requirement for international road haulage workers was new, it would breach the standstill clause.

counterpart to Art 12 which had been held not directly effective in *Demirel*).[74] The five intervening Member States, the Commission, and the Advocate General were against direct effect for the latter provision and the ECJ followed suit invoking the same reasoning as in *Demirel*.

The two remaining post-*Sevince* rulings on the employment restrictions standstill clause stemmed from questions from the Dutch Council of State framed in terms of the interpretation of that provision. In the first, the Court did not employ express direct effect language but did underscore that the standstill clause could be relied on before Member State courts, and concluded that it precluded the introduction of national legislation making the granting of residence permits or their extension conditional on disproportionate charges compared to those for EU nationals.[75] The second paid no customary lip-service to direct effect.[76] The basic issue in *Toprak & Oguz* was whether national provisions on the acquisition of residence permits introduced after the entry into force of Decision 1/80 and relaxing the provisions applicable on its entry into force could be tightened without being any more restrictive than the rules applicable when Decision 1/80 entered into force. Unsurprisingly, the Member State defending its new regime did so precisely on the ground that the relevant date was when the Decision entered into force (1 December 1980), a position supported by Germany and Denmark. Creative judicial interpretation followed with the Court finding that the relevant date to assess whether new rules gave rise to 'new restrictions' was when the new rules were adopted.[77] In effect, any liberalization post-1 December 1980, sets a new benchmark from which a Member State can no longer retreat. To reach this conclusion, the Court relied on the objectives pursued by Article 13 as it articulated them, reiterating earlier judgments, creating conditions conducive to the gradual establishment of freedom of movement of workers, the right to establishment, and the freedom to provide services by prohibiting national authorities from creating new obstacles to those freedoms. The critic might

[74] C-37/98 *Savas* [2000] ECR I-2927. Uncharacteristically this came with a detailed justification including by analogizing with an almost identically worded but since repealed standstill clause (Art 53 TEC) and the direct effect holding on the employment restrictions standstill clause in *Sevince*. Commentators had expressed reservations as to its direct effect (Martin and Guild (1996: 262–3)).

[75] C-242/06 *Sahin* [2009] ECR I-8465.

[76] C-300/09 and 301/09 *Toprak and Oguz* [2010] ECR I-12845.

[77] An approach called for by Hoogenboom (2010: 713–15) albeit articulating some of its shortcomings.

well emphasize that none of these objectives are actually directly apparent on a reading of Decision 1/80. That the Court bolstered its conclusion by relying on equally generous interpretations of internal EU law standstill clauses, will be disconcerting for Member States seeking to defend their measures insofar as it further attests to the cross-fertilization from internal to external EU law.[78]

The services and establishment standstill clause first held directly effective in *Savas* has led to three further preliminary rulings reiterating its direct effect.[79] The first (*Tum*) and second (*Soysal*) were of considerable consequence. The significance of *Soysal*, where the standstill clause was held to preclude a German visa requirement for Turkish nationals which did not exist when the Additional Protocol entered into force, is touched on in Section 2.2. In *Tum* Turkish nationals challenged decisions refusing their entry into UK territory to establish themselves in business and ordering them to leave. This refusal resulted from the application of new immigration rules. Only three Member States intervened, two of which argued, relying on *Savas*, which convinced the Advocate General, that Member States were exclusively competent to determine who is permitted lawful first entry and that the standstill clause could only be invoked by those lawfully present. The ECJ held that whilst the standstill clause does not confer a right of entry and does not render inapplicable the relevant substantive law it replaces, it operates as a quasi-procedural rule stipulating *ratione temporis* which Member State legislative provisions apply in this context. Or in plainer English, the standstill clause required the new immigration rules to give way and that those in force in 1973 be applied instead. The Court insisted that this did not call into question Member State competence to conduct their national immigration policy and that the mere fact that the clause imposed a duty not to act which limits their room for manoeuvre did not mean that the very substance of their sovereign competence in respect of aliens was undermined. To many Member States

[78] C-40/00 *Commission v France* [2001] ECR I-4539 concerning the Sixth VAT Directive and C-101/05 *A* [2007] ECR I-11531 concerning free movement of capital.

[79] C-16/05 *Tum* [2007] ECR I-7415. A preliminary ruling concerning Art 41(1) was sought in C-296/05 *Günes*, but once the *Tum* ruling was sent to the Dutch Council of State it decided it was no longer needed: see Order of 21 November 2007 ([2008] OJ C64/46); C-228/06 *Soysal* [2009] ECR I-1031. In C-186/10 *Tural Oguz*, Judgment of 21 July 2011 the ECJ responded to a UK court reference that the clause could be relied upon by a Turkish national who breached a condition of his leave to remain by setting up a business.

this distinction will ring hollow, for it further intrudes in the applicability of their immigration policy, as far as Turkish nationals are concerned.[80]

Article 9 of Decision 1/80: Turkish children and access to education and educational benefits The final judgment to consider is the *Gürol* ruling.[81] A German court asked a direct question as to the direct effect and interpretation of the first sentence of Article 9 of Decision 1/80. This provides that Turkish children resident with parents who are or have been legally employed in the Member State are to be admitted to general education, apprenticeship, and vocational training courses under the same educational entry qualifications as children of Member State nationals. Germany and Austria, alongside the Commission and the Advocate General, accepted that the first sentence was directly effective and the Court unsurprisingly followed suit. But, strikingly, it went on to hold the second sentence to be directly effective which provides that 'They [the children] *may* in that Member State be eligible to benefit from the advantages provided for under the national legislation in this area.'[82] This was drafted in terms that, as academic commentary had suggested, granted such wide latitude to Member States as to rule out direct effect.[83] The choice of the verb 'may' over an imperative form such as 'shall' or 'will' should not be overlooked, for it was surely the result of careful consideration at the drafting stage. Not surprisingly, Germany and Austria argued that this wording imposed no obligation, but the Commission asserted otherwise and crucially so held the Court. Non-discriminatory access to courses including those provided abroad, as in *Gürol* itself, would, it was held, be purely illusory if Turkish children were not assured of an equal right to the relevant grant. This was considered the only interpretation making it possible to attain in full the objective pursued by Article 9 of guaranteeing equal opportunities for Turkish children and those of host State nationals in education and vocational training. But asserting that this is the objective of the provision does not make it so. If that were, indeed, the objective, as contrasted with ensuring equal treatment with respect to entry qualifications, then the expressed intention of the parties could have reflected this

[80] The Court also substantiated its reading by drawing on a fundamental freedoms judgment: C-372/04 *Watts* [2006] ECR I-4325.

[81] C-374/03 *Gürol* [2005] ECR I-6199. See for a supportive account, Van der Mei (2009: 377–9).

[82] Emphasis added.

[83] Hedemann-Robinson (2001: 547); Martin and Guild (1996: 274); Peers (1996a: 26–7).

directly rather than, as they did, expressly opting not to use imperative language.[84] It is no solution for the Court to assert that, like the first sentence, it lays down an obligation of equal treatment when the language chosen is not unconditional. The general rule of treaty interpretation, codified in the Vienna Convention on the Law of Treaties (Art 31) is that a treaty is to be interpreted in good faith in accordance with the ordinary meaning to be given to its terms in their context and in light of its object and purpose. A term should be given its ordinary meaning since it is reasonable to assume that until the contrary is established this is most likely to reflect what the parties intended.[85] And it would be unpersuasive to suggest that in *Gürol* the contrary was convincingly established. Austria and Germany were not alone in their ordinary meaning interpretation, for at least one other Member State has changed its law in the wake of the ruling.[86]

2.1.2.2 *Social security provisions*

The seminal *Kziber* judgment is the fountain from which nearly all later jurisprudential developments pertaining to social security provisions in EU Trade Agreements have stemmed.[87] Here, a Belgian court had asked whether Belgium could refuse on nationality grounds to grant a Moroccan national's child a particular unemployment benefit given the social security equal treatment clause in the Morocco Cooperation Agreement (Art 41(1)). France and Germany argued that it did not have direct effect. They were joined by the Commission in arguing that this was precluded in the main because Article 41(2) expressly provided for the Cooperation Council to take measures to ensure the application of the principles in Article 41 and no such measures had emerged. The Court held that Article 41(1) provided

[84] The Commission argued that if the second sentence were held not directly effective, then the first could be read to include study grants. The drafting of the first sentence ('same educational entry qualifications') was clearly intended to preclude the 9/74 *Casagrande* [1974] ECR 773 conclusion pertaining to Art 12 of Regulation 1612/68 which referred to 'under the same conditions' (see also Peers (1996a: 26–7)). Sympathy for the proposed interpretative creativity is understandable given that the Turkish national involved was born and brought up in Germany. However, in an era of growing anti-EU sentiment fuelled at least in some part by judicial creativity then it behoves the Commission to avoid such transparent infidelity to legislative intent.

[85] Aust (2007: 235).

[86] In England this took place via the Education (Student Fees, Awards and Support) (Amendment) Regulations 2007 (SI 2007/1336); in Wales via the Assembly Learning Grants and Loans (Higher Education) (Wales) Regulations 2007 (SI 2007/1045 (W. 104)).

[87] C-18/90 *Kziber* [1991] ECR I-199.

in clear, precise, and unconditional terms for a prohibition on nationality discrimination for Moroccan workers and their family members in social security.[88] That Article 41(2) foresaw Cooperation Council implementing measures did not call into question the direct applicability of a text that was not subordinated in its execution or effects to any further implementing measures, nor did it condition the immediate applicability of the non-discrimination principle. And direct effect was held not to be contradicted by the purpose and nature of the agreement.[89] The direct effect finding bore a stark resemblance, unmentioned by the Court in contrast to its Advocate General, to the approach to internal EU law as famously evinced in *Reyners* where the absence of implementation measures was not permitted to stand in the way of the direct effect holding.

A textually contentious substantive scope interpretation was also given, for the Member States had argued that unemployment benefits did not come within social security under Article 41.[90] The curt response was that 'social security' needed to be understood by analogy with the EU Social Security Regulation; a conclusion reached absent any supporting reasoning and subject to powerful criticism given that the Agreement makes no provision for free movement of workers.[91] For the ECJ, unemployment benefits did fall within Article 41 absent a clear manifested intent towards their exclusion, and the benefit at issue was simply a particular form of unemployment benefit. This finding, however, was in stark tension with its own earlier finding that the benefit at issue was a 'social advantage' within Article 7(2) of the basic Free Movement of Workers Regulation (1612/68), a provision not replicated in the Agreement at issue.[92] Unsurprisingly, the judgment generated accusations of judicial activism.[93]

The financial ramifications of the bold *Kziber* judgment would be significant for not only would this put the Member States on notice for all existing social security practices that may be of a discriminatory nature, but indeed

[88] That it provided that the prohibition was subject to the following paragraphs of Art 41(1) which contained certain limitations was not considered to remove the unconditional character of the discrimination prohibition with respect to all other social security questions.

[89] Broadly, to promote Moroccan economic development.

[90] A broad interpretation of 'worker', contrary to the arguments of the Member States, encapsulating both active members of the workforce and in certain contexts those who have left it, was also proffered.

[91] Hailbronner and Polakiewicz (1992: 58); Peers (1996a: 36–7).

[92] 94/84 *Deak* [1985] ECR 1873 which the Advocate General had relied on in rejecting the interpretation that found favour with the Court.

[93] Hailbronner and Polakiewicz (1992: 58–9); Peers (1996a: 36–8).

all future social security developments would need to accommodate Moroccan workers and their family members. Furthermore, Member States were well aware that the particular clause at issue had a direct counterpart in the Agreements with two other Maghreb States (Algeria and Tunisia) and in Turkey Association law. Germany responded to *Kziber* as it had to *Sevince*, by seeking to have the judgment reconsidered (*Kus*). In *Yousfi* a Belgian court had asked a question on the direct applicability and interpretation of Article 41(1). The ECJ reiterated *Kziber* and rejected Germany's reconsideration request on the ground that no new fact had been submitted.[94] In the third of the social security judgments, the ECJ predictably responded to a French court's question on the interpretation of the equivalent Algeria Cooperation Agreement provision (Art 39(1)) by holding that it too had direct effect.[95]

The fourth judgment, *Taflan-Met*, concerned Decision 3/80 of the EU–Turkey Association Council.[96] Questions were put forward by a Dutch court as to the applicability and interpretation of provisions pertaining to social security aggregation for workers. The significance of the dispute was attested to by six Member State interventions.[97] They argued that Decision 3/80 was not binding in the absence of implementing measures and was not

[94] C-58/93 *Yousfi* [1994] ECR I-1353. Like treatment was accorded to the three intervening Member States' submission that the term 'social security' in Art 41(1) could not include the disability benefits at issue because they were only expressly added to the EU Social Security Regulation in 1992. The Court underscored that it had already brought such benefits within the Regulation and, as *Kziber* had held, social security was to be given the same definition as in the EU Social Security Regulation.

[95] C-103/94 *Krid* [1995] ECR I-719. The dispute concerned an Algerian national but the question also pertained to the Tunisia Agreement on which the ECJ remained silent. A French argument seeking to draw a distinction, based on internal EU law and the EU Social Security Regulation, between personal rights and derived rights was also rejected (a distinction stemming from 40/76 *Kermaschek* [1976] ECR 1669, which was later overturned: C-308/93 *Cabanis-Issarte* [1996] ECR I-2097); that rejection was emphatically reiterated in the fifth and sixth cases: first in a Morocco Agreement case in response to views expressed by the Netherlands, the referring Dutch court and the Dutch Social Security Board (C-126/95 *Hallouzi Choho* [1996] ECR I-4807), then in response to a Belgian court reference which generated Belgian submissions seeking to have the personal/acquired social security rights dichotomy accepted for the Algeria Agreement: C-113/97 *Babahenini* [1998] ECR I-183.

[96] C-277/94 *Taflan-Met* [1996] I-4085.

[97] Until this point, only one EU Agreement case had seen as many interventions (C-280/93 *Germany v Council* considered in Chapter IV) and, that aside, only the trilogy of Europe Agreement cases (C-63/99 *Gloszczuk*; C-235/99 *Kondova*; C-257/99 *Barkoci and Malik*) and C-72/09 *Rimbaud*, considered below, C-308/06 *Intertanko*, considered in Chapter V, and C-366/10 *Air Transport Association of America* (noted in Chapter VI) have generated more interventions.

directly effective. The Court held that despite the Decision not providing for a date for its entry into force, an argument sufficient to resolve the dispute for the Advocate General, it followed from the binding character attached to the Decisions by the Agreement that in the absence of any provision on entry into force it did so on the day it was adopted. The relevant provisions were, however, held not directly effective, essentially because like the initial EU Social Security Regulation it required further implementing measures.[98] It was thus concluded that Decision 3/80 could not be applied.

Nearly three years later in *Sürül*, the seemingly clear implications of *Taflan-Met*, that any direct effect of Decision 3/80 was ruled out, were disavowed.[99] In responding to questions from a German court whether rights could be derived directly from the social security equal treatment provision of Decision 3/80 (Art 3), the Court concluded it was directly effective in the face of staunch opposition from five intervening Member States, but in line with the Commission and the Advocate General. *Taflan-Met* was distinguished as being concerned with the social security co-ordinating rules of Decision 3/80 which required further implementing measures, as contrasted with the non-discrimination provision which did not.[100] That provision was held to lay down in clear, precise, and unconditional terms a nationality discrimination prohibition.[101]

In the wake of *Kziber*—and *Sevince* asserting jurisdiction over Association Council Decisions and their capacity for direct effect in the first place—it would appear counter-intuitive, once the entry into force hurdle was surmounted, for the equivalent Turkey Agreement-related provision, with its

[98] Indeed, it was noted that a Council Regulation was proposed by the Commission in 1983 containing supplementary rules for implementing Decision 3/80. This failure to adopt is usually attributed to Greek resistance: see Conant (2002: 184), Sharpston (2003: 244).

[99] C-262/96 *Sürül* [1999] ECR I-2685.

[100] The ECJ reiterated a point astutely made by the Advocate General, namely, that the proposed Council Regulation, like the implementing Regulation for the basic EU Social Security Regulation, contained no provisions for giving effect to the equal treatment provision.

[101] The Court added that Art 3 constituted the implementation and concrete expression in the social security field of the general nationality discrimination prohibition in Art 9 of the Agreement which refers to its general counterpart currently in Art 18 TFEU. In terms of its scope *ratione personae*, the Court drew on the EU Social Security Regulation (1408/71), predictably given that Decision 3/80 expressly draws on and cross-refers to it, and related jurisprudence on the definition of 'worker'. As for material scope, the German law residence document requirement for 'aliens' was caught by the non-discrimination prohibition. The Court, acknowledging the uncertainty *Taflan-Met* may have created, did limit the judgment's temporal effects. For criticism see Peers (1999a: 632–3).

more integrationist agenda, to be deprived of direct effect. In this sense *Sürül* was the inevitable by-product of the bold *Kziber* judgment. Clearly, when dealing with EU Agreements where their provisions are frequently framed in similar, if not identical, terms a bold ruling regarding one Agreement will often be capable of direct transposition to other Agreements.[102] This also explains why the ECJ was unlikely to bow to pressure in *Sürül*: the jurisprudence on the Morocco and Algeria Agreements was by then firmly established and had been built initially in the face of opposition from only two Member States, alongside the Commission. The fact that it had increased to five Member States for the Turkey Agreement, with the Commission having changed sides since *Kziber*, would not be reason enough to inject a large dose of inconsistency into its case law on the equal treatment social security provisions of EU Agreements.

The additional nine social security judgments also concerned individuals challenging either the refusal to award a specific benefit, the level of the award, or the withdrawal of a benefit.[103] These nine cases have dealt with the Agreements with Turkey and Morocco in three of which the questions referred were expressly framed in terms of direct effect,[104] and in the three where the ruling amounted to preserving the domestic measure at issue, its response was not framed in terms of direct effect.[105] Of the six cases where matters were conceptualized in terms of direct effect,[106] three were Turkey Agreement cases and three concerned the Morocco Cooperation Agreement. Of the

[102] Peers suggested, when commenting on *Taflan-Met* and *Sürül*, it would have been 'illogical' to do otherwise: (1999a: 629).

[103] The first seven cases came from Belgium, France, Germany, and the Netherlands, the remaining nine were divided between references from courts in these Member States and in addition Austria: C-179/98 *Mesbah* (Belgian); C-33/99 *Fahmi* (Dutch); C-23/02 *Alami* (Belgian); C-358/02 *Haddad* (Belgian); C-336/05 *Echouikh* (French); C-276/06 *El Youssfi* (Belgian); C-102/98 *Kocak* (German); C-373/02 *Öztürk* (Austrian); C-485/07 *Akdas* (Dutch).

[104] C-102/98 *Kocak*; C-336/05 *Echouikh*; and C-485/07 *Akdas*.

[105] Two cases involved far-fetched attempts to be brought within the scope of the Morocco Agreement: C-33/99 *Fahmi* [2001] ECR 2415; C-358/02 *Haddad* [2004] ECR I-1563. In C-179/98 *Mesbah* [1999] ECR I-7955 the Commission unsuccessfully sought an analogous reading to internal EU law (C-369/90 *Micheletti* [1992] ECR I-4239) such that the Moroccan nationality of a dual EU/Moroccan national could be invoked to obtain equal treatment in social security. The ECJ underscored that that jurisprudence concerned a fundamental freedom not at issue in the Morocco Agreement and that it was for Belgian law to determine the nationality of a Moroccan worker for the purposes of applying Art 41.

[106] In C-373/02 *Öztürk* the terminology employed was that of a precise and unconditional principle capable of being applied by a national court.

latter three,[107] the most recent two also involved its replacement where the Court transposed its extant jurisprudence on the direct effect and scope of the equal treatment social security provision of the Morocco and Algeria Agreements to its identical counterpart in the newly created Euro-Mediterranean Association Agreement with Morocco.[108] Of the three Turkey Agreement cases, the first was significant because while giving a clean bill of health to German legislation, the ECJ accepted, drawing on internal EU law, that the social security provision also prohibits all forms of covert discrimination.[109] The third concerned a Turkey Association Council Decision 3/80 provision (Art 6(1)) which provides that certain identified benefits 'shall not be subject to any reduction, modification, suspension, withdrawal or confiscation by reason of the fact that the recipient resides in Turkey or in the territory of a Member State other than that in which the institution responsible for payment is situated.'[110] The ECJ predictably concluded, in line with the Commission submissions, that it was directly effective as it laid down a precise obligation of result.[111] More controversially, the interpretation proffered meant that legislation withdrawing the award of a supplementary invalidity benefit for those not living in the Netherlands had to be disapplied vis-à-vis Turkish nationals falling within the scope *ratione personae* of that provision, even though the exportability of such benefits could be denied to EU nationals and which accordingly may have appeared in tension with

[107] In the first, Art 41(1) was held to preclude legislation only permitting periods of work completed on Belgian territory to count for the purposes of a supplementary benefit for non-Belgian nationals: C-23/02 *Alami* [2003] ECR I-1399.

[108] C-336/05 *Echouikh* [2006] ECR I-5223; C-276/06 *El Youssfi* [2007] ECR I-2851. Neither left any doubt as to the incompatibility of the national legislation with the social security non-discrimination provision (Art 65(1)).

[109] C-102/98 *Kocak* [2000] ECR I-1287. The outcome was contrary to Commission submissions that there was indirect discrimination. The German legislation imposed certain non-discriminatory requirements as to the amendment of a date of birth for social security and pension purposes. In C-373/02 *Öztürk* [2004] ECR I-3605 the Grand Chamber found that the non-discrimination provision precluded the application of Austrian legislation making a certain old-age pension conditional upon having received Austrian unemployment benefits for a set period. Austria and Germany both contested the proposition that the provisions were discriminatory.

[110] It corresponds directly to Art 10 of Regulation 1408/71.

[111] 485/07 *Akdas*. A Commission official had predicted this as exportability of benefits, unlike social security coordination rules, was not the subject of further implementing measures in the unadopted Commission Regulation (Verschueren 1999: 381–2).

the Additional Protocol provision precluding Turkey from receiving more favourable treatment than that granted under EU law between Member States.[112]

2.1.2.3 *Provisions on non-discrimination as regards working conditions, remuneration, and dismissal*

Numerous EU Trade Agreements contain provisions that essentially provide that workers from the respective third States shall be free from any nationality discrimination with regard to working conditions, remuneration, and dismissal as compared to the relevant EU Member States' own nationals.[113] The Court first interpreted such a provision in the *El-Yassini* case where a UK court sought an interpretation of Article 40 of the Morocco Cooperation Agreement.[114] The Full Court response commenced by finding Article 40(1) directly effective. It was held to prohibit in clear, precise, and unconditional terms, nationality discrimination against employed Moroccan workers as regards working conditions or remuneration and this finding was held not to be contradicted by the purpose and nature of the Agreement.[115]

In rejecting any notion of the social security non-discrimination provision in the Morocco Agreement being programmatic in *Kziber*, the Court had referred to this also being so for Article 40. It had thus been clear for some eight years that the ECJ considered this provision directly effective.[116] The three intervening Member States (and the Commission) sought to preclude the transposition of the Turkey Agreement jurisprudence linking

[112] See for a cogent defence: Eisele and van der Mei (2012). This led to the Commission proposing a new Association Council Decision: COM(2012) 152 final.

[113] All bar two of the Europe Agreements contained such a provision (Cyprus and Malta). The earlier versions of this clause did not expressly include dismissal (eg Morocco and Turkey Agreements) but more recent formulations do (eg the Euro-Med Agreements with Algeria, Tunisia, and Morocco, the Europe Agreements (EAs), the Partnership and Cooperation Agreements (PCAs), the Stabilisation and Association Agreements, the Cotonou Agreement, the Swiss Free Movement of Persons Agreement).

[114] C-416/96 *El-Yassini* [1999] I-1209. Mr El-Yassini was refused a residence permit extension as the initial reason for its grant no longer existed given the breakdown of his marriage to a UK national.

[115] The object of which is to promote cooperation and contribute to Moroccan economic and social development and strengthen relations between the Contracting Parties.

[116] In C-18/90 *Kziber* the Member States, and the Commission, had essentially conceded this point because their submissions against the direct effect of the social security non-discrimination provision were partially premised on it being unlike Art 40 for it foresaw further Cooperation Council implementation measures.

lawful employment to a residence right. The Court responded by invoking Article 31 of the VCLT 1969 and considered it necessary to assess the Morocco and Turkey Agreements in light of their object and context. It held that, unlike the Turkey Agreement, the Morocco Agreement did not anticipate the possibility of accession or provide for the progressive attainment of freedom of movement for workers guided by the relevant EU Treaty provisions nor had the Cooperation Council adopted a Decision analogous to Decision 1/80. These 'substantial differences' precluded analogous application of the Turkey Agreement rules to the Morocco Agreement. It was held that Member States could refuse a residence permit extension for a Moroccan national where the initial reason for granting leave to stay no longer existed, subject to the caveat that a residence permit extension refusal where a work permit had been granted for a longer period would need justification on the ground of a legitimate national interest such as public policy, public security, or public health. In taking up this caveat, the Advocate General's Opinion was being followed but the latter reached this conclusion by expressly drawing an analogy with a fundamental freedoms judgment,[117] as well as the Turkey Agreement *Kus* ruling. The ECJ, however, remained conspicuously silent as to the source of its conclusion. A factor illuminating this unwillingness to read into Article 40(1) a right to remain, subject to the aforementioned caveat, is that the counterpart provision in the Morocco Euro-Med Agreement, not yet in force at the time of *El-Yassini*, came with an explanatory joint declaration to the effect that it could not be invoked to obtain renewal of a residence permit, the granting, renewal, and refusal of which was to be governed by each Member State's legislation.[118] The Court was thus warned by the Contracting Parties (in reality the Member States) against transposing its Turkey Agreement jurisprudence on the right to remain to the Euro-Med Agreements.

Nine more rulings have arisen on the equivalent provision in seven Agreements stemming from litigation in three different Member States.[119] National courts framed their questions expressly in terms of direct effect

[117] C-292/89 *Ex parte Antonissen*.

[118] The joint declaration was referred to by the Advocate General but not by the ECJ.

[119] C-162/00 *Pokrzeptowicz-Meyer* (Germany–Poland EA); C-171/01 *Wählergruppe* (Austria–Turkey Agreement); C-438/00 *Kolpak* (Germany–Slovakia EA); C-265/03 *Simutenkov* (Spain–Russia PCA); C-97/05 *Gattoussi* (Germany–Tunisia Euro-Med); C-4/05 *Güzeli* (Germany–Turkey Agreement); C-152/08 *Kahveci* (Spain–Turkey Agreement); C-351/08 *Grimme* (Germany–Swiss FMP Agreement, Art 9(1) of Annex I); C-101/10 *Pavlov* (Austria–Bulgaria EA).

twice.[120] Nonetheless, three cases aside one of which employed a direct effect conceptualization,[121] the ECJ responded with a preliminary direct effect entitled subsection asserting the direct effect of the relevant provision. In two cases the issue was essentially whether *El-Yassini*, and its caveat, applied. The first was the *Güzeli* case on Article 10(1) of Decision 1/80 of the Turkey Agreement.[122] Here, the Commission and Slovakia had argued that *El-Yassini* was applicable by analogy, whilst Germany contested its ratio as well as its applicability to the Turkey context. The ECJ left it to the national court to determine whether the situation was similar to the caveat articulated in *El-Yassini*.[123] The *Gattoussi* case which followed gave rise to a German frontal assault on the *El-Yassini* residence permit extension caveat in a case on the Euro-Med Agreement with Tunisia (Art 64(1)).[124] Germany emphasized the differences between it and the provision in the Morocco Cooperation Agreement, especially the joint declaration which reflected the Contracting Parties intention to preclude reliance on the non-discrimination prohibition to claim a right to remain. That this was the provision to which the joint declaration expressly applied, did not alter the conclusion reached on its predecessor in the Morocco Cooperation Agreement to which the equivalent joint declaration did not apply: the *El Yassini* caveat still applied.

Five rulings are notable for transposing internal EU law interpretations to EU Agreements (as well as in some cases for the direct effect holding). The 2002 *Pokrzeptowicz-Meyer* judgment concerned the relevant provision of the Europe Agreement with Poland (Art 37(1)).[125] The direct effect finding by the Full Court saw it conclude that Article 37(1) laid down a clear, precise, and unconditional discrimination prohibition. A German

[120] Both cases coming from Austria where the express question of direct applicability was raised: C-171/01 *Wählergruppe*; C-101/10 *Pavlov*.

[121] C-152/08 *Kahveci* [2008] ECR I-6291. And a case where the referring court expressly framed its first question as one of direct applicability, a question directly answered by the Advocate General, but where the response was that the relevant provision did not preclude the national legislation at issue: C-101/10 *Pavlov* (Austria–Bulgaria EA). Direct effect was never in doubt as equivalent provisions in the Europe Agreements with Poland and Slovakia had been held directly effective: C-162/00 *Pokrzeptowicz-Meyer* [2002] ECR I-1049; C-438/00 *Kolpak*.

[122] First held directly effective in C-171/01 *Wählergruppe* considered below.

[123] The Advocate General's approach was in line with the German submissions, namely, that using Art 10 would undermine Art 6 where a Turkish worker does not satisfy the conditions for a residence permit extension via the latter.

[124] C-97/05 *Gattoussi* [2006] ECR I-11917.

[125] C-162/00 *Pokrzeptowicz-Meyer* [2002] ECR I-1049.

Land argument that direct effect was negated by an indent providing that it was 'Subject to the conditions and modalities applicable in each Member State' was to no avail,[126] as the Court held that this would render the provision meaningless and deprive it of any practical effect.[127] Crucially, the ECJ concluded that a free movement of workers judgment holding the German legislation in breach of Article 45(2) TFEU could be transposed to Article 37(1) of the Polish Europe Agreement such that the indirectly discriminatory legislation breached the latter.[128]

The *Wählergruppe* ruling concerned a challenge to Austrian legislation on eligibility for the general assembly of a workers chamber on the grounds of its incompatibility with Article 10(1) of Decision 1/80.[129] An affirmative direct effect finding was quickly reached. Earlier judgments had established that, under an EU Regulation, migrant EU workers were eligible for election to occupational guilds.[130] Austria underscored that unlike the EU Regulation, which expressly referred to trade union and related rights, no such terms were used in the Turkey Agreement and a narrower scope was also justified because of its less ambitious aims. The ECJ employed the interpretative parallelism logic in holding that Article 10(1) was to be interpreted in line with EU free movement of workers law thus resulting in the national legislation being in breach.

In *Kolpak* a Slovakian handball player challenged a German sports federation rule restricting non-EEA nationals in certain matches.[131] The crux of the case was whether the *Bosman* ruling,[132] that found nationality restrictions on EU nationals imposed by sporting federations to be prohibited by Article 45 TFEU, could be transposed to the working conditions non-discrimination clause of the Slovakia Agreement. The fifth Chamber predictably transposed the Full Court's direct effect findings in *Pokrzeptowicz-Meyer* on the Poland Agreement. This was followed by holding that its Article 38(1) could apply to a sports federation rule, as

[126] Extra-judicial reservations were acknowledged due to this phrasing: Wathelet (1996: 619). Martin and Guild (1996: 297) suggested the Member States added this provision to avoid direct effect.

[127] The only intervening Member State, like the Commission, supported direct effect, consistent with prior academic commentary: eg Cremona (1995: 112).

[128] C-272/92 *Spotti* [1993] ECR I-5185. Indirect discrimination was first brought within an EU Trade Agreement in C-102/98 *Kocak*.

[129] C-171/01 *Wählergruppe* [2003] ECR I-4301.

[130] C-213/90 *ASTI I* [1991] ECR I-3507; C-118/92 *ASTI II* [1994] ECR I-1891.

[131] C-438/00 *Kolpak* [2003] ECR I-4135.

[132] C-415/93 *Bosman* [1995] ECR I-4921.

found with Article 45 TFEU in *Bosman*, and a citation to the *Pokrzeptowicz-Meyer* holding that it establishes an equal treatment right as regards employment conditions of the same extent as Article 45(2) TFEU. The *Bosman* ruling was essentially transposed to the Slovakia Agreement provision thus leaving the sports federation rules doomed.

Kolpak was significant in both being the first time that horizontal direct effect was accorded to an EU Agreement,[133] and for the ease with which it transposed the *Bosman* ruling the logic of which was imbued throughout with the fact that the sporting rules challenged a fundamental freedom. Indeed, in rejecting attempts at justification in *Bosman* it was underscored that accepting the nationality clauses would deprive Article 45 TFEU 'of its practical effect and the fundamental right of free access to employment which the Treaty confers individually on each worker in the [EU would be] rendered nugatory.' The Europe Agreements conferred no such fundamental right of free access to employment and yet the outcome for the relevant sports federation rules was identical.[134]

That the *Kolpak* logic was not confined to immediate accession contracting partners,[135] was confirmed when the Grand Chamber's *Simutenkov* ruling transposed the *Kolpak* ruling to Article 23 of the PCA with Russia such that Spanish football federation rules would have to give way.[136] That the PCA provided that Article 23 was to be implemented on the basis of Cooperation Council recommendations did not, the Court held, make its applicability subject to the adoption of any measure.[137] Nor was the absence of an association or accession dimension considered to prevent certain provisions having direct effect. The absence of an association with a view to gradual integration into the EU was held not to warrant a different interpretation of Article 23(1) of the Russia PCA than that provided in *Kolpak*.

Here, then, less than ten years after the seminal *Bosman* ruling which would then have appeared to be the quintessential of judgments in need of a

[133] Grounds which two Member States invoked for non-transposition of the *Bosman* ruling.

[134] Hillion, however, emphasized that Member State derogations were subject to an effectiveness test rather than the EU law proportionality test: (2008: 829).

[135] As it could have been read, see eg Van den Bogaert (2004: 274) underscoring the accession dimension.

[136] C-265/03 *Simutenkov* [2005] ECR I-2579.

[137] This provision, and the more limited objectives of the Russia PCA, led Cremona (1995: 112) to suggest that this 'may undermine ... direct effect', views expressed prior to an express direct effect finding of the counterpart provision in any EU Trade Agreement.

fundamental freedoms underpinning, we find it transposed to a 'mere' PCA. Admittedly, this transposition was not built in the face of substantial Member State opposition.[138] It may have been relevant that *Kolpak* and *Simutenkov* had been preceded by national court 'pre-emptive strikes' finding the provisions directly effective and applicable to sports federations.[139] The judgment, as Hillion put it, symbolized the active transposition of notions of EU substantive and constitutional law into EU bilateral agreements, regardless of their teleological variation.[140]

Just over three years later the Court, transposing *Kolpak* and *Simutenkov*, ruled that the same national rules would have to give way vis-à-vis the relevant non-discrimination provisions of Turkey Association law (Art 37 of the Additional Protocol and Art 10(1) of Decision 1/80).[141] The Turkey Agreement has a strong integrationist agenda, however the earlier transposition of the *Bosman* and *Kolpak* rulings to the Russia PCA leave little doubt that it would be duly transposed to EU Agreements containing an equivalent provision.[142]

2.1.2.4 *Establishment equal treatment provisions*

The Europe Agreements all contained a provision on establishment in the EU Member States for self-employed nationals, and those seeking to establish a company, from the relevant third State. This led to five rulings pertaining to four different Agreements. The first three were handed down on the same day in response to rulings sought by a UK court in which it directly asked whether the relevant provision of the Poland (Art 44(3)), Bulgaria (Art 45(1)), and Czech (Art 45(3)) Agreements were directly effective.[143] In all three, the analysis commenced with an identically

[138] As far as can be gauged from their submissions. In C-438/00 *Kolpak* three Member States were against the transposition of *Bosman*, but Germany and the Commission were in favour. In C-265/03 *Simutenkov* only Spain intervened and it, in contrast to the Commission, remained steadfastly against transposing *Kolpak* outside the Europe Agreement context.

[139] On this 'pre-emptive strike', to use the terminology of Hillion, see Hillion (2008: 825).

[140] Hillion (2008: 832–3).

[141] C-152/08 *Kahveci*.

[142] However, the terminology in the Agreements with the former Soviet republics is 'shall endeavour to ensure' rather than 'shall ensure' (employed in most language versions of the Russian PCA). The Advocate General's Opinion in *Simutenkov* appeared to rule out direct effect where such phrasing has been employed.

[143] C-63/99 *Gloszczuk* [2001] ECR I-6369; C-235/99 *Kondova* [2001] ECR I-6427; C-257/99 *Barkoci and Malik* [2001] ECR I-6557.

reasoned affirmative conclusion.[144] The ECJ looked at the wording of the provision in the respective Agreements which was held to lay down in clear, precise, and unconditional terms a nationality discrimination prohibition against the relevant third country nationals. The sentence that followed found the equal treatment rule to lay down a precise obligation to produce a specific result which individuals could rely upon to set aside discriminatory legislation.

The direct effect finding was a foregone conclusion given the bold approach generally taken in EU Trade Agreements, and whilst this trilogy of cases gave rise to a strikingly high number of Member State interventions (nine, ten, and seven respectively), this sought to shape the substantive scope interpretation.[145] All intervening Member States, the Commission, and Advocate General contested the requested interpretation in line with Article 49 TFEU in order to limit the express proviso in the Europe Agreements permitting Member States' laws and regulations regarding inter alia entry, stay, and establishment.[146] The ECJ followed suit.[147]

The two rulings that followed concerned the provisions in the three Europe Agreements already considered, alongside that in the Slovakia Agreement.[148] The first reference was sought prior to the aforementioned trilogy and the questions included whether Polish and Czech nationals could directly rely on the Agreements. The ECJ reiterated the judgments from the preceding month on direct effect and scope of the relevant provisions; but also transposed an Article 49 TFEU interpretation, that of the

[144] This line of rulings, unlike those in the previous subsection, did not come with direct effect-entitled subsections (contrast the Advocates General Opinions in C-63/99 *Gloszczuk* and C-268/99 *Jany*).

[145] Only one Member State (the UK) appeared to contest direct effect with four in support: see the Advocates General Opinions in C-63/99 *Gloszczuk*, paras 26 and 42, and C-257/99 *Barkoci and Malik*, para 32.

[146] Provided they are not applied in a manner nullifying or impairing the benefits accruing under the terms of a specific provision.

[147] It acknowledged that under its Art 49 TFEU and Turkey Agreement case law, rights of entry and residence were conferred as corollaries of the right of establishment, but held that this interpretation could not be transposed as the relevant Europe Agreements created a framework for gradual integration into the EU with a view to possible accession rather than creating an internal market. Prior entry clearance requirements were held in principle permissible under the three Europe Agreements, thus preserving the challenged domestic decisions: see further Hillion (2003).

[148] C-268/99 *Jany* [2001] ECR I-8615; C-327/02 *Panayotova* [2004] ECR I-11055. The challenges were to ministerial decisions rejecting residence permit applications to work as self-employed prostitutes.

expression 'activities as self-employed persons' to the equivalent expression—'economic activities as self-employed persons'—in the Europe Agreements, and the public policy derogations were also interpreted in line with those of the EU Treaty. The second reference seeking interpretations of the Bulgaria, Poland, and Slovakia Agreements saw the Grand Chamber reiterate both the earlier direct effect findings and the interpretations as to scope.[149]

In addition, the ECJ proffered an interpretation of the self-employed workers equal treatment provision in the bilateral free movement of persons Agreement with Switzerland (Art 15 of Annex I) which included self-employed frontier workers.[150] As this was the first time this Agreement had been addressed,[151] it was surprising that a direct effect analysis was not provided. Only two years earlier in *Gattoussi* (noted above) involving a provision arising for the first time concerning the Tunisia Euro-Med Agreement where the national court had also only expressly framed its question in terms of interpretation, and where, as in *Stamm*, an affirmative direct effect finding was also wholly predictable,[152] the Court nonetheless expressly addressed direct effect.[153] The next Swiss Free Movement of Persons Agreement ruling offered another example of provisions interpreted without reference to direct effect.[154] As with the Swiss Agreement, the preliminary rulings interpreting the freedom of establishment provision of the EEA Agreement (EEAA) did not give any express consideration to the direct effect issue.[155]

[149] A reading of the relevant provisions, in line with the three intervening Member States as contrasted with the Commission submissions and the Advocate General's Opinion, was proffered which amounted to a defence of the Dutch legislation by holding that there was in principle no requirement to permit short-duration legal entrants to make a within-territory application for establishment.

[150] The Bundesgerichtshof's interpretation of German law on agricultural leases would thus have to give way: C-13/08 *Stamm* [2008] ECR I-11087.

[151] In a withdrawn case an Advocate General had addressed it (including a direct effect analysis): C-339/05 *Zentralbetriebsrat der Landeskrankenhäuser Tirols* [2006] ECR I-7097.

[152] Peers (2000: 140) emphasized that the Agreement and many of its provisions, including that at issue in *Stamm*, can confer direct effect.

[153] The provision was framed in almost identical terms to the equivalent Morocco Cooperation Agreement provision held directly effective in *El Yassini* (see above).

[154] In C-351/08 *Grimme* [2009] ECR I-1077 it rejected the argument that legal persons were granted the same right of establishment as natural persons, thus preserving the validity of domestic legislation (it also rejected an argument relying on the services provisions and non-discrimination clause pertaining to employed workers of the Agreement).

[155] In C-471/04 *Keller Holding* [2006] ECR I-2107, Art 31 EEAA was not actually raised by the referring court but an interpretation was proffered, drawing on the interpretative parallelism provision in Art 6 EEAA, in line with that of the right of establishment under EU law and thus

2.1.3 *Other provisions*

The other provisions category can be quickly dispensed with. Of the nine rulings, five were on the EEAA in which the questions were not framed in terms of direct effect, and one in which an EEAA question was not expressly asked. In the first four, jurisdiction was declined because they concerned the Agreement's application in EFTA States prior to its accession.[156] The fifth and sixth rulings both concerned the free movement of capital provision, Article 40 EEAA, and no attention was paid to direct effect.[157] Two Swiss Free Movement of Persons Agreement cases also saw interpretations of relevant provisions without any express consideration of direct effect.[158]

Finally, one ruling concerned Turkey Agreement provisions on the creation of the Association Council and the submission of disputes to it.[159] A court asked whether a Portuguese customs authorities decision was valid without first initiating the Turkey Association Council Dispute

proscribing the German legislation at issue. In C-157/07 *Krankenheim* [2008] ECR I-8061 aspects of the German tax system were held to constitute a restriction under Art 31 EEAA but were justified by the need to guarantee the coherence of the German tax system.

[156] The first two concerned failures to comply with EEAA obligations to transpose EU Directives: C-140/97 *Rechberger* [1999] ECR I-3499 and C-321/97 *Andersson* [1999] ECR I-3551. The third and fourth concerned the same factual scenario, the compatibility of national legislation with a free movement of capital standstill clause in the EEAA: C-178/99 *Salzmann* [2001] ECR I-4421 and C-300/01 *Salzmann* [2003] ECR I-4899.

[157] In C-452/01 *Ospelt* [2003] ECR I-9743 no express EEAA question was advanced but the ECJ ruled that Art 40 EEAA applied and had the same scope as its EU counterpart; it did not have enough information to determine whether the national legislation at issue unjustifiably discriminated against EEA nationals. In C-72/09 *Rimbaud* [2010] ECR I-10659 the ECJ, in line with nine intervening Member States, held that Art 40 EEAA did not preclude French legislation which made a tax exemption for companies with their seat in an EEA country that is not an EU Member State, conditional on an administrative assistance convention combating tax avoidance or on the fact that, pursuant to a treaty prohibiting nationality discrimination, those legal persons must not be taxed more heavily than companies established in France.

[158] In C-541/08 *Fokus Invest AG* [2010] ECR I-1025 a provision on equal treatment concerning purchases of immovable property by residents in the host State was confined to natural persons (Art 25, Annex I). In C-70/09 *Hengartner* [2010] ECR I-7233, the referred question was surprisingly confined to Art 49 TFEU when the dispute clearly involved Swiss nationals. The ECJ interpreted the relevant services provisions of the Agreement in a manner preserving the validity of a higher regional tax on Swiss nationals. These cases were included in s 2.1.3 rather than the persons section as they involved rather different types of provisions to those in the s 2.1.2 cases. Alternatively, they can, along with C-72/09 *Rimbaud*, simply be seen as three more persons-related cases (including legal persons) taking the tally to 79 persons rulings since C-65/77 *Razanatsimba*.

[159] C-251/00 *Ilumitrónica* [2002] I-10433.

procedures; a curious request because the provision expressly provides that disputes 'may' be submitted to it, and it was found that this did not constitute an 'obligation of submission'.

2.2 Challenges to EU action

Preliminary rulings challenges to EU measures have given rise to a dozen rulings coming from courts in six different Member States, concerning eight different Agreements.[160] The first three were touched in Chapter II (*Schroeder*; *Schlüter*, and *Haegeman II*) and all saw the relevant interpretations preserve the EU measure. Nine further cases have arisen, the first of which came some 20 years after the preceding Article 267 challenge (*Haegeman II*).[161] In *Lubella* the Court was asked whether a Commission Regulation complied with interim Trade Agreements with Poland, the Czech and Slovak Federal Republic, and Hungary; the issue being whether the Commission immediately entered into consultations with the other Contracting Party.[162] The sole intervening Member State and the Commission argued that the Agreements were not infringed.[163] The ECJ simply held that the provision (Art 15) 'is effective only between the contracting parties and provides merely for a formal step to be taken after the adoption of protective measures ... [and] cannot in any event be effectively relied on to contest the validity of the protective measures themselves.'

In the next case, an Italian court referred questions as to validity vis-à-vis the Lomé Convention of a Council Regulation, and Commission

[160] The Greek Association Agreement (40/72 *Schroeder*—Germany and 181/73 *Haegeman II*—Belgium); a Swiss Tariff Agreement (9/73 *Schlüter*—Germany); an Interim Europe Trade Agreements with three Contracting Parties (C-64/95 *Lubella*—Germany); the Lomé Convention (C-369/95 *Somalfruit*—Italy); the Yugoslavia Cooperation Agreement (C-162/96 *Racke*—Germany); a Cooperation Agreement with six Arab States (C-74/98 *DAT-SCHAUB*—Denmark); the dispute settlement provisions of the Turkey Agreement (C-251/00 *Ilumitrónica*—Portugal) and provisions of Turkey Agreement Association Council Decisions (C-372/06 *Asda Stores*—UK) and the Additional Protocol (C-228/06 *Soysal*—Germany); the EEAA (C-286/02 *Bellio*—Italy); a Framework Cooperation Agreement with Latin American States (C-377/02 *Van Parys*—Belgium).

[161] The GATT and WTO-related cases are considered in Chapter IV.

[162] C-64/95 *Lubella* [1996] ECR I-5105.

[163] The Commission underscored that the day after the measures came into effect it informed the Polish representative and that this constituted compliance which the Advocate General accepted.

implementing Regulations, limiting imports of Somali bananas.[164] That Somalia had not ratified the Convention led a Member State, the Commission, and the Council, to contest jurisdiction and the Advocate General to conclude that the Convention was irrelevant. Curiously, but without an intelligible explanation, the ECJ considered that the Convention compatibility of the Regulations was not obviously hypothetical but found no factors to suggest that their validity was affected by the Convention.

The *Racke* judgment that followed was also enigmatic.[165] A preliminary reference asked whether a Council Regulation suspending trade concessions provided for in the Yugoslavia Cooperation Agreement was valid. That Agreement contained a provision permitting its denouncement on six months' notice which the Council invoked on 25 November 1991, a Decision that came into effect on 27 November 1991, nearly two weeks after the Council Regulation suspending the trade concessions.[166] Ultimately, Racke wanted to benefit from the Agreement's preferential tariffs (Art 21) and the fact that it only expressly permitted denouncement with a six-month notice period. Accordingly, but for justification of the suspending Regulation using customary international law, supported by the Commission and Council and contested by Racke, the EU would be breaching the Agreement. Before the ECJ, the case appears to have been framed in terms of whether the Regulation itself was void for incompatibility with customary international law and it was held justified by the fundamental change of circumstances doctrine.[167] Prior to reaching this conclusion it was considered necessary to determine whether the tariff provided for in the Agreement was directly effective, the logic apparently being that only an affirmative response permitted the trader to benefit from reduced duties were the Regulation held to be invalid. A brisk two-part direct effect test followed. It commenced with the wording of the provision, which required EU implementing measures, but there being no discretion as to their adoption they were held to confer domestically judicially enforceable individual rights.[168] This direct effect finding was to no avail for Racke as

[164] C-369/95 *Somalfruit* [1997] ECR I-6619.

[165] C-162/96 *Racke* [1998] ECR I-3655.

[166] A German Finance Court found the suspension justified as a fundamental change of circumstances under customary international law and the VCLT given the outbreak of war in Yugoslavia and an appeal to the Federal Finance Court led to the preliminary reference.

[167] See generally Eeckhout (2011: 387–91, 393–5).

[168] This was held to be consistent with the purpose and nature of the Agreement the aim of which was to promote trade development.

the suspending Regulation was held unaffected by the customary international law rules invoked. Whilst the case was thus a customary international challenge to the suspending Regulation, one wonders if it could have been framed more expressly in terms of non-compliance with the Agreement itself. After all, if the suspending Regulation and the denouncing Council Decision, which appeared to operate with immediate effect contrary to the Agreement's terms, could not be supported by customary international law rules, this would attest to a breach of the Agreement itself.

The fourth case concerned an attempt to have a Commission Regulation on export refunds interpreted in line with a Cooperation Agreement concluded with six Arab States and specifically a non-discrimination provision as to how the EU applies the arrangements between those six States, their nationals, or their companies and firms.[169] The ECJ reiterated the Commission submission that the Regulation applied without distinction to the Arab States and did not discriminate between them. Interestingly, the Commission had, in the words of the Court, argued: 'this is only a framework agreement which lays down certain objectives and principles but implies that a proper trade agreement will subsequently be concluded, and therefore cannot be of direct application.'

The fifth ruling was the *Ilumitrónica* case noted earlier.[170] A Commission Decision was challenged on the same grounds as the Portuguese customs authorities Decision. As the Court found nothing in the reference identifying the Decision, it was unable to adjudicate the point. In the next case the referred questions concerned whether the EU free movement of goods provisions and their EEAA counterpart precluded a particular interpretation of two Decisions.[171] The ECJ pointed to a sector-specific counterpart to Article 34 TFEU applicable to the dispute and the relevant justificatory provision to Article 36 TFEU (Art 13 EEAA) and held in line with the two intervening Member States, the single intervening EEA State, the Commission, and the Advocate General, that the EU measures were justified under Article 13 EEAA.

The *Van Parys* ruling that followed concerned the WTO compatibility of the EU's banana imports regime.[172] A Belgian court queried the validity

[169] C-74/98 *DAT-SCHAUB* [1999] ECR I-8759. A Danish exporter argued that one particular interpretation would be inconsistent with the non-discrimination prohibition.

[170] C-251/00 *Ilumitrónica* [2002] ECR I-10433.

[171] C-286/02 *Bellio* [2004] ECR I-3465.

[172] C-377/02 *Van Parys* [2005] ECR I-1465.

of EU measures in relation to a Framework Cooperation Agreement's provisions providing for GATT most-favoured-nation treatment. The Commission and Council rejected the capacity to use the provision to challenge the EU measures as it did not go beyond WTO obligations, and the Court held that the reasoning it applied to the WTO challenge applied equally here. The ruling turned on the WTO argumentation, considered in Chapter IV, with the Cooperation Agreement creatively invoked to seek to bypass the outcome of unsuccessful WTO validity review.

The *Asda Stores* ruling in 2007 concerned a UK customs dispute where a trader contested provisions in a Commission Regulation that resulted in several questions concerning whether provisions of Turkey Association law required the EU to apply for Turkey Association Council recommendations and imposed requirements prior to imposing anti-dumping duties to inform and/or notify the Association Council, the Customs Union Joint Committee, and traders and, if so, the consequences of non-compliance.[173] The final question asked whether the relevant Turkey Association provisions were directly effective so that traders could rely on their breach to resist anti-dumping duties. As the duties are domestically imposed, it is in effect challenging domestic-level activity, but that domestic activity simply sought to give effect to EU Regulations and this could accordingly be viewed as indirectly challenging the EU measure. Curiously, the Court started with the final question, reasoning that if the provisions were not directly effective their interpretation would be of no interest to the traders. Several provisions were held not to be directly effective.[174] It was also held that notification requirements only created an obligation between the parties to the Agreement and that a simple formality of inter-institutional information is not capable of direct effect. However, a provision (Art 47 of Decision 1/95) requiring importing State authorities to ask importers to indicate the origin of certain products was held to be a clear, precise, and unconditional obligation, not subordinate in execution or effect to further measures, and thus directly effective. Reverting back to the first batch of questions, several were dispensed with as involving non-directly effective

[173] C-372/06 *Asda Stores* [2007] ECR I-11223.

[174] One provision because it required the intervention of other parties and was thus not unconditional (Art 44(1), Decision 1/95); four others because they either provided for the possibility of taking certain measures or encouraged coordinated action (Art 45, Decision 1/95) without containing an obligation (Art 47(1)–(3) of the Additional Protocol and Art 46 of Decision 1/95).

provisions. And it was reiterated that the information and notification requirements provisions were a simple formality of inter-institutional information governing only relations of international law between the EU and Turkey which could not be regarded as containing an obligation to inform individuals. In short, there was no obligation under Turkey Association law to inform individuals.

The most recent ruling is the only one to have actually impacted on the relevant EU measure. Whilst the outcome in *Soysal* (C-228/06) concerning the establishment and services standstill clause in the Turkey Agreement's Additional Protocol, noted above, flowed inexorably from the *Savas* ruling, this caught the EU legislature by surprise,[175] because the impugned German law implemented the Common Visa List Regulation (Council Regulation 539/2001) that lists Turkey as a country whose nationals must obtain a visa when crossing the EU's external borders. For the Court, this could not call into question its conclusion and it pointed to the consistent interpretation obligation flowing from the primacy of EU Agreements. This ruling appeared to authorize Member State authorities including their courts, in States where the visa requirement post-dates their obligation to apply the Additional Protocol, to ignore the Visa List Regulation. To call this consistent interpretation would be disingenuous for it required an expressly *contra legem* reading.[176]

2.3 Concluding assessment

One striking factor concerning the 131 preliminary rulings pertaining to EU trade agreements is the sharp dissonance between judicial activity concerning challenges to domestic action and EU action. As Figure III.3 illustrates, challenges to EU action have constituted 9 per cent of this case law as contrasted with 91 per cent for challenges to domestic action.

One factor that might be assumed to contribute to this dearth of individuals challenging EU measures via the preliminary rulings procedure is the existence of an alternative direct route to such a challenge before the EU

[175] Indeed, the Commission appeared to defend the regime by emphasizing that the visa requirement introduced offered the advantage of Schengen free movement in contrast to the visa-free but Germany-exclusive access applicable when the Additional Protocol entered into force.

[176] For Peers (2011: 115) the direct conflict of the two sources of law was overlooked, which he rightly noted could not be solved by consistent interpretation.

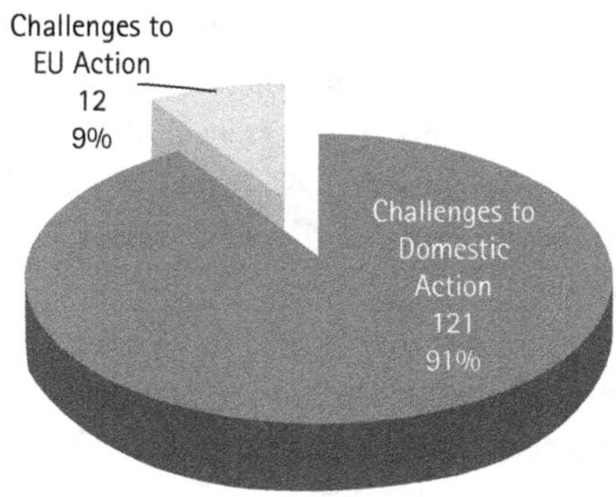

Figure III.3 Preliminary rulings concerning EU Trade Agreements (131 rulings,[177] challenges to domestic action/EU action)

Courts which is not an option available to individuals with domestic measures.[178]

One gleans little from the few challenges to EU action, not least given that some, especially the plea concerning the Lomé Convention (*Somalfruit*) and the unidentified challenged decision (*Ilumitrónica)*,[179] hardly appeared realistic prospects for success. *Soysal* is clearly of interest for it effectively sanctioned, for certain Member States in certain limited contexts, non-application of an EU Regulation. The EU legislature has been slow to respond to this for it took over two years for even a formal proposal to amend the Visa List Regulation to allow Member States to derogate from the visa requirement where required by the standstill clause.[180] *Soysal* aside, perhaps the most interesting detail is the Commission's recourse to the argument against direct application of a Cooperation Agreement where it was a Commission measure being challenged (*DAT-SCHAUB*). Lawyers are tasked with winning cases, but it remains striking that in the goods and persons case law challenging national measures, the Commission has rarely opposed direct effect and has frequently sought the boldest of substantive readings, and yet resorts so casually to this argument on that rare occasion where a Commission measure is challenged. The *Lubella* ruling was also noteworthy insofar as the ECJ did not, unlike the Advocate General,

[177] Two cases are categorized as both challenges to EU and domestic action: C-251/00 *Ilumitrónica* and C-228/06 *Soysal*. The total of 133 challenges in Figure III.3 is explained by the fact that C-251/00 *Ilumitrónica* and C-228/06 *Soysal* are categorized as both challenges to EU and domestic action.

[178] However, the stringent standing requirements would suggest otherwise.

[179] Presumably the absence of an 'obligation of submission' in the Turkey Agreement dispute procedures would in any event have resolved this aspect of the dispute.

[180] COM(2011) 290 final (24.5.2011), on which no further action seems to have taken place.

actually acknowledge Commission compliance but rather asserted that the provision in the Interim Trade Agreements was only effective between the Contracting Parties and could not be relied upon to contest the validity of the relevant measures; the ECJ has arguably rejected more persuasive arguments to shield domestic action from review vis-à-vis EU Trade Agreement provisions.

The 121 preliminary rulings concerning challenges to domestic action in contrast provide a rich body of case law for analysis. The points that the remainder of this subsection seeks to articulate in this respect can be grouped around four sub-categories: first, the contrasting levels of judicial activity; secondly, use of the direct effect lens; thirdly, the nature and application of the direct effect test; and, fourthly, the scope of the interpretation proffered of the relevant EU Agreement provisions.

As to the **contrasting levels of judicial activity**, whilst there was an initial burst of activity as to goods-related provisions, the post-*Kupferberg* period has only generated a further 27 rulings. In contrast, the sphere of persons which generated a first ruling in 1977 (*Razanatsimba*), and no further ruling until 1987 (*Demirel*), has given rise to a further 75 rulings. As Figure III.4 illustrates, over 60 per cent of the rulings to date have concerned the persons-related provisions in EU Trade Agreements.[181]

If we break this down further, we find that of the 77 persons-related cases, a clear majority (51, or 66 per cent) are accounted for by Turkey Agreement

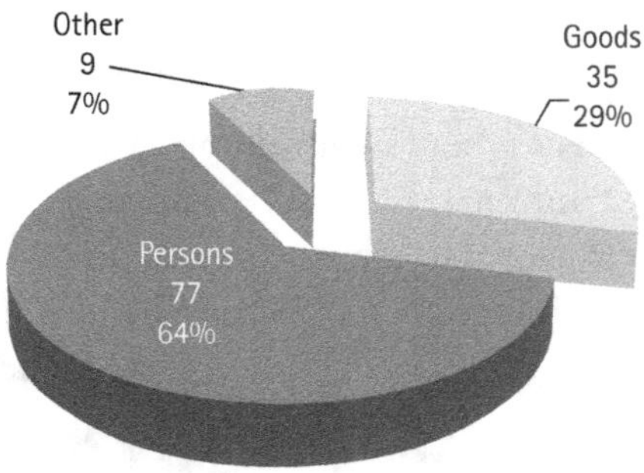

Figure III.4 Preliminary rulings concerning EU Trade Agreement challenges to domestic action (121 rulings)[182]

[181] It would be over 70 per cent if we looked simply at the case law since 1990.

[182] C-251/00 *Ilumitrónica* is included as the 'other' categorization because provisions of the Turkey Agreement on the Association Council were involved even though the dispute itself did concern goods. As noted above at n 158, three cases in the other categorization (C-541/08; C-70/09; C-72/09) could instead be included in the persons categorization.

litigation. Put another way, 42 per cent of the preliminary rulings Trade Agreement cases involving challenges to domestic action have concerned the persons-related provisions of the Turkey Agreement. Given that Germany has a vastly greater number of Turkish workers and their family members present than any other Member State, some may not be surprised to find that German preliminary references account for fully 33 (65 per cent) of those 51 cases.[183] In effect, then, German preliminary references on Turkey Agreement persons provisions in challenges to domestic action account for over one-quarter (27 per cent) of the 121 preliminary rulings.

In terms of the **use of the direct effect lens**, a dissonance has emerged in the manner in which it has been employed in the contrasting spheres of goods and persons-related provisions. In the goods line of case law, only six rulings saw matters conceptualized in the express language of direct effect, three being the first express direct effect conclusions pertaining to EU Agreements (*Bresciani*, *Pabst*, and *Kupferberg*). Two of the later cases to do so resulted from the need to respond to challenges to the direct effect of the relevant provisions (*Anastasiou*[184] and *Chiquita Italia*). The sixth case rejected the direct effect of a provision and thus clearly required conceptualization in direct effect terms (*Katsivardas*). Additionally, most recently in *Camar* a direct effect analysis was evaded in a manner reminiscent of the early EU Agreement cases where interpretations were proffered preserving the validity of challenged measures.

Of course, with 'internal EU law' it constitutes normal practice simply to proffer interpretations without forever reiterating the direct effect of particular provisions. For many, this absence of constant recourse to the language of direct effect where a presumption of judicial enforceability analogous to that of internal EU law is apparent, is to be celebrated. It might initially seem that the failure expressly to resort to this language is conditioned by the framing of questions by the national courts and submissions before the ECJ.[185] This, however, is clearly belied by the

[183] Perhaps more surprising is the fact that none of the cases have resulted from rulings sought by courts in Belgium or Denmark. On Eurostat figures from 2011, the greatest number of Turkish nationals reside respectively in Germany, Austria, the Netherlands, Belgium, and Denmark (the latter two swap places if we adjust for population size). The ECJ case law only emanated from courts in five different Member States (in descending order: Germany, the Netherlands, Austria, the UK, and Spain).

[184] None of the rules of origin cases post-*Anastasiou* employed the language of direct effect.

[185] There are goods-related cases where the Court avoided express questions as to direct effect, as in 270/80 *Polydor* and 174/84 *Bulk Oil*.

persons-related jurisprudence. For where the persons provisions have been at issue, express conceptualization in terms of direct effect has usually followed notwithstanding that the referred questions were rarely framed in such terms. Indeed, in the social security and non-discrimination as regards working conditions line of cases the initial assertion of direct effect of such a provision and subsequent affirmations are expressly attributed their own specifically entitled direct effect subsection.[186] And only a handful of the persons-related rulings have not expressly conceptualized matters in terms of direct effect and, perhaps tellingly, the main examples stem from recent cases concerning the Swiss Agreement (*Stamm*; *Grimme*) and the EEAA (*Keller Holding*; *Krankenheim*) which are precisely the Agreements premised on extending EU free movement law to the States concerned, thus perhaps explaining why it was felt unnecessary to embark on express direct effect analysis. Ultimately, despite the reluctance to use express direct effect language in the goods line of cases (evinced most recently in *Camar*), other than when left without alternative (*Bresciani*; *Pabst*; *Kupferberg*; *Anastasiou*; *Chiquita Italia*; *Katsivardas*), direct effect largely remains the conceptual lens for the impact of these Agreements in the domestic legal order.

Turning to the actual **nature and application of the direct effect test**, it has been flexibly and boldly applied. Where the two-part test has been employed, the Court has only rarely diverged from commencing with the express wording of the relevant provision.[187] And on no occasion has the second part of the test alone, concerned with the purpose and nature of the Agreement, stood in the way of according direct effect to a provision. The indications that particularly special and close relationships between the EU and the other Contracting Parties—initially fostered via the *Bresciani* and *Pabst* rulings—that were dispelled in *Kupferberg* was further consolidated with the express direct effect finding for the first time of a Cooperation Agreement provision with the 1991 *Kziber* ruling and most recently with the *Simutenkov* ruling on the PCA with Russia.[188] Crucially, the application of the test has led to affirmative findings, frequently in the

[186] Exceptions are C-101/10 *Pavlov* and C-351/08 *Grimme*.

[187] 12/86 *Demirel* and C-277/94 *Taflan-Met* being two exceptions since *Kupferberg*.

[188] As well as rejecting the argument in *Katsivardas* that individuals cannot rely upon Cooperation Agreement provisions.

face of substantial Member State opposition.[189] The classic example since *Kuferberg* was *Sürül* which involved a third of the then Member States arguing unsuccessfully against direct effect. That case is testament to a fascinating dynamic. The ECJ has been able to put in place aspects of the doctrinal edifice with limited Member State opposition (eg *Kziber* on the direct effect of the non-discrimination social security provision of the Morocco Agreement). Accordingly, when the Member States present a more united front—five Member States argued against direct effect of the Turkey Agreement counterpart in *Sürül*—they are doing so against the grain of the previously constructed doctrinal edifice. The ECJ was, therefore, able simply to transpose the logic to ensure consistency across similar provisions of EU Trade Agreements. This bears some parallel with what occurred in the foundational era: the seminal *Bresciani* and *Pabst* findings as to the direct effect of provisions of the Yaoundé Convention and the Greek Association Agreement saw no Member States intervene, accordingly when they turned out in force in *Kupferberg* to contest the direct effect of the equivalent provision in the Portugal Agreement to that held directly effective in *Pabst* their pleas fell on deaf ears. Inevitably, alternative outcomes in cases like *Kupferberg* and *Sürül* would have been viewed as egregious instances of judicial capitulation to political pressure. The more interesting counterfactual would be to speculate on whether the affirmative direct effect findings in path-breaking cases such as *Pabst* and *Kziber* would have been forthcoming had the ECJ been faced with the level of Member State opposition exhibited in *Kupferberg* and *Sürül* vis-à-vis the same provisions in different Agreements. After all, the Member States were advancing perfectly viable textual arguments against direct effect. What cannot be gainsaid is that the outcome in *Kziber* was of immense significance, for had the French, German, and Commission submissions been followed it is difficult to see how an alternative outcome could have been reached for the Tunisia, Algeria, and Turkey Agreements. One commentator presciently remarked in the wake of *Kziber* that it was 'up to politicians to decide, whether it should give rise to different strategies as regards the framing of international agreements'.[190] They have heeded that suggestion because the Member States have refused, except with EFTA countries and in the upgrading of the trio of 1976 Maghreb Cooperation Agreements (Algeria,

[189] The rare exception in which the Commission unsuccessfully joined the Member States in arguing against direct effect is C-18/90 *Kziber*, but it changed sides on the same point for the C-262/96 *Sürül* ruling.

[190] Neuwahl (1991: 330).

Morocco, and Tunisia) into Euro-Med Agreements, to include that clause in other Agreements.[191] If proof is needed that a generous approach to direct effect (and the substantive scope interpretation of norms) has consequences for the obligations to which executive and legislative actors are willing to agree, then this provides it.[192]

Furthermore, even where there has been limited Member State intervention against direct effect as in *Kziber*, *Gürol*, and *Sevince*, weighty textual arguments have been brushed aside. In *Gürol* the interpretation of the relevant provision appeared to fly in the face of the text. Whilst *Kziber*, along with rulings such as *Sevince*, *Sürül*, and *Simutenkov*, are manifestations of a willingness to transpose a key aspect of how it treats internal EU law, namely, not allowing explicitly textually envisaged implementation measures to preclude an affirmative direct effect finding as to a justiciable core of the relevant provision.[193] The significance of the latter point should not be underestimated. Developments taking place seemingly at the purely internal EU law level can in due course shape the judicial approach to external EU law, and it seems likely that there is judicial awareness of the sensitivity of relying expressly on the internal EU analogy.[194]

There are other notable manifestations of the flexibility and boldness on the direct effect question that deserve reiterating. One is the willingness to permit Agreements to have horizontal direct effect (*Kolpak*; *Simutenkov*; *Kahveci*) which can be read as inconsistent with the famous *Faccini Dori* holding, refusing to extend horizontal direct effect to Directives, that the EU only has the power to enact obligations for individuals with immediate effect where it is empowered to adopt Regulations;[195] for in some contexts such a power now appears possible via EU Agreements.[196] Another significant manifestation was that non-publication of the Association Council

[191] Maresceau (2006: 262). The judges were fully aware of this consequence for the negotiations: see Wathelet (who served from 1995–2003) (1996: 619).

[192] It might be thought preferable to have judicially enforceable obligations rather than vaguely worded non-judicially enforceable aspirations. But this can preclude otherwise beneficial treaty-making from taking place: Jackson (1992).

[193] This is precisely where the domestic courts of automatic treaty incorporation States have a strong peg on which to hang unwillingness to engage judicially with provisions of certain Agreements.

[194] Contrast the Advocate General's willingness in C-18/90 *Kziber* to rely on 2/74 *Reyners* by analogy on the direct effect finding with the Court's silence.

[195] C-91/92 *Faccini Dori* [1994] ECR I-3325, para 24.

[196] The Agreements where horizontal direct effect has been affirmed were all concluded via Decisions. Peers (1996a: 30) had anticipated a reluctance to grant horizontal direct effect.

Decisions at issue in *Sevince* did not stand in the way of a direct effect finding nor did the absence of a date of entry into force for Association Council Decision 3/80. In both contexts, textually powerful contrary submissions were advanced, indeed, five Member States in *Taflan-Met* and the Advocate General viewed the absence of an express entry into force date for the Decision as conclusive. It seems rather unlikely that domestic courts dealing with treaty law would have been so unwilling, particularly when faced with vigorous submissions from their executive branch, to allow non-publication and absence of a clear entry into force date to impede the domestic applicability of treaty law. The aforementioned judgments brought the Association Council Decisions to life and sowed the seed for a line of case law that has had an immeasurable impact on the lives of Turkish workers and their family members. Whilst that is undoubtedly a most laudable outcome, the cogency of the textual objections marshalled to the contrary should not be ignored.[197]

In the final analysis, the ECJ's contribution can only be assessed on how it has dealt with the cases that have presented themselves and on this basis one cannot but conclude that the results can be situated within a similar maximalist enforcement paradigm to that of internal EU law. Inevitably, as with internal EU law, there will be rulings rejecting the direct effect of particular provisions. But amongst this data-set of 121 rulings, the cases doing so can be counted on one hand.[198] And it is revealing that mainstream academic criticism of those particular conclusions has not been forthcoming.[199] In sum, there can be no doubt that the direct effect findings have represented a strikingly bold line of jurisprudence. But without seeking to diminish the judicial contribution, it must also be acknowledged that the ECJ has mainly addressed a handful of different types of provision across a select batch of mainly bilateral Trade Agreements. And the provisions litigated have primarily, though certainly not exclusively, concerned non-discrimination and standstill clauses which frequently have a similar counterpart in EU law proper. These are exactly the types of treaty provision which courts in automatic treaty incorporation States would be most comfortable applying, and the ECJ itself in its own direct effect determination

[197] The limited critical comment on the Turkey Agreement case law suggests it may have had this effect. For two recent uncritical accounts, see Karayagit (2011) and Tezcan/Idriz (2009); indeed, the former dismissively categorizes the submissions of the UK and the Netherlands in C-16/05 *Tum* as those of proponents of 'Fortress Europe'.

[198] 12/86 *Demirel*; C-277/94 *Taflan-Met*; C-37/98 *Savas*; C-160/09 *Katsivardas*.

[199] The *Taflan-Met* logic was criticized for implying, though later disavowed by the ECJ, that the social security equal treatment provision in Decision 3/80 was devoid of direct effect.

of internal EU law was also especially receptive to such provisions.[200] Accordingly, a contrasting approach to non-discrimination and standstill provisions in 'external EU law' would inevitably have exposed the ECJ to a prima facie potent double-standards critique.

Turning to the **scope of the interpretation proffered** of the relevant provisions, it is essential to recognize that limiting ourselves, when assessing the judicial contribution, to a mere yes/no tick-box approach on the direct effect question generates a relatively superficial picture. A considerably richer picture emerges with an analysis of the substantive interpretation accorded to the relevant provisions. Admittedly, a single section providing coverage of such a substantial body of cases inevitably risks bias of selection in terms of those singled out for closer consideration. Nevertheless, it is hoped that enough has been done to substantiate the basic conclusion that here too there has been a marked willingness to pursue a bold line, usually consistently with Commission submissions,[201] frequently in the face of stiff Member State opposition and occasionally Advocates General as well.[202]

In fact, Member State submissions have more commonly centred on influencing the scope of relevant provisions rather than direct effect, which is to be expected given that most rulings concern provisions that established jurisprudence holds to be directly effective. Inevitably across such a large body of cases, there are rulings that can be picked out which commentators consider to be overly restrictive on a particular point,[203] but this does not detract from the broader trends. Ultimately, we have seen a judicial actor building a bold line of jurisprudence as to the substantive scope of the provisions, often with limited foundation in the text or at least in the face of perfectly coherent textual arguments to the contrary. This has been most noticeable where we see the transposition of the substantive interpretative logic from internal EU law. This has been especially apparent with the heavily litigated Turkey Agreement. As with the direct effect finding itself, this substantive interpretation transposition has often not been precluded by vociferous Member State opposition as with, for example, *Bozkurt* (C-434/93) where the internal EU law meaning of legal

[200] See Pescatore (1983).

[201] On occasion the Court has been bolder than the Commission submissions, eg C-207/91 *Eurim-Pharm*; C-317/01 & 369/01 *Abatay & Sahin*; C-188/00 *Kurz*; C-228/06 *Soysal*. And on occasion less so: C-434/93 *Bozkurt* (on the right to remain for someone permanently incapacitated); C-179/98 *Mesbah*; C-327/02 *Panayotova*.

[202] Both C-16/05 *Tum* and C-294/06 *Payir* offer recent examples of this in the Turkey Association law context.

[203] See, eg, Hedemann-Robinson (2001: 556), Peers (2011: 422–3).

employment was transposed to the Turkey Agreement contrary to the views of the four intervening Member States. But such transposition has by no means been confined to the Turkey Agreement.[204] The *Kziber* ruling saw the EU seek to transpose the EU Social Security Regulation meaning of social security to the Morocco Cooperation Agreement against the views of the intervening Member States without even proffering a justification. Perhaps most surprisingly, the logic from the seminal *Bosman* ruling was transposed not only to the Europe Agreements (a reading contested by three intervening Member States in *Kolpak*), but also to a PCA in the *Simutenkov* ruling. It is significant that we are dealing here with Agreements that do not have the interpretative parallelism anchor for which recourse can be had in the Turkey Agreement context. But even with the Turkey Agreement, we have seen far-reaching conclusions reached via analogy with internal EU law to which the Turkey Agreement does not refer. Thus in *Toprak & Oguz* the ECJ relied on earlier dynamic readings of standstill clauses in relation to free movement of capital and the VAT Directive in support of a dynamic reading of the employment restrictions standstill clause thus precluding Member States from retreating from liberalizations post-entry into force of that standstill clause. When *Toprak & Oguz* is combined with the earlier *Abatay* ruling, rejecting the permissibility of new restrictions subject to non-applicability for existing lawfully employed workers, one further realizes how crucial to the effectiveness of the employment restrictions standstill clause the ECJ has been. Those outcomes were not inevitable and wholly predictable readings of the text. In both cases, the ECJ stance was adopted in the face of contrary interventions from three Member States, and in *Abatay* they were supported by the Commission and the Advocate General.

Furthermore, we have seen instances where the ECJ was potentially influenced by its approach to internal EU law whilst exhibiting an unwillingness to acknowledge the analogy. Thus, the creation of the *El Yassini* caveat on residence permit extension refusals in the Morocco Agreement context came with a fundamental freedoms analogy as support in the Advocate General's Opinion, that was wholly absent from the ECJ ruling. And its maintenance in the Tunisia Euro-Med Agreement context (*Gattoussi*) came notwithstanding the assault from Germany; the latter armed with a joint declaration that suggested that the Member States had

[204] Such substantive transposition was rejected, in line with powerful Member State submissions, in the trilogy of Europe Agreement cases: C-63/99 *Gloszczuk*; C-235/99 *Kondova*; C-257/99 *Barkoci and Malik*.

responded to the link created by the ECJ between lawful employment and residence permits in the Turkey Agreement context by seeking to preclude any judicial constraint on the Member States' exclusive competence to determine the right to remain.[205]

In sum, the judicial interpretation as to scope has, like the direct effect question itself, evinced a strong attachment to the maximalist enforcement paradigm with the Court time and again resisting arguments from Member States (as well as occasionally Advocates General and more rarely the Commission) to provide less generous readings of the text.

3. Direct Actions

The direct actions line of cases divides into two core categories concerning, respectively, challenges to domestic or EU action allegedly incompatible with EU Agreements.

3.1 Challenges to domestic action

The direct action mechanism for challenging domestic measures is provided for by the infringement procedures. The *Haegeman II* ruling, consolidated by *Kupferberg*, left little doubt that if the textually more dubious preliminary ruling procedure could be employed for policing compliance with EU Agreements, then so could the infringement procedure which posed no equivalent textual hurdle.[206] It was not until 1988 that the first EU Agreement infringement proceeding ruling arose, with cases two, three, and four coming in respectively 1989, 1992, and 1993.[207] These four cases share certain traits. First, jurisdiction was taken for granted with no reference to Article 216(2) TFEU or *Haegeman II* or *Kupferberg*. Secondly, they were all challenges to domestic action for being incompatible with EU law proper and EU Trade Agreements, and in all bar one infringements of both were

[205] In some quarters the judgment led to cries of judicial activism: Herzog and Gerken (2008).

[206] The infringement procedure is a tool for policing failures to fulfil EU Treaty obligations, and Art 216(2) expressly stipulates that EU Agreements bind the Member States.

[207] 194 & 241/85 *Commission v Greece* [1988] ECR 1037; 340/87 *Commission v Italy* [1989] ECR 1483; C-65/91 *Commission v Greece* [1992] ECR I-5245; C-228/91 *Commission v Italy* [1993] ECR I-2701.

found.[208] The relevant national measures were not solely alleged to breach EU Agreements and, accordingly, could be referred to as cases pertaining to 'incidental infringements of EU Agreements'.[209] The third case is prima facie the closest to a pure infringement given that the national measure did not apply to intra-EU trade as such, but rather the refusal to issue certain import permits breached both the Sweden Agreement and an EU Regulation on import arrangements. However, it concerned much more than a product-specific import prohibition applicable to one non-Member State.[210] Moreover, Greece displayed a cynical disregard for EU law and the Commission's role in the infringement procedure by refusing to cooperate.[211] Clearly, the Commission had plenty of reason to pursue these proceedings vigorously wholly independently of the Sweden Agreement.[212]

With the exception of a GATT Agreement case,[213] it took another nine years for the next EU Agreement infringement ruling. The *Irish Berne* case concerned a pure EEAA infringement ruling brought against Ireland for failing to adhere to the Berne Convention as required by the EEAA.[214] Curiously, one Member State intervened to contest the alleged breach by another Member State that conceded that it was in breach. The UK was

[208] In 194 & 241/85 following a finding of an Art 34 TFEU violation for intra-EU trade, the violation of the Lomé Convention counterpart (Art 3(1)) was found. In 340/87 following an infringement finding on intra-EU trade (Arts 28 and 30 TFEU), the ECJ essentially rejected the alleged breach of the standstill counterpart to Art 30 TFEU in the Norway Agreement (Art 6) because of an absence of reasoned argumentation. The charge in the extra-EU trade context was the subject matter of C-125/94 *Aprile* considered earlier. In C-65/91 the national import restriction applying to, inter alia, certain Swedish imports simultaneously infringed Council Regulation 288/82/EEC on common import rules and the Swedish Agreement (Art 13). In C-228/91 an inspections practice based on national legislation simultaneously infringed both Art 34 TFEU with respect to intra-EU trade and a standstill provision in the Norway Agreement on new measures unduly obstructing trade (Art 15(2)).

[209] In C-194 & 241/85 infringement proceedings were brought separately against a national measure pertaining to ACP bananas, where the Lomé Convention was invoked, later being joined with the already initiated proceedings against a national measure in intra-EU trade. However, the two measures arose out of Greece's organization of the market for bananas, and had the same practical consequence, namely an import prohibition whether in intra-EU or direct ACP trade (for the former an import licence requirement was imposed with a systematic refusal to issue, and for the latter an outright import prohibition).

[210] It was suspected of both applying to all non-Member States and not being confined to a single product.

[211] A duty of cooperation infringement was duly found.

[212] Sweden had, however, been pressing the Commission for some time before the Court application was made.

[213] C-61/94 *IDA*, see Chapter IV.

[214] C-13/00 *Commission v Ireland (Irish Berne)* [2002] ECR I-2943.

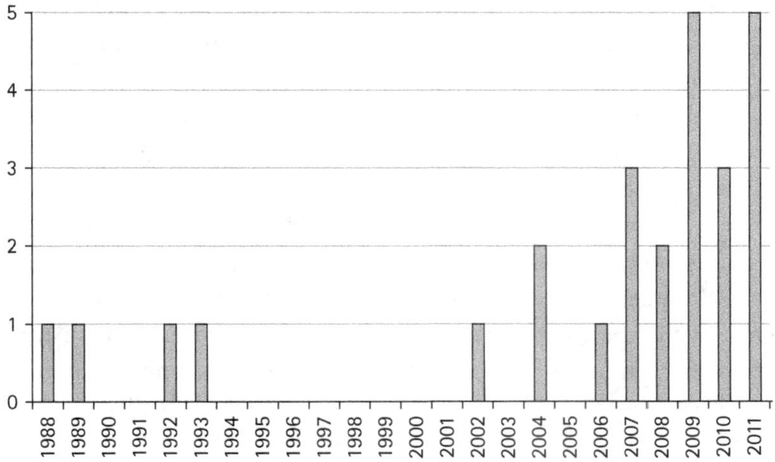

Figure III.5 Infringement rulings concerning EU Trade Agreements (26 cases, 1988–2011 (03/10/11))[215]

seeking to ensure its input into the emerging judicial construct pertaining to jurisdiction over mixed agreements,[216] and argued that the Berne Convention did not fall wholly within EU competence and therefore neither did the obligation to adhere to it.[217] The ECJ rejected these submissions on procedural grounds, but nevertheless commenced by affirming its jurisdiction before confirming the breach of both Article 216(2) and the EEAA. Its logic on jurisdiction was that the Berne Convention provisions covered 'an area which comes in large measure within the scope of [EU] competence'. It pointed, inter alia, to the protection of literary and artistic work being 'to a very great extent governed by [EU] legislation' and concluded that there was an EU interest in ensuring adherence to the Berne Convention.[218]

There has been a sizeable increase in Trade Agreement infringement rulings in the wake of the *Irish Berne* case as illustrated in Figure III.5.

Of the 26 infringement rulings concerning EU Trade Agreements, 22 have come since the turn of the century and 21 in the post-*Irish Berne*

[215] C-61/94 *IDA*, a case on an EU-concluded GATT Agreement considered in Chapter IV, is not included in this figure.

[216] This issue had also previously arisen in a batch of WTO-related cases, considered in Chapter IV.

[217] The Commission argumentation revealed a weakness in the UK's logic which conceded that Berne Convention provisions fell within EU competence, namely, that adherence could only be to the Convention as a whole.

[218] See further Eeckhout (2011: 302–3); Koutrakos (2006: 202–4).

period. Put another way, four times the number of Trade Agreement infringement rulings have been generated in less than a decade than in all the previous years.

This increased activity (2004–2011, 21 cases) exhibits two distinctive features. First, only one is a pure infringement, the remaining 20 can all be seen as incidental breaches. That one pure infringement case is noteworthy because it concerned the Turkey Agreement which has generated a voluminous body of case law (as Section 2 illustrated) but was not the exclusive Agreement in an infringement ruling until 2010.[219] In that case, Dutch residence permit charges for Turkish nationals were held disproportionate compared to those for similar documents for Member State nationals thus breaching non-discrimination clauses and standstill clauses in the Turkey Agreement.[220]

Secondly, the vast bulk of this activity has concerned one Agreement, the EEAA. Of the two cases not involving the EEAA, one is the previously mentioned *Turkish Residence Permit Charges* case and the other a case in which a Sicilian environmental tax on gas imported from Algeria infringed Articles 28 and 207 TFEU as well as the Algeria Cooperation Agreement's customs duties and quantitative restrictions prohibition.[221] The other 19 cases all involved alleged breaches of the fundamental freedoms and the counterpart EEAA provisions. All bar five shared the same pattern of the Court finding national measures in breach of one or more of the fundamental freedoms and then holding that they also breached the counterpart EEAA provisions;[222] in three of the remaining five the counterpart breach

[219] C-92/07 *Commission v Netherlands* [2010] ECR I-3683. The only previous infringement ruling appearing to involve the Turkey Agreement was C-465/01 *Commission v Austria*.

[220] Respectively, Art 9 of the Agreement, Art 10 of Decision 1/80 and Art 41 of the Additional Protocol, and Art 10 of Decision 1/80.

[221] C-173/05 *Commission v Italy* [2007] ECR I-4917.

[222] C-465/01 *Commission v Austria* [2004] ECR I-8291 (discriminatory legislation breached Art 45 TFEU and the EEAA counterpart in Art 28, and breaches of the non-discrimination provisions concerning working conditions in other EU Agreements were also found); C-219/03 *Commission v Spain*, Judgment, 9 December 2004 (breaches of Arts 56 and 63 TFEU and Arts 36 and 40 EEAA); C-345/05 *Commission v Portugal* [2006] ECR I-10633 (breaches of Arts 45 and 49 TFEU and Arts 28 and 31 EEAA, it not being considered necessary to address Art 63 TFEU and Art 40 EEAA); C-104/06 *Commission v Sweden* [2007] ECR I-671 (breaches of Arts 45 and 49 TFEU and Arts 28 and 31 EEAA); C-522/04 *Commission v Belgium* [2007] ECR I-5701 (breaches of Arts 45, 49, and 56 TFEU and Arts 28, 31, and 36 EEAA, it not being considered necessary to address Art 63 TFEU and Art 40 EEAA); C-248/06 *Commission v Spain* [2008] ECR I-47 (breaches of Arts 49 and 56 TFEU and Arts 31 and 36 EEAA); C-265/06 *Commission v Portugal* [2008] ECR I-2245 (breaches of Arts 34 and 36 TFEU and Arts 11 and 13 EEAA); C-406/07

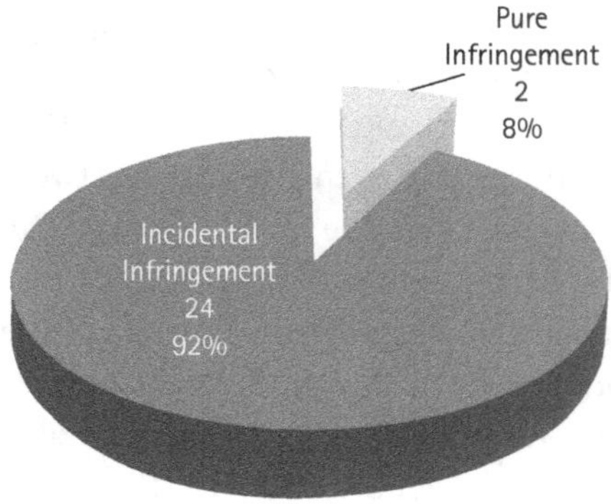

Figure III.6 Infringement rulings concerning EU Trade Agreements (pure infringement/incidental infringement) (03/10/11)

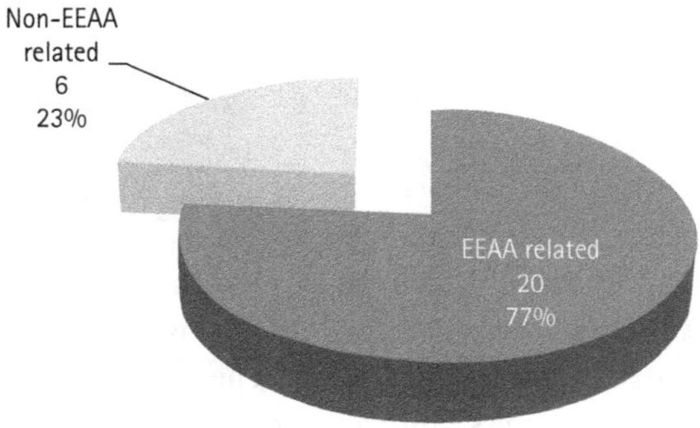

Figure III.7 Infringement rulings concerning EU Trade Agreements (EEAA/non-EEA-related) (03/10/11)

was not established,[223] in another neither internal EU law nor an EEAA breach were established[224] and, finally, one case saw the Member State

Commission v Greece [2009] ECR I-62 (breaches of Arts 49 and 63 TFEU and Arts 31 and 40 EEAA); C-562/07 *Commission v Spain* [2009] ECR I-9553 (breaches of Art 63 TFEU and Art 40 EEAA); C-153/08 *Commission v Spain* [2009] ECR I-9735 (breaches of Art 56 TFEU and Art 36 EEAA); C-20/09 *Commission v Portugal*, Judgment of 7 April 2011 (breaches of Art 63 TFEU and Art 40 EEAA); C-155/09 *Commission v Greece* [2011] ECR I-65 (breaches of Arts 18, 21, 45, and 49 TFEU and Arts 4, 28, and 31 EEAA); C-10/10 *Commission v Austria*, Judgment of 16 June 2011 (breaches of Art 63(1) TFEU and Art 40 EEAA); C-387/10 *Commission v Austria*, Judgment of 29 September 2011 (breaches of Art 56 TFEU and Art 36 EEAA).

[223] C-267/09 *Commission v Portugal*, Judgment of 5 May 2011 (breach of Art 63(1) TFEU, but not of Art 40 EEAA as the restriction could be justified in the EEAA context); C-540/07 *Commission v Italy* [2009] ECR I-10983 (breach of Art 63(1) TFEU but not of Art 40 or 31 EEAA as justified in that context); C-487/08 *Commission v Spain* [2010] ECR I-4843 (breach of Art 63 TFEU, but insufficient evidence supplied to determine alleged breach of Art 40 EEAA).

[224] C-105/08 *Commission v Portugal* [2010] ECR I-5331 (alleged breaches of Arts 56 and 63 TFEU and Arts 36 and 40 EEAA dismissed as Commission had not proved the alleged failure to fulfil obligations).

respond to the pre-litigation procedure by amending its legislation concerning EU Member States with the Commission proceeding successfully to challenge the legislation's compatibility vis-à-vis the EEAA.[225]

Bringing together these infringement rulings, two important findings deserve underscoring. First, on the divide between pure and incidental infringements, there have been two pure EU Agreement infringement rulings. One concerned the EEAA (*Irish Berne*) and the other the Turkey Agreement (*Residence Permit Charges*).[226] As illustrated in Figure III.6, 92 per cent of the rulings have thus concerned incidental infringements.

Secondly, only six cases have not concerned the EEAA, and four of these predate its birth.[227] As illustrated in Figure III.7, that equates to 77 per cent of the rulings having involved the EEA.[228]

3.2 Challenges to EU action

In the 40 years since the unsuccessful challenge to an EU measure in relation to an EU Trade Agreement in *Haegeman I* (touched on in Chapter II), an additional 26 challenges involving an assortment of EU Trade Agreements have been identified. In 12 cases the Agreements being invoked were not substantively addressed. The EU Courts dispensed with seven of these cases on admissibility grounds.[229] Of the remaining five, two

[225] C-521/07 *Commission v Netherlands* [2008] ECR I-4873 (breach of Art 40 EEAA). Because of the pre-litigation context it has been classified as an incidental rather than pure EU Agreement infringement ruling.

[226] Both 194 & 241/85 *Commission v Greece* and C-521/07 *Commission v Netherlands* were classified as incidental infringements for the reasons enunciated earlier.

[227] C-465/01 *Commission v Austria* is included as an EEAA-related case although it did also find infringements of other EU Trade Agreements.

[228] This figures rises to 91 per cent if we only include infringement rulings (22) since the birth of the EEAA.

[229] Three were actions brought against measures not having legal effects: 114/86 *UK v Commission* [1988] ECR 5289 (an annulment action in which the UK unsuccessfully invoked the Lomé Conventions); C-50/90 *Sunzest v Commission* [1991] ECR I-2917 (annulment action invoking Cyprus Association Agreement); and T-75/96 *Söktas v Commission* [1996] ECR II-1689 (damages action relying on the Turkey Agreement; the application for interim measures had been unsuccessful on the same grounds: T-75/96R *Söktas v Commission* [1996] ECR II-859); two were damages actions dispensed with for not having been brought within the five-year time limit laid out in Art 46 of the Statute of the Court (T-367/08 *Abouchar v Commission* [2009] ECR II-128 alleging a breach of the Lomé Convention and T-210/09, *Formenti Soleco v Commission*, order of 19 May 2011, involving alleged breaches by the Commission of the Turkey

annulment actions brought by individual Member States saw the ECJ annul the respective Commission Decision and Regulation on alternative grounds without considering the alleged EU Agreement infringements.[230] In a combined annulment and damages action, the applicability *ratione temporis* of the EEAA was rejected.[231] An additional annulment action was held devoid of purpose,[232] and finally a damages action relying on an alleged Lomé Convention infringement that was declared admissible by the GC was overturned by the ECJ.[233]

The remaining 14 cases, however briefly, do substantively explore the relevant Agreements. Five involved unsuccessful challenges to EU action relying on the successive Trade Agreements with the ACP States in which the claims arguably ranged from the unconvincing to the patently unmeritorious.[234] Three cases concerned Turkey Agreement provisions. Two

Association Agreement and Association Council Decision 1/95); 247/87 *Star Fruit Company SA v Commission* [1989] ECR-291 was an action for failure to bring infringement proceedings against France for allegedly failing to comply with, inter alia, the Lomé Convention which the ECJ would not countenance as commencement of infringement procedures is at the Commission's discretion; T-47/95 *Terres Rouges v Commission* [1997] ECR II-481, saw the ECJ accept the Commission's standing-based inadmissibility objection (individual concern), supported by the Council and two Member States, in an annulment action against a banana-related Regulation allegedly breaching Lomé IV.

[230] C-267/94 *France v Commission* [1995] ECR I-4845 (International Convention on the Harmonised Commodity Description and Coding System) and C-159/96 *Portugal v Commission* [1998] ECR I-7379 (EC–China Textiles Agreement).

[231] T-185/94 *Geotronics v Commission* [1995] ECR II-2795, upheld in C-395/95 P *Geotronics v Commission* [1997] ECR I-2271.

[232] Because to the extent that it constituted a Decision, it had been revoked: 82/85 *Eurasian Corporation v Commission* [1985] ECR 3603 (Cooperation Agreement with Thailand on manioc production).

[233] C-214/08 P *Guigard v Commission* [2009] ECR I-91 (the ECJ holding that as this was a contractual dispute the GC had no jurisdiction).

[234] C-280/93 *Germany v Council* [1994] ECR I-4973 was an annulment action against a Council Regulation, organizing the EU banana market, alleging that it infringed the customs duty prohibition in Lomé IV (Art 168(1)). The ECJ's terse two-paragraph response, in line with the submissions of the Council, six Member States, and the Advocate General's Opinion, was that the banana tariff quota scheme came within a different provision (Art 168(2)(a)(ii)) and that the EU obligation was to maintain the advantages from prior to Lomé IV and thus the Council Regulation was able to impose a levy without breaching the Convention. The GC invoked this ruling, in line with Council and Commission submissions, in dispensing with a private party challenge to the same Council Regulation as allegedly incompatible with Lomé IV and the Banana Protocol: T-521/93 *Atlanta* [1996] ECR II-1707. A recently decided damages action involved both Lomé IV and its successor (Cotonou) as a banana-exporting company sought damages allegedly suffered as a result of the EU's banana regime. The GC acknowledged the direct effect of the customs duty and charges having equivalent effect prohibition (Art 168) but

were successful annulment actions brought by individual traders against Commission Decisions finding remission of customs duties unjustified and in certain cases requiring recovery of customs duties.[235] They were included hesitantly within this section because in neither case was the issue whether the Decisions themselves breached relevant Turkey Agreement law, but rather whether their improper implementation by Turkish authorities and Commission implementation monitoring deficiencies was such that the Commission made a manifest error of assessment in applying EU import duty rules. The GC first held that this was so in *Kaufring* in 2001, and in 2008 the ECJ's *CAS* judgment reached a similar conclusion in a factual setting with parallels to *Kaufring*.[236] These two judgments are significant because they hold that the Commission is obliged to police compliance with an EU Agreement by third States and failure to fulfil this obligation had legal consequences for the legality of Commission Decisions based on secondary EU law.

The remaining Turkey Agreement case was a damages action brought by a trading company, Yedaş Tarim, against the Council and Commission for losses allegedly resulting from implementation of the Turkey Agreement and the Association Council Decision on the customs union (No 1/95). It was alleged that the institutions breached various provisions of the Turkey Agreement,[237] annexed financial protocols, and its Additional Protocol.

this was, however, to no avail due to an absence of any explanation as to why the EU measure was in breach, whilst the relevant Banana Protocol provision (Art 1 of Protocol 5 of Cotonou) was held not directly effective because it clearly depended on further measures: T-128/05 *SPM v Council & Commission* [2008] ECR II-260; upheld on appeal C-39/09 P *SPM v Council and Commission* [2010] ECR I-38. T-71/99 *Meyer v Commission* [1999] ECR II-1727 was a combined annulment and damages action against a Commission Decision refusing emergency aid. The Lomé provision invoked (Art 366) established the Agreement's duration and the procedure for its revision and was held not to cover any payment of special emergency aid to individuals established in an ACP State. C-342/03 *Spain v Council* [2005] ECR I-1975 was an annulment action brought against a Council Regulation opening a tariff quota which Spain contested, inter alia, as incompatible with a Cotonou Agreement provision providing for the EU to inform the ACP States in good time where it intends to take a measure which might affect their interests as far as the Agreement's objectives are concerned. In line with the Council and Commission submissions, and the Advocate General, it was held that there was no infringement because they had been duly informed.

[235] Respectively Joined Cases T-186/97, T-187/97, T-190–2/97, T-210/97, T-211/97, T-216/97, T-217/97, T-218/97, T-279/97, T-280/97, T-293/97, and T-147/99 *Kaufring v Commission* [2001] ECR II-1337 and C-204/07 P *CAS v Commission* [2008] ECR I-6135, setting aside judgment in T-23/03 *CAS v Commission* [2007] ECR II-289.

[236] On a successful appeal from a GC judgment.

[237] Articles 2(1), 3(1), and 6.

The GC held that for reliance upon these provisions to establish the unlawfulness of the institutions' conduct it was necessary to consider whether the provisions were directly effective.[238] The GC then invoked *Demirel*, and the holding therein that the Agreement does not establish the detailed rules for attaining its aims, in concluding that the Turkey Agreement is not included in the norms in light of which it reviews the lawfulness of EU acts. For good measure, the specific provisions invoked were held to be insufficiently precise and unconditional as well as subject to further implementing measures.[239]

An additional unsuccessful damages action was brought against the Council and the Commission for failing to suspend the Lebanon Association Agreement due to violations of fundamental rights.[240] The GC emphasized that the provision relied upon pertaining to suspension (Art 86) imposed no obligation to terminate or suspend the Agreement, and that even if the institutions had manifestly and gravely exceeded the limits of their discretion and thus infringed Article 86, which the applicant had not established, that provision did not give rights to individuals.[241]

One of the remaining cases saw the rejection of the argument that provisions of the Finland Trade Agreement precluded the application of the EU prohibition on anti-competitive agreements (Art 101 TFEU) on the ground that those provisions presupposed that the EU had rules enabling it to take action against agreements regarded as incompatible with the Finland Agreement.[242] Another was an annulment action against Commission countervailing charges Regulations on the grounds, inter alia, of an alleged breach of the principle of legitimate expectations, which alongside the Framework Cooperation Agreement with Chile created a climate of

[238] T-367/03 *Yedaş Tarim v Council and Commission* [2006] ECR II-873.

[239] The alleged Financial Protocol violation was rejected for failure to identify the relevant provisions, as was reliance on the Additional Protocol as the applicant was relying on the preamble which was held to have 'no inherent legal significance'. *Yedaş Tarim* was upheld on appeal, however the sweeping rejection of review vis-à-vis the Turkey Agreement was not addressed as contrasted with concluding that the GC did not err in law in concluding that Arts 2(1), 3(1), and 6 were programmatic in nature: C-255/06 P *Yedaş Tarim v Council and Commission* [2007] ECR I-94.

[240] T-292/09 *Mugraby v Council and Commission*, Order of 6 September 2011. Actions for failure to act were rejected as manifestly inadmissible.

[241] The Court emphasized that the provision could not be directly effective as it was not sufficiently clear or precise and was subject to the adoption of subsequent measures by EU institutions.

[242] Joined Cases 89, 104, 114, 116, 117 & 125–9/85 *Ahlström v Commission* [1988] ECR 5193.

confidence precluding the adoption of a unilateral measure without prior negotiation. The GC simply held that a reading of the Agreement—albeit without actually providing a reading!—revealed that it did not intend to amend the Council Regulation which provided the basis for the subsequent, Commission-imposed, charges.[243]

There are two unsuccessful challenges which are notable because of the defending institutions' argumentation. One involved an alleged breach of a Romania–Europe Agreement provision on consultation requiring, inter alia, the Association Council to be informed of a dumping case as soon as it was initiated.[244] The Council resorted to the argument that the relevant provision did not have direct effect. The GC's interpretation of the provision was such that the alleged breach was not sustained while considering it unnecessary to examine whether it could be relied upon. It reached essentially the same outcome in a challenge to a Commission aid Decision allegedly infringing EEAA provisions pertaining to consultation where the Commission argued that no individual right could be derived from any infringement of EEAA procedural rules.[245]

Finally, the most striking judgment was an annulment action against a Council Regulation, withdrawing tariff concessions on gearboxes produced by an Austrian company, alleging that it infringed, inter alia, the EEAA and the Trade Agreement with Austria.[246] The Regulation was adopted shortly after EU approval of the EEAA and less than two weeks before its entry into force. In its *Opel Austria* ruling the GC addressed a plea concerning infringement of the international law obligation not to defeat the object and purpose of a treaty before its entry into force, together with a plea alleging infringement of the EEAA, and in conjunction found these pleas well founded.[247] It held that the customary international law principle of good faith, recognized by the ICJ and codified in the VCLT (Art 18), was a corollary of the EU law principle of legitimate expectations; a principle which traders may rely on where the EU has deposited their instruments of approval of an Agreement the date of entry into force of which is known, to

[243] T-489/93 *Unifruit Hellas* [1994] ECR II-1201. Upheld in C-51/95 *Unifruit Hellas* [1997] ECR I-727.

[244] T-33/98 *Petrotub* [1999] ECR II-3837. The appeal, which did not raise the Europe Agreement point, is considered in Chapter IV.

[245] T-244/94 *Stahl* [1997] ECR II-1963 (the appeal, which did not involve the EEAA, was upheld: C-441/97 P *Stahl* [2000] ECR I-10293).

[246] Articles 10, 26, and 62 of the former and Arts 23 and 27 of the latter.

[247] T-115/94 *Opel Austria v Council* [1997] ECR II-39.

challenge EU measures adopted since its approval but prior to its entry into force and which are contrary to what would be its directly effective provisions upon entry into force. Whilst the direct effect analysis was as curt as those frequently conducted in the EU Trade Agreement context, it was curious that the GC cited *Bresciani* alongside *Kupferberg* as confirmation that unconditional and sufficiently precise provisions of EU Agreements have direct effect, for this is but one aspect of the classic two-part direct effect test consolidated in *Demirel*. In any event, it quickly concluded that the customs duties prohibition (Art 10 EEAA) was indeed directly effective.

The bulk of the judgment then focused on whether the Council Regulation infringed Article 10 EEAA. The Council had argued that it was not to be interpreted in the same manner as its EU law counterpart (Art 30 TFEU) because of major differences between the TFEU and the EEAA. This was never likely to succeed given the presence of the interpretative parallelism provision of Article 6 EEAA, and alongside reliance on this provision the GC provided a detailed analysis of the EEAA objectives in rejecting that argument. The Commission, at the forefront of pushing for the most expansive reach for EU Trade Agreements where domestic measures are challenged, invoked dubious legal reasoning in defence of EU measures. Thus, it argued that the EEAA and TFEU prohibitions were not identical in substance and that parallel interpretation would run contrary to other EEAA provisions. This was appropriately rejected and the reintroduced duties were held to be a prohibited charge within Article 10 EEAA;[248] the Regulation was contrary to that provision and the Council infringed the applicant's legitimate expectations by adopting the Regulation prior to the Agreement's entry into force but following deposit of the EU instruments of approval. The Council also breached legal certainty by knowingly creating a situation in which two contradictory rules of law would coexist.[249] In sum, infringements of the general principles of legitimate expectations and legal certainty resulted in annulment of the Council Regulation.

In an annulment action, the legality of the measure is assessed in light of the facts and state of the law at the time it was adopted. For the Regulation in *Opel Austria* this was prior to the EEAA's entry into force, even if

[248] The GC invoked in support C-163/90 *Legros*, where it was held that the term 'charge having equivalent effect' in the counterpart provision in an EFTA Agreement, which have much more limited objectives than the EEAA, would be deprived of much of its effectiveness if interpreted more narrowly than the same EU Treaty term.

[249] In deliberately backdating the Official Journal issue in which the Regulation was published, the Council committed an additional legal certainty infringement.

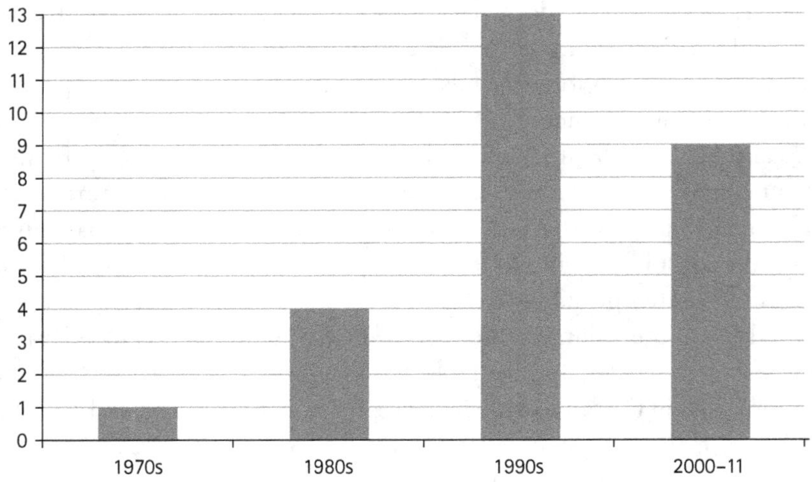

Figure III.8 Direct challenges to EU action invoking EU Trade Agreements (27 cases)

publication took place later. This posed an obvious obstacle to straightforward legality review vis-à-vis the EEAA. Accordingly, whilst the EU measure's incompatibility with the directly effective EEAA customs duty prohibition was clearly acknowledged, it was the general principles of EU law that offered the mechanism for bypassing the procedural incapacity to challenge a measure for infringing an Agreement where the measure was adopted post-approval but pre-entry into force of the Agreement.[250]

The 27 rulings are represented by decade in Figure III.8.[251]

3.3 Concluding assessment

The direct actions jurisprudence has given rise to 53 cases. As illustrated in Figure III.9, the split between infringement proceedings and challenges to EU action is strikingly even with 49 per cent in the case of the former and 51 per cent in the case of the latter,[252] although of course initiation of infringement proceedings are intended to operate as an incentive to

[250] For critical comment, see Kuijper (1998: 13–16).

[251] A case heard by the ECJ on appeal is counted once as are joined cases.

[252] This is so even if one excludes the two cases (*Kaufring* and *Cas*) that were hesitantly included in the challenges to EU action category, above at n 235.

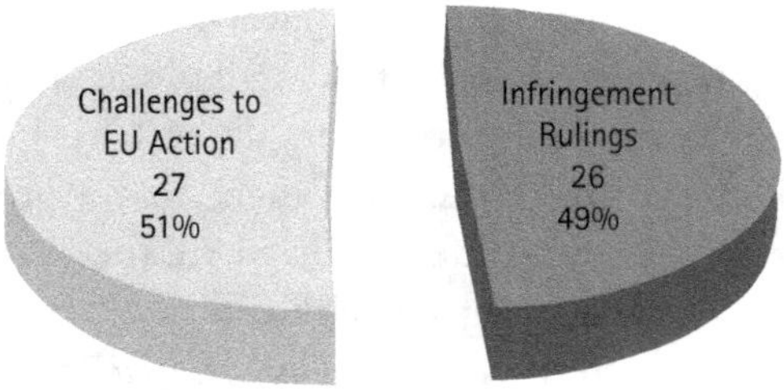

Figure III.9 Direct actions alleging infringements of EU Trade Agreements (53 cases, challenges to EU action/infringement rulings)

compliance upon Member States without the need for a ruling, in contrast to the initiation of Luxembourg-based litigation against the EU institutions.

The split between successful challenges is a rather different matter. Thus, in only one direct action has an infringement of an EU Trade Agreement by an EU measure been found and there the annulment was the result of linking this breach to a violation of the general principles of EU law (*Opel Austria*).[253] In contrast, if we look to infringement rulings, the alleged violation of an EU Trade Agreement has proved unsuccessful on only five occasions,[254] which is unsurprising given that infringement rulings overwhelmingly uphold the Commission stance.[255] Likewise, direct action challenges to EU action are also overwhelmingly unsuccessful,[256] and thus it is perhaps unsurprising in general terms that the ratio of initiated actions to successful actions has not been greater. Nor would it be fair to say that there has been a patently meritorious argument in any of those judgments in which an annulment action invoking an EU Agreement had not been upheld. Ultimately, the annulment action cases pertaining to EU

[253] Two cases, however, did see successful annulments without the need to address the arguments concerning the EU Agreements themselves (C-267/94 *France v Commission* and C-159/96 *Portugal v Commission*), and two of the cases involved successful annulment actions due to Commission implementation monitoring deficiencies (*Kaufring* and *Cas*).

[254] C-340/87; C-267/09; C-540/07; C-487/08; C-105/08, of which all bar C-105/08 found breaches of internal EU law.

[255] As is evident from the annual statistics produced by the Court. To take the most recent data: in 2010, 83 of 95 rulings declared an infringement; in 2009, 133 of 143 rulings declared an infringement; in 2008, 94 of 103 rulings declared an infringement, and in 2007, 127 of 143 rulings declared an infringement.

[256] See generally Tridimas and Gari (2010); Chalmers (2005).

Agreements have been so few, and even fewer where the EU Courts have actually engaged with the Agreements at stake, that only two additional comments need be made. The first is to underscore how willingly the political institutions resorted to the argument that a provision does not have direct effect or does not confer rights where the provisions are relied upon to challenge EU action (eg *Petrotub* and *Stahl*) or support strongly contestable substantive interpretations (*Opel Austria*) where their activity was challenged. The *Yedaş Tarim* ruling was also curious for there the GC sought to insulate EU action from Turkey Agreement review.

Finally, it is ultimately quite surprising how little judicial activity flowing from the direct action route to contest domestic or EU action has taken place. As regards challenges to EU action, Figure III.8 above illustrated that the 1980s witnessed a greater number of such challenges than the 1970s, and the 1990s an increase on the preceding decade. However, a range of factors aside from the growth in number of Agreements would also lead one to expect increased challenges, notably the considerable increase in both numbers of Member States and EU-level legislative and executive activity capable of being challenged, as well as greater recourse to majority voting which encourages Member State litigation. It is, accordingly, surprising that since the turn of the century there have been less rulings than in the 1990s, and that the case law since 2000 accounts for barely one-third of the rulings. The challenges to domestic action attests to a prima facie starkly different trend with only four infringement rulings predating 2000 (15 per cent) and the remainder (85 per cent) having occurred since then. The vast bulk of that activity is not only of the incidental infringement variety but also concerned exclusively with the EEAA.

4. Conclusions

As illustrated by Figure III.10, over 70 per cent of the 184 EU Trade Agreement cases have been generated via preliminary rulings.

And as Figure III.11 illustrates, nearly 80 per cent of the combined preliminary rulings and direct actions cases have involved challenges to domestic action.

Clearly, then, the EU Courts have been overwhelmingly called upon to adjudicate the compatibility of domestic action, rather than EU action, with EU Trade Agreements. And if we inspect more closely the challenges to

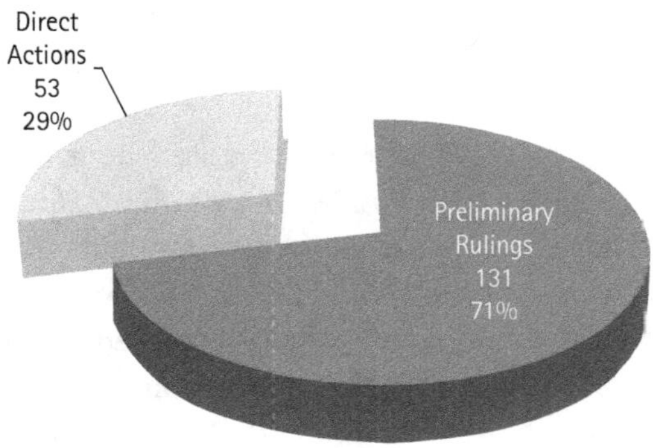

Figure III.10 EU Trade Agreement cases (184 cases, preliminary rulings/direct actions)

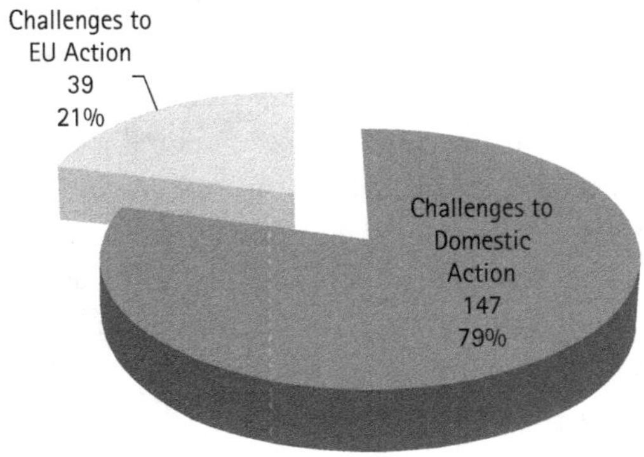

Figure III.11 EU Trade Agreement cases (186 cases, challenges to domestic action/EU action)[257]

domestic action there was a clear willingness to adjudge them incompatible with EU Trade Agreements. This is wholly predictable for the 26 infringement rulings, given that infringement rulings generally overwhelmingly uphold the Commission line. Of more significance is the case law largely generated via preliminary rulings in which the ECJ rejected reasonable Member State attempts to ensure that it would not be in a position to adjudge their action incompatible with EU Agreements, as with the non-publication and absence of entry into force provision arguments employed vis-à-vis

[257] C-251/00 *Ilumitrónica* and C-228/06 *Soysal* are included in both categories. The total of 186 challenges in Figure III.3 is explained by the fact that C-251/00 *Ilumitrónica* and C-228/06 *Soysal* are categorized as both challenges to EU and domestic action.

Association Council Decisions (*Sevince* and *Taflan-Met* respectively), as well as by contesting its jurisdiction over certain provisions of mixed agreements (as in *Demirel* and *Irish Berne*[258]). In addition, the ECJ has addressed EU Agreements even when the issue was not raised by a question from the national court (*Nijman*; *Ludwigs-Apotheke*; *Ospelt*; *Keller Holding*; *Hengartner*), including by leaving the national court in little doubt that the domestic measure appeared to breach an EU Agreement (*Simba*).

In the preliminary ruling context, it is supposedly ultimately for the national court to draw the appropriate conclusions from the ruling,[259] but the boldness of that line of case law, as evidenced by the direct effect findings and the substantive interpretation accorded to the provisions, cannot be denied. A maximalist approach to treaty enforcement has evidently taken hold with respect to EU Trade Agreements which has brought to bear powerful EU law enforcement tools for the policing of international treaty obligations entered into by the EU. It is perhaps not surprising, then, to find that in the particularly sensitive context of the persons line of authorities, a study published in 2002 documented a considerable level of Member State resistance, if not wilful non-compliance.[260]

With the exception of *Soysal*, no preliminary ruling involving challenges to EU action invoking EU Agreements was successful, and in *Soysal* itself the ECJ curiously avoided engaging with the direct implications of what a decree to employ consistent interpretation actually entailed. Only one direct action has found an infringement of an EU Trade Agreement and the annulment of the EU measure required tortuous reasoning linked to general principles of EU law (*Opel Austria*). Little should be read into such a crude statistic. The ratio of challenges to domestic action versus EU action has been of the order of three to one and, more significantly, challenges to EU action involving EU Trade Agreements have rarely appeared meritorious, as evinced partly by the numerous direct actions where it was not even necessary to address the substance of the Agreements themselves. Accordingly, one might surmise that the litigation activity before the EU Courts as to the EU's Trade Agreements indicates that the EU has been more assiduous in its compliance with its international, and indeed EU (Art 216(2) TFEU), obligations than have its constituent Member States. That said,

[258] Though in C-13/00 *Irish Berne* the Member State subject to infringement proceedings had conceded the breach.

[259] For recent consideration of the level of specificity in the rulings, see Tridimas (2011).

[260] See Conant (2002: ch 7).

a clear majority of challenges to domestic action have been concerned with the persons-related provisions in EU Trade Agreements (around 100 of the 147 cases can be so classified). However, because of the absence of EU legislative competence, which only began to emerge with the Maastricht Treaty, EU institutions had not been able to legislate to determine whether and under what conditions third country nationals—family members of EU nationals aside[261]—could enter and remain on the territory of EU Member States. In short, the contrasting litigation patterns will partly be accounted for by the fact that the EU has only recently acquired immigration competence and thus did not have legislative output in potential tension with these Agreements.

Nevertheless, the result is that it would be possible to suggest that to the extent that the maximalist treaty enforcement logic has been unleashed in the Trade Agreements context, it has, at least as a matter of practice, been so in a one-sided fashion in relation to the domestic action of the EU's constituent parts. It is in this sense, above all, the Member States and their authorities that have had to grapple with the bold readings, and the implications for the domestic legal order, of this additional external, and now supra-constitutionalized, body of EU law.

[261] Already included with the 1968 Free Movement of Workers Regulation (1612/68).

IV

The GATT and WTO Before the EU Courts: Judicial Avoidance Techniques or a Case Apart?

1. Introduction

This chapter assesses the EU Courts' case law in relation to the legal effects accorded GATT and WTO norms in the EU legal order. Strikingly, particularly during the GATT era, this has been amongst the most criticized case law to have emanated from the Luxembourg Courts. This line of jurisprudence commenced with a seminal case on the 1947 GATT in which the ECJ first advanced its principled stance against reviewing EU measures vis-à-vis the GATT. And it has proceeded to reach a similar outcome with respect to its successor, the WTO and the Agreements therein.

The chapter is divided into two main sections. The first assesses the GATT-era case law and in doing so provides a corrective to the largely one-sided and revisionist accounts that have emerged; accounts which in particular fail to show a sufficiently nuanced understanding of the nature of the GATT or the implications of general domestic legal review in relation to its norms. The second main section provides an assessment of the WTO-era case law which has also witnessed the emergence of a principled stance against review. And it too has generated a predominantly critical academic response viewing this largely as nothing more than unprincipled recourse to avoidance techniques to immunize EU action from review in relation to legally binding WTO norms. The argumentation advanced herein will put forth an alternative account of the judicial stance and in doing so will also highlight other manifestations of judicially sanctioned legal impact that WTO norms are having in the EU legal order.

2. GATT Agreements Before the EU Courts

This section assesses the case law concerning GATT Agreements that arose before the EU Courts via two main subsections which consider, first, the principled judicial stance adopted vis-à-vis GATT Agreements and, secondly, the remaining manifestations of EU judicial application of GATT norms.

2.1 The reasoning in *International Fruit*: lasting first impressions

The ECJ first addressed itself expressly to the legal effect of GATT norms in a seminal judgment in 1972. The bulk of this section provides an assessment of the brief reasoning enunciated therein which was reiterated throughout the GATT-era case law.

2.1.1 *The* International Fruit *judgment and its GATT-era progeny*

In 1970 the Commission adopted Regulations protecting the EU market from certain agricultural imports which were challenged in relation to the GATT by importers in a direct action and a separate action in a Dutch court. In the direct action, the GATT arguments were not addressed, nor were any reasons for not doing so provided.[1] In any event, the alleged GATT incompatibility of the Regulations was soon before the ECJ again for the Dutch court put forth two questions: whether the validity of EU measures also refers, within the meaning of Article 267, to their validity under international law and, if so, whether the relevant Regulations were invalid as contrary to Article XI GATT.[2]

On the first question, the starting point was that preliminary rulings jurisdiction extends to all grounds capable of invalidating acts of EU institutions including 'whether . . . they are contrary to a rule of international law'. Two criteria for validity review were announced: first, the EU must be

[1] 41–4/70 *International Fruit Company v Commission* [1971] ECR 411.

[2] 21–4/72 *International Fruit Company* [1972] ECR 1219. However, it had previously rejected an attempt by Italy to defend itself in infringement proceedings by invoking GATT rules as against its EU obligations: 10/61 *Commission v Italy* [1961] ECR 1.

bound by the relevant international law provision; and, secondly, for invalidity to be relied upon before a national court the said provision must also be capable of conferring rights. On being bound, the ECJ reasoned that by concluding the Treaty of Rome the Member States could not thereby 'withdraw from their obligations to third countries', indeed their desire to observe the GATT was made clear by Member State declarations when the EC Treaty was presented to the GATT's Contracting Parties under Article XXIV GATT and also by Treaty provisions (particularly what became Arts 206 and 351(1) TFEU). Furthermore, the gradual transfer of trade policy powers to the EU showed the Member States' wish to bind the EU by their GATT obligations, a transfer of powers put into concrete form in the GATT and recognized by the other Contracting Parties. In short, GATT bound the EU insofar as it assumed the powers previously exercised by the Member States in areas governed by the Agreement.

Moving on to the conferring rights criterion, it was held that 'the spirit, the general scheme and the terms of the General Agreement must be considered'. The ECJ recited the GATT's preamble to the effect that it 'is based on the principle of negotiations undertaken on the basis of "reciprocal and mutually advantageous arrangements".' And continued by asserting that the GATT 'is characterized by the great flexibility of its provisions, in particular those conferring the possibility of derogation, the measures to be taken when confronted with exceptional difficulties and the settlement of conflicts between the contracting parties.' The flexibility allegation was supported by reference to various GATT provisions: the central dispute settlement provisions, Articles XXII and XXIII, and the various measures that the Contracting Parties may or must take if an Article XXIII action is brought; the possibility, under Article XIX GATT, of unilaterally suspending obligations and withdrawing or modifying tariff concessions where some producers suffer or are threatened with serious damage. The aforementioned reasoning, a mere seven paragraphs, resulted in the conclusion that Article XI was not capable of conferring rights and, accordingly, could not affect the validity of the Regulations.

The *International Fruit* reasoning was reiterated, occasionally in condensed form, in a number of judgments from 1973 to 1995 whether in challenges to EU or domestic action, regardless of the GATT provision invoked,[3] and even in a much-anticipated Member State annulment action

[3] In chronological order: 9/73 *Schlüter* [1973] ECR 1135 (attempted reliance on Art II before national courts in challenge to EU measures); 266/81 *SIOT* [1983] ECR 731, 267–9/81 *SPI and*

which saw the GATT's features held to preclude it from being taken into account in considering the legality of a Regulation.[4] There were some exceptions to this reiteration of the *International Fruit* reasoning,[5] the most interesting of which was arguably the *Dürbeck* ruling where the alleged

SAMI [1983] ECR 801, and 290–1/81 *Singer and Geigy* [1983] ECR 847 involved attempted reliance, in challenging Italian measures, on respectively Art V; Arts II, III, VI, VIII and EU-concluded GATT tariff protocols; and Art II and EU-concluded GATT tariff protocols; C-469/93 *Chiquita Italia* [1995] ECR I-4533 (attempted reliance on Art III GATT in challenging an Italian banana consumption tax, the ECJ previously avoided a direct question from an Italian court as to the compatibility of that tax with Art III GATT, both the Advocate General, Italy, and the Commission had argued that it could not be relied upon as it did not confer rights: 193/85 *Cooperativa Co-Frutta* [1987] ECR 2085). In T-115/94 *Opel Austria*, considered in Chapter III, the plea alleging the Council Regulation breached Art VI GATT and the EU-concluded GATT Anti-Dumping Code (ADC) was not addressed given the annulment on other grounds.

[4] C-280/93 *Germany v Council* [1994] ECR I-4973. The GC reiterated the ruling in rejecting a private party damages action based on the alleged GATT incompatibility of the same Regulation T-521/93 *Atlanta* [1996] ECR II-1707 (upheld in C-104/97 P *Atlanta* [1999] ECR I-6983).

[5] In 38/75 *Spoorwegen* [1975] ECR 1439 the ECJ responded to a direct question from a Dutch court as to whether it was bound to apply GATT provisions even though it may conflict with EU law, that the EU had not unilaterally increased a duty bound under the GATT. In 90/77 *Stimming v Commission* [1978] ECR 995 an importer sought damages due to the EU increasing levies on certain imports, which was rejected seemingly in line with the Commission submission that the applicant was unable to specify the infringed GATT rules. In 191/88 *Co-Frutta v Commission* [1989] ECR 793 an annulment action against a Commission measure allegedly breaching Art XI saw the Commission inadmissibility objection that the applicant was not individually concerned upheld. In C-38/95 *Ministero delle Finanze v Foods Import Srl* [1996] ECR I-6543 a national court referred questions in an appeal before it concerning a lower court decision holding certain duties not payable because the relevant EU measure breached the GATT. The trader involved argued the GATT breach point to which the Commission objected because the national court referred questions as to interpretation only and not validity. The Advocate General invoked *International Fruit*. The ECJ did not deal with the GATT challenge point but provided an interpretation of EU law such that the relevant product was not exempt of duties, however its interpretation of EU law on the waiver of recovery of duties may have proved beneficial to the trader involved. In C-189/88 *Cartorobica SpA* [1990] ECR I-1269 a preliminary reference concerned a challenge to an EU anti-dumping duty as incompatible with the ADC and the basic implementing regulation (ADR) but the ECJ essentially found that the provisions invoked did not actually concern the anti-dumping duty. In a challenge to a Council Regulation imposing anti-dumping duties, the GC did not respond expressly to the alleged ADC infringement but did conclude that the Council had not exceeded its margin of appreciation: T-159/94 & T-160/94 *Ajinomoto Co v Council* [1997] II-2461 (upheld on appeal C-76/98 & 77 P). In a challenge to a Council Regulation imposing anti-dumping duties for breach of the ADC, the GC held that irrespective of whether it was applicable (China was not a GATT Contracting Party) neither it nor the ADR required what the applicant contended: T-170/94 *Shanghai Bicycle v Council* [1997] ECR II-1383. In C-178/87 *Minolta v Council* [1992] ECR I-1577 the ECJ found it unnecessary to consider a claimed violation of Art VI GATT and the ADC by a Council Regulation imposing anti-dumping duties as the applicant had not proved that the relevant sales were at different levels of trade.

GATT incompatibility of a Commission Regulation was rejected via reliance on information supplied by the Commission that a GATT panel had 'criticized' the EU, but found the measures not to infringe Article I or II of the GATT.[6]

2.1.2 *Reappraising the* International Fruit *logic*

> The Court's reasoning sinks below criticism.
>
> (Conforti (1993: 30))

The reasoning first employed in *International Fruit* was the subject of frequent and widespread opprobrium.[7] The focus of this criticism has been on the application of the twin-pronged test for review. Before turning to its application, it is useful to commence with a few comments as to the test itself.

2.1.2.1 *The twin-prong test for review*

Although in *International Fruit* the ECJ had been faced with an international agreement, it responded, as the Advocate General had before it, and in line with the question referred, in general terms, at least in the context of a preliminary ruling, as to the relationship between international law and EU law. It established that the EU's secondary legislation can be reviewed vis-à-vis a rule of international law. However, the Court took the conclusion it reached for granted, and unlike its Advocate General, did not invoke any detailed argumentation in support. The persuasiveness of reasoning that the absence of any express limitations on grounds of validity under Article 267 amounts to an obligation to examine validity in relation to international law was unsurprisingly questioned as soon as the ink was dry on the judgment.[8]

The first prong has a seemingly innate logic. One need only pose the question why validity review should be possible in relation to provisions of international law by which the EU is not bound, to sense, at least prima facie, the elementary logic of this requirement. One could seek a domestic analogy and consider how controversial it would be for a domestic court to

[6] 112/80 *Dürbeck* [1981] ECR 1095. The Advocate General did invoke *International Fruit*. The information supplied was, however, erroneous: see for criticism Petersmann (1983: 408–10).

[7] Examples include Petersmann (1983; 1985; 1995); Conforti (1993); Kuilwijk (1996); Kaddous (1998); Cebada Romero (2002: 407–36).

[8] Kapteyn (1974: 756).

embark on direct validity review of a domestic measure in relation to international law provisions that are not binding on the State. Matters are, however, considerably more complex in the EU context because it is composed of States which have their own internationally binding obligations which can both pre-exist and post-date the Treaty of Rome. The crucial question becomes when is the EU so bound. Article 351(1) TFEU specifically speaks to the situation of pre-existing treaties concluded by the Member States with third parties. It provides that the rights and obligations arising from such agreements between one or more Member States and one or more third countries shall not be affected by the provisions of the Treaty. One might argue that it follows that the EU is bound by all prior agreements of the Member States.[9] Alternatively, it can be argued that had the drafters intended all such agreements to be binding on the EU they could have stated it in the express terminology of Article 216(2). That Article 351(1) was not determinative of the matter was made apparent in the *International Fruit* decision; were it otherwise, the Court could simply have invoked Article 351 to support the contention that the GATT binds the EU rather than also underlining the Treaty-based transfer of competences to the EU.[10]

However, it is the second hurdle, requiring the international provision to be capable of conferring rights, that has generated greater comment.[11] In *International Fruit* the ECJ articulated no justification for this requirement. One justification would be to ensure a measure of symmetry between the approach to the relationship between EU law and the domestic legal order, and that between EU law and international norms.[12] Put simply, if a hurdle is in place for the enforceability of EU norms in the domestic legal order, such a hurdle should also apply to international norms. This logic took hold after *International Fruit* with respect to EU Agreements as Chapter II illustrated,

[9] To this effect see Rideau and Rainaud (1974: 35) and similarly Schermers (1975: 80).

[10] The Commission and Advocate General had both considered the EU bound by the GATT. Art 351 TFEU was not the basis for this conclusion and their reasoning was essentially followed by the ECJ.

[11] In *International Fruit*, the ECJ did not use the language of direct effect but the Advocate General had used the language of rights conferral and direct effect synonymously. In *SPI & SAMI*, it referred to *International Fruit* and *Schlüter* as having answered in the negative questions concerning direct applicability, and in *SIOT* it referred to the GATT provision invoked as not having direct effect for the reasons stated in *International Fruit*.

[12] Logic invoked by the Advocate General in *International Fruit*.

and inevitably once such symmetry takes hold there, its applicability cannot be coherently contested for treaties not even concluded by the EU.

Nevertheless, a critique emerged. Schermers suggested that one would be inclined to reject this condition all together.[13] The reasoning is essentially one of normative prescription, a vision of domestic courts—including the ECJ—faithfully applying all binding norms of international law. In the words of Schermers: 'What is the meaning of a binding rule of international law if there is no international court which has (compulsory) jurisdiction and if national (and [EU]) courts refuse to apply it in the vast majority of cases? If ever we want to establish some form of an international legal order all courts should apply its binding legal rules.'[14] In keeping with this vision, he expressed a preference for the ECJ 'to apply all rules of international law binding upon the Communities and not merely the self-executing rules'. Clearly, simply as a matter of empirical observation, there is a great deal of meaning to binding rules of international law even absent strict judicial enforceability by international and national courts. International norms operate as constraints on the behaviour of nations, and crucially their legislative and administrative output, notwithstanding that domestic courts may not apply them.[15] To argue that greater respect for particular international norms would result if there were an international court with compulsory jurisdiction and if national courts routinely apply such norms would appear axiomatic.[16] In contrast, to imply that the meaning of an international norm is suspect when it is not going to be judicially applied is wholly unpersuasive.

As for the actual type of criterion being used, the Court looked to 'the spirit, the general scheme and the terms' of the GATT in its conferring rights determination. Criticism was forthcoming for applying the test employed in the relationship between EU and domestic law rather than the intent of the parties test.[17] The concern appeared to be that a *Van Gend en Loos*-type test would result in fewer agreements qualifying as conferring

[13] Schermers (1975: 80). Criticism of this criterion continues, eg Cebada Romero (2002: 392–3, 426).

[14] (1975: 80).

[15] A scholar with Schermers' expertise in international law would be only too well aware of this.

[16] The EU itself is the paradigmatic example.

[17] However Riesenfeld (1973: 507) expressed a strong preference for this test over what he considered the rather specious test employed in various national systems that looks to the intent of the parties.

rights when contrasted with a strict intent of the parties test.[18] Were the ECJ to look for a parallel to the EU Treaty in all international agreements as a condition precedent to their capacity to be used to review EU or national measures, then few if any would not be found wanting. Other treaties lack even the limited textual evidence in favour of direct applicability marshalled in *Van Gend en Loos*. An international lawyer concerned with domestic judicial enforceability would inevitably be anxious that if this kind of evidence were looked for it would scupper the chances for greater enforcement of treaties through the medium of EU law. Such concerns proved misplaced as the ECJ's jurisprudence on EU Agreements was to illustrate.

2.1.2.2 *Applying the twin-pronged test to the GATT*

The most frequently heard, and prima facie compelling, critique of the *International Fruit* reasoning was that it constituted a misrepresentation of the GATT. In the cases cited, the ECJ generally avoided engaging with the specific provisions with which EU or national measures were allegedly incompatible, it apparently sufficed to contend that the Agreement in which the provisions were housed, characterized as it is by 'great flexibility', detracts from the notion that the particular provision invoked could possibly confer rights. In effect, one could say that the appearance of provisions that are clear, precise, and unconditional[19] is belied by the spirit, general scheme, and terms of the Agreement. But was the GATT really characterized by the great flexibility of its provisions? Many commentators over the years have taken issue with these observations. Essentially, the argument runs that this was a caricature of the GATT, the reality being that it was injected with a much greater degree of legalism and accordingly much less flexibility.[20] The assumption, not always expressly stated, is that indeed the GATT should in principle meet the criteria enunciated for review. The argument advanced, contrary to received wisdom,[21] is that the ECJ was

[18] Sacerdoti (1976: 246), which was articulated in the GATT-specific context.

[19] Not a point conceded by the ECJ, and indeed in C-280/93 they were expressly referred to as 'not unconditional'.

[20] eg Petersmann (1983; 1985; 1995); Dillon (2002: 361); Kaddous (1998); Kuilwijk (1996); Cebada Romero (2002); Pescatore (2003: 336–8).

[21] Received wisdom as judged by the general tenor of academic contributions on the invocability of the GATT. Exceptions in English do exist, notably the brief and perceptive coverage by Eeckhout (1997: 29–33). As well as early defences from the Commission legal service director general and an ECJ judge, respectively, Ehlermann (1986) and Everling (1986).

largely on firm ground in what is unquestionably a superficial assessment of the GATT.

The safeguard clause Some commentators intimate that there was something amiss in relying on the safeguard clause. Kuilwijk argued that it could only 'be invoked under strictly defined circumstances' and that 'The clause itself is not flexible at all'.[22] He continued: 'By saying that the GATT clause is too flexible, the Court confuses GATT law with GATT practice.'[23] If substantiated, such assertions constitute a chink in reading Article XIX as an exemplar of the GATT's flexibility. However, the ECJ did not actually assert that the clause was too flexible, but rather that the Agreement was characterized by the great flexibility of its provisions. The context of the argument being that this was one of the provisions evincing the flexibility inherent in the Agreement itself, which is difficult to contest given that the objective of a general safeguard clause is, indeed, to inject a measure of flexibility. In this respect, Kuilwijk's attempt to contest the Court's position misses its target. More importantly, it is rather telling that Kuilwijk was content to leave the reader with the impression that there was nothing flexible about Article XIX without any mention of the criteria for its applicability. A brief foray into the criteria provides a rather different picture.

To 'escape' GATT obligations, the language of Article XIX:1(a) required, somewhat oversimplified, imports in increased quantities causing or threatening serious injury and resulting from both unforeseen developments and GATT obligations. From the very earliest of days, these requirements were interpreted loosely.[24] A 1948 Working Party report concluded that the increased quantities of imports included a relative increase.[25] A few years later, a Working Party report took a very generous approach to the 'unforeseen developments' and to the causation requirement such that

[22] Kuilwijk (1996: 133–4). Even more boldly at p 342 he asserted 'The safeguard clause itself never has been flexible...' In like vein, Petersmann (1983: 432) argued that the GATT 'admits...suspension of obligations (Art XIX) only under exceptional and specified conditions...'; in a later piece (1988: 25) he referred to GATT law providing for generously drafted safeguard clauses, and one assumes this included Art XIX.

[23] Kuilwijk (1996: 134), reiterated at 342.

[24] Sykes (1991: 255) (referring to the criteria as being virtual nullities).

[25] Thus no actual increase in imports need occur, indeed, they could well have decreased providing they retained a greater share of the reduced domestic market than they had earlier obtained: see Jackson (1969: 558–9).

the author of the acknowledged GATT law 'bible',[26] queried: 'If the nature of the development can be foreseen and yet the degree of its impact on imports is that which fulfils the "unforeseen development" prerequisite, can this not be the case in every substantial increase in imports?'[27] That Working Party's determination of whether serious injury had been sustained or threatened, concluded that the Contracting Party invoking Article XIX was 'entitled to the benefit of any reasonable doubt' and that the complaining party had 'failed to establish that no serious injury has been sustained or threatened'.[28] Jackson contended that the net result was 'to render tariff concessions and other GATT obligations less stable'.[29] That the doyen of GATT lawyers put it in such stark terms renders it surprising that Kuilwijk referred to the strictly defined circumstances and the absence of flexibility of the safeguard clause.

Much was certainly happening outside the context of Article XIX inconsistent with the spirit, if not necessarily the letter, of the GATT, notably, the Voluntary Export Restraints (VERs) that had come into vogue by the early 1970s. In this sense, the safeguard clause could be viewed as too exacting in that were it less so recourse to VERs outside the strictures of Article XIX may not have been needed.[30] One can interpret Kuilwijk's discussion as hinting in this direction. This would be the only way in which he can be interpreted to have marshalled support, if only implicitly, for the strictly defined circumstances and inflexibility of the safeguard clause. There is nothing inappropriate in pointing out that the consultation requirement of Article XIX, and the compensation or retaliatory responses to which it can give rise, have constrained its role as a general escape clause and that it had failed to satisfy the needs of the post-war trading regime. Kuilwijk, however, seized on the VERs as support for the notion that the Court made the most elementary of blunders by confusing GATT law with GATT practice. This allegation is immediately followed by a discussion of VERs, with the implication being that this may have been what the ECJ had in mind in terms of flexibility in that Article XIX was not providing an effective discipline because it was largely being ignored. But there is simply no opening in the mere seven sentences of paragraph 26 of *International*

[26] Hudec (1993: 7).

[27] Jackson (1969: 561).

[28] This 'procedural rule' permitted much freer access to Art XIX than its language appeared to allow: Dam (1970: 103).

[29] (1969: 563).

[30] See eg Tumlir (1973).

Fruit to suggest that any such thing was intended. Indeed, the ECJ confined itself to merely paraphrasing Article XIX, accurately when compared with the text.[31] It is, thus, impossible to see from where any inkling that the ECJ confused Article XIX with the practice of employing VERs could be derived. And yet in the summary and conclusion to Kuilwijk's work the point is put in even starker terms: '[the ECJ] . . . took the rather peculiar view that this neglect [of Article XIX] was a sign of GATT's institutional weakness'.[32] The Court, however, told us nothing of any neglect of Article XIX nor did it need to in order to make the rather axiomatic point that the capacity to resort to unilateral safeguard measures is evidence of the flexibility of the GATT.[33]

This brings us to a related though more veiled criticism of reliance on the safeguard argument alluded to by Kuilwijk when he points out that unilateral safeguard measures are also allowed under the EC Treaty in certain circumstances.[34] The implication is that there was something amiss in invoking the Article XIX safeguard measure as exemplifying flexibility, given that the EU Treaty itself allowed for unilateral safeguard measures. The point was made more explicitly in a piece shortly after *International Fruit* to which Kuilwijk refers in which Waelbroeck essentially argues that although the EU system is more stringent, notably because of a posteriori control by the Commission and potentially also the Council, it is only a difference of degree not substance.[35] But as both acknowledged, the old Article 109(1)TEC was concerned with balance of payments difficulties and accordingly did not play the role of a general safeguard clause as did Article XIX. This makes any comparison misplaced because insofar as balance of payments problems were being addressed it would be via Article XII and Article XVIII:B and not the general safeguard regime of Article XIX.[36]

[31] Kuilwijk (1996: 133) acknowledges that the decision 'was based on the bare text of Article XIX' which renders it surprising that in the safeguard context the Court was considered to be confusing GATT law with GATT practice.

[32] (1996: 342).

[33] According to the chronological list of Art XIX actions in the GATT *Analytical Index* (1984), 61 invocations of Art XIX had taken place by mid-1972, that is shortly before *International Fruit*. The disclaimer is added that the figures may be incomplete due to insufficient information available in the GATT Secretariat.

[34] (1996: 136).

[35] (1974).

[36] The latter was aimed at the problems of a particular domestic industry and the former a problem of liquidity to which a free trading regime can expose nations. As Sampson (1987: 144) explains: 'In the late 1950s and early 1960s . . . many countries did not need to resort to Article

Indeed, the more appropriate comparator would have been the old Article 226 which did perform the role of a general safeguard clause comparable to Article XIX. That this general safeguard clause lapsed following the culmination of the transitional period[37] is itself testament to one of the differences between the EU and GATT regimes. But even if it had remained in operation, it would have been of little use to those implying there was some sophistry in invoking the GATT's general safeguard clause. To the contrary, it exemplifies a further sharp difference between the two, namely, that Article 226 did not allow for unilateral safeguard measures.[38] This was clearly, then, a qualitatively different regime from that put in place by Article XIX of GATT,[39] one which constituted a difference of substance and not merely of degree. Given the rigidity inherent in the old Article 226 procedure, policed as it was by the Commission, Council, and ECJ, it is unsurprising that the Court considered the GATT counterpart to be an indicator of its great flexibility.

Despite the conspicuous shortcomings in Kuilwijk's attempt to counter the invocation of the safeguard clause, the conclusion reached was that 'The alleged flexibility of the safeguard clause never should have prevented the Court from granting direct effect to precise and unconditional GATT rules.'[40] At the risk of pedantry, the way this and related sentences are formulated could mislead the reader unacquainted with the *International Fruit* reasoning.[41] It bears repeating that the safeguard argument was not in and of itself the reason for the judicial unwillingness to use GATT provisions as a review criterion. Rather it formed part and parcel of a broader argument premised on the GATT being characterized by great flexibility such that the ECJ was in principle unwilling to employ it in this fashion. The capacity unilaterally to suspend GATT obligations, especially when read alongside the other arguments, does suggest that the 'precise' and

XIX as they applied balance-of-payments restrictions (under Article XII) that served the same purpose.'

[37] Until 31 December 1969.

[38] Any doubts as to this were dispelled in 7/61 *Commission v Italy* [1961] ECR 317.

[39] As Trebilcock and Howse (1999: 613) pointed out 'A striking feature of the [Art XIX] regime is that the importing country is responsible for the substantive determinations, and while notification to the GATT is mandatory there is no requirement of surveillance or external confirmation.'

[40] Kuilwijk (1996: 134–5).

[41] eg, he stated (1996: 137) 'the Court construed GATT's main safeguard clause as being too flexible to allow direct effect. There never has been any ground for such interpretation . . .'. The terminology has also been taken up by later commentators: see Kaddous (1998: 387).

'unconditional' GATT rules to which Kuilwijk, amongst others,[42] referred may not be quite so precise and unconditional after all. This was the unambiguous message of the Court.

Provisions conferring the possibility of derogation This brings us to the related reference to provisions conferring the possibility of derogation. It is related because Article XIX would also qualify as such a provision,[43] and because the same objective is served by referring to the derogation provisions and Article XIX, namely, to invoke evidence in support of the 'great flexibility' characterizing the GATT. However, one searches in vain for elaboration of the derogation provisions that support the flexibility allegation. It is not that a detailed consideration of all the specific derogations was called for, but merely to leave the issue in this fashion opened the decision to criticism. Accordingly, it is worth briefly touching upon some of the major clauses which might have been invoked in support.

The Court could, for example, have referred to the waiver provision in Article XXV(5) which certainly constitutes a derogation clause, indeed, by far the most powerful of them. It enables the Contracting Parties to take a decision waiving a GATT obligation of a Contracting Party. The procedural thresholds are high for it must be approved by a two-thirds majority and the majority must constitute more than half the Contracting Parties. The objective of such a provision is to inject flexibility and is thus perfectly consistent with the logic of the Court's allegation, reiterating the Advocate General who explicitly invoked the waiver provision, as to flexibility. By the time of *International Fruit* some 67 waivers had been granted under Article XXV(5),[44] most controversially a wide-ranging waiver accorded the US in the agricultural domain which the Advocate General had been eager to bring to the Court's attention.[45] Curiously, Kuilwijk asserted that 'Article XXV:5 never has been a good example to prove the flexibility of GATT'.[46] The drafters, the negotiators, and the Contracting Parties who had been granted waivers would surely disagree. Neither is support to be

[42] eg Petersmann (1983; 1986; 1995).

[43] The Court, however, cited it independently in the context of the measures to be taken when confronted with exceptional difficulties.

[44] These figures are drawn by tallying the waiver decisions—not including the extensions, amending decisions, and new decisions but including the waivers for measures of more than one Contracting Party—from the table of waivers in the GATT *Analytical Index* (1994).

[45] On the US waiver, see Dam (1970: 260); Jackson (1969: 735).

[46] (1996: 132).

found for such a proposition in the relevant scholarly literature. The Jackson treatise contended that 'The legal technicalities of GATT provide a considerable measure of flexibility allowing "pragmatic" solutions to real concrete problems. The waiver provision . . . as well as the escape clause, are illustrations of this.'[47] Whilst Hudec argued that 'Even in its most legalistic days the GATT was quite generous with waivers . . . '.[48]

Another core provision attesting to flexibility was Article XXVIII which allows for the renegotiation of tariff concessions. This provision provided 'a periodic right to withdraw concessions for any reason whatsoever'.[49] Here we thus find another provision providing clear testimony to the GATT's flexibility.[50] There are also permissible derogations that apply specifically to the provision invoked in *International Fruit* itself (Art XI), notably the balance of payments exceptions in Article XII (and in Art XVIII:B with respect to developing countries) and an agricultural exception in Article XI:2(c). The latter was cited by both the Advocate General and the Commission in *International Fruit*; the Court was unlikely to be keen on making this provision an explicit tenet of its reasoning due to its case-specific applicability, that is, quantitative restrictions in the agricultural domain.[51]

An overall sense of why the ECJ was on safe ground in underlining the derogation provisions was provided by the leading GATT legal treatises at the time of *International Fruit*. The leading French treatise was published in 1968 and argued that: 'Dans la technique du G.A.T.T., non seulement l'exception confirme la règle mais, bien plus, elle constitue la règle'.[52] Flory's account clearly supported the invocation of the derogation provisions as exemplifying the great flexibility of the GATT. The same can be said of the seminal GATT treatise published the following year. It is telling

[47] (1969: 755).

[48] (1971: 1334).

[49] Hudec (1971: 1313).

[50] The ECJ admittedly did not mention this provision explicitly and there was little danger that the critics would draw attention to any provisions bolstering the flexibility argument. It was, however, mentioned by Petersmann (1983: 432) as follows: 'the General Agreement admits unilateral withdrawal of trade concessions (Article XXVIII) . . . only under exceptional and specified conditions . . . '.

[51] Avoiding references to the derogation clauses that only apply in a specific context, like that of agriculture, made it easier for the *International Fruit* reasoning to be given more general application.

[52] Flory (1968). He referred to the substantive rules as 'assortis de si nombreuses exceptions que l'on est parfois tenté de se demander si les principes eux-mêmes subsistent et demeurent toujours valables.'

that Part III of this treatise was headed 'Exceptions to GATT Obligations' and contained well over 200 pages, whereas Part II headed 'Law of GATT Obligations', which also included some of what were considered to be the 'minor exceptions' such as Article XI:2, contained less than 350 pages. Jackson provided detailed consideration of the manifold derogations that can apply and rightly refers to them as having 'provided the necessary flexibility without which the General Agreement might never have endured in the face of the pressures that have buffeted it.'[53] The key phrase of 'flexibility' again makes an appearance. The other major treatise was published in 1970 by an author adopting a markedly anti-legalist approach famously remarking that '"Illegality" is an uncertain and ambiguous concept when applied to the General Agreement'.[54] It is thus submitted that the ECJ was on solid ground in underlining that the derogations were both flexible and conferred great flexibility on the system. The practice as it then existed, recognized in the work of the leading scholars in the field, was unmistakable testimony to this.

The dispute settlement system If the ECJ was on secure ground in pointing to the derogations and the safeguard clause as exemplars of the flexibility of the GATT system, what of the reference to the dispute settlement system? The Court, following the Advocate General, limited itself to paraphrasing Articles XXII and XXIII and while there was strictly nothing inaccurate in doing so, the system had moved much further than one could have anticipated on the basis of that bare text. The provisions did not enshrine a system of third party adjudication, an embryonic form of which took hold by the 1950s.[55] It is accordingly not surprising that the ECJ was criticized for apparently wilful misrepresentation of the dispute settlement system. On the other hand, by the early 1970s the dispute settlement system had been deep in a process of decline,[56] with the US and the EU being the main proponents of an anti-legalistic and non-confrontational GATT agenda.[57] Given it was not possible to foresee what the future would hold, to have painted a picture of the system as it had existed in the late 1950s, rudimentary as it may have been, would also have misrepresented the extant reality. More importantly, were a more

[53] Jackson (1969: 352).
[54] Dam (1970: 352).
[55] See generally Hudec (1975: 66 et seq); Jackson (1989: 95).
[56] Hudec (1975; 1993).
[57] For the EC in particular see Hudec (1993: 33).

nuanced picture of the dispute settlement process presented this would only have bolstered the *International Fruit* reasoning rather than detract from it. In a seminal 1971 article, the commentator most closely acquainted with the dispute settlement system discussed its flexibility:

> proceedings have generally been conducted with as much room as possible for negotiated solutions. Formal legal rulings have seldom been sought before the parties are in deadlock. The rulings themselves have usually been expressed in terms that are soft and tentative and have almost invariably been accompanied by an invitation to continue negotiations. And, in fact, the parties have very often gone back to the bargaining table after a ruling and worked out a bilateral settlement.[58]

Hudec brought out clearly the large discretion inherent in all stages of the process giving ample room for (frequently taken) negotiated settlements. The Jackson treatise also underlined that throughout the panel procedure an attempt was made to achieve conciliation.[59] The system thus encouraged the parties to the dispute to produce as far as possible a result palatable to them given the economic and political exigencies of the time. If indeed judicial resolution of disputes can ever be seen simply as the mechanical application of a legal rule to a particular factual scenario, one can confidently state that such a vision did not even come close to accurately representing GATT reality at the time of *International Fruit*. Indeed, panels drawn from diplomats rather than lawyers, hence Hudec's coinage of 'a diplomat's jurisprudence',[60] was still dominant in the 1980s. It was not until the early 1980s that an Office of Legal Affairs was created for the GATT which generated a marked improvement in the legal quality of panel reports,[61] but the willingness of the losing party to block reports—the system operated with a consensus requirement at most stages of the process including adoption[62]– became increasingly common with the growth in panel activity since the 1980s.[63] The remarkable evolution of the GATT dispute settlement system since the initial *International Fruit* judgment cannot be gainsaid and perhaps many would have found the initial

[58] Hudec (1971: 1335).

[59] Jackson (1969: 176). Jackson (1969: 166) considered it very difficult to ascertain where dispute settlement leaves off and either trade bargaining or policy formulation begins.

[60] Hudec (1970).

[61] Hudec (1993: 137–8).

[62] Some of the veto possibilities were removed by a 1989 agreement: see Petersmann (1991).

[63] Lester and Mercurio (2008: 156) ('as time progressed, the frequency of the use of the "veto" power increased').

International Fruit reasoning, which merely paraphrased GATT provisions, more palatable were it to have come with recognition of the increasingly legalized nature of the dispute settlement process. Ultimately, however, the critics were not merely seeking judicial recognition of the evolution of the dispute settlement system, but a different substantive outcome, one in which the GATT was accepted as a general review criterion.

Back in *International Fruit* the Commission strenuously emphasized that for the ECJ to hold a measure invalid due to its GATT incompatibility would interfere with the diplomatic dispute settlement procedures. The Council had joined the Commission in running this argument in *Schlüter* the following year, and over 20 years later, in the challenge to the bananas regime (C-280/93), this argument was employed by the Council joined by the Commission and six intervening Member States. The political pressure from this consistent and unified response from the political institutions cannot be underestimated. But we should not merely conclude that the ECJ bowed to political pressure. Rather, the cogency of the logic invoked should be assessed. And as far as dispute settlement was concerned, the system had certainly evolved considerably from its more pronounced diplomatic roots. Nevertheless, this takes little away from the broader objection of the political institutions. A result that the ECJ might achieve in a particular dispute might well not accord with that which would have been reached were the dispute settlement procedures employed. Clearly, if a measure were invalidated for its alleged GATT incompatibility this would preclude the Commission from reaching a negotiated solution to any alleged inconsistencies of the said measure. For the ECJ to have accorded itself the role of overseer in these circumstances would have constituted a substantial incursion into the Commission's potential role in the dispute settlement procedures and, more generally, in its role as EU representative within the GATT. One can dress this up in the language of flexibility of the provisions, adding various examples to boot, as the Court did. Indeed, each of the examples can be taken in turn to illustrate that there was nothing inaccurate in the curt and uninformative analysis of the GATT. In this sense, much of the criticism of the *International Fruit* reasoning, premised as it is on a misrepresentation of the GATT system, is not convincing.

2.1.2.3 *Broader considerations against review: the declining normativity of GATT agricultural norms and beyond*

The preceding subsection was not intended to suggest that the seven paragraphs in *International Fruit* devoted to assessing the GATT, much of which is mere selective paraphrasing and was articulated yet more concisely in later judgments, actually sheds light on the complex system that was the GATT. *International Fruit* and its offspring were far from a model of clarity and carefully reasoned analysis. A finer grasp of the issues involved can be gleaned from the Advocates General Opinions and the reports for the hearings of the relevant cases. But much reading between the lines is needed. ECJ judgments, as has rightly been noted, 'may well be satisfactory but readers must often supply for themselves the reasons, political or juridical, which grounded the decision.'[64] *International Fruit*, and its progeny, exemplified this proposition. Whilst we do get a strong sense of the reasoning which grounded the decision, fundamentally that we are not dealing with hard and fast legal rules, as attested to by the assortment of applicable derogations and the nature of the dispute procedures, it is nonetheless essential for this to be supplemented by an understanding of some of the more openly political considerations lurking in the background.

The most significant of such considerations, that has rarely received open recognition in the largely one-sided critiques, is the place of agriculture in the GATT. Whilst it formally always applied to agricultural trade, the reality was that this sector had largely escaped GATT discipline.[65] The US was the first Contracting Party to make it clear that it was not willing to see its agricultural policies constrained.[66] A 1951 congressional amendment obliged the President to implement *ad valorem* fees up to 50 per cent or such quantitative limitations as necessary in order to prevent agricultural imports materially interfering with various domestic farm programmes. This led in the mid-1950s to the US receiving a GATT waiver, unlimited in time, from its obligations under the most-favoured-nation clause of Article I and the quantitative restrictions interdiction in Article XI.[67] Essentially, this was forced through the GATT machinery, all parties fully aware that the granting of a waiver was not going to determine whether the dictates of the amendment to an Act of Congress would be followed.[68]

[64] Rudden and Phelan (1997: 6).

[65] See Jackson (1998: 2). Agriculture was not alone in this respect, Jackson (1998: 3) also pointed to trade in textiles having escaped normal GATT discipline.

[66] Hudec (1971: 1338) noted that during the GATT's first decade flat non-compliance usually led to a waiver being sought which could be considered implicit recognition of the rule's continuing validity.

[67] There was also a less significant congressional amendment from 1951 that equally flew in the face of GATT rules and required import quotas on particular dairy products.

[68] Dam pointed out (1970: 260) that the breadth of the waiver 'coupled with the fact that the waiver was granted to the contracting party that was at one and the same time the world's largest

By the end of the 1950s most Contracting Parties were likewise unwilling to see their domestic agricultural policies hemmed in by GATT rules. The GATT certainly granted greater flexibility for agricultural products:[69] it remained, however, overly ambitious and the developed countries promoting greater self-sufficiency found themselves producing surpluses which not only led them to restrict agricultural imports, but also to 'dump' the excess on the international market with additional trade-distorting effects. The arrival of the EEC with its attachment to a burgeoning protectionist agricultural agenda consolidated the de facto demise of the GATT's rules as they pertained to agriculture.[70] Agricultural protectionism that flew in the face of the letter of the GATT was yet more rife by the time of the 1994 *Bananas* ruling (C-280/93), when the Council and Commission strenuously contested the GATT's capacity to form a general review criterion, than at the time of *International Fruit* itself. It is telling that these two seminal cases, coming at different points in the GATT's evolution, concerned challenges to EU agricultural measures. In effect these challenges were seeking to have GATT agricultural rules resurrected vis-à-vis the EU and policed by the EU Courts. This would be a one-sided resurrection of the rules, for the protectionist agenda of other powerful Contracting Parties, most prominently the US, would remain and with no need to fear domestic judicial challenge. The ECJ was certainly aware of this context and in such circumstances the rejection of the GATT as a review criterion could be expected. This, however, may be the very reason why some have criticized the ECJ, seeing it as having 'needlessly weakened the GATT'.[71] The logic seemingly being that requiring strict adherence to the rules, which the GATT system itself was incapable of generating and, indeed, can be viewed as having de facto accommodated non-compliance, would have bolstered the GATT.[72] It is difficult to believe, however, that the EU's political institutions and the Member States would have been willing to countenance such one-sided enforcement of the GATT bargain. Perhaps a waiver for the EU's

trading nation and the most vocal proponent of freer international trade, constituted a grave blow to GATT's prestige.'

[69] Thus Art XI does have an agricultural exception: Art XI:2(c). It is, however, only applicable when domestic production is likewise being restrained. The US pursued a waiver precisely because its legislation authorized restrictions regardless of restraints on domestic production.

[70] Hudec (1975).

[71] Pescatore (1986: xvii) (it is not, however, clear whether Pescatore was simply recounting the views of others).

[72] Schermers (1983) advanced similar logic.

protectionist agricultural agenda could have been sought which would at least provide some semblance of GATT conformity. In any event, it had long been emphasized that the size and weight of the project could have justified renegotiating the GATT rules to produce those that would have been negotiated in 1947 had the EU existed and that, in fact, this is essentially what happened, albeit not openly and directly.[73]

The de facto status of GATT discipline in relation to agricultural trade is also testimony to a further distinction between the GATT and the other trade-related EU Agreements, considered in Chapter III, and thus weakening the oft-heard double standards critique.[74] After all, with the other EU Agreements the EU negotiators were able formally to accommodate the increasingly protectionist Common Agricultural Policy. Even if judicial enforcement of such Agreements were to be one-sided this would not constitute a threat to the EU's emerging agricultural policy. Independently of this distinction, the other Agreements were not characterized by the same level of flexibility that had come to characterize the GATT. Whilst it can be conceded that satisfactory reasons for the different treatment meted out to different Agreements was not provided,[75] it should equally be acknowledged that the reasons are not hard to find.[76]

One final significant critique concerns the relevance of the *International Fruit* reasoning where the challenge is brought by a Member State as many had assumed a different outcome would prevail.[77] This proved to be mistaken, as illustrated with the *Germany v Council* ruling where the reasoning was considered equally applicable. This logic generated considerable

[73] Hudec (1993: 196).

[74] Authors running this critique include: Kuilwijk (1996); Petersmann (1983); Kaddous (1998 104, 389 et seq).

[75] As suggested by Griller (2000: 445).

[76] Satisfactory reasoning is not a characteristic trait of ECJ rulings which can partly be attributed to the collegiate nature of its decision-making. Arnull (2006: 10) notes that 'Sometimes disagreements may be concealed by cursory reasoning on important issues.' One suspects that *International Fruit* and its progeny are such examples. Judge Pescatore who sat for *International Fruit* and *Schlüter* and was the judge-rapporteur for the trilogy of Italian cases in 1983 (266/81 *SIOT*; 267–9/81 *SPI* and *SAMI*; 290–1/81 *Singer and Geigy*), strongly disapproved of the outcome as is evident from his published views. Indeed, in an interview he attributed his disapproval with that trilogy of cases, reiterating the *International Fruit* reasoning in challenges to national measures, as contributing to his decision to retire.

[77] Not least both a Director General of the Commission legal service and an ECJ judge: see, respectively, Ehlermann (1986: 138–9) and Everling (1986: 98). Contrast Waelbroeck (1974: 621) who thought the same conditions would apply.

criticism,[78] but as Eeckhout has argued, the success of a challenge should not depend on the route by which it is brought before the EU Courts or who is bringing the challenge.[79] If the clear implication of the *International Fruit* reasoning was that GATT rules were not sufficiently unconditional for domestic judicial enforcement then the fact that the EU measure is being challenged via a different procedure and with a different challenger should be irrelevant. A closely related point is that the GATT's dispute settlement procedures would be bypassed regardless of the procedure by which the challenge is brought and regardless of the litigant. The EU, if challenged, might defend a particular position in dispute settlement and this is imperilled if the ECJ reviews EU measures vis-à-vis its own interpretation of GATT rules. Admittedly, in the *Bananas* case a panel had already found the measures in breach of GATT rules, but the EU vetoed adoption of the ruling.[80] Some might suggest that it is the ECJ's place to make up for such shortcomings in the GATT's dispute settlement system in the interests of ensuring a more rules-based international order. However, that non-adopted panel ruling triggered negotiations within the GATT framework between the EU and various affected Contracting Parties concluded after the *Bananas* judgment.[81]

The aforementioned questions are just a handful of those that could be asked about the potential impact of judicial enforceability of GATT law. It is also essential to take a step back and consider the broader constitutional setting. The foundational court-created concepts of the EU legal order—direct effect and supremacy—were not yet a decade old at the time of *International Fruit*, and resistance in various national legal orders had already made its presence emphatically felt. At such a critical juncture in the acceptance of the foundational tenets of the EU legal order, it seems at least arguable that to accord the GATT the status of a review criterion, when one could reasonably infer that the structure of the system was unlikely to lead the courts of the automatic incorporation Member States to reach such a conclusion for domestic purposes, would have been a very

[78] Kaddous (1998: 378); Cebada Romero (2002: 421–6); Hahn and Schuster (1995); Everling (1996: 421–3); Petersmann (1995: 1134–5, 1164–70).

[79] Eeckhout (1997: 24–5; 2011: 295–6). Contrast Bronckers (2001), Ehlermann (2003: 417–18), Tancredi (2012: 250–1, 267–8).

[80] EEC—Import Regime for Bananas (*Bananas II*)—DS38/R Report of the Panel (11.2.94).

[81] See Eeckhout (1997: 31–2).

controversial result indeed.[82] Such a result could justifiably have been interpreted as binding the Member States beyond that which they had bargained for in acceding to the GATT and potentially to GATT interpretations which would not accord with the results that might be achieved through its dispute settlement procedures. This is accentuated when one considers that the European project resulted in the Member States giving up their independent regulatory capacity in the external commercial policy sphere. For the result would be that, not only had they lost such autonomous regulatory capacity, but its collective use through the EU regulatory framework would be subject to validity review as against ECJ interpretations of the dictates of GATT 'law', which the Member States would be unlikely to have contemplated in transferring the powers. In other words, Member States where the direct effect of the GATT had been rejected, or would be likely to be rejected,[83] would to all intents and purposes find that it could be judicially enforced vis-à-vis their external commercial policy, now in an EU guise, through the back door and potentially in their own courts. There seems no doubt of the court's awareness of the implications at stake,[84] and it is noteworthy that a judge who sat for the string of 1983 judgments rejecting the direct effect of GATT provisions, and EU-concluded GATT tariff protocols, stated extra-judicially that 'the Court must reflect upon the necessary acceptance of its judgments'.[85]

2.2 Exceptions to the non-judicial applicability of the GATT

That the EU Courts were not in principle willing to allow GATT norms to be used as a direct review criterion, did not mean that such norms were not judicially applicable at all. Three important ways in which they were cognizable before EU Courts, with varying degrees of legal consequence, were recognized.

[82] Hilf (1986: 157–8, 176) suggested that the courts of most of the Member States, apparently Italy aside, had rejected its direct applicability. Italy, it should also be reiterated, applies the *lex posterior* rule.

[83] To say nothing of the non-automatic treaty incorporation States.

[84] The submissions before the Court made this only too clear, those of Member States in 266/81, as recounted in the report for the hearing, were particularly illuminating.

[85] Everling (1986: 98).

2.2.1 *The consistent interpretation doctrine*

GATT norms could be employed as an aid to the interpretation of EU legislation via the doctrine usually known as consistent interpretation. Application of this interpretive principle first appeared shortly before the *International Fruit* ruling where tariff agreements concluded within the GATT framework were drawn upon in interpreting the Common Customs Tariff.[86] Reliance or attempted reliance on GATT norms when interpreting EU legislation was repeated in a growing number of rulings,[87] but it was not until 1996 that some explicit justification for this doctrine was offered.[88] In that case it was held that the primacy of EU Agreements over EU secondary legislation, the first such express judicial affirmation, meant that the latter was, as far as possible, to be interpreted consistently with the former. The logic is clear and familiar from domestic courts when dealing with international obligations: where possible superior norms are to shape the interpretation of inferior norms in order that breach of the former, and thus international responsibility, can be avoided. It, thus,

[86] 92/71 *Interfood* [1972] ECR 231, paras 6–9.

[87] Three of the cases concerned the EU-concluded GATT Customs Valuation Agreement: in 290/84 *Hauptzollamt Schweinfurt* [1985] ECR 3909 an importer and the Commission drew on that Agreement in interpreting the EU implementing Regulation which appears to have been supported by the ECJ; that same Regulation and Agreement were relied upon in 183/85 *Itzehoe* [1986] ECR 1873 with the ECJ, in contrast to the Advocate General, rejecting the Commission's proposed interpretation; in C-17/89 *Deutsche Olivetti* [1990] ECR I-2301 the ECJ drew on the Customs Valuation Agreement, as Art 2(3) of the implementing Regulation required (1224/80), in determining the customs value of goods. In 187/85 *Fediol v Commission* [1988] ECR 4155 the ECJ offered an interpretation of 'subsidy' for the anti-subsidy proceedings Regulation which it asserted was not inconsistent with the GATT and GATT Agreements. In C-105/90 *Goldstar v Council* [1992] ECR I-677, a company sought to have a Council anti-dumping duty Decision annulled by virtue of its alleged incompatibility with the Basic Anti-Dumping Regulation (ADR) interpreted in light of the ADC, and the ECJ read the relevant provision compatibly with the ADC. In C-175/87 *Matsushita* [1992] ECR I-1409, a company alleged that the ADR breached the ADC and the ECJ appeared to reject a consistent interpretation. In C-179/87 *Sharp v Council* [1992] ECR I-1409, a requested interpretation of the ADR in line with the ADC was not followed because the applicant had failed to prove that in establishing dumping the normal value and export price had been compared at different levels of trade. In C-70/94 *Werner* [1995] ECR I-3189 and C-83/94 *Leifer* [1995] ECR I-3231, an interpretation of the prohibition of export QRs in the Exports Regulation (2603/69/EEC) was proffered which was considered to be supported by Art XI GATT. Finally, in T-163/94 and T-165/94, *NTN Corporation and Koyo Seiko v Council* [1995] ECR II-1381, a Council Regulation was annulled for breach of the ADR interpreted in light of the ADC.

[88] C-61/94 *Commission v Germany* (IDA) [1996] ECR I-3989.

constitutes the mirror image of the obligation of consistent interpretation upon domestic courts and authorities in the context of Directives, which ultimately has its grounding in the primacy of EU law of which the cooperation duty in Article 4(3) TEU can be viewed as a manifestation.[89]

2.2.2 *The* Fediol *and* Nakajima *principles*

Consistent interpretation illustrated that GATT norms could indirectly influence the interpretation of EU and potentially domestic legislation,[90] but their capacity to have a more potent legal impact first became apparent with the 1989 *Fediol* judgment.[91] This case concerned a Regulation allowing EU producers to lodge complaints as to 'illicit commercial practices' by third countries.[92] A trade federation challenged a Commission Decision adopted under that Regulation. The ECJ reiterated the jurisprudence commencing with *International Fruit*, but held that this did not mean individuals could not rely on the GATT to obtain a ruling on whether the conduct in the lodged complaint constituted an 'illicit commercial practice'.[93] The Regulation defined 'illicit commercial practices' by reference to their incompatibility with international law, and referred expressly to the GATT in the preamble, and on this basis the ECJ concluded that GATT provisions formed part of the rules to which the Regulation referred. The Court reiterated the GATT's broad flexibility whilst holding that this did not prevent it from interpreting its rules with reference to a specific case to establish the compatibility of specific commercial practices.[94]

The obvious question that *Fediol* raised was whether it could be reconciled with the general rejection of the GATT as a review criterion. Eeckhout appeared to see no inconsistency. For him, judicial review of the Commission's examination of the legality of third country commercial practices, an examination required by the Regulation, would not be meaningful if GATT provisions could not be looked at.[95] That is certainly so,

[89] See Chapter I.

[90] No such assertion was made by the ECJ during the GATT era.

[91] 70/87 *Fediol v Commission* [1989] ECR1781.

[92] Known in its current format as the Trade Barriers Regulation (Regulation 3286/94).

[93] The Commission's admissibility objections included that the applicant could not call the interpretation of GATT provisions into question because they do not give rise to individual rights.

[94] The submissions that the relevant practices were GATT-incompatible were, however, rejected.

[95] Eeckhout (2011: 359).

but it does still clearly require the judicial interpretation of GATT provisions. And in *Fediol* itself this included Article XI, the very provision the ECJ had been unwilling to engage with in *International Fruit*. Clearly, then, there was not some inherent factor precluding EU judicial interpretations of GATT provisions, but then that much was already apparent by virtue of the doctrine of consistent interpretation.

The consequences of the *Fediol*-type review is, however, not to be confused with general review of measures for GATT compatibility. *Fediol* is concerned with ensuring that a Regulation is being faithfully applied and thus that the Commission's determination of illicit practices does not remain unchecked. The consequences of holding that the Commission erroneously interpreted the GATT would result in a violation of the Regulation and thus, in principle, the annulment of the Commission Decision adopted thereunder. Moreover, if the Commission considered a judicial interpretation advanced in a *Fediol* review case to sit uneasily with GATT norms, there would be no legal impediment to pursuing its interpretation with the relevant third State including via initiation of GATT dispute procedures. The consequences, however, of general review of EU measures for GATT compliance would be altogether different. In an annulment action it would lead in principle to *ex tunc* annulment.[96] This would in theory also open up the EU to damages liability. Clearly, this would interfere with the GATT's dispute settlement procedures and with the potential for a negotiated settlement. *Fediol* review provides no such interference and thus can be reconciled with the *International Fruit* logic.

A second potentially potent impact of GATT norms would, however, have very different consequences from *Fediol* review. In the *Nakajima* annulment action a company argued that the basic Council Anti-Dumping Regulation (ADR) breached the ADC.[97] The Council averred that GATT rules did not confer individual rights and it was not directly applicable, with *International Fruit* being invoked in support. Nakajima, the ECJ held, was not relying on the direct effect of the GATT provisions but rather was incidentally questioning the ADR under Article 277 TFEU. The ECJ concluded that the ADR was adopted, as evinced in its preamble, in order to comply with international obligations and that the Court is, as it had consistently held, under an obligation to ensure compliance with

[96] On the consequences of annulment generally, see Lenaerts et al (2006: 318–20).

[97] C-69/89 *Nakajima v Council* [1991] ECR I-2069.

the GATT.[98] It proceeded to review the ADR vis-à-vis the GATT Code and upheld its legality. During the GATT era two further cases arose in which *Nakajima* review was conducted with the ADR remaining unscathed.[99]

It has been suggested that the *Nakajima* principle did not compromise the logic of the *International Fruit* line of case law and that essentially the internalization of GATT duties via the ADR renders the analysis of the nature and purpose of the GATT irrelevant to its enforcement.[100] This is, however, contestable. GATT norms do not become less flexible because an EU Regulation pays them lip-service in its preamble; nor does this result in the flexibility with which the dispute settlement system imbued GATT norms—which appeared so central to the *International Fruit* reasoning—becoming any less so. The ECJ assumed the capacity to challenge EU measures adopted pursuant to the ADR—and the ADR itself—in relation to specific GATT norms.[101] Individuals and Member States could in this limited context challenge the GATT compatibility of EU measures, which constrains the capacity of the EU institutions to advance their own interpretation of particular GATT norms. Put simply, this principle did, in contrast to *Fediol* review, compromise the *International Fruit* logic.[102]

[98] In fact it had certainly not consistently held as such.

[99] C-188/88 *NMB v Commission* [1992] ECR I-1689; T-162/94 *NMB v Commission* [1996] ECR II-427. In addition, one case concerning a GATT-era Agreement, C-150/95 *Portugal v Commission (BHA)* [1997] ECR I-5863, has been viewed as an example of the *Nakajima* principle (Snyder 2003: 343–4). At issue was the Blair House Agreement (BHA) between the EU and the US limiting EU oilseed production. It was implemented via a Council Regulation amending an earlier Regulation and Portugal alleged these measures, as well as a Commission Regulation adopted thereunder, breached the BHA. The ECJ referred to an interpretation it put forth of the amended Regulation as according with the BHA, in that sense it might be viewed as applying consistent interpretation, as well as to the implementing Regulation being an accurate transposition of the BHA in a certain respect. It concluded that an examination of the legality of the contested Regulation disclosed nothing constituting an infringement of the BHA. There was, however, no reference to *Nakajima* and it is debatable whether review vis-à-vis the BHA was actually conducted.

[100] Koutrakos (2006: 262).

[101] Whilst the consequences of a successful plea of illegality only leads to inapplicability of the EU measures with respect to the parties in the proceedings, the institution that adopted the act is obliged to withdraw or amend it: see Lenaerts et al (2006: 352).

[102] Thus, for Member States it provides an opportunity to use ECJ litigation to unpick EU measures for alleged GATT non-compliance.

2.2.3 *Infringement proceedings*

A further crucial manifestation of the judicial application of GATT norms was provided when in Commission initiated infringement proceedings the ECJ engaged in a detailed interpretation of the International Dairy Arrangement (IDA) in concluding that Germany was not permitted to authorize imports at lower than the minimum price set therein.[103] Having only recently rejected Germany's attempt to have GATT norms employed as a legality criterion for the EU's bananas regime, the *IDA* ruling finding a GATT Agreement infringement by that same Member State inevitably accentuated existing criticism.[104] The appearance of double-standards was palpable: infringement proceedings, it now seemed,[105] could be employed to challenge GATT-inconsistent action by Member States, but GATT-inconsistent action of the EU institutions could not be challenged using the EU judicial architecture.[106] The flexible dispute settlement procedures applied equally to the IDA and, accordingly, it could be argued that if the dispute settlement system is a factor that envelops GATT norms and is a testament to their flexibility, it must be equally so with respect to the IDA provisions. Or is it the case, as Eeckhout rhetorically suggested, that the EU alone may opt to benefit from flexibility?[107]

The most powerful response to the prima facie compelling double-standards critique arguably flows from the consequences for the EU as a unified international actor if there were no enforcement role in such circumstances. The *IDA* case dealt with a pure EU Agreement, that is, an Agreement within the sphere of the EU's exclusive competence concluded solely by the then EC. It would be illogical if Member States could chart separate courses with respect to such Agreements. It thus illustrates a dimension of federalization in EU external relations law: federal-type legal systems will usually allow for the policing of sub-unit compliance with the international treaty obligations assumed by the centre; for the alternative would leave the sub-units in a position to violate obligations

[103] C-61/94 *Commission v Germany (IDA)* [1996] ECR I-3989. This was also held to breach an EU Regulation on inward processing relief.

[104] See eg Cebada Romero (2002: 425–6).

[105] There might be an argument that they could not unless it was a GATT-concluded agreement like the IDA.

[106] Subject to the *Nakajima* and *Fediol* principles.

[107] (1998: 565).

assumed by the centre with the latter powerless to respond, hardly a conducive scenario for treaty negotiations. Critics of where the *IDA* case left matters could freely concede this; after all, the EU Treaty was drafted in a fashion that yields this centre versus constituent-units enforcement tool with ease via the combined reading of Articles 216(2) and 258 TFEU. But they might argue that the EU Treaty equally yields a tool of constituent-unit versus centre enforcement via a reading of Articles 216(2) and 263 TFEU. This logic can be bolstered by underlining that the EU's component States remain sovereign entities with treaty-making power on the international stage, unlike the constituent units of federal legal orders, and frequently are themselves signatories to EU Agreements. One response is that we are not dealing with comparable situations. In rejecting the GATT's capacity to be employed as a direct review criterion of EU action, we are concerned with enforcing EU obligations vis-à-vis the GATT, whilst in *IDA* we are concerned with enforcing Member State obligations vis-à-vis the EU.[108] Where it is not a pure EU Agreement, unlike in *IDA*, one could equally suggest it would constitute indirect enforcement of Member State obligations in relation to the GATT. Ultimately, it is necessary to engage with whether there is a case for the EU to be allowed to profit from GATT flexibility in a manner that Member States acting individually may not. It is suggested that there is such a case. There is no inconsistency between:

1. precluding Member States from using GATT norms enforced by the ECJ to undo political agreement reached by majority in the Council; and
2. permitting the Commission to enforce GATT norms against a recalcitrant Member State.

The political agreement reached in the Council that the outvoted Member State (Germany) challenged in the *Bananas* litigation formed the basis for negotiations with the affected GATT Contracting Parties; the temporary legal resolution of the dispute employing the GATT framework would have been jeopardized were outcome 1 different. Outcome 2, on the other hand, ensures that the EU is able to act as a unified actor on the international stage. The illogical alternative would permit Member States to advance

[108] This argument was advanced by Bourgeois (2000: 112–13) and reiterated by Antoniadis (2007: 67–8). The EU was never a GATT member, as contrasted with being a party to certain GATT Agreements, so seeking to enforce EU obligations vis-à-vis the GATT can be about enforcing Member State obligations, the signatories, vis-à-vis the GATT albeit the allegedly incompatible regulatory output will usually stem from the EU law-making process.

conflicting positions on the interpretation of GATT Agreements; conflicting positions which would likely have resulted in initiation of GATT dispute procedures against the EU.[109] And, of course, the Commission would represent the EU in such disputes and should therefore be able to advance a common EU position.[110] Thus, one clear benefit of allowing contrasting positions for GATT interpretations to be resolved internally, as in *IDA*, is that reliance need not be placed on third party-initiated dispute procedures to resolve conflicting internal EU interpretations. Admittedly, this might not seem fair on the one or more Member States that do not agree with the reading advanced by the Commission or the ECJ reading, should that follow as in *IDA* itself, but ultimately it remained theoretically possible for a GATT panel to have endorsed a different reading of the relevant GATT obligations. Moreover, the *IDA* outcome ensured Article 216(2) TFEU was given effect in relation to Member States (as was the well-known mantra that EU Agreements are an integral part of EU law). In this sense, some might view the *IDA* outcome as preferable to insisting on ostensible parity whereby neither Member States nor EU institutions can invoke the GATT as a review criterion for EU or national action.

3. WTO Agreements Before the EU Courts

On 1 January 1995 the World Trade Organization and its 'covered agreements' including the provisions of the GATT 1947, now renamed the GATT 1994, came into force for the EU and its Member States. The new regime was considerably more 'rules-oriented'[111] than its predecessor. The new dispute settlement system, enshrined in the Dispute Settlement Understanding (DSU), was considered to be the 'jewel in the crown' of the transformed international trading order.[112] Crucially, the losing party to a dispute could no longer block the adoption of a negative report. And a new two-tier system was created with panels as the first tier and a World Trade

[109] GATT Contracting Parties would be able to attack the non-uniformity that would result if Member States could track their own course.

[110] Albeit one with which not all Member States are content, as is the corollary of having majority voting.

[111] Jackson (1997).

[112] Van den Bossche (2008: 93).

Court[113]—its official title is the Appellate Body—constituting a new second tier. The safeguards regime was also considerably strengthened. These changes unsurprisingly led many to consider that the *International Fruit* reasoning could no longer stand in the increasingly legalized WTO era.

3.1 The legal effect of the WTO per se in the EU legal order

3.1.1 *The principled stance against review vis-à-vis the WTO: the* Portuguese Textiles *reasoning*

No sooner had the WTO come into force, than the European Court docket began to accumulate challenges invoking WTO Agreements. But in a number of judgments the EU Courts avoided this controversial issue,[114] until finally addressing it head-on in the *Portuguese Textiles* judgment some weeks short of the fifth anniversary of the WTO's entry into force.[115]

[113] Weiler (2001b: 11–12) refers to it as a court in all but name, whilst expressing his preference for the name World Trade Court.

[114] The first was an interim measures application seeking damages and the suspension of the leg-hold traps Regulation which allegedly breached Art XI GATT; the Commission and Council contested the argument that the WTO era altered the position on reviewability: T-228/95 R *Lehrfreund Ltd v Council and Commission* [1996] ECR II-111. The ECJ refused to consider the compatibility of a Commission Decision and a Council Directive vis-à-vis the WTO's Agreement on the Application of Sanitary and Phytosanitary Measures (SPS Agreement) because the national court itself, as contrasted with the individual litigants, had not raised the issue: C-183/95 *Affish* [1997] ECR I-4315 and C-106/97 *Dutch Antillian Dairy Industry Inc* [1999] ECR I-5983; the EU bananas regime's compliance with GATT 1994 was avoided because the bananas at issue came from Ecuador which had not initially been a Contracting Party: C-364/95 and C-365/95 *T. Port III* [1998] ECR I-1023; in C-53/96 *Hermès* [1998] ECR I-3603 the direct effect of the Agreement on Trade-Related Aspects of Intellectual Property Rights (TRIPs Agreement) was raised, but it was not considered necessary to address the issue as it was not raised by the national court; the GC also found the Anti-Dumping Agreement (ADA)—invoked in an annulment action against a Council Regulation—not to be applicable temporally to a dispute: T-48/96 *Acme Industry v Council* [1999] ECR II-3089; the ECJ ignored that the WTO era had commenced when it rejected a Member State allegation that a Council Regulation breached GATT 1994 while reiterating the *Bananas* holding that it was only in the *Nakajima* and *Fediol* contexts that EU rules were reviewable: C-352/96 *Italy v Council (Rice Tariffs)* [1998] ECR I-6937; the UK's attempt to contest a reading of the Plant Protection Products Directive as incompatible with the Agreement on Technical Barriers to Trade (TBT Agreement) was rejected on the basis that the reading was neither discriminatory nor did it create an unnecessary barrier to international trade: C-100/96 *The Queen v MAFF, ex parte British Agrochemicals Association Ltd* [1999] ECR I-1499.

[115] C-149/96 *Portugal v Council (Portuguese Textiles)* [1999] ECR I-8395.

Portugal brought annulment proceedings against a Council Decision concluding trade in textiles agreements, alleging it breached GATT 1994 and the Agreements on Textiles and Import Licensing. The Full Court commenced, invoking *Kupferberg* in support, by looking at whether the WTO Agreements determined the legal means of ensuring they were applied in good faith domestically and concluded that they did not. The ECJ acknowledged the Portuguese submission that the WTO differed significantly from the GATT 1947, but underscored the scope for negotiation provided for and invoked various provisions of the DSU in support. Attention was drawn to the fact that the DSU allowed for compensation, and provided for the means by which the party invoking the dispute procedures could trigger negotiations leading to mutually acceptable compensation, as a temporary measure in the event that Dispute Settlement Body (DSB) rulings and recommendations were not implemented within the reasonably allotted period of time. It concluded that to require judicial organs to refrain from applying WTO-incompatible domestic law would deprive the legislative or executive organs of the Contracting Parties of this possibility of entering, even temporarily, negotiated arrangements.

But matters were not left with this conclusion alone. The ECJ turned more specifically to the WTO's application in the EU and developed a reciprocity argument against its general capacity to form a review criterion for EU measures. The WTO like its predecessor was considered, the preamble cited in support, to be founded on negotiations with a view to reciprocal and mutually advantageous arrangements. This distinguished it from Agreements introducing a certain asymmetry of obligations, or creating special relations of integration with the EU, such as the Agreement interpreted in *Kupferberg*. This was followed by reference to the WTO's subject matter and purpose having led some of the EU's most important commercial partners to conclude that it is not a judicial review criteria for domestic law. This, the ECJ told us, consistently with *Kupferberg*, was not in itself such as to constitute a lack of implementation reciprocity, but when added to the aforementioned distinction between the WTO and EU Agreements it may lead to disuniform WTO application. And, thus, for the EU judicature to ensure EU compliance with WTO rules would deprive the EU legislative or executive organs of the scope for manoeuvre enjoyed by their trading partner counterparts. The interpretation reached—that WTO rules are not amongst those used to review EU measures—was considered to correspond to the preamble in the Concluding Decision. And, finally, applicability of the *Fediol* and *Nakajima* principles in the

WTO era was affirmed, albeit they were considered inapplicable on the facts.

The *Portuguese Textiles* holding was reiterated in a number of cases pending at the time of that ruling which involved several different WTO Agreements in both preliminary rulings and annulment actions and were marked by powerful institutional and Member State submissions against direct effect.[116] One deserves special mention. A Dutch annulment action against the Biotech Directive included pleas that it breached the TRIPs and TBT Agreements.[117] The Council, European Parliament, and Commission, argued against review vis-à-vis the WTO Agreements. And it seemed the Court would follow suit for it commenced by duly reiterating *Portuguese Textiles*. However, it went on to assert that the 'plea should be understood as being directed, not so much at a direct breach by the EU of its international obligations, as at an obligation imposed on the Member States by the Directive to breach their own obligations under international law,

[116] In C-300 & 392/98 *Christian Dior* [2000] ECR I-11307 the Commission, the Council, and various Member States successfully argued against the direct effect of TRIPs in a ruling relying on *Portuguese Textiles* that was later reiterated by the Full Court in line with submissions from the Council, Commission, and several Member States in C-89/99 *Groeneveld* [2001] ECR I-5851. In C-307/99 OGT *Fruchthandelsgesellschaft* [2001] ECR I-3159 a German court contested the EU's bananas regime in light of GATT 1994. Both the Commission and Council argued against individual reliance on such provisions and the ECJ reiterated *Portuguese Textiles* and rejected the applicability of *Nakajima* and *Fediol*. In two challenges to a Council Regulation allegedly breaching the Safeguards Agreement, the Netherlands Antilles failed to surmount the individual concern test (C-452/98 *Nederlandse Antillen v Council* [2001] ECR I-8973), whilst the Netherlands claimed, contrary to the views of the Council, Commission, and three intervening Member States, that the Agreement's provision was directly effective leading the ECJ to reiterate *Portuguese Textiles* and find *Nakajima* and *Fediol* inapplicable (C-301/97 *Netherlands v Council* [2001] ECR I-8853). In addition, four cases avoided engagement with pleas of WTO breaches: a plea that a Commission Regulation breached the Safeguards Agreement, Art XIII:2(c) GATT 1994, and Art 216(2) TFEU was not addressed as the Regulations were annulled on other grounds in T-32/98 and T-41/98 *Netherlands Antilles v Commission* [2000] ECR II-201 (but set aside due to the Netherlands Antilles not having standing: C-142/00 P *Commission v Netherlands Antilles* [2003] ECR I-3483); in C-147/96 *Netherlands v Commission* [2000] ECR I-4723 an inadmissibility objection to a Dutch annulment action against a Commission letter allegedly breaching the SPS Agreement because the letter produced no binding legal effects was accepted; in T-7/99 *Medici Grimm v Council* [2000] ECR II-2671 a Council Regulation was annulled without expressly addressing the ADA breach plea; in C-248/99 P *France v Monsanto and Commission* [2002] ECR I-1 an SPS Agreement breach plea was rejected as unfounded as in reality it was not directed at the challenged Commission decision.

[117] C-377/98 *Netherlands v Parliament and Council (Biotech)* [2001] ECR I-7079.

while the Directive itself claims not to affect those obligations.'[118] The Court then conducted the compatibility review as against the TRIPs and TBT Agreements, from which the Directive emerged unscathed. How this can be reconciled with the *Portuguese Textiles* holding, that it is only in the *Nakajima* and *Fediol* context that review is possible, was left unexplained. The reasoning has been referred to as 'elliptical',[119] but impenetrable is more appropriate. Further clarification of that reasoning has never appeared and the case remains an aberration.

Despite the stance adopted in *Portuguese Textiles* and its reiteration in most of the then pending cases, litigants continued with WTO-based challenges to EU action. Between the GC and the ECJ 15 such cases were dispensed with generally either on procedural grounds or by reiterating the *Portuguese Textiles* reasoning, usually in line with institutional and Member State submissions.[120]

[118] Paragraph 55. Article 1(2) of the Directive expressly stated that it was without prejudice to the Member States' Treaty obligations, pointing specifically to TRIPs and the Convention on Biological Diversity.

[119] Eeckhout (2011: 298).

[120] A preliminary ruling rejected the alleged incompatibility with the TBT Agreement of a Council Regulation by reiterating *Portuguese Textiles* in line with the submissions of the Council, Commission, the sole intervening Member State, and the Advocate General: C-27/00 & 122/00 *Omega Air* [2002] ECR I-2569. A preliminary ruling rejected a challenge to an EU Directive allegedly breaching TRIPs with *Portuguese Textiles* reiterated in line with the submissions of the Parliament, Council, Commission, and five Member States, and with neither, as in *Omega Air*, the *Nakajima* nor *Fediol* principles considered applicable: C-491/01 *British American Tobacco* [2002] ECR I-11453. A preliminary ruling rejected an alleged Commission breach of Art VII GATT 1994 and the Agreement on its implementation because of no demonstration of incompatibility: C-422/00 *Capespan* [2003] ECR I-597. In rejecting annulment and damages actions against two Commission Regulations as allegedly breaching the Safeguards Agreement, *Portuguese Textiles* was reiterated and the *Nakajima* and *Fediol* principles were found inapplicable: see respectively Joined Cases T-332/00 & T-350/00 *Rica Foods v Commission* [2002] ECR II-4755, and Joined Cases T-94/00, T-111/00 & T-159/00 *Rica Foods v Commission* [2002] ECR II-4677 (both upheld on appeal C-40/03 P *Rica Foods v Commission* [2005] ECR I-681 and C-41/03 P *Rica Foods v Commission* [2005] ECR I-6875). An appeal challenging the TRIPs compatibility of a decision of the Office for Harmonization in the Internal Market (OHIM) saw *Portuguese Textiles* reiterated: C-238/06 P *Develey v OHIM* [2007] ECR I-9375. The GC rejected an alleged WTO breach, in a bananas damages plea, due to the late stage at which it was introduced while reiterating, in line with Council and Commission submissions, that the WTO did not create domestically judicially enforceable rights nor did infringement give rise to EU non-contractual liability: T-56/00 *Dole v Council and Commission* [2003] ECR II-57. A damages action for compensation allegedly suffered as a result of Commission Decisions relied on an alleged SPS Agreement breach and was rejected as manifestly inadmissible due to a failure to demonstrate the damages alleged: T-4/04 *Achaiber Sing v Commission* [2006] ECR II-41. An alleged TRIPs breach was classified as a new inadmissible plea, although the GC nonetheless opined that the EU Regulation was not in tension with

3.1.2 *Engaging with the* Portuguese Textiles *reasoning*

No sooner was the ink dry on the *Portuguese Textiles* ruling than the academic criticism came flooding in.[121] This subsection evaluates and builds upon the reasoning advanced and, in doing so, engages with common strands of criticism.

The ECJ's starting point was to apply the test set in *Kupferberg* of only determining an Agreement's internal legal effect where that question was not resolved by the Agreement itself. It was in this first step of the analysis that various DSU provisions were directly invoked. What then of this first stage of analysis? Would requiring judicial organs to refrain from applying WTO-inconsistent rules deprive legislative or executive organs of their DSU-enshrined possibility of entering into negotiated arrangements?

The *Portuguese Textiles* ruling took place against a backdrop of controversy in WTO circles as to whether there is an obligation to withdraw an

that Agreement: T-212/02 *Commune de Champagne v Council and Commission* [2007] ECR II-2017. An annulment action against a Commission Regulation allegedly running counter to TRIPs saw the Commission's inadmissibility objection on standing grounds upheld: T-170/04 *FederDoc v Commission* [2005] ECR II-2503. In T-123/00 *Thomae v Commission* [2002] ECR II-5193 the GC annulled a contested Decision without engaging with the alleged TRIPs infringement by the European Agency for the Evaluation of Medicinal Products. In C-244/03 *France v Parliament and Council* [2005] ECR I-4021 the ECJ rejected as inadmissible partial annulment of the Cosmetics Directive in a case where France alleged its incompatibility with Art III:4 GATT 1994. In two Italian court references concerned with the compatibility of an EU–Hungary Wine Agreement and a related EU Regulation with inter alia the TRIPs Agreement, the interpretation of TRIPs essentially confirmed the validity of EU action: C-347/03 *ERSA* [2005] ECR I-3785, C-231/04 *Confcooperative* [2006] ECR I-61. In an unsuccessful patent infringements proceedings (inadmissible) and damages action (manifestly lacking foundation in law) against the ECB, the applicant appeared to allege a TRIPs breach: T-295/05 *Document Security Systems v ECB* [2007] ECR II-2835.

[121] Examples include: Bronckers (2001) (at least where Member States bring the challenge); Cebada Romero (2002: 467 et seq); Griller (2000); Van den Broek (2001); Schmid (2001); Uerpmann-Wittzack (2003); Zonnekeyn (2000); Lavranos (2004: 36–40). In the case of Petersmann, a sustained critic of the GATT-era jurisprudence, the criticism commenced with a brief reference (2000a: 1380–1) and has been reiterated and developed in numerous pieces since, eg (2001), (2002), (2007), (2011). Defences were initially few and far between. The first came from the Commission's principal legal adviser who had responsibility for the external relations team (Rosas (2000a)). A sustained defence emerged with Eeckhout's contribution (2002) largely reproduced in his external relations monograph (2004, 2011). A further external relations monograph emerged which also provided a reasoned defence (Koutrakos (2006)). Thus, in stark contrast to the GATT era, the WTO-era debate saw established EU law scholars providing carefully reasoned defences of the ECJ's stance.

incompatible measure. Views were initially expressed on both sides,[122] and the debate has continued since.[123] What rapidly became the most-cited argument in the debate was that of an eminent GATT and WTO scholar responding to the argument that there was no such obligation.[124] Following a careful analysis of the relevant DSU and WTO provisions, Jackson concludes that there is overwhelming support for the view that the result of an adopted dispute settlement report 'that rules that the laws or other measures of a respondent nation are inconsistent with its obligations is to create an international law obligation to comply with that report…'.[125] This conclusion was further reinforced by both the text, object and purpose, context, and practice of the GATT and WTO over more than five decades and also by an analysis of the central policy goals of the dispute settlement system. His prediction that if the issue came before the Appellate Body it would likely rule that there is an international law obligation to carry out those reports remains untested.

The Jackson view is significant because it is frequently cited to discredit the *Portuguese Textiles* reasoning.[126] In actual fact, however, the Jackson view does nothing to discredit the reasoning advanced on this point. Even a cursory glance at the DSU provisions is clear testimony to them having been faithfully recited.[127] This is not, one must add, equivalent to the GATT era where the ECJ could legitimately be criticized for simply reciting several sentences from a text that had come to bear little resemblance to

[122] Bello (1996), and Reiff and Forestal (1998) that there was no binding obligation to withdraw, whilst Jackson (1997) advanced the opposing view.

[123] Those arguing against an obligation for withdrawal include Sykes (2000) and Schwartz and Sykes (2002). Pauwelyn (2000: 340) (considers the Jackson view to be correct); see also Pauwelyn (2003a: 948) (in support of the Jackson view that compensation and suspension of concessions cannot close or settle a case but also suggesting that a bilateral settlement can close a case); Carmody (2002: 319) (appears to support the Jackson approach); Fukunaga (2006: 395–8) (arguing for obligation and against efficient breach theory); Cottier and Schefer (1998: 85) (supporting obligation); Footer (2007: 79) (supporting the Jackson line); Trachtman (2007) (suggesting though the issue is not free from doubt, the Jackson view is probably better); Collins (2009: 227) (suggests it is arguable that DSU contemplates remedies other than strict compliance).

[124] Jackson (2004) (responding in particular to Schwartz and Sykes (2002) who expressly contest what they refer to as the Jackson view (1997)).

[125] Jackson (2004: 123).

[126] Examples include: Desmedt (2000: 99–100); Griller (2000: 453); Van den Broek (2001: 432–4); Zonnekeyn (2000: 300–2); Uerpmann-Wittzack (2009: 143) (does not cite Jackson but does cite the same view including a reference to Pauwelyn (2000) who advances the Jackson argument).

[127] Curiously the ECJ did not refer to the 'usually' in Art 3.7 DSU, see para 38.

the reality of the GATT dispute settlement system. The DSU text was the product of careful and painstaking negotiations and clearly does provide for negotiated compensation as at least a potential[128] temporary alternative to full implementation of a DSB recommendation. Jackson and those subscribing to this position of course recognize this as, indeed, they must given that this is what the text of the DSU provides. In fact, Jackson situates this temporary DSU additional time within the context of the need for an escape valve to enable losing governments to improve the management of a politically thorny situation in their domestic legal and governmental context.[129] What Jackson contested was the notion that compensation (or suspension of concessions) can constitute permanent resolution of a dispute as the advocates of the efficient breach reading of the DSU suggest.[130] But there is no inconsistency between this reading and that proposed by the ECJ. Indeed, the Court itself was at pains to reiterate the DSU text on the temporary nature of compensation and this not being preferable to full implementation. No view was expressed on the legal obligation debate, faithful recitation of the DSU text aside, but then it is not the ECJ's place to do so when there is a quasi-judicial mechanism established for interpreting WTO law.[131] It should, nevertheless, be noted that the Jackson view is more nuanced than one oft-cited commentary on *Portuguese Textiles* which considers there to be an unconditional obligation to comply with dispute settlement decisions and that there is no authorization to depart even on a temporary basis.[132] This need not concern us here because if intended in such uncompromising terms it flies in the face of a text, and the views of mainstream WTO scholarship advancing the Jackson line, which clearly permits compensation in lieu, at least temporarily, of implementation of the

[128] The winning party must request negotiations to this effect: see Palmeter and Mavroidis (2004: 265–6).

[129] (2004: 122).

[130] eg Sykes (2000); Schwartz and Sykes (2002).

[131] An authoritative interpretation can be provided by the Members via Art IX:2 WTO Agreement.

[132] Griller (2000), at eg p 450, 'the alleged lack of a categorical obligation from a WTO Dispute Settlement Decision'; p 451 'the binding force of panel and Appellate Body rulings is unconditional, and . . . there is no authorisation to depart from such findings, not even on a temporary basis'; p 452 'they [compensation and retaliation] do not offer an alternative to compliance'; p 454 'the DSU requires . . . unconditional compliance with dispute settlement decisions'.

ruling.[133] For similar reasons, suggestions that the ECJ ignored the legally binding effect of WTO law and the WTO obligation to terminate illegal measures by misinterpreting the DSU do not withstand scrutiny.[134]

The DSU was only expressly cited in ascertaining whether the WTO Agreements determine the legal means by which their good-faith application must be domestically ensured. The conclusion that they do not cannot be faulted, and the ECJ's critics concede this.[135] This is not surprising, for the WTO is not some rare species of multilateral treaty which seeks expressly to require its wholesale direct domestic judicial enforcement.[136] The vast number of initial Contracting Parties, and thus the great variety of domestic treaty-implementation approaches among the initial Contracting Parties, is a factor that made it unlikely that it would be drafted in a manner elucidating the domestic effect it is to have.[137] And certainly there is little danger that a DSB ruling would be adopted reaching a conclusion comparable to that in *Van Gend en Loos*, not least as this would fly in the face of Article 3.2 DSU which provides that DSB rulings cannot add to the rights and obligations provided in the WTO.[138]

Where the critics find fault is in how the determination of the WTO's internal EU legal effect was dealt with. And there are two issues that were

[133] Griller suggests (2000: 453) there is something amiss in the ECJ insinuating that there is a power to negotiate the temporary replacement of compliance by compensation. There is, however, no 'insinuating'. Rather, this is expressly stated in the DSU text, and repeated by the ECJ and leading WTO scholars. How can it not be the case that this is in lieu of implementation for there would be no need for compensation to be negotiated if you have withdrawn or amended the incompatible measure? They are, in other words, mutually exclusive options. If you have removed the incompatible measure upon culmination of the reasonable period of time (RPT) there is no need for a compensation arrangement.

[134] See for that assertion, Petersmann (2001: 83). It is worth contrasting the early observation of a prominent international law scholar: 'according to the . . . DSU . . . a breach of a GATT rule does not entail a mechanical duty to undo an unlawful act' (Tomuschat (1999: 366)).

[135] eg Griller (2000: 454).

[136] Certain of the WTO Agreements do require domestic judicial enforcement in at least an indirect fashion vis-à-vis domestic legislative implementation. Thus, the ADA clearly anticipates legislative implementation of its provisions and judicial review of administrative action imposing anti-dumping duties (Arts 13 and 18.4); as does the Subsidies and Countervailing Measures Agreement with respect to countervailing duties (Arts 23 and 32.5). The TRIPs Agreement requires civil judicial enforcement of IP rights (Art 42). The Customs Valuation Agreement requires judicial appeal of a customs valuation determination (Art 11).

[137] A Swiss proposal to insert a provision providing for its direct effect was quickly rejected: Kuijper (1995a: 226).

[138] A panel ruling shortly after the *Portuguese Textiles* ruling reads like the mirror image to *Van Gend en Loos*: *United States—ss 301–310 of the Trade Act of 1974* (WT/DS152/R). It is surely no coincidence that one of the panellists was the eminent EU scholar, JHH Weiler.

linked in reaching the conclusion that, subject to the *Fediol* and *Nakajima* principles, review vis-à-vis WTO norms was not possible. It commenced by providing a response that was aimed, it seemed, both at the double-standards critique that had dogged its GATT-era jurisprudence, and at pre-empting or minimizing its re-emergence in the WTO era. But this attempt to distinguish between Agreements, introducing an asymmetry of obligations or creating special relations of integration as in *Kupferberg*, and the WTO and GATT, as founded on negotiations with a view to reciprocal and mutually advantageous arrangements, was quickly and rightly criticized.[139] After all, both the GATT and WTO are asymmetrical in terms of how developing countries are treated.[140] The ECJ went on, however, to introduce its judicial reciprocity argument[141] and the scope for manoeuvre enjoyed by the EU's counterparts. This was clearly the core argument and it is clouded by attempting to distinguish the WTO from other Agreements based on the former being premised on reciprocal and mutually advantageous arrangements.

The WTO is clearly distinguishable from other Agreements by virtue of its idiosyncratic dispute settlement system,[142] and invoking the GATT/WTO preambular sentence is not only superfluous,[143] but also opens the reasoning up to unnecessary criticism when the core of the argument is sound. As well as a way to respond to double-standards criticism, it also seemed to serve a further function, namely, to evade the constraint imposed by the *Kupferberg* holding that non-judicial application by other parties is *not in itself* such as to constitute a lack of implementation reciprocity, for the ECJ reiterated the distinction it drew between types of Agreement in concluding that here, in contrast to *Kupferberg*, it might lead to disuniform WTO application. Again, this was unnecessary because *Kupferberg* supplied the 'not in itself' rider to implementation reciprocity which could be satisfied by the distinctive characteristics of the dispute system. Indeed, the *Portuguese Textiles* judgment would ultimately have been more coherent with a succinct first part and a second part which employs and builds upon the distinctive characteristics of the dispute settlement system alone in rejecting WTO norms as a general review criterion; rather than a second

139 Peers (2001a: 120–1); Eeckhout (2002: 95). More recently Maresceau (2006: 259).

140 See generally chapter 15 of Trebilcock and Howse (2005).

141 In doing so the ECJ repeated the distinction it had drawn between the WTO and other agreements (para 45).

142 For a different attempt at emphasizing its distinctive character, see Koutrakos (2006: 278).

143 Rosas (2000a: 813) also considered this unnecessary.

part that seeks to combine arguments and is clearly building on the conclusions of the DSU analysis in the first part, albeit without any cross-referencing.

Why, then, does the dispute settlement system pose a central obstacle to the use of the WTO as a general review criterion? The germ of the point is advanced but arguably, to be grasped, a combined reading of the part one and two reasoning is necessary. The part one reasoning, read alone, points to the absence of judicial reciprocity and the scope for manoeuvre for legislative and executive organs and links this to the preambular sentence in the WTO. What makes for more convincing reasoning is to underscore that, as part one concludes, this room for manoeuvre is DSU-enshrined. That is to say, what other Contracting Parties have concluded as to judicial application is not in itself significant,[144] it becomes significant when allied to the nature of the Agreements.[145] The ECJ alluded to this,[146] but it is left undeveloped and appears to be linked to the preambular sentence, this point coming in the paragraph directly following the questionable attempt at distinguishing types of Agreement. The point should instead be linked directly not to the subject matter of the Agreements, but rather to the Treaty-enshrined room for manoeuvre. In other words, it is not because commercially important Contracting Parties reject domestic judicial application, that the ECJ's conclusion is legally persuasive, nor does it become more so through reference to the preambular sentence. Such a conclusion merely gives undeserved credence to allegations that the judgment was politically motivated.[147] To the contrary, it is precisely because the DSU is framed in the manner that it is, that these allegations are unconvincing; likewise for the suggestion that whichever way the case was decided was an issue of judicial policy-making with formal legal reasoning only serving to

[144] At the time of the judgment what they had indeed concluded may not have been completely clear, but the US made its position clear in its legislation implementing the WTO Agreements (Leebron 1997).

[145] And, indeed, it is the nature of the Agreements that is likely to lead them to such conclusions.

[146] Paragraph 43.

[147] Accusations of this nature have come from Zonnekeyn (2000); Van den Broek (2001); AG Colomer in C-431/05 *Merck*, para 79, below; Petersmann (2001) (uses the language of 'judicial protectionism'). Peers refers to its 'political argument' (2001a: 122). Where a reciprocity condition is present in a constitutional reception norm for treaties, as with art 55 of the French Constitution, matters are different for there such a conclusion based on the practice elsewhere is legally defensible (though in France that provision has become a dead letter).

dress up and disguise the judicial decision.[148] For if we accept that the treaty text does provide for alternatives to immediate full implementation, as it has been submitted we must, then perfectly coherent legal reasoning is being advanced. The reasoning, indeed, need not have rested there. Disputes can also temporarily be resolved via counter-measures.[149] And the DSU expressly permits mutually satisfactory solutions over withdrawal of incompatible measures, also left unmentioned by the ECJ.[150]

It accordingly defies legal (rather than simply political) logic for the Contracting Parties to go to great lengths to put in place a dispute settlement regime that allows for various temporary, and a permanent, post-DSB decision mechanism for closing a dispute in the form of a mutually satisfactory solution, if these options are in practical terms to be ruled out because traders and the EU's Member States have been given a powerful domestic tool to seek compliance. And this would be further complicated because the normal consequences of a successful challenge to an EU measure under Articles 263 and 267 is *ex tunc* annulment. Whilst judgments could be issued that operate prospectively,[151] this barely begins to address the tensions with the DSU remedial framework. It preserves neither the aforementioned temporary (compensation or retaliation), nor permanent (mutually satisfactory solution), means of dispute closure, that could follow from an adverse DSB ruling. Nor does it preserve the RPT for implementation that the DSU permits where immediate compliance is 'impracticable'.[152] The DSU contracts out of general international law, it is *lex specialis* in this respect, and sets forth its own system of remedies.[153] Thus *restitutio in integrum* is not the objective of the WTO's dispute settlement system and remedies are, in principle prospective.[154] The WTO dispute settlement system thus creates a very different remedial system to that of other treaties, not least those

[148] Eeckhout (2004: 306).

[149] First acknowledged in C-27/00 & 122/00 *Omega Air*, para 89.

[150] See also Rosas (2000a: 809).

[151] Eeckhout (1997: 54); Bourgeois (2000: 121).

[152] Article 21.3. This is a period which can be set in various ways (Art 21.3(a)–(c)), including via arbitration and via negotiations between the implementing member and the complaining party: see Lester and Mercurio (2008: 162); Van den Bossche (2008: 298). Indeed, parties are also permitted mutually to agree extensions to the reasonable implementation period: see eg Davey (2006: 13).

[153] For detailed coverage on the extent of contracting out, see Pauwelyn (2003b: 218–36), and Gomula (2010).

[154] See generally Trachtman (2007).

where immediate compliance with rulings is sought and damages are retrospective.

Whilst the importance accorded to negotiation between the parties was emphasized, it has been shown that greater textual support could have been marshalled in support of the post-DSB decision scope for manoeuvre and negotiation. Perhaps more striking was the absence of any express reference to the pre-DSB decision, DSU-enshrined, room for manoeuvre and negotiation that could be invoked as legal argumentation against general domestic judicial enforceability of WTO norms. This was surprising because the challenge in *Portuguese Textiles* was not to an EU measure subject to an adverse DSB ruling. Pre-DSB decision, DSU-enshrined, room for manoeuvre that domestic judicial enforceability interferes with can clearly be identified. Dispute settlement proceedings commence with consultations with a view to reaching a mutually agreed solution. And well over half of initiated consultations do not lead to a DSB decision: mutually agreed solutions constitute a large percentage of the disputes that do not lead to rulings, other forms of settlement have also emerged and cases have also been dropped.[155] Disputes can be settled at many stages prior to adoption of a DSB decision.[156] Article 3.7 DSU itself expresses a clear preference for mutually agreed solutions between the parties over solutions reached through adjudication.[157] Clearly, domestic judicial enforcement that can result in *ex tunc* annulment would leave little scope to pursue the DSU-enshrined preference for mutually agreed solutions even prior to adoption of reports.

If all this pre- and post-DSB decision room for manoeuvre does indeed exist, which admittedly some of the critics seem loath to accept in the post-DSB decision context, then what other lines of criticism are advanced? Perhaps the most common is to emphasize that the judicial reasoning flew in the face of Article 216(2) TFEU and, albeit less frequently, the case law on EU Agreements forming an integral part of EU law.[158] Even if Article 216(2) was considered to provide a basis for resolving problems as to the internal effect of EU Agreements, there is no reason why it should be

[155] Davey (2005: 45–8). See more recently Van den Bossche (2008: 169, 173).

[156] Examples given by Davey (2005) include following panel establishment, on the eve of first submissions or even on the eve of a ruling.

[157] Van den Bossche (2008: 173, 269).

[158] Examples include Griller (2000: 472); Petersmann (2001: 83); Van den Broek (2001: 439) (arguing that Art 216(2) and the *Haegeman–Kupferberg* line of case law are being deprived of effect); Uerpmann-Wittzack (2009: 138, 147).

employed to give the substantive provisions a legal effect in tension with the procedural provisions concerning dispute settlement. Cases like *Haegeman*, cited by the critics, mean that the DSU provisions, rather than just the substantive provisions as they might have it, are also part of EU law.[159] Not employing a substantive WTO provision, for example Article III GATT 1994, in reviewing an EU measure does not deprive the WTO's DSU provisions of their effect nor does it preclude the relevant substantive provision of ultimately being given legal effect, for example potentially via triggering of dispute procedures. The contrary, of course, has the opposite effect for it would deprive the DSU provisions of their intended legal effect or at least the effect that the EU's political institutions had expected. In short, whilst Article 216(2) and case law are invoked by the critics, they can also be invoked to support the *Portuguese Textiles* reasoning.

A further argument sometimes invoked in support of the rejection of general legality review is the absence of a preliminary ruling procedure enabling the Appellate Body to provide interpretations of WTO norms.[160] Such arguments can appear to have more of an explicitly policy-based logic than a strictly legal logic. However, they can be tied back directly to the WTO having been endowed with a sophisticated dispute settlement system. So too, it might be responded, has the ECHR and that has never proved a convincing argument against its domestic judicial enforceability in automatic incorporation legal orders. That is certainly so, but human rights treaties start from a fundamentally different premise, namely, the exhaustion of local remedies.[161] This is not so for the WTO, the DSU of which can be viewed as generally seeking to start from the opposite premise,[162] that the DSU creates the exclusive forum for reviewing the legality of its members' measures (see Art 23 DSU). Suggestions that the EU Courts might be able to distinguish between cases where WTO law is clear and those where it is not, such that they, and Member State courts, could employ WTO law as a review criterion in the former case even if not the latter, pose their own problems. Given how critical the Appellate Body has been on occasion of the first instance panels that are composed of trade and

[159] I draw partially in making this point on Rosas (2000a: 811).

[160] For this point see eg Eeckhout (2011: 376–7) and Rosas (2000a: 812).

[161] See generally chs 3 and 13 of Amerasinghe (2004).

[162] See Bhuiyan (2007: 20–3) arguing that in the WTO there is no requirement for exhaustion of domestic remedies.

international law specialists,[163] is it really to be expected that the EU Courts—the judgments of which are themselves guilty of a laconic and terse style[164]—are well placed to be a general first instance WTO court for EU and Member State measures? Is not the appropriate forum for determining the WTO compliance of the EU's hormones or genetically modified organisms regime, or its subsidies for civil aircraft, that provided for in the DSU? The first two offer especially good examples as they involved the SPS Agreement, core provisions of which remain shrouded in controversy and have yet to be the subject of interpretation by the WTO's Appellate Body. Ultimately, one cannot build the argument for per se review vis-à-vis WTO Agreements on the basis of easy cases, for easy cases, as a glance at WTO litigation attests, are far from standard fare and even where they may appear to be so the panel and Appellate Body rulings they can generate provide the basis for the development of WTO jurisprudence. Again, this should not be viewed as merely policy arguments against per se review for they do link back to the nature of the dispute settlement system that the DSU has created; as, indeed, does a related consideration, that the system is not built for domestic judicial enforceability as it would have unintended consequences such as the member becoming an aggressive litigant in order to redress the imbalance resulting from one-sided domestic enforceability.[165] The same could also be said for a further legitimacy-based argument, namely, that an enhanced status for WTO norms in the EU, cloaking them with the imperial gowns of constitutionalism (direct effect and supremacy),[166] would serve to heighten the legitimacy concerns that have engulfed the WTO and thus harm the WTO system rather than bolster it.[167] In addition, from a purely practical perspective, the EU Courts had been fighting a losing battle for many years to deal with their ever-expanding docket and to have become a general WTO court of first

[163] The classic example being the *Asbestos* dispute (WT/DS315). The zeroing dispute has also proved to be a point of tension between various panels and the Appellate Body: see Hermann (2008: 1517).

[164] It is worth noting that both the panel rulings in the GMO (WT/DS291, WT/DS292, WT/DS29) and Civil Aircraft disputes (WT/DS316) were over 1,000 pages long.

[165] This is the argument advanced by a former Appellate Body member and former Director General of the Commission legal service: Ehlermann (2003: 415–16).

[166] To borrow the terminology of Eeckhout (2002: 101).

[167] See for similar logic Eeckhout (2002: 100); Rosas (2000a: 815–16).

instance, as a number of the critics had hoped, would inevitably have exacerbated such problems.[168]

Given all the fertile ground identified for rejecting general (or per se) WTO domestic judicial enforceability, it is no surprise to have seen such frequent interventions to this effect from Member States and the EU's political institutions. Likewise, given the stakes, it is understandable, albeit a unique occurrence, to have seen the preamble to the Council Decision concluding the Agreements express a negative view as to the possibility of domestic judicial enforceability.[169] Both the interventions and the Council Decision might be viewed as undue political pressure and, even though the ECJ was careful not to attribute a direct impact to the Decision,[170] it would be naïve to suggest that they do not influence the Court. However, we need to ask ourselves why the political institutions have taken the unprecedented step of stating their position in the preamble and also to be forceful and generally united in their stance before the Court. They have gone to such lengths because the doctrinal edifice that has been judicially constructed exhibits a willingness, at least theoretically, to use EU Agreements as a review criterion and thus a strong case to the contrary has to be made which was provided, in particular, by the DSU, as the ECJ duly recognized.

3.2 The legal effect of WTO rulings in the EU legal order

3.2.1 *The principled stance against review vis-à-vis WTO rulings: reinforcing the* Portuguese Textiles *reasoning*

In the wake of the *Portuguese Textiles* judgment, and the cases reiterating the reasoning, the focus turned to how the EU Courts would respond where a litigant invoked an adverse DSB ruling in challenging a measure.[171] Even some commentators supportive of the absence of general legality review in

[168] In and of itself this is hardly a compelling argument against the review function; whether it was a concern that had impact is another matter.

[169] The presence of this provision gave rise to great debate and contrasting views as to its potential purchase: see eg Kuijper (1995a: 236); Mengozzi (1995: 127–33); Eeckhout (1997: 37–40); Gaja (1995). The EU and Member States' Schedule of GATS commitments expressly states that the GATS shall have no self-executing effect.

[170] The ECJ noting that its conclusions correspond to those in the preamble.

[171] This had been the subject of much speculation since the creation of the WTO: Cottier (1998: 369–75); Eeckhout (1997: 51–5); Peers (1999b).

relation to WTO norms and the *Portuguese Textiles* reasoning, to say nothing of those against, considered the existence of a contrary DSB decision to warrant a different conclusion.[172] A rather curious stance given that the *Portuguese Textiles* reasoning appeared to be articulated with an eye to such challenges, otherwise why the focus on the post-DSB decision room for manoeuvre with no explicit reference to the pre-DSB decision scope for manoeuvre? Several weeks before the *Portuguese Textiles* ruling, the ECJ rejected reliance on a DSB decision concerning the bananas regime due to the late stage of the plea.[173] In the post-*Portuguese Textiles* era, both the GC and the ECJ dispensed with further challenges invoking adverse DSB decisions as against the bananas regime.[174] In 2003 the Full Court chided the GC for failing to give adequate consideration to arguments based on a DSB decision.[175] The *Biret* cases had their origin in the Hormones Directives which prohibited administering certain substances to farm animals and the placing on the market of meat derived from animals to which those substances had been administered. A DSB ruling established that this breached the SPS Agreement,[176] but it was well over three years post the expiry of the implementation period before the legislative response

[172] At least where the implementation period had expired: Eeckhout (2002; 2004; 2005; 2011); and seemingly in certain contexts Peers as well (2001a: 117–18).

[173] C-104/97P *Atlanta* [1999] ECR I-6983. The GC previously dispensed with an annulment action because the applicant had established no link between that DSB decision and the action brought: T-254/97 *Fruchthandelsgesellschaft mbH Chemnitz v Commission* [1999] ECR II-2743.

[174] The first three saw the GC respond, drawing on *Portuguese Textiles*, that the WTO was not intended to confer judicially enforceable individual rights, and that *Nakajima* and *Fediol* were not applicable because the Commission Regulation did not expressly refer to any specific WTO obligations or provisions: T–18/99 *Cordis* [2001] ECR II–913; T-30/99 *Bocchi* [2001] ECR II–943; T–52/99 *T. Port v Commission* [2001] ECR II–981 (the appeal was dismissed: C-213/01 P *T. Port v Commission* [2003] ECR I-2332). In two further actions the new argument that an exception existed for review vis-à-vis DSB decisions not complied with during the prescribed time limit was rejected as out of time: T-2/99 *T. Port v Council* [2001] ECR II-2093; T-3/99 *Bananatrading* [2001] ECR II-2123. A preliminary reference challenging the amended bananas regime was rejected by simply reiterating the *Portuguese Textiles* judgment and holding that the *Nakajima* and *Fediol* principles did not apply to the amended bananas regime: C-307/99 *OGT Fruchthandelsgesellschaft* [2001] ECR I-3159. The GC also dispensed with a non-contractual liability claim for unlawful or lawful action on the basis that the applicants had not established that they suffered any damages: T-99/98 *Hameico v Council and Commission* [2003] ECR II-2195.

[175] C-93/02 P *Biret v Council* [2003] ECR I-10497 and C-94/02 P *Biret and Cie v Council* [2003] ECR I-10565. In fact, the ECJ inappropriately employed the reasoned order procedure in C-307/99 *OGT*, ibid, where litigants had invoked a panel ruling, not an issue it had previously considered, and the bananas regime was as amended following a DSB decision, rather than the initial regime as in earlier cases: see also Peers (2001b: 609).

[176] *EC—Measures Concerning Meat and Meat Products* (WT/DS26/AB/R, WT/DS48/AB/R).

appeared.[177] A French subsidiary and its parent company brought WTO incompatibility-based damages actions. The GC reiterated the principled stance against legality review and non-contractual liability by citing *Portuguese Textiles* and the host of cases decided since. The *Nakajima* and *Fediol* principles were held inapplicable as the Directives were adopted prior to the SPS Agreement's entry into force. The relevance of the DSB decision was dispensed with via reliance on an earlier ECJ judgment (C-104/97 P *Atlanta*), inappropriately given that the DSB plea had been dispensed with due to the late stage at which it was introduced.[178] The ECJ held that it did not suffice to deal with the argument that the legal effects of the DSB decision called into question the finding that WTO rules did not have direct effect and provided grounds for legality review in a damages action. The judgments were nonetheless upheld on other grounds, and the ECJ thus managed to avoid addressing the legal effect of a DSB decision upon expiry of the implementation period.[179]

Less than 18 months after the *Biret* judgments both the GC and the ECJ pronounced on the legal effect of DSB decisions in cases concerning that hobbyhorse of litigants, the bananas regime. The EU bananas regime was successfully challenged using WTO procedures with the EU's amended regime (the 1999 regime) coming into force on the very day that the reasonable period of time for implementation culminated;[180] but a DSB ruling in May 1999 also found it to be WTO-incompatible.[181]

As a result of the 1999 regime, Van Parys and three companies forming part of the Chiquita group brought their respective challenges. The Chiquita group sought damages for losses allegedly suffered. Van Parys

[177] Directive 2003/74/EC.

[178] The ECJ had observed that the DSB decision could only be taken into consideration if the GATT itself had direct effect. Clearly in the wake of *Portuguese Textiles*, and the *OGT* order (C-307/99), the GC was given grounds for the conclusion it reached in the *Biret* cases.

[179] Despite the *Biret* judgments (C-93/02 P and C-94/02 P), the GC, in a bananas damages action, rejected reliance on a DSB decision by reciting *Portuguese Textiles* and finding no allegation or proof supporting the applicability of the *Nakajima* and *Fediol* principles: T-64/01 & T-65/01 *Afrikanische Frucht-Compagnie* [2004] ECR II-521.

[180] Council Regulation 1637/98/EC.

[181] The US and Ecuador were authorized to retaliate and the US duly did. The dispute was brought to a temporary close in 2001 via an EU–US and Ecuador mutually agreed solution that led to a WTO waiver, and a 2005 EU bananas regime which led to renewed Art 21.5 compliance proceedings and a DSB decision in 2008 establishing the new regime's breach of GATT 1994 which itself led to a 2009 Agreement between the EU and 11 Latin American banana-supplying countries which seeks to bring closure to this long-running dispute. For details see: <http://www.wto.org/english/tratop_e/dispu_e/cases_e/ds27_e.htm>.

brought actions contesting import licence rejections before the Raad van State which sought a preliminary ruling as to whether the 1999 regime infringed, inter alia, the WTO.

The *Chiquita* judgment emerged first.[182] The plea, seeking to establish illegal conduct for damages liability, relying exclusively on the *Nakajima* principle, was rejected. In doing so, the GC reinforced the *Portuguese Textiles* reasoning. It found that the holding that legality review would deprive the legislative or executive organs of their DSU-enshrined negotiation space could not be confined to cases where the implementation period had not expired, for even after its expiry and after compensation or suspension of concessions the DSU continues to reserve an important place for negotiation. In support of this, Article 21.6 DSU was invoked. This provides that six months after the establishment of the implementation period, the issue of implementation, unless the DSB decides otherwise, is placed, and remains, on the DSB's agenda including, as provided by Article 22.8 DSU, where compensation has been provided or suspension of concessions or other obligations has been authorized but the DSB ruling has not been implemented. The GC quoted directly from Article 22.8 DSU which expressly permits a mutually satisfactory solution to be reached over removal of the inconsistent measure. It was noted that when the present action was brought the dispute was still on the DSB agenda and the GC concluded that the EU Courts could not review the legality of the 1999 regime without depriving Article 21.6 DSU of its effectiveness. A strange conclusion to reach it must be conceded, but arguably it could be read more charitably given the reliance on Article 22.8 DSU which permits a mutually satisfactory solution while a dispute is pending on the DSB agenda. The GC struggled to evade the *Nakajima* principle and appeared to be resorting to semantics when it accepted that the EU 'intended to comply with its WTO obligations' when adopting the 1999 regime, but held that this did not show that it 'intended to implement [WTO] obligations . . . within the meaning of . . . *Nakajima*'.[183]

Within a month the Grand Chamber ruled in *Van Parys*.[184] It concluded that WTO Agreements did not give EU nationals a right to rely on them in

[182] T-19/01 *Chiquita v Commission* [2005] ECR II-315.

[183] The first submissions of the Commission and its rejoinder contained a detailed, though unconvincing, attempt at distinguishing between intending to comply and intending to implement.

[184] C-377/02 *Van Parys* [2005] ECR I-1465.

challenges to the validity of EU legislation where the DSB has held that both that legislation and subsequent legislation adopted to comply with WTO rules was incompatible with those rules. The judgment commenced with recitation of settled case law rejecting WTO legality review except where the *Nakajima* or *Fediol* principles apply. In the very next paragraph, the ECJ held that the EU 'did not intend to assume a particular obligation in the context of the WTO' by undertaking, after the DSB decision, to comply with WTO rules. Support for this proposition commenced with the *Portuguese Textiles* reasoning that even where a DSB decision holds a measure WTO-incompatible, the dispute settlement system nevertheless accords considerable importance to negotiation between the parties. The *Portuguese Textiles* reasoning was then rehashed and expanded. The ECJ now, like the GC in *Chiquita*, drew attention to the possibility of concessions or other obligations being suspended.[185] The dispute remaining on the agenda until resolved, that is, removed or a mutually satisfactory solution being reached, was also a new addition (Arts 22.8 and 21.6 DSU). As was the recourse to dispute procedures being provided for (Art 21.5 DSU) where there is disagreement over the compatibility of compliance measures, including an attempt to reach a negotiated settlement.

Turning to the specifics of the dispute before it, it was noted that the EU having declared its intention to comply: amended its regime upon expiry of the period allocated; that this was held still to infringe Articles I and XIII GATT 1994; that the US was authorized to take countermeasures; that the EU regime was re-amended in 2001; and, that agreements were negotiated with the US and Ecuador with a view to bringing the EU regime into WTO conformity. The Court pointed out that the aforementioned outcome by which the EU sought to reconcile its WTO obligations with those to the ACP States, and with the requirements inherent in implementing the Common Agricultural Policy, could be compromised if the EU Courts could review EU measures vis-à-vis the WTO upon expiry of the implementation period. The expiry of that period did not imply that the EU had exhausted the DSU possibilities of finding a solution, and thus to require the EU Courts, merely on the basis of the expiry of the time limit, to review measures in light of the WTO 'could have the effect of undermining the . . . [EU's] position in its attempt to reach a mutually acceptable solution to the dispute in conformity with those rules.' It followed that the

[185] As it had previously in C-27/00 & 122/00 *Omega Air*.

Regulations at issue could not be interpreted as measures intended to ensure the enforcement of a particular WTO obligation, nor did they expressly refer to specific WTO provisions. This rejection of WTO review even where a DSB decision was at issue was finalized via reiteration of the judicial reciprocity argument with the additional observation that admitting this lack of reciprocity would risk introducing an anomaly in the application of WTO rules.

The *Chiquita* and *Van Parys* rulings did not leave all questions of principle concerning the legal effect of DSB decisions resolved.[186] There remained an important batch of cases of which, bar one, all had been pending prior to *Chiquita* and *Van Parys* landing on the respective EU Court dockets. EU traders had brought damages actions due to the DSB-authorized increased US duties on their goods, the product of the EU's failure to bring its measures into WTO conformity following expiry of the implementation period in the *Bananas* dispute. Thus, unlike in the other *Bananas* cases, here we were not dealing with banana traders but rather EU exporters of different products suffering the consequences of DSB-authorized US cross-sector retaliation. Six separate, but essentially identical, judgments were given on the same day by the GC's first ever Grand Chamber formation.[187] The GC reiterated the *Chiquita* and *Van Parys* reasoning, albeit without citing either judgment,[188] in concluding that review vis-à-vis WTO rules was not possible and, thus, no unlawful conduct, the first hurdle for damages liability, could be established. For no-fault liability three conditions were laid down and it was the third, the requirement of unusual and special damage, that was unsatisfied because suspension of tariff concessions was considered among the vicissitudes inherent in the current system of international trade.[189] Two of these judgments led to

[186] In one curious recent case a company faulted a Commission State aid decision for complying retroactively with a DSB decision but the GC held that the contested decision indicated that approval of aid would breach the common market, an assessment prior to the EU's WTO responsibilities assessment: T-584/08 *Cantiere v Commission* [2011] ECR II-63.

[187] T-69/00 *FIAMM* [2005] ECR II-5393; T-135/01 *Fedon & Figli* [2005] ECR II-29; T-151/00 *Laboratoire du Bain* [2005] ECR II-23; T-301/00 *Groupe Fremaux* [2005] ECR II-25; T-320/00 *CD Cartondruck AG* [2005] ECR II-27; T-383/00 *Beamglow* [2005] ECR II-5459.

[188] The reference to depriving Art 21.6 DSU of its effectiveness in *Chiquita* was not, however, to be repeated.

[189] The first condition was actual and certain damage which was clearly met given the large increases in duties and the consequent reduction in total value of relevant US imports. The second was a causal link between the damage suffered and the EU institutions' conduct, also

appeals which were joined.[190] In its *FIAMM* judgment the Grand Chamber found, in line with the Council, Commission, and the sole intervening Member State, both the appellants' pleas concerning non-contractual liability for lawful and unlawful conduct unsuccessful. On the first, the *Portuguese Textiles* reasoning as reinforced in *Van Parys* was reiterated with emphasis on case law drawing no distinction between legality review via annulment proceedings or a compensation action.[191] A distinction, much mooted in academic circles[192] and advanced by the litigants, between direct effect of WTO rules themselves imposing the substantive obligations and that of a DSB decision was rejected. Here the ECJ first underscored the existence of post-DSB decision discretion and scope for negotiation, asserting that 'such leeway must be preserved'. It then invoked Article 3.2 DSU in concluding that a DSB decision could not require a WTO party to accord individuals a right they do not hold by virtue of the WTO absent the DSB decision. As to no-fault liability, it held that it has not accepted the existence of liability for lawful acts particularly of a legislative nature, and that as EU law stood, there was no liability for conduct falling within its legislative competence where a failure to comply with the WTO cannot be relied upon before the EU Courts.[193]

3.2.2 *Engaging with the reinforced* Portuguese Textiles *reasoning*

The reinforced *Portuguese Textiles* reasoning employed to dispense with cases seeking to review the legality of EU measures in relation to DSB decisions, was inevitably to draw criticism. The critics can be divided into at least three different camps. First, those in favour of general legality review vis-à-vis WTO norms and thus inevitably in favour where the

satisfied because withdrawal of concessions resulted from retaining a WTO-incompatible import regime in accord with the normal and foreseeable operation of the dispute settlement system.

[190] C-120/06 P & C-121/06 P *FIAMM v Council and Commission* [2008] ECR I-6513.

[191] The ECJ added, reiterating the Advocate General, that a determination that a measure is unlawful has the force of *res judicata* and compels the institution concerned to remedy the illegality.

[192] eg Eeckhout (1997: 53–5). Contra, Kuijper in Kuijper and Bronckers (2005: 1335).

[193] A qualifier was added to the effect that where an EU legislative measure restricts the right to property or freedom to pursue a trade or profession, such as to impair their very substance in a disproportionate and intolerable manner, perhaps because no provision for compensation is made, it could give rise to non-contractual liability. However, here exporters to non-Member State markets must be aware that their position may be affected by circumstances which include, as Art 22 DSU expressly envisages, suspension of concessions including cross-sectoral suspension.

implementation period has expired.[194] Secondly, those who defend the general rejection of legality review but support post-implementation expiry review.[195] Thirdly, those who may not support general post-implementation period review, but who at least do so for the purposes of damages liability.[196]

What these different stances all have in common, however, is emphasis on the obligation to implement WTO rulings, with the Jackson view often cited to this effect.[197] There is, thus, again the explicit or implicit message that there was something amiss in the DSU coverage.[198] But as the preceding subsection sought to show, the ECJ was in fact on sturdy ground in its initial *Portuguese Textiles* reasoning. The DSB decision led challenges provided the EU Courts with an opportunity to bolster that reasoning. The first example of this was actually provided when the Court held in the *Biret* judgments that no review would be possible for such decisions prior to the expiry of the implementation period. This conclusion was consistent with the views of a leading GATT/WTO scholar who had suggested: 'During that period, it is evident that any court action based upon the findings... remains suspended'.[199] The ECJ's ruling on this point can thus be interpreted as bolstering the general denial of WTO-based legality review.[200] For if legality review during the implementation period would render ineffective 'the reasonable period for compliance... provided for in the dispute settlement system', then one might argue that the same is a fortiori applicable where dispute settlement establishing a breach has not even taken place. Certainly it would seem anomalous for litigants who can

[194] Petersmann (2007; 2011); Lavranos (2004: 36–40; 2005).

[195] Eeckhout (2002; 2004; 2005; 2011).

[196] Thies (2004; 2006). This appears to be the position advanced by Dani (2010: 324 et seq). Contrast also the positions of AG Alber in the *Biret* cases with his earlier opinion in *Omega Air*.

[197] Eeckhout (2005: 16–17); Lavranos (2005: 456); Dani (2010: 321).

[198] In the case of Petersmann (2007) this is explicit, thus it is asserted that the GC position against direct applicability in *FIAMM* relies on obvious misinterpretations of WTO rules. And a sentence from the judgment is quoted in support 'applicants are wrong in inferring from Articles 21 and 22 of the DSU an obligation on the WTO member to comply, within a specified period, with the recommendations and rulings of the WTO bodies.' Petersmann does not, however, proceed to explain why this is an obvious misinterpretation. Clearly, the text does permit other solutions temporarily of which compensation is one. Other prominent WTO scholars accept this, eg Cottier (1998); Jackson (2004); Pauwelyn (2000). See also Tancredi (2012: 253–9) for nuanced engagement with the post-DSB decision scope for manoeuvre.

[199] Cottier (1998: 372).

[200] Mendez (2004: 525).

point to a DSB decision confirming the EU is breaching WTO rules, to be in a worse position for the purposes of legality review, at least during the allotted implementation period, than applicants without a DSB decision in support of their claim.[201]

The expanded reasoning now also drew attention to the fact that unresolved disputes remained on the DSB agenda and that possibilities other than compensation existed in the post-implementation period, notably suspension of concessions and mutually satisfactory solutions. The *Bananas* dispute was rightly used to highlight the kind of negotiations that can take place in the post-implementation period to seek to ensure that a WTO-compatible outcome emerges. The new reference when developing the *Portuguese Textiles* reasoning to Article 21.5 DSU, in both *Van Parys* and the GC innocent exporters cases, provided an unused peg on which to hang non-review in the post-DSB implementation period argument in certain circumstances. Where the EU institutions have responded with legislative or administrative action during the implementation period, the EU Courts could, were a new challenge brought, also consider that any such review would be in tension with Article 21.5 DSU.[202] Why, after all, should the EU Courts be able to give rulings that entitle individuals to sidestep the DSU-enshrined procedure for this type of implementation compliance review? Article 216(2) TFEU and *Haegeman*, as suggested above, are an inadequate response because Article 21.5 DSU can also be said to be binding on the EU and to be part of EU law. The purpose of Article 21.5 is to prevent unilateral determinations by the winning disputant, but its presence should be of relevance to the courts of the losing party which cannot, in contrast to the WTO dispute settlement system, offer a definitive answer on WTO compliance.[203]

The EU Courts have not yet employed this argument and one suspects this might be so for two reasons. First, being contingent on EU institutional activity, it could be viewed as detracting from the general proposition being advanced of no review in the post-implementation period regardless of activity. Secondly, invoking the Article 21.5 argument arguably raises a tension with the *Nakajima* and *Fediol* principles. It would then be necessary to concede that a measure is intended to implement WTO obligations,

[201] Admittedly this is possible where the *Fediol* and *Nakajima* principles apply.

[202] See on Art 21.5, Van den Bossche (2008: 300–5).

[203] Dani's account (2010) in favour of possible damages liability seeks to accommodate Art 21.5 DSU.

which sounds like it should trigger the *Nakajima* or *Fediol* principles. Ultimately, the solution might simply be to reject the applicability of the *Nakajima* and *Fediol* principles in the DSB decision context, as the case law appears inclined to, and to acknowledge the reasoning that bolsters rejection of legality review in the DSB context.[204]

A further argument that the EU Courts' DSU analysis could have led them to advance was the tension that would be posed between review and the existence of a negotiated compensation settlement or DSB-authorized sanctions.[205] The Commission argued that compensation and suspension of concessions re-established the overall balance of WTO concessions and damages liability results in the EU 'paying twice'. There is certainly some logic to this. If, for example, arbitrators have authorized a certain level of sanctions as a rebalancing mechanism, would this not be undermined by domestic damages awards in the EU?[206] Indeed, one commentator suggested it would be somewhat absurd to award past damages in a system which functions on the basis of prospective damages.[207] Such issues were left unexplored, but a suitable response was given to the argument that the consequences of EU damages are merely pecuniary,[208] namely, as the ECJ responded in *FIAMM*, this compels the institution concerned to remedy the illegality. This, thus, takes the ground from under those suggesting that review in the post-implementation period could be confined to damages actions because it maintains the room for manoeuvre.[209]

Finally a basic point needs emphasizing. It is the DSU's drafting that sustains the arguments, run by the political institutions and the Member States in litigation before the EU Courts, against review even in the wake of a DSB decision. Some may consider it disingenuous for the ECJ to in effect run with what is effectively that reasoning when it could instead boldly bolster the rule of law in international trade relations. But that would simply be to provide a one-sided bolstering of the domestic legal effect of the WTO DSB decisions. If the DSU allows the WTO's Contracting Parties scope to at minimum drag their heels on implementing

[204] See further the section below on *Nakajima/Fediol*.

[205] An additional intriguing possibility mooted by Kuijper was that compensation could violate WTO law as illegal export aid: Kuijper and Bronckers (2005: 1340).

[206] For a response, see Kuijper and Bronckers (2005: 1346); Thies (2006: 1159).

[207] See Kuijper and Bronckers (2005: 1335).

[208] See eg Thies (2006: 1158).

[209] As no-fault liability does not compel such an outcome, a case for it in certain instances can be made: see Thies (2009: 908–11).

DSB decisions, then that is precisely because this is what the Contracting Parties came up with. It is not for the EU Courts to remedy this but for the Contracting Parties within the scope of DSU reform to do so if they so desire.[210] Whether they will make significant changes to this end may be unlikely for as was once remarked: 'Even from a systemic point of view, compensation or other forms of bilateral settlement—as opposed to insisting on full and immediate compliance under all circumstances—may actually save the system from collapse, rather than question the integrity of the WTO legal regime.'[211]

3.3 Exceptions to the non-judicial applicability of the WTO

As with the GATT era, that the EU Courts were in principle unwilling to allow WTO norms to be used to review EU or national measures still left in place several mechanisms for judicial application of WTO law. And, in addition, a new exception was to emerge.

3.3.1 *The consistent interpretation doctrine*

The ECJ arguably first employed consistent interpretation in the WTO era vis-à-vis the general principles of EU law.[212] It was, however, in three preliminary rulings concerning domestic trademark and industrial design disputes that followed that the ECJ expressly affirmed the consistent interpretation doctrine while offering interpretations of a TRIPs provision (Art 50) concerning judicial remedies for the protection of intellectual property rights.[213] The doctrine was also employed in several preliminary

[210] See briefly on DSU reform, Van den Bossche (2008: 308–11).

[211] Pauwelyn (2003a: 949). See also Colares (2011) who takes issue with proposals for further legalization of the WTO dispute settlement system.

[212] C-200/96 *Metronome Musik* [1998] ECR I-1953, see further Snyder (2003: 324–5).

[213] C-53/96 *Hermes* (interpretation proffered for the national court to apply in the domestic trademark dispute); C-300/98 & C-392/98 *Christian Dior* [2000] ECR I-11307 (views proffered on whether industrial designs may qualify as IP rights under TRIPs, but it was considered to be an issue left to the domestic legal system); C-89/99 *Groeneveld* [2001] ECR I-5851 (a more robust interpretative approach in trademark dispute). In a damages action against the Commission, the consistent interpretation doctrine vis-à-vis national rules for protection of rights in a field to which TRIPs applied was reiterated: T-279/03 *Galileo v Commission* [2006] ECR II-1291 (appeal was dismissed: C-325/06 P *Galileo* [2007] ECR I-44). However, the applicants could not invoke

rulings to interpret the Trade Marks Directive and the Trade Marks Regulation in conformity with TRIPs including referring to Appellate Body interpretations for the first time.[214] Several preliminary rulings also saw affirmation of consistent interpretation in relation to the TRIPs Agreement, the GATS, the Rules of Origin Agreement, and the Information Technology Agreement (ITA);[215] and the doctrine in all but name was employed to allow the TRIPs Agreement to influence the interpretation of the Software Copyright Directive.[216]

that obligation as they failed to plead or identify such national rules and as TRIPs did not have direct effect they could not rely on it directly and the GC thus declared inadmissible the alleged breach of Art 8 of the Paris Convention for the Protection of Industrial Property, compliance with which is required by TRIPs.

[214] The references to two Appellate Body reports occurred in C-245/02 *Budvar* [2004] ECR I-1989 which offered interpretations of TRIPs provisions in the context of a national trademark dispute. Two previous GC judgments had referred to an Appellate Body ruling: T-13/99 *Pfizer v Council* [2002] ECR II-3305 and T-70/99 *Alpharma v* Council [2002] ECR II-3495. The other examples were C-49/02 *Heidelberger* [2004] ECR I-6129 and C-246/05 *Häupl* [2007] ECR I-4673 on the Trade Marks Directive, and T-237/08 *Abadía v OHIM* [2010] ECR II-1583 where a company failed to convince the GC that the Trade Marks Regulation should be interpreted vis-à-vis TRIPs in the way it proposed in order to annul an OHIM decision.

[215] In C-275/06 *Promusicae* [2008] ECR I-271 a party invoked TRIPs provisions to influence the reading of several EU Directives (2001/29/EC; 2000/31/EC; 2004/48/EC), whilst the Grand Chamber reiterated the consistent interpretation doctrine, TRIPs was not considered to require the EU Directives to be interpreted differently from the interpretation it had reached as to their meaning. In C-428/08 *Monsanto v CefetrA* [2010] ECR I-6765, the ECJ held that although the Biotech Directive must as far as possible be interpreted in light of the TRIPs Agreement, the TRIPs provisions did not affect its interpretation of the Biotech Directive. In C-335/05 *Řízení* [2007] ECR I-4307, a German court asked whether the Thirteenth VAT Directive should be interpreted in light of a GATS provision such that the applicant should be refunded certain charges levied under domestic law, and the ECJ held that it did not need to be restrictively interpreted because it did not prevent GATS compliance. In C-447/05 & C-448/05 *Thomson Multimedia* [2007] ECR I-2049, a preliminary ruling on a reference from a French court, lip-service was paid to the doctrine in interpreting the EU customs code vis-à-vis the Rules of Origin Agreement, though it is not clear whether it had any impact. In C-260/08 *HEKO* [2009] ECR I-11571 the ECJ affirmed the consistent interpretation doctrine while holding that the Rules of Origin Agreement, which the Commission invoked, did not constitute complete harmonization and allowed the WTO members a margin of discretion in adapting their rules of origin with a panel report invoked in support: see to the same effect C-373/08 *Hoesch Metals and Alloys* [2010] ECR I-951. In Joined Cases C-288/09 & C-289/09 *BSB and Pace*, Judgment of 14 April 2011, the ECJ's tariff classification interpretation allowed it to avoid addressing whether, as a UK tribunal had asked, a positive customs duty would breach the ITA and Art II:1(b) GATT 1994, and while it underscored that the ITA could not be directly relied upon, the consistent interpretation doctrine applied which suggests it viewed its interpretation of the Combined Nomenclature Regulation (2658/87) as ITA-consistent if not directly influenced by the ITA.

[216] C-393/09 *Bezpečnostní softwarová asociace* [2010] ECR I-13971. The Advocate General simply referred to the interpretation he offered as being confirmed by TRIPs.

The anti-dumping field has seen clear examples of the GC applying consistent interpretation to EU measures of which perhaps the most noteworthy occasion was the first.[217] The *BEUC* case was a consumer organization-initiated annulment action of a Commission Decision refusing to consider it an interested party for the purposes of the ADR.[218] The GC held that the ADR sought to implement the ADA. It was thus considered right for the Commission to interpret the ADR in light of the ADA, however, its detailed interpretation led it to conclude that the Commission's interpretation could not be upheld and its decision was annulled. The case reveals a significant potential consequence of consistent interpretation, namely, that it can lead indirectly to the annulment of both EU and domestic measures.[219] Where EU measures adopted under a parent measure, and domestic measures, are inconsistent with the parent measure as interpreted consistently with an EU Agreement, then the subordinate measures can be annulled.[220]

Two final significant developments should be noted. First, the GC rejected the application of consistent interpretation to the EU Treaty

[217] In T-188/99 *Euroalliages* [2001] ECR II-1757, the ADA was used in part to justify the admissibility of a challenge to a subordinate measure adopted under the ADR as well as to support a rejection of an alleged ADR infringement. Snyder's suggestion (2003: 343) that this was an application of *Nakajima* (which he labels the transposition exception) and that the ADA was used as a criterion to assess and invalidate the EU Regulation is thus not accurate. The case is simply a manifestation of consistent interpretation, the ADA being used to interpret the ADR but not resulting in the annulment of the challenged measure. In an annulment action against a Council Regulation, the GC read the ADR provision consistently with its ADA counterpart, an interpretation considered consistent with a panel report, which did not result in annulment of the subordinate measure: T-35/01 *Shanghai v Council* [2004] ECR II-3663. T-45/06 *Reliance Industries*, is considered below. In T-409/06 *Sun Sang Kong Yuen Shoes Factory v Council* [2010] ECR II-807, the applicants alleged the Commission inappropriately applied a provision of the ADR read in conjunction with an annex to the ADA and the GC held that the relevant ADR provision implemented the ADA annex and a paragraph to the ADA 'and must be interpreted in the light thereof in so far as possible' with a panel ruling also cited but no violation found. In addition, applicants sought a particular reading for the ADA according to which the ADR was to be interpreted which was not accepted: C-76/01P *Eurocoton v Council* [2003] ECR I-10091, a somewhat similar unsuccessful attempt was apparent in C-422/02 P *Europe Chemi-Con v Council* [2005] ECR I-791.

[218] T-256/97 *BEUC v Commission* [2000] ECR II-101. In addition, various companies unsuccessfully sought to put forth a reading of the ADR in accordance with the ADA in order to have a Commission Decision annulled: T-132/01 *Euroalliages v Commission* [2003] ECR II-2359.

[219] Accordingly, it was not an example of the *Nakajima* principle as has been suggested, eg the Advocate General's Opinion in C-313/04 *Egenberger* below, and Snyder (2003: 344).

[220] In T-256/97 *BEUC* the Commission sought to save a subordinate measure that on a natural reading would seem to breach its parent measure.

itself.[221] It was argued that the Commission's interpretation of Article 102 TFEU breached various TRIPs provisions and that so did the contested decision. *Portuguese Textiles* was reiterated in rejecting ordinary legality challenges and *Nakajima* and *Fediol* were not considered applicable. The GC employed the strict language of the *IDA* case (C-61/94) to conclude that consistent interpretation only applies where the Agreement prevails over EU law provisions which was not so with primary EU law.

Secondly, commentators have rightly drawn attention to the WTO and its jurisprudence having an unacknowledged impact on judgments.[222] Case law has emerged that smacks of consistent interpretation albeit without express acknowledgement. In a recent example a Commission Regulation was annulled for incompatibility with its parent Regulation.[223] This interpretation deviated from the traditional interpretation given by EU customs authorities but was consistent with an Appellate Body ruling condemning that traditional interpretation.[224] A reference to the ruling did appear in the ECJ's recitation of the applicants' claims, but there was no acknowledgement that it was influenced by this ruling. Bronckers has used the term 'muted dialogue' to capture such cases which he views as a dialogue between European Courts and WTO tribunals. The term 'unacknowledged consistent interpretation' will be employed here instead because it is considered a more accurate representation of what is occurring.[225]

3.3.2 *The* Fediol *and* Nakajima *principles*

In the WTO era it has been the *Nakajima* principle, rather than *Fediol*, that has been routinely invoked.[226] In the DSB context, all attempts proved

[221] T-201/04 *Microsoft* [2007] ECR II-3601. In T-55/99 *CETM v Commission* [2000] ECR II-3213 an attempt to use the WTO Subsidies Agreement definition of subsidy to influence the classification of a measure as State aid within EU law was rejected.

[222] Snyder (2003); Bronckers (2008).

[223] C-310/06 *FTS International* [2007] ECR I-6749.

[224] As Bronckers astutely observed (2008: 889–90).

[225] Keeping track of such cases is a most difficult task for, unlike in *FTS* (C-310/06), there may not be a reference to WTO norms in any part of the judgment. Or where there is such a reference, as in the *BSB and Pace* ruling (C-288/09 & C-289/09), there is no reference to dispute settlement decisions of relevance (the ECJ's interpretive approach and conclusion sat comfortably with a DSB decision adopted six months earlier: *EC and its Member States—Tariff Treatment of Certain Information Technology Products* (WT/DS375/R, WT/DS376/R, WT/DS377/R)).

[226] Commission Trade Barriers Regulation decisions were the subject of litigation, but not *Fediol* review: T-317/02 *FICF v Commission* [2004] ECR II-4325 and T-90/03 *FICF v Commission* [2007] ECR II-73.

unsuccessful and the *Van Parys* and *FIAMM* rulings, alongside the GC judgment in *Chiquita*, appeared to close the door to its potential as a mechanism for review vis-à-vis DSB decisions.[227] The first WTO-era case in which *Nakajima* review was conducted was the *Rice Tariffs* case. Italy alleged that a Council Regulation breached Article XXIV:6 of GATT 1994 (and the understanding concerning the interpretation of Art XXIV), a provision concerning tariff renegotiations resulting from the formation of customs unions.[228] It was held that the Regulation was seeking to implement a particular GATT obligation. In short, *Nakajima* applied and the ECJ was required to review the Regulation against Article XXIV:6 and the Understanding.[229] In terms of the actual review, it was simply held that the requirement to conclude a 'mutually satisfactory compensatory adjustment' is fulfilled when an agreement is concluded by the parties (as indeed was the case in the dispute at hand).

The 2001 *Kloosterboer* ruling has been considered an application of *Nakajima*;[230] it was a challenge to a Commission Regulation allegedly incompatible with its parent Council Regulation and the Agriculture Agreement.[231] The Advocate General found relevant provisions of the implementing Regulation void because they distorted the clear meaning of the basic Regulation. He went on, however, to assess its validity in light of the Agriculture Agreement, considering that the basic Regulation implemented a WTO obligation. An Appellate Body report was relied upon and the implementing Regulation was also considered invalid on this basis. The ECJ did not take this second step and, whilst the WTO background to the amended Basic Regulation was acknowledged, the analysis simply found the implementing Regulation to breach the basic Regulation. This was accordingly not 'an ideal example' of *Nakajima*.[232] It was simply a direct judicial application of EU legislative measures transposing Treaty norms. This is routine EU Court activity. In the WTO context that is so whether

[227] However, with *Nakajima*, review can in theory still take place vis-à-vis the WTO Agreements as interpreted by the DSB and, indeed, indirectly even via consistent interpretation.

[228] C-352/96 *Italy v Council (Rice Tariffs)* [1998] ECR I-6937. The 1995 EU enlargement triggered renegotiations resulting in EU trade agreements pursuant to Art XXIV:6 which were partially implemented by the Council Regulation.

[229] This was the first *Nakajima* application outside the anti-dumping context unless one considers C-150/95 *BHA*, like Snyder did, an application of *Nakajima*.

[230] Snyder (2003: 344–5).

[231] C-317/99 *Kloosterboer* [2001] ECR I-9863.

[232] As Snyder (2003: 345) puts it, albeit using the terminology of the transposition exception. Holdgaard (2008a: 316) also 'suggested it may be seen as a successful application of... Nakajima'.

we are dealing with the ADR, that implements the ADA, or the basic Anti-Subsidy Regulation, that implements the Subsidies Agreement,[233] or the myriad of other EU measures implementing WTO rules. Certainly, a distinctive feature was drawn to our attention in the form of the pleadings and the Advocate General's Opinion. Perhaps this was of influence and we have an unacknowledged application of the consistent interpretation doctrine at play: the Agriculture Agreement influencing the interpretation of the basic Regulation. There is no evidence that this is so and the reading accorded the basic Regulation did not seem in need of a helping hand from WTO sources and, even if that were necessary, it would not constitute *Nakajima* review but rather consistent interpretation.

Application of the *Nakajima* principle did prima facie result in an annulment in the *Petrotub* judgment. The applicants sought the annulment of a Council Regulation basing this partly on the absence of an explanation, required by the WTO's ADA (Art 2.4.2), as to why a particular dumping calculation method had been used. On appeal the ECJ held that it was indeed necessary to take account of Article 2.4.2 ADA.[234] The standard *Portuguese Textiles* line was repeated. However, the *Nakajima* principle was considered applicable for the ADR preamble showed it was adopted to transpose ADA rules, and was intended to implement particular obligations in Article 2.4.2 ADA. It was, thus, for the ECJ to review the legality of the EU measure in light of Article 2.4.2 ADA. The reasoning then took a curious turn for the duty of consistent interpretation was invoked. That the ADR did not expressly specify that the Article 2.4.2 ADA requirement was considered explicable by the existence of the duty to state reasons in Article 296 TFEU. The ECJ held that once Article 2.4.2 ADA was transposed, its requirement to state reasons was subsumed under Article 296 TFEU. There being no reference as to why the particular dumping calculation method was used, the relevant Council Regulation was annulled.

[233] In one curious case the GC held that a Regulation imposing countervailing duties infringed both provisions of the basic anti-subsidy Regulation and what were considered substantially the same provisions of the WTO Subsidies Agreement: T-58/99 *Mukand v Council* [2001] ECR II-2521.

[234] C-76/00P *Petrotub v Council* [2003] ECR I-79. The GC acknowledged the *Nakajima* principle but considered that the relevant ADA provision did not constitute a rule to be applied and, further, that the relevant ADR provision (Art 2(11)), did not mention any specific obligation to give an explanation: T-33 & 34/98 *Petrotub SA and Republica SA v Council* [1999] ECR II-3837.

Petrotub has been viewed as simply an application of *Nakajima*,[235] however a more promising suggestion, worth teasing out further, is that it was a special case of consistent interpretation.[236] Clearly, a Regulation was annulled. But the measure that implemented the ADA *à la Nakajima* was the annulled measure's parent Regulation. At least two options initially appeared available for annulling such subsidiary measures. One would be to hold that *Nakajima* applies, conduct the review, and as the ADR does not provide for the ADA's specific reason-giving requirement, then the relevant article on calculating dumping margins (Art 2(11)) can be annulled leading to annulment of the subordinate measures. Clearly, this avenue was not adopted. Alternatively, consistent interpretation could be invoked to hold that the ADR can be read consistently with the ADA reason-giving requirement and that, accordingly, measures adopted under the ADR that do not do so breach their parent measure and can be annulled. It was not this option either that was pursued. It is not that Article 2(11) ADR was alone read as requiring the ADA reason-giving requirement, rather the ADA requirement was read into Article 296 TFEU. Had Article 296 TFEU not existed, the only peg for the outcome reached, annulling the subsidiary measures but not the parent Regulation, would have been using consistent interpretation to read the parent Regulation in conformity with the ADA requirement. Accordingly, it could be suggested that *Nakajima* was irrelevant to the outcome for consistent interpretation enabled the WTO-compatible outcome to be reached. The reference to both *Nakajima* and consistent interpretation in the same judgment is not puzzling, it is simply that the former only needs to bite if the latter cannot ensure a WTO-compatible reading. An alternative reading would be that *Nakajima* was not irrelevant and that it was not consistent interpretation alone that did the work here; rather, it was because the ADR was viewed *à la Nakajima* as seeking to implement the ADA, that this species of consistent interpretation was able to lead to a reading for Article 296 TFEU that subsumed within it the need for a reasoning requirement stemming from a WTO Agreement. This was thus different from how consistent interpretation alone had ever previously been employed. Here it was influencing the interpretation

[235] See eg AG Alber and AG Maduro in, respectively, C-93/02 P *Biret*, para 61 and C-120/06 P & C-121/06 P *FIAMM*, para 41. Antoniadis (2007: 69) explored *Petrotub* in a section on the *Nakajima* and *Fediol* principles and it was not given further consideration in the consistent interpretation section. Koutrakos (2006: 282–5) accorded the judgment its own independent section, however the coverage itself largely situated it within the *Nakajima* camp.

[236] See Kuijper (Kuijper and Bronckers 2005: 1326–8).

accorded primary EU law, albeit in its application to a very specific context. If the *Nakajima* principle generated the outcome in this case, it was a curious conclusion because it never previously having had such effect, it will need to be distinguished from what is normally understood by the *Nakajima* principle. Furthermore, if it is to be accepted that a particular type of legislative activity, going beyond that required for concluding an EU Agreement, can impact upon the reading of EU primary law, which would not be possible via the conventional consistent interpretation doctrine alone,[237] then some justification for this should be forthcoming.

There are five further post-*Petrotub* cases where the *Nakajima* principle was invoked that have not been touched thus far.[238] In *Egenberger* a German court considered that a Commission Regulation concerning import arrangements implemented WTO obligations *à la Nakajima* and that it breached a GATT 1994 non-discrimination principle applicable to State-owned enterprises and a provision of the Import Licensing Agreement.[239] The Commission called on the ECJ to revisit its *Nakajima* principle and essentially to leave the consistent interpretation doctrine alone in its place. The Grand Chamber annulled the relevant provisions

[237] At least according to the GC in T-201/04 *Microsoft*, and more recently T-18/10 *Inuit Tapiriit Kanatami* (see further Chapter V), an issue on which the ECJ is yet to expressly pronounce.

[238] Such pleas were likely in a number of additional anti-dumping annulment actions for otherwise alleged WTO breaches would have been pointless given the *Portuguese Textiles* line of authority. In three cases, allegations of ADA infringement were not addressed as the Regulations were annulled on other grounds: T-107/04 *Aluminium Silicon Mill Products v Council* [2007] ECR II-669, T-498/04 *Zhejiang Xinan Chemical Industrial Group v Council* [2009] ECR II-1969, T-143/06 *MTZ Polyfilms v Council* [2009] ECR II-413; in T-462/04 *HEG v Council* [2008] ECR II-3685 alleged breaches of the ADA and Subsidies Agreement were not upheld as concerned one plea because the facts did not fall within the scope of the relevant ADA provision, and as concerned alternative pleas because either it had not been shown how, or it had not been argued that, the provisions differed from the provisions in the Council Regulations which were not being breached and gave effect to the Agreements. In Joined Cases T-407/06 & T-408/06 *Zhejiang Aokang Shoes v Council* [2010] ECR II-747, an alleged breach of an ADA provision requiring investigating authorities to set out the facts and considerations on the basis of which definitive duties are imposed, was rejected as this had been done by the Commission; in T-119/06 *Usha Martin v Council and Commission* [2010] ECR II-4335 a proportionality-based challenge in which an ADA incompatibility was invoked was rejected without comment on the ADA. T-274/02 *Ritek v Council* [2006] ECR II-4305 was rather different for the GC engaged with whether the *Petrotub* reason-giving requirement read into Art 2(11) of the ADR was satisfied, suggesting that the contrary had been specifically agued; the GC also rejected the argument that a particular 'zeroing' technique condemned by the Appellate Body as violating the ADA applied in the specific context at issue.

[239] C-313/04 *Egenberger* [2006] ECR I-6331.

on the basis of internal EU law pleas and found it unnecessary to address the *Nakajima* plea.[240] The following year in its *IKEA* ruling the ECJ addressed a challenge to a Regulation in light of, inter alia, the ADA and a DSB decision finding that the dumping calculation method the EU had used breached the ADA.[241] The Advocate General had considered the *Nakajima* principle applicable and reviewed the Regulation vis-à-vis the ADR and the ADA jointly and found it in breach. This, it is however submitted, is to be distinguished from *Nakajima* review; it was, rather, consistent interpretation: the ADR being read in light of the ADA, which precludes the particular dumping calculation method results in annulment of the measure adopted thereunder. The ECJ, however, explicitly rejected the applicability of *Nakajima* but nevertheless found the dumping calculation method used breached the ADR and accordingly annulled a provision of the contested Regulation. In short, the ECJ's conclusion was consistent with the DSB decision and this is, thus, arguably an example of 'unacknowledged consistent interpretation'.[242]

In the *Wine Labelling Regulation* case Italy contested the TRIPs compatibility of a Regulation which amended the Labelling Regulation in response to WTO consultations where Members expressed strong views as to its WTO compliance.[243] The amending Regulation's preamble expressly identified this context albeit without reference to a particular WTO obligation, which was enough to reject the applicability of *Nakajima*, and the Wine Labelling Regulation's reference to regard being had to obligations arising from EU Agreements was considered too general for the Commission to have meant to implement specific WTO obligations.[244] The basic Regulation on the common organization of the wine market was, however, considered to implement specific WTO obligations, referring, as it did, expressly to specific TRIPs provisions. But it was held that it limited itself to protecting within the EU geographical indications from third party

[240] The Advocate General conducted *Nakajima* review and found the challenged Regulation, relying also on WTO rulings, to breach the WTO provisions (having first found it to breach certain EU law provisions).

[241] C-351/04 *Ikea Wholesale* [2007] ECR I-7723. For detailed comment, see Hermann (2008).

[242] See also Bronckers (2008: 889).

[243] T-226/04 *Italy v Commission* [2006] ECR II-29.

[244] The GC had previously cited its *Chiquita* judgment (T-19/01) holding that as an exception to the non-direct individual reliance on the WTO, the *Nakajima* principle was to be interpreted restrictively which is a proposition neither reiterated nor disavowed in the two significant ECJ judgments, *Van Parys* and *FIAMM*, that followed *Chiquita*.

WTO members, whereas the case at hand concerned 'traditional names' of EU Member States. In short, the basic Regulation was held to implement a specific application of the expressly cited TRIPs provisions and, therefore, those very TRIPs provisions could not be used *à la Nakajima* for review in a different application.[245]

In the *Huvis* case, a company refused a particular cost adjustment alleged that this, based on Article 2(10) ADR, infringed Article 2.4 ADA and the principle of sound administration.[246] The GC reiterated the *Petrotub* ruling to the effect that Article 2(10) ADR intended to implement Article 2.4 ADA and that it was accordingly required to review the legality of the contested Regulation vis-à-vis that specific ADA provision. Article 2.4 ADA was found to contain certain requirements not expressly restated in Article 2(10) ADR. However, the GC held that these requirements formed part of the general principles of law and, in particular, the principle of sound administration and that it had to determine whether the institutions had taken the requirements into account in applying the ADR.

The *Huvis* logic should be familiar from *Petrotub* for the GC was asserting that a requirement in the ADA, not re-enacted in the ADR, could be read into a different category of EU law. If this is the case, then earlier observations concerning *Petrotub* apply. What independent function did the *Nakajima* principle play? Was this not simply consistent interpretation being applied to the general principles rather than secondary EU law? As it turned out, the institutions were held to have complied with Article 2.4 ADA and the principle of sound administration in their application of Article 2(10) ADR. Presumably, had that not been so the infringement would have been of the principle of sound administration. And yet the GC concluded that the institutions did not infringe Article 2(10) ADR, interpreted in light of Article 2.4 ADA; adding in a separate sentence that therefore they did not breach the principle of sound administration either. This manner of concluding suggests that the ADR was being interpreted in consistent interpretation fashion using the ADA to include the requirements in the latter that had not been re-enacted in the former. And, accordingly, that failure to have satisfied these non-transposed

[245] Presumably this would mean that importers of third country WTO products (or exporters) would be able to have *Nakajima* review conducted vis-à-vis the same provisions.

[246] T-221/05 *Huvis v Council* [2008] ECR II-124. The company challenged a Council Regulation claiming it infringed the ADR and the ADA, and that the ADR itself infringed the ADA but this did not lead to consideration of *Nakajima* for the relevant provision was annulled due to infringement of the ADR.

requirements of the ADA violates the ADR, which would equally violate the principle of sound administration. This, then, could simply be seen as a manifestation of the consistent interpretation doctrine. A more tortuous route would be that the ADA requirements were read into the principle of sound administration, which is then read back into the ADR. But neither of these options are what the GC actually stated it was doing. The key paragraph 77 quite clearly appears to read the requirements exclusively into the general principles of EU law and they seem to form the relevant review criterion.

Finally, the *Reliance Industries* case offered an ideal, but unseized, opportunity to clarify the *Nakajima* principle.[247] A company challenged Council and Commission expiry reviews of anti-dumping and countervailing duties. The first limb of the plea was that the EU measures initiating the expiry review infringed the ADR and the basic Anti-Subsidy Regulation interpreted in accordance with their counterpart provisions in the ADA and the WTO Subsidies Agreement. The GC responded by reciting case law on review only being possible in the *Nakajima* and *Fediol* scenarios. It was held that the preambles to the basic Regulations made it clear their purpose was to transpose the ADA and Subsidies Agreement rules and that the relevant provisions were adopted to implement particular obligations in their corresponding provisions in the WTO Agreements.[248] It was held to follow that the basic Regulation provisions were to be interpreted as far as possible in light of the corresponding WTO provisions. In other words, from establishing the *Nakajima* applicability the Court actually proceeded into the terrain of consistent interpretation and, indeed, the provisions of the relevant basic Regulations were then interpreted consistently with their WTO counterparts, Appellate Body reports being engaged with to boot, and the challenged EU expiry review measures emerged unscathed.

An additional argument advanced sought actual *Nakajima* review. The logic was that if consistent interpretation could not lead to the two basic Regulations being interpreted consistently with their counterpart WTO provisions, then they should be annulled. Here the Commission continued

[247] T-45/06 *Reliance Industries* [2008] ECR II-2399.

[248] As concerned the ADA, authority existed for this proposition in the form of *Petrotub*, which was invoked albeit it concerned a specific ADA provision (Art 2.4.2) not at issue in *Reliance Industries*, but this was the first *Nakajima* finding on the Subsidies Agreement. The suggestion by Bronckers (2008: 887), who cites *Reliance Industries*, that the EU Courts have only recognized an explicit intention to follow WTO law in the anti-dumping legislation and the Trade Barriers Regulation (*Fediol*) is thus inaccurate as already illustrated by C-352/96 *Italy v Council (Rice Tariffs)*.

its campaign against the *Nakajima* principle, as conventionally understood, for it argued essentially that consistent interpretation and *Nakajima* were one and the same thing, and that if consistent interpretation did not permit WTO-compatible interpretation then any conflict could not be relied on to annul provisions of the basic Regulations. The plea was rejected as being based on an incorrect assumption, that consistent interpretation did not permit a WTO-consistent reading of the basic Regulations.

Ultimately, that the GC did split its coverage of the issue of consistent interpretation and legality review may provide a more coherent manner for addressing future cases where both consistent interpretation and the *Nakajima* principle arise. The Commission may be expected to continue its quest to have the *Nakajima* principle reconsidered, which would spare the EU Courts the intellectual acrobatics to which various cases have attested. A tension does actually remain between the *Nakajima* principle and the *Portuguese Textiles* logic for it was born prior to the ECJ's express attachment to a judicial reciprocity logic linked to the DSU. And there is no evidence that other WTO members have a similar exception. That said, perhaps we can find a justification for it alongside particularly powerful manifestations of the consistent interpretation doctrine, if indeed the two can be distinguished, in the fact that it has largely been operating in a field, anti-dumping, in which the EU has transposed close to verbatim the text of the relevant WTO Agreement. To allow such norms to influence the interpretation of EU law,[249] might thus be viewed as a manifestation of the ECJ contributing to a more rules-based international trading order and, indeed, judicial comity in relation to the Appellate Body in particular. And the Court can certainly be put on notice as to those occasions in which use of *Nakajima* and the consistent interpretation doctrine is in tension with the 'EU interest' and the DSU-sanctioned room for manoeuvre.[250] Clearly, however, this line of case law does not raise the same profound questions that are generated by contemplating general WTO-compliance review of EU action.

3.3.3 *Domestic judicial review vis-à-vis WTO norms in areas outside the EU's exercised legislative competence*

The WTO era brought forth a debate, the extent of jurisdiction over mixed agreements, that had been the subject of much academic speculation but

[249] As far as influencing the interpretation of domestic law that serves an additional objective of ensuring that the Member States comply with EU obligations.

[250] eg that the Commission is advancing a different line in WTO dispute settlement.

little judicial clarification.[251] The WTO is a mixed agreement and so the question soon arose. The first occasion was the *Hermès* ruling where three Member States and the Council, contrary to the Commission, asserted that the ECJ had no jurisdiction to rule on the interpretation of Article 50 TRIPs given that the dispute was one of national trademark law.[252] The ECJ noted that the WTO was concluded without any allocation between the EU and the Member States of their respective obligations. However, the EU's Trade Mark Regulation was already in force by then and rights thereunder could, it was held, be safeguarded by provisional measures provided under Member State law for national trademark law purposes. And these national provisional measures were to be applied, as far as possible, in light of Article 50 TRIPs. In other words, the consistent interpretation doctrine applied. The ECJ accordingly held that it had jurisdiction to interpret Article 50 and it was immaterial that the dispute concerned national trademark law because, where a provision can apply to situations falling both within the scope of national and EU law, as here, it is in the EU's interest that it is interpreted uniformly to forestall future differences of interpretation. Consistent interpretation was applied to a trademark dispute outside the scope of EU law, concerning, as it did, a national trademark. The ruling gave rise to two different interpretations.[253] The broad interpretation was that it asserted jurisdiction over all provisions of a mixed agreement falling within non-exclusive competence.[254] On this reading certainly all of TRIPs was within the Court's jurisdictional reach because the EU was competent to legislate across all of it,[255] thus forestalling future differences of interpretation. The narrow reading took the judgment to simply confirm jurisdiction where a provision can apply to both areas of EU and Member State competence.

The *Christian Dior* ruling, concerning a domestic industrial design, provided both further clarification and obfuscation.[256] The Court asserted its jurisdiction to define the obligations the EU has assumed. This is logical as the ECJ needs this interpretative jurisdiction to determine the EU's

[251] As illustrated by *Demirel*, *Sevince*, and *Irish Berne* considered in Chapter III.

[252] C-53/96 *Hermès*.

[253] See Koutrakos (2002: 36) and Heliskoski (2000: 403 et seq) both articulating the two different readings.

[254] Dashwood (2000: 173–4); Rosas (2000b: 214–15).

[255] *Opinion 1/94* [1994] ECR I-5267 is confirmation of this.

[256] C-300 & 392/98 *Christian Dior* [2000] ECR I-11307.

obligations under any given mixed agreement.[257] The core of *Hermès* was then rehashed, but with a new reference to an earlier holding (*Opinion 1/94*) asserting an obligation of close cooperation on the Member States and EU institutions in fulfilling their WTO commitments. That obligation required the Member State and EU Courts, for practical and legal reasons, to give Article 50 a uniform interpretation as it is a procedural provision to be uniformly applied in every situation falling within its scope which only the ECJ could ensure via the preliminary ruling procedure in cooperation with domestic courts. Accordingly, jurisdiction over Article 50 was not confined to domestic trademark law. The ECJ held that the consistent interpretation duty applied in a field where the EU had legislated, but that where it had not the field would fall outside the scope of EU law and within Member State competence and it was for their legal orders to determine whether individuals could rely directly on Article 50(6). An additional exception to the principled stance against WTO legality review was thus created, albeit applicable only before domestic courts vis-à-vis domestic norms. Many questions were left unanswered with this curt reasoning: what is outside the scope of EU law? How do we define a field? Would harmonizing legislation be required or would minimum standards suffice?[258]

In the *Merck* case, a Portuguese Supreme Court asked whether the Court had jurisdiction to interpret a TRIPs provision on the period of patent protection and, if so, whether national courts were required to apply it.[259] On jurisdiction the Grand Chamber reiterated the core of its *Christian Dior* ruling. In determining whether there was any EU legislation in the sphere of patents, it was concluded that the EU had not exercised its powers in this sphere or that internally this exercise had not been sufficiently important for this sphere to fall within the scope of EU law. Accordingly, it was not contrary to EU law for Article 33 TRIPs to be directly applied by a national court.

The Advocate General had controversially called for unlimited jurisdiction across all of TRIPs. The argumentation invoked in support was mainly a combination of the status of the WTO as part of international law, the duty of cooperation, and the deficiencies in the existing approach. Little was

[257] See also Holdgaard (2008b: 1239).

[258] See further Koutrakos (2002: 451).

[259] C-431/05 *Merck* [2007] ECR I-7001. In C-89/99 *Groeneveld* [2001] ECR I-5851, like C-53/96 *Hermès*, the application of Art 50 TRIPs in a domestic trademark dispute was at issue but it offered no enhanced understanding pertaining to mixed agreements.

adduced as to deficiencies, but it is easy to point to problems that fidelity to a test based on the exercise of legislative competence poses. It will tend to be left to a case-by-case determination and before the EU Courts if it is to be authoritative. The freedom of domestic courts and the domestic legislature to make determinations as to the legal effect of WTO provisions would be on a timer of sorts. Thus, Member State courts and legislatures are free to determine the legal effect of Article 33 TRIPs, though for how long remains to be seen given that patent harmonization remains on the EU's agenda. Indeed, questions as to what type of legislative activity is necessary for a field to fall within the sphere of EU law will need answering.[260] As for Article 4(3) TEU, this was invoked in underscoring the Member States' obligation with respect to the implementation of EU Agreements and it was asserted that it could be more easily complied with if essentially the ECJ could ensure uniform interpretation even outside those areas where the EU had legislated.[261]

A related argument invoked in calling for a broader approach to jurisdiction is linked to international responsibility and runs essentially as follows:[262] as the EU and Member States did not allocate their respective obligations under the WTO, the EU is jointly and severally liable for all WTO obligations and jurisdiction should be at least coterminous with international responsibility. There is, however, dissent from the mainstream view that joint and several liability flows from mixed agreements in areas of shared competence absent a declaration of competence.[263] It would have been intuitively unattractive to expect that the EU could have been held internationally responsible by, for the sake of hypothesis, Portuguese non-compliance, following *Merck*, with Article 33 TRIPs. But if that were

[260] In *Merck* the ECJ recognized the existence of EU legislative activity in the sphere of patents but introduced the notion that it was not of 'sufficient importance'. See further Koutrakos (2010: 129–33).

[261] The duty of close cooperation in the sphere of mixed agreements founded on Art 4(3) TEU had already been advanced in support of a wider jurisdiction than that resulting from the emerging case law, eg Cremona (2000: 31); Bourgeois (2000: 88, 122).

[262] Variants are considered by Eeckhout (2004: 240 et seq, 270) and AG Tesauro in C-53/96 *Hermès*.

[263] See discussion in Cremona (2006: 344–8) and Kuijper and Passivirta (2004: 122). Of the three Advocates General contributing views, two advanced the joint and several liability line (AG Jacobs in C-316/91 *EP v Council* [1994] ECR I-625 and AG Tesauro in C-53/96 *Hermès*) and one the contrary (AG Mischo in C-13/00 *Commission v Ireland (Irish Berne)* who suggested that the very existence of a mixed agreement announced to non-Member States that the Agreement did not fall wholly within EU competence).

possible there would likewise be an intuitively appealing logic to jurisdiction and certainly the possibility of infringement proceedings.

However, a broad assertion of jurisdiction will not come cost-free. Admittedly one consequence, if jurisdiction were successfully linked to international responsibility and the absence of declarations of competence, might be easily resolved: the Council could see to it that declarations of competence were forthcoming in future treaty negotiations and were kept current to keep track of changing EU competence. But this is of considerable sensitivity to the Member States. The Council intervention against jurisdiction in *Hermès* was a strong indicator and the UK argued that the broad approach to jurisdiction being advanced by the Commission, equivalent to that of the Advocate General in *Merck*, would lead Member States to caution in concluding mixed agreements with a greater inclination for entirely separate arrangements. Such concerns should not be surprising for a bold approach has been taken to the legal effects of EU Agreements.[264] The Member States are thus duly concerned that, even in areas where they retain their treaty-making competence, they may find its exercise in the form of a mixed agreement deprives them, and their domestic courts, of the capacity to determine the domestic legal effect of any of those norms in favour of a supranational court that has generally adopted a markedly internationalist perspective to this question. It might be thought that such political ramifications should not carry any weight, however in *Hermès* the Commission framed its arguments for broader jurisdiction in terms of 'expediency'. Moreover, the ECJ's compromise position was advanced for unidentified practical and legal reasons in *Christian Dior*. As a final note, it bears repeating that whilst jurisdiction in the TRIPs cases was not as expansive as some had called for,[265] it was broader than the position advocated by the Council and those Member States submitting observations.[266]

[264] GATT and WTO Agreements might be put to one side, although even here Member States have Commission-led policing of their obligations to contend with.

[265] Including the Commission, the submissions of which underscored the notion of joint liability and there being a 'Community interest' in jurisdiction. The Commission was only willing to concede an absence of jurisdiction in those areas of exclusive Member State competence.

[266] With the extension of exclusive competence (Art 207(1) TFEU) it has been argued that all of TRIPs now comes within the scope of EU law and that it will no longer be possible to allow national law to determine the legal effects of TRIPs in areas where the EU has not legislated: Eeckhout (2011: 285–6).

3.3.4 *Infringement proceedings*

Infringement rulings against a Member State for breaching WTO rules have not yet arisen. But there is little doubt that such proceedings can be initiated (following the *IDA* logic) and that the ECJ would review national measures against WTO obligations.[267] There is upon closer inspection, as outlined above in relation to the GATT, a defensible logic that can be advanced to support EU measures being in principle free from WTO review by the ECJ, yet this not being so for Member State measures. Arguably, the EU should be able to advance a common stance in areas falling within its competence, with the necessary corollary being that not all Member States need agree with the interpretation advanced of an EU Agreement, but must nonetheless be willing to abide by an ECJ-sanctioned interpretation of it. In the WTO context, this might be viewed as allowing the EU to benefit from the WTO-enshrined scope for manoeuvre while depriving the Member States of that same ability. It might be phrased in a more palatable way as follows: in areas of EU competence the Member States can only benefit from that flexibility to the extent that their position is adopted at EU level, but they are not free simply to track their own paths in tension with a common EU line. This would also give the lie to the assertion that the ECJ views WTO law as not 'meant to be legally binding'.[268]

4. Conclusions

The GATT-era section of this chapter has, against the grain of a now dated debate, defended the principled stance against review vis-à-vis GATT norms. Whilst it was acknowledged that the *International Fruit* reasoning was most certainly capable of more convincing articulation, it was also emphasized that some critics have been guilty of putting forth revisionist accounts of a GATT system as having a more legalistic than diplomatic

[267] Craig and de Búrca (2011: 353) state expressly that infringement proceedings can be brought 'with regard to the WTO agreements'. The then head of the Commission legal service external relations team also implied as much: Kuijper (2006: 271–2). See also AG Maduro's Opinion in C-120/06 P & C-121/06 P *FIAMM*, para 40.

[268] The assertion of Lenaerts and Corthaut (2006: 300).

dispute settlement system and that was not characterized by the great flexibility of its provisions. These revisionist accounts may have gained currency in the debate concerning the legal effect accorded to the GATT in the EU, but they bore little resemblance to the picture then painted of the GATT system by its leading scholars, and also frequently ignore the declining GATT normativity pertaining to agriculture.

There were a total of 37 cases identified with litigants invoking, or the EU Courts in any event employing, GATT Agreements. The small numbers are to be expected because there was little incentive for individual litigants to run GATT-based challenges given the established jurisprudence, and the rejection of Member State challenges came as the GATT era drew to a close. Of these 37 cases, Figure IV.1 provides a breakdown by type of invocation of GATT Agreements.

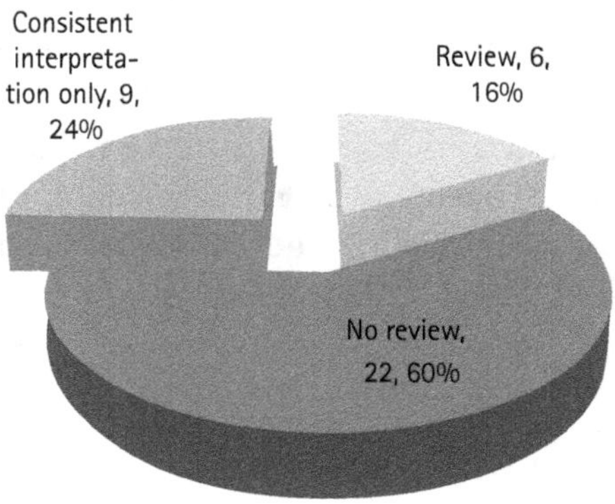

Figure IV.1 GATT Agreements case law (37 judgments)

The consistent interpretation category is exclusively composed of cases where consistent interpretation was employed or relied upon successfully or otherwise to influence interpretation of EU legislation but where no express allegation of a breach of GATT law was apparent. That form of consistent interpretation can, of course, lead to annulment of a subsidiary EU measure.[269] Two of the consistent interpretation cases are in the no-review categorization precisely because there were express GATT breach allegations but no actual review was conducted.[270] As well as the obvious cases where the *International Fruit* reasoning was employed, the no-review categorization includes an upheld standing inadmissibility

[269] As in T-163/94 & T-165/94 *NTN Corporation*.
[270] C-105/90 *Goldstar* and C-175/87 *Matsushita*.

objection,[271] cases seemingly ignoring alleged GATT violations,[272] several anti-dumping cases where even if direct review of the EU measures had taken place this would have been to no avail,[273] a case where a measure was annulled on other grounds,[274] and two cases that some have viewed as examples of review but where a clean bill of health was provided to EU measures and where we would otherwise surely have seen *International Fruit* reiterated.[275]

Four of the six review cases constitute the birth of the *Nakajima* principle and the three further applications, or at least a variant, of that principle though none led to annulment of the contested measure.[276] One is the *Fediol* exception, which likewise did not lead to annulment of the contested measure, and, finally, the infringement ruling against Germany (*IDA*). In short, a maximum of five cases resulted in direct review of EU action vis-à-vis GATT law, as contrasted with the indirect review possible via consistent interpretation, and one instance of GATT review of Member State action.

Turning to the WTO section, this chapter assessed both the judicial contribution and academic debate. Whilst in respect of the judicial stance, the expression *plus ça change, plus c'est la même chose* might appear fitting, it is in fact only superficially so. The reality, as a growing body of WTO scholars have recognized, is that the break from the diplomatic past has not been as pronounced as the initial euphoria that greeted the birth of the WTO in some quarters would suggest.[277] The DSU-sanctioned scope for manoeuvre is the most central, but not sole,[278] manifestation of this. It is fitting, then, that this has formed the centrepiece of the ECJ's principled stance against review in relation to WTO norms whether the litigant has an unimplemented DSB decision in support or not. The analysis conducted herein accordingly leads to the conclusion that whilst the WTO has

[271] 191/88 *Co-Frutta v Commission.*

[272] 41–44/70 *International Fruit Company*; T-159/94 & T-160/94 *Ajinomoto Co*; C-38/95 *Ministero delle Finanze v Foods Import Srl*; 193/85 *Cooperativa Co-Frutta.*

[273] T-170/94 *Shanghai Bicycle*; C-189/88 *Cartorobica*; C-178/87 *Minotta.*

[274] T-115/94 *Opel Austria.*

[275] 112/80 *Dürbeck* was viewed by Lenaerts and Van Nuffel (2011: 868) as an example of review, as was 38/75 *Spoorwegen* by Bebr (1983: 47) and both were viewed as essentially review by Kapteyn (1993: 1015).

[276] C-188/88 *NMB*; T-162/94 *NMB*; C-150/95 *Portugal v Commission* is the variant given there was no reference to the *Nakajima* principle though some form of review vis-à-vis the BHA may have been conducted.

[277] As recognized by, eg, Pauwelyn (2005).

[278] eg waivers and renegotiations.

patently been on the receiving end of distinct judicial treatment to that of other EU Agreements, this is not inconsistent with the presence of a receptive treaty-enforcement model. The WTO has been treated as a case apart because it is indeed a case apart; an EU Agreement with certain unique characteristics, chief of which is the DSU, warranting distinctive treatment. It is instead the alternative of a blind adherence to domestic judicial enforcement writ large in the face of a Treaty transparently drafted to indicate that its Contracting Parties intended no such outcome, underscored in the EU context via the Council Decision concluding the Agreement and the institutional submissions to the Court, that would have given the greatest cause for concern. Not only would such an outcome have had unpredictable consequences for the EU, the Member States, and the WTO, it would also have challenged the EU's capacity to sign up to a Treaty without according the EU and domestic courts a principal role in policing compliance. A likely retort is that the *Kupferberg* option of expressly determining the domestic legal effect via the Treaty itself would have remained. However, this is a nuclear option which would be likely to have predictable consequences for the respect accorded to those norms in other Contracting Parties by both courts and non-judicial actors.

Ninety-four cases have been identified as challenging domestic or EU action with litigants invoking or the EU Courts in any event employing WTO Agreements. Figure IV.2 illustrates the breakdown.

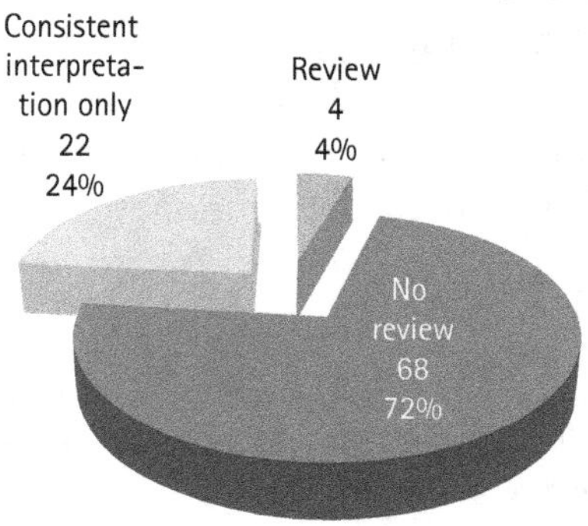

Figure IV.2 Challenges to domestic or EU action invoking WTO Agreements (94 judgments), review conducted/no review conducted/consistent interpretation only

The consistent interpretation category, some 22 cases, is exclusively composed of those cases where consistent interpretation was employed or relied upon, successfully or not, to influence the interpretation of EU legislation but where no express allegation of breach of WTO law was apparent.[279] On that basis, there have been at least 68 cases in which the ECJ was offered the opportunity to engage in direct WTO review of either domestic (in a few rare instances) or EU action but declined.[280] However, the no-review category is deceptive because it includes a number of cases such as *Acme Industries* where reliance on the ADA was rightly rejected on temporal grounds, as well as *Merck* where review in relation to domestic measures was left to the national court, along with three other cases where the Court offered TRIPs interpretations for domestic courts to grapple with.[281] The no-review categorization also includes those cases where *Nakajima* review proper was sought but not conducted.[282] Moreover, nine of the cases that did not lead to review vis-à-vis WTO norms saw a challenged measure annulled on other grounds,[283] and four of these could be viewed as manifestations of 'unacknowledged consistent interpretation'.[284]

Clearly, placing together all the consistent interpretation cases,[285] including those where *Nakajima* review proper was sought but not conducted, and the unacknowledged consistent interpretation cases, and potentially even cases like *Petrotub* and *Huvis* which are perhaps better understood as novel manifestations of consistent interpretation rather than *Nakajima* review, one gets a truer sense of the significant impact that consistent interpretation is having. But the real impact of consistent interpretation only becomes apparent when one considers the real interlocutors for such rulings: ultimately, the rulings primarily put the EU's political actors on notice of their need to ensure textual fidelity to WTO law or risk

[279] C-100/96; T-256/97; T-55/99; T-188/99; T-35/01; C-76/01 P; T-132/01; C-49/02; C-245/02; C-422/02; T-274/02; T-279/03; C-246/05; C-335/05; C-447 & 448/05; C-275/06; T-409/06; T-237/08; C-260/08; C-373/08; C-428/08; C-393/09.

[280] The figure is likely to be higher given that some of the 22 cases in the exclusively consistent interpretation category may have included direct WTO breach pleas, including *Nakajima* or *Fediol* pleas, not clearly articulated in the rulings themselves (T-274/02 *Ritek* and T-279/03 *Galileo* are potential examples).

[281] C-53/96 *Hermès*; C-300 & 392/98 *Christian Dior*; C-89/99 *Groeneveld*.

[282] The terminology of *Nakajima* review proper is used to refer to express review of an EU implementing measure vis-à-vis the relevant WTO Agreements, as contrasted with what is essentially consistent interpretation where the implementing measure is read in conformity with the Agreement.

[283] T-7/99 *Medici*; C-317/99 *Kloosterboer*; T-123/00 *Thomae v Commission*; C-313/04 *Egenberger*; T-107/04 *Aluminium Silicon*; C-351/04 *Ikea*; C-310/06 *FTS*; T-143/06 *MTZ Polyfilms*; T-498/04 *Zhejiang Xinan Chemical Industrial Group v Council*.

[284] C-317/99 *Kloosterboer*; C-313/04 *Egenberger*; C-351/04 *Ikea*; C-310/06 *FTS*.

[285] T-58/99 *Mukand* could also be viewed as a consistent interpretation case rather than direct WTO review.

successful challenges in EU Courts to subsidiary measures taken under EU legislation that essentially implement WTO obligations.[286]

That only four cases can be considered examples of review of EU action in relation to WTO norms, might not be a considerable surprise to many given the principled stance against review and the fact that no infringement rulings have arisen. But that principled stance does allow for *Fediol* and *Nakajima* review which is precisely why such low numbers should be surprising. Three cases at most can be considered applications of the *Nakajima* principle: *Rice Tariffs*, *Petrotub*, and *Huvis*. However, only one (*Petrotub*) led to annulment of an EU measure and in actual fact arguably it, alongside *Huvis*, is more appropriately viewed as a novel and powerful manifestation of consistent interpretation rather than *Nakajima* review vis-à-vis WTO law. The elliptical *Biotech* ruling is the remaining case and the cynic might well note that review was accepted in circumstances where a clean bill of health for the EU measure was easily achieved. If one excluded *Biotech*, *Petrotub*, and *Huvis*, that would leave only one case. Regardless of how one classifies *Petrotub* and *Huvis*, what is clear is that in practice it is unquestionably consistent interpretation rather than the *Nakajima* and *Fediol* principles that constitute the real manifestations of judicial receptiveness to WTO norms. Perhaps, in due course, the ECJ may indeed backtrack on *Nakajima* such that only the doctrine of consistent interpretation remains. In practical terms this would not be the major loss that some might assume because, as demonstrated, *Nakajima* review has never independently led to annulment of an EU measure.[287] Moreover, consistent interpretation, in contrast to *Nakajima* review, exhibits less tension with the *Portuguese Textiles* reasoning. *Fediol* review which has only ever resulted in review once, much less successful review, would be even less sorely missed. In any event, even consistent interpretation alone may be testament to a more receptive approach than that of the courts of other economically powerful WTO members.[288]

The final comment to underscore is that the image of a WTO lawlessness zone in the EU needs to be laid to rest. The judicial manifestation of this is

[286] They are also a message to domestic authorities to interpret EU and domestic law in light of WTO norms.

[287] Although its existence is likely to impact on the EU's political institutions activity, beyond that is encouraging them to avoid referencing WTO norms in their legislative and administrative action for fear of exposure to *Nakajima* review.

[288] For the US equivalent of the consistent interpretation doctrine in the WTO context, see Davies (2007) and Gattinara (2009).

provided by the growing receptivity to WTO norms in interpreting EU and domestic measures even if they can only be used directly as a review criterion in the rarest of circumstances. There has certainly been no judicial sanctioning of an EU hermetically sealed from the WTO. Indeed, the powerful legal consequences of consistent interpretation should not be understated for the EU Courts are regularly being presented with, and often seize, the opportunity to provide rulings consistent with WTO norms, on occasion as interpreted by the Appellate Body and Panels, whether they acknowledge this is what they are doing or not.[289] This can and does lead to EU measures being annulled. To generate a true picture of the extent of this activity is a most difficult task, given the possibility of unacknowledged consistent interpretation, requiring considerable expertise in the intricacies of both EU and WTO law. It will undoubtedly be the occasional high-profile disputes such as *Bananas* and *Hormones* where full compliance is questionable, or tardy at best, that will continue to attract all the headlines. However, there certainly has been a sea change in approach on the part of the political institutions to their WTO obligations. WTO-compliance considerations play an increasingly prominent role in the legislative drafting stage.[290] And the EU's response record to adverse WTO rulings has been positive indeed,[291] albeit often somewhat overshadowed by the long-running critique of the bananas regime.

[289] Scott (2004: 5) perceptively observed that the room for manoeuvre carved out by the DSU 'may be just as effectively—if frequently less visibly—undermined by way of interpretative fidelity to the WTO'.

[290] Bourgeois and Lynskey (2008); de Búrca and Scott (2001). Lawyers with WTO law expertise advise on the compatibility of measures, a development which commenced in the GATT era: Kuijper (1995b: 60).

[291] Wilson (2007: 400–1).

V

The Non-Trade Agreements Before the EU Courts: The Emergence of Judicial Avoidance Techniques in Challenges to EU Action

1. Introduction

This chapter assesses the case law of the EU Courts in the context of essentially challenges to domestic and EU level action involving those Agreements that do not fall into the category of the preceding two chapters. The catch-all category of 'non-trade Agreements' is thus potentially large given the extent of the EU's treaty-making practice. In actual practice it has given rise to a surprisingly low number of cases before the EU Courts and, indeed, much of the case law which has arisen is of very recent vintage. That there is limited case law from the EU Courts, in what is an increasingly expansive category of treaty-making, is itself a significant finding given that the established case law would arguably have provided litigants with every reason to invoke these EU Agreements where their interests were at stake. Nevertheless, despite the paucity of rulings, there is a great deal to be gleaned from a number of the cases that have arisen and the recent growth in rulings is undoubtedly an indicator of things to come. Most significantly of all, the recent *Intertanko* ruling suggests a fundamental reassessment in approach to a core plank of the EU's external relations constitution that results in a considerably less generous gateway for the use of EU Agreements as review criteria than had previously been thought possible.

This chapter is divided into two main sections assessing the two main fashions in which the case law has arisen.

2. Challenges to Domestic Action

Despite the broad treaty-making ambit of the EU, the EU Courts have only had to deal with challenges to action at the Member State level on a handful of occasions.

2.1 Preliminary rulings

The preceding chapters have illustrated that the EU Courts have been called upon to deal with over 150 preliminary rulings in which litigants have sought to challenge domestic action for its alleged incompatibility with EU trade-related Agreements. Strikingly, it was not until 2004 that the ECJ was faced with an alleged incompatibility of national action with a non-trade Agreement.[1]

2.1.1 *The* EDF *ruling: the Barcelona Convention and the Mediterranean Sea Protocol*

The 2004 *EDF* ruling concerned a judicial challenge brought by an association of fishermen against the French electricity provider EDF, because of discharges of fresh water from a hydroelectric power station into a saltwater marsh (the Étang de Berre), which communicated directly with the Mediterranean Sea. The action alleged that the discharges breached a Protocol to the Convention for the Protection of the Mediterranean Sea against Pollution (the Barcelona Convention), in particular a provision requiring that such discharges be subject to prior authorization from the competent domestic authorities which had not occurred here. The EU was a party, alongside its Member States, to both the Protocol and the Barcelona Convention. The Cour de Cassation put forth two questions: first, whether the provision in the Protocol must be held directly effective so that interested parties can rely on it before domestic courts to halt unauthorized discharges; secondly, whether it prohibited the discharges at issue.

The ECJ invoked the *Demirel* direct effect test and asserted it would commence by examining the wording of the provision. A single sentence

[1] C-213/03 *Pêcheurs de l'Étang de Berre v EDF* [2004] ECR I-7357.

followed, holding that it clearly, precisely, and unconditionally laid down a Member State obligation to subject discharges to prior authorization. This was followed by a further sentence reiterating the Commission view that the domestic authority discretion in issuing authorizations in no way diminishes the clear, precise, and unconditional nature of the discharge prohibition absent prior authorization.[2] These two sentences were the extent of the direct textual analysis of the provision. The conclusion was, however, then bolstered by reference to the purpose and nature of the Protocol. It was held to be clear from its articles that its purpose was to prevent, abate, combat, and eliminate certain causes of pollution of the Mediterranean Sea and that to this end Contracting Parties were required to take all appropriate measures. One cannot demur from this exposition of purpose, nor the assertion that followed that the prior authorization requirement contributes to the elimination by Member States of pollution. Here, however, it was followed directly by the assertion that recognition of the provisions' direct effect can only serve the Protocol's purpose and reflect the nature of the instrument which is intended to prevent pollution resulting from the failure of public authorities to act.[3] Clearly, if such reasoning were to be employed when looking to the purpose and nature of an EU Agreement in drawing conclusions as to whether particular provisions are directly effective, then it becomes difficult to conceive of provisions that should be deprived of this status. Certainly, treaties will frequently require action from public authorities and accordingly would have their purposes, ultimately ensuring that States Parties comply with the obligations enunciated therein, served by domestic courts policing compliance. To put it another way, if we operate at this level of abstraction then it would rarely be the case that a treaty will not have its purpose served by domestic judicial enforcement.[4] As to the

[2] In running this argument the Commission (written submissions) invoked a well-known case holding that the existence of discretion upon national authorities did not preclude individual reliance on a Directive to determine whether this discretion had been exceeded: C-287/98 *Linster* [2000] ECR I-6917. *Linster* and other similar cases, notably C-72/95 *Kraaijeveld* [1996] ECR I-5403, are manifestations of judicial boldness vis-à-vis internal EU law and the difficulties presented by the traditional direct effect lens. It is, thus, noteworthy that whilst reiterating the Commission conclusion there was no citation of this line of cases.

[3] The ECJ ruled that the same conclusion applied to the provision as amended, which had not yet come into force, even though it also provided that the prior authorization procedure required the domestic authorities to take due account of relevant decisions or recommendations of the meetings of the Contracting Parties.

[4] The obvious exception would be that rare example of a treaty drafted to exclude domestic judicial enforcement.

second question, the ECJ concluded that the relevant provision did, indeed, absent prior authorization, prohibit the relevant freshwater discharges.

The *EDF* case was clearly of considerable import for it indicated that it was by no means only the predominantly bilateral trade agreements that would receive a receptive hearing before the EU Courts. The direct effect finding was not a foregone conclusion. Admittedly, it had been supported by France, and the Commission, but the counter-argument advanced by EDF was not without merit.[5] EDF emphasized the interdependence of various provisions of the Protocol. The requirement, in the provision held directly effective, to take due account of provisions in an Annex to the Protocol, was considered vague. A provision concerning the formulation of common standards, not yet defined vis-à-vis the discharge at issue, before a prior authorization system was put in place was also invoked. Moreover, it was argued that this being an EU Agreement those standards could principally be at EU level and, as yet, no relevant Directive existed and accordingly the Commission would also have failed to fulfil its obligations.

2.1.2 *The Aarhus Convention and access to justice*

The EU became a party in 2005 to the UN Economic Commission for Europe Convention on Access to Information, Public Participation in Decision-Making and Access to Justice in Environmental Matters (commonly known as the Aarhus Convention). In *LZ VLK* the ECJ addressed an express question from the Slovakian Supreme Court as to the direct effect of Article 9 and in particular subsection (3) requiring that each Contracting Party ensures that members of the public, meeting the criteria, if any, laid down in national law, have access to administrative or judicial procedures to challenge acts and omissions by private persons and public authorities which contravene national environmental law provisions.[6] The Grand Chamber found that the dispute fell within the scope of EU law. It emphasized that the dispute concerned whether an environmental association could be a party to administrative proceedings concerning the grant of derogations to the protection for a species mentioned in the Habitats Directive (92/43/EEC). The Court acknowledged the existence of the

[5] Indeed, the essence of the argument had proved successful before the Cour d'appel d'Aix en Provence from which the case was then appealed to the Cour de Cassation.

[6] C-240/09 *Lesoochranárske zoskupenie VLK v Ministerstvo životné ho prostredia Slovenskej republic*, *(LZ VLK)* Judgment of 8 March.

EU's declaration of competence under the Aarhus Convention that clearly stated that the Article 9(3) obligations, with the exception of their applicability to EU institutions, were the responsibility of the Member States until the EU adopted provisions to implement the obligations. However, for the Court even if a specific issue had not yet been the subject of EU legislation it may fall within the scope of EU law if it is related to a field covered in large measure by it. It underscored in this respect that it was irrelevant that the Aarhus Convention implementing Regulation (1367/2006) only concerned the EU institutions, for where a provision could apply both to situations falling within the scope of EU law, it was in the interest of EU law that, to forestall future differences of interpretation it should be interpreted uniformly.[7]

The ECJ followed the Advocate General in rejecting the direct effect of Article 9(3).[8] For the Court, Article 9(3) did 'not contain any clear and precise obligation capable of directly regulating the legal position of individuals. Since only members of the public who meet the criteria, if any, laid down by national law are entitled to exercise the rights provided for in Article 9(3), that provision is subject in its implementation or effects, to the adoption of a subsequent measure.' Once the jurisdiction hurdle was surmounted, the direct effect conclusion was wholly foreseeable given the express wording of Article 9(3) for even the ECJ's traditionally generous approach to the direct effect of provisions of EU Agreements would struggle where a provision expressly cross-references national legal criteria for its applicability.[9] However, it was far from predictable that it would require domestic courts nonetheless to interpret their domestic procedural law in such a way as to enable an environmental organization, such as the one in the proceedings (LZ), judicially to challenge an administrative decision liable to be contrary to EU environmental law. It reached this conclusion by first emphasizing that Article 9(3) was intended to ensure

[7] C-53/96 *Hermès*, which first used this reasoning to establish jurisdiction over Art 50 TRIPs, was invoked in support.

[8] For the Advocate General this was because it left national law to determine the criteria that trigger its applicability and she added that to attribute that provision direct effect and thus bypass 'the possibility for Member States to lay down the criteria triggering its application, would be tantamount to establishing an *actio popularis* by judicial fiat rather than legislative action.' She also distinguished *Kolpak* and *Simutenkov*, relied upon by LZ, as cases where Member States were setting 'fairly limited procedural criteria, rather than wide-ranging substantive criteria'.

[9] The French Conseil d'État had also previously rejected the direct effect of Art 9(3): Judgment of 5 April 2006, *Mme A, MB and others* (No 275742).

environmental protection and that, in the absence of EU rules, it was for the domestic legal system of each Member State to lay down the detailed procedural rules governing actions for safeguarding individual rights derived from EU law. For the ECJ it was inconceivable that Article 9(3) could be interpreted in such a way as to make it, in practice, impossible or excessively difficult to exercise EU law rights. It was for the national courts, insofar as concerned species protected by EU law and particularly the Habitats Directive, and in order to ensure effective judicial protection in fields covered by EU environmental law, to interpret its national law to the fullest extent possible consistently with the objectives of Article 9(3). Put simply, then, the ECJ reached a conclusion that combined reliance on its effective judicial protection case law with a particularly demanding manifestation of the principle of consistent interpretation, in all but name, essentially to dictate the outcome of the domestic proceedings,[10] and potentially to impact significantly on all manner of domestic proceedings throughout the EU.[11]

Clearly, then, the *LZ VLK* ruling is of considerable significance. The Court was extremely generous in according itself jurisdiction as to the direct effect determination. The declaration of competence combined with the absence of EU implementing legislation for Article 9(3) other than vis-à-vis the EU institutions would surely have led most to conclude, as it did the Advocate General, that the dispute did not fall within the scope of EU law and that it was accordingly for national courts to make the direct effect determination.[12] By reaching the contrary conclusion the Court was able, notwithstanding its rejection of direct effect, substantially to bolster the impact Article 9(3) will be accorded across the EU Member States in a manner that, as one commentator suggested, blurred the distinction between direct effect and consistent interpretation.[13] Furthermore, the broad reading on jurisdiction can be viewed as encouraging the Commission to monitor Member State compliance with Article 9(3), and encourage potential non-compliance to be drawn to its attention, for without this ruling the declaration of competence combined with the absence of EU legislative activity would have sowed strong doubt as to the Court's

[10] The Slovakian Supreme Court proceeded to quash the relevant domestic decisions and required that the NGO be granted access to the review procedures: see Krawczyk (2012: 60–1).

[11] Jans (2011b) has, however, noted Dutch Council of State decisions that followed in which the interpretative obligation enunciated was not considered.

[12] See also the powerful criticism of Jans (2011a) and more briefly Krawczyk (2012: 57–9).

[13] Jans (2011a).

willingness to entertain infringement proceedings for non-compliance with those provisions.[14]

The *LZ VLK* ruling was rapidly followed by the *Trianel* ruling in which the ECJ invoked the Aarhus Convention in offering an interpretation of the Environmental Impact Assessment (EIA) Directive.[15] That Directive, as amended by Directive 2003/35 EC with a view to giving effect to Aarhus Convention obligations, transposes nearly verbatim Article 9(2) of the Aarhus Convention which requires States to permit certain members of the public access to review procedures to challenge administrative decisions, acts, or omissions. An environmental NGO sought to challenge an administrative decision but a court found that it did not have *locus standi* as it was not relying on the impairment of a substantive individual right as required by German law. That German Administrative Court effectively asked whether the amended EIA Directive, and the Aarhus Convention according to the Advocate General's Opinion,[16] precluded the applicability of that German standing rule to environmental NGOs. Essentially, both the Advocate General and ECJ concluded that the Directive precluded the applicability of that German standing rule to environmental NGOs and invoked the Aarhus Convention in doing so. The ECJ made two specific references to the Aarhus Convention in this respect. First, in asserting that the relevant EU 'provisions must be interpreted in the light of, and having regard to, the objectives of the Aarhus Convention, with which—as is stated in [the EIA Directive]—EU law should be properly "aligned".' And, secondly, in concluding that while Member States determine which infringed rights can give rise to an environmental action they cannot deprive environmental protection organizations which fulfil the conditions laid down in Article 1(2) of the EIA Directive—which the Advocate General noted mirrored Article 2(5) of the Convention—of playing the role granted to them both by the EIA Directive and the Aarhus Convention.

The ECJ could surely have reached precisely the same substantive conclusion without expressly referring to the Convention but both the Advocate General and Court references to it in the substantive parts of their opinion and judgment suggest that their conclusions were directly influenced

[14] Commission reluctance to monitor the application of EU environmental agreements had in any event long been identified, see Krmer (2000: 5, 284).

[15] C-115/09 *Bund für Umwelt und Naturschutz Deutschland*, Judgment of 12 May 2011.

[16] Paragraph 2. The referred questions as articulated in the case do not, however, refer expressly to the Aarhus Convention.

by it.[17] It is perhaps not wholly coincidental that this express reliance on the Aarhus Convention appeared in a ruling concerning the same rule of national law before the Aarhus Convention Compliance Committee in a complaint that had been stayed pending the outcome of the EU ruling.[18]

2.2 Infringement proceedings: the *Étang de Berre* ruling

The *Étang de Berre* case saw the ECJ address its first, and thus far only, infringement case alleging non-compliance with a non-trade Agreement.[19] In and of itself this was therefore a significant moment, for the Commission had long been chided by one of its own officials for not pursuing Member State infringements of environmental agreements,[20] the very type of Agreement at issue. The case arose out of the same factual background as the *EDF* ruling. The Commission brought infringement proceedings against France for allegedly failing to reduce pollution from land-based sources, as required by provisions of the Barcelona Convention and, in addition, for breaching the Mediterranean Sea Protocol provision at issue in the *EDF* ruling by not instituting a compatible prior authorization system for discharges. France which had argued in favour of direct effect in *EDF*, and thus by definition accepted ECJ jurisdiction over the prior authorization provision, was now disingenuously arguing that there was no jurisdiction over the provisions being invoked because they did not fall within the scope of EU law; there being no EU Directive regulating the discharges of fresh water and alluvia, the argument ran, resulted in the Convention and Protocol provisions covering such discharges not falling within EU competence.[21]

[17] In contrast, in an earlier case the interpretation of the same provision merely acknowledged that it implemented the relevant Aarhus Convention provision (although the Advocate General relied heavily on the objectives and aims of the Aarhus Convention): C-263/08 *Djurgården-Lilla Värtans Miljöskyddsförening* [2009] ECR I-9967. The current chair of the Compliance Committee has remarked that the criteria at issue in that case requiring environmental associations to have 2,000 members for a right of appeal that was found incompatible with the EIA Directive, were also incompatible with the Aarhus Convention: Ebbesson (2011: 259).

[18] ACCC/C/2008/31. The Advocate General's Opinion acknowledges that this was drawn to the attention of the Court.

[19] C-239/03 *Commission v France (Étang de Berre)* [2004] ECR I-9325.

[20] See Krmer (2000: 5, 284).

[21] The Commission's rejoinder pointed to the 'flagrant contradiction' in the argumentation of France in these two cases. In *EDF* the ECJ had not engaged with the issue of jurisdiction and the

The French argument was dispensed with employing reasoning of considerable significance to the use of the EU institutional machinery for policing compliance with mixed agreements. The ECJ underscored that the Protocol had been concluded under shared competence and that mixed agreements have the same status in the EU as pure EU Agreements insofar as the provisions fall within the scope of EU competence. The Court continued that from this it had inferred that in ensuring compliance with commitments in EU Agreements the Member States fulfil an obligation to the EU, which assumes responsibility for their due performance.

The ECJ then held that the provisions of the Convention and Protocol covered a field that fell in large measure within EU competence. This was supported by reference to environmental protection, the subject matter of the Convention and Protocol, being in the main regulated by EU legislation, with three water pollution protection Directives being invoked in support. As the Convention and Protocol created rights and obligations in a field covered in large measure by EU legislation, it followed that there was an EU interest in both EU and Member State compliance.[22] This finding, the ECJ held, could not be called into question by the fact that the discharges at issue had not yet been the subject of EU legislation.

The ECJ thus asserted jurisdiction over mixed agreement provisions despite the fact that the EU had not actually legislated for the specific type of water pollution at issue. Certainly, it may have been only a matter of time before such legislation appeared and it does raise its own problems to adopt a stance on jurisdiction over mixed agreements that is dependent, at least where a declaration of competence does not exist, on the emergence of EU legislation directly on point.[23] Nevertheless, it is clear that the less

report for the hearing disclosed no attempt by EDF to contest jurisdiction. The association of fishermen did argue for the most expansive of approaches to jurisdiction under a mixed agreement, namely, that, at least where there had been no division of competence, once the EU has adhered to all the provisions of an Agreement, they are part of EU law; that position, however, begs the very question of whether when there is no declaration of competence the EU does indeed adhere to all the provisions.

[22] On the elusive concept of the 'Union interest' in general, see Cremona (2008) and, along with Neframi (2012: 343–9), at 144–56 in the specific mixed agreements context.

[23] eg jurisdiction over provisions would have a markedly temporal dimension; varying over time as the EU legislates and potentially with domestic case law on questions such as direct effect altering over time in line with the position advanced by the ECJ. This applies with a more expansive approach to jurisdiction but in a much less pronounced fashion because if legislation is looked for in a field, or related to a field as it was put in C-240/09 *LZ VLK*, which falls in large measure within EU competence, it by definition permits less scope for diversity. Indeed, the

expansive approach to jurisdiction sought by France could have been adopted.[24] The Court's willingness to expand its jurisdictional reach to the provisions at issue arguably owed something to the possibility of the EU's international responsibility.[25] Thus, although the ECJ did not expressly refer to this, the fact was that it was dealing here with a Convention and Protocol concluded without any declaration of competence and therefore raising the possibility of the EU being jointly liable for any breaches by the Member States.[26] Indeed, this is one reason why the expansive approach to jurisdiction adopted in the later *LZ VLK* ruling, which relied on the *Étang de Berre* ruling, was surprising. For if the *Étang de Berre* ruling was implicitly shaped by potential EU responsibility, in *LZ VLK* we had a declaration of competence that seemed expressly intended to negate the EU's joint responsibility for non-compliance with Article 9(3) at the Member State level. In short, if the extent of jurisdiction sanctioned in *Étang de Berre* was being shaped, if only implicitly, by international responsibility, then *LZ VLK* could be viewed as severing that link.

The ECJ also rejected the French argument that it was only under an obligation of means, effectively an obligation to prove that it had created

temporal problem is only reduced rather than overcome through the jurisdictional approach pursued in C-239/03 *Étang de Berre*, for on that judicial reasoning had such a case arisen in the late 1980s, ie prior to the passage of the Water Pollution Directives that appeared instrumental to establishing jurisdiction, then the field would not have been in large measure covered by EU legislation, only for jurisdiction to be triggered some years later through the passage of the said measures.

[24] A more expansive approach was theoretically possible. The Commission submissions asserted that the simple fact that the EU is party to the Barcelona Convention and the Mediterranean Sea Protocol and that they are mixed agreements concluded in areas of shared competence, meant that the Member States are required to respect them in their entirety; and that this is an obligation owed to the EU that has assumed responsibility for their faithful implementation. Although it acknowledged the recent case law, including vis-à-vis TRIPs, it is clear that the Commission has been advancing the most expansive possible reading of jurisdiction. It was suggested that the ECJ saw an EU interest in holding the Member States to account for the whole of a mixed agreement where it is a matter of shared competence (Cremona 2006: 338–9; 2008: 152), however, the fact that the EU interest point was linked to the Convention and Protocol creating rights and obligations in a field covered in large measure by EU legislation and that the three Water Pollution Directives were cited, suggests that in their absence there would have been no EU interest in ensuring Member State compliance.

[25] See also Kuijper (2010: 209–10). Hoffmeister (2010: 265) also suggested that had the French thesis prevailed 'the Union might have faced the awkward situation of being held liable internationally without having the means to enforce the agreement internally.'

[26] As previous case law suggested: see C-316/91 *European Parliament v Council* [1994] ECR I-625.

sufficient legal means to limit the pollution resulting from the discharges. The Commission went for the broadest possible reading, namely, that it was under an obligation to achieve a particular result. The ECJ did not explicitly adopt that approach but found it to be a '"particularly rigorous obligation"... to "strictly limit" pollution... and to do so by "appropriate measures".' France was found wanting, essentially because the pre-litigation procedure attested to large quantities of harmful discharges from the hydroelectric power station and, in addition, there was no prior authorization system in place. In short, France was held to have failed to fulfil its obligations under the Barcelona Convention, the Mediterranean Sea Protocol, and accordingly also Article 216(2) TFEU.

3. Challenges to EU Action

This section is structured around the small number of cases that have arisen. It first touches upon a miscellaneous array of unsuccessful challenges. The subsection that follows engages briefly with the increasingly controversial tension between the EU standing requirements and Aarhus Convention obligations. The final subsection focuses on three cases that can be viewed as representing opposing approaches to the legal effects of EU Agreements in the EU legal order.

3.1 Miscellaneous unsuccessful challenges

Some five cases fall into this category including the very first occasion when the ECJ was required to address the validity of an EU measure because of its alleged incompatibility with an EU Agreement outside the purely trade sphere.[27] In the 1998 *Compassion in World Farming* (*CIWF*) ruling, CIWF

[27] There were also two cases challenging a Council Regulation adopted to fulfil EU commitments under environmental agreements (the Vienna Convention for the Protection of the Ozone Layer and a related Protocol on Substances that Deplete the Ozone Layer) in which the ECJ invoked the consistent interpretation doctrine vis-à-vis EU Agreements but this did not appear to influence the interpretation of the relevant Regulation, the validity of which was upheld, nor was there any indication from the judgment or the Advocate General that EU Agreements were invoked at the behest of the national courts or the litigants: C-284/95 *Safety Hi-Tech* [1998] ECR 1-4301; and C- 341/95 *Bettati v Safety Hi-Tech* [1998] ECR 1-4355.

had brought a challenge, referred by a UK court, to the Calves Protection Directive alleging it was incompatible with the European Convention on the Protection of Animals Kept for Farming Purposes and a Recommendation adopted thereunder.[28] This aspect of the case was uncontroversially dispensed with, a position supported by the Council, Commission, and the two intervening Member States. The Court emphasized that the Convention did not define standards in the relevant area, indeed, the provisions were indicative only and were limited to providing for the elaboration of recommendations to the Contracting Parties to apply the principles. As to the Recommendation, it expressly provided that it was not directly applicable and was to 'be implemented according to the method that each Party considers adequate, that is through legislation or through administrative practice' and accordingly was held not to contain legally binding obligations. The same Convention arose in a preliminary ruling several years later, where a national court had rejected reliance on it in challenging a Directive by relying on the reasoning in the *CIWF* ruling.[29] Before the ECJ the relevant party did not rely on this claim but did invoke the Convention in seeking recognition of a general principle of EU law on animal welfare that could invalidate a provision of an EU Directive. The Court held that it was not possible to infer any such principle from the Convention, which 'does not impose any clear, precisely defined and unqualified obligation'.

The other three cases share a common trait in that in none did the EU Courts invoke the mantra of EU Agreements being an integral part of EU law or refer to Article 216(2) TFEU. In the first to arise, Spain challenged an implementing Regulation as being in breach of both its parent Regulation, which implemented a programme adopted under the EU-concluded North-West Atlantic Fisheries Organization (NAFO) Convention, and a bilateral EU–Canada Agreement concluded within the NAFO framework.[30] Having upheld the validity of the implementing Regulation vis-à-vis its Parent Regulation, the ECJ held that as the relevant EU–Canada Agreement provision was framed in virtually identical terms to those of the parent Regulation, the plea must be rejected, the logic clearly being that it had already passed muster under the virtually identically phrased parent Regulation.

[28] C-1/96 *Ex parte Compassion in World Farming* [1998] ECR I-1251.

[29] C-189/01 *Jippes* [2001] ECR I-5689.

[30] C-179/97 *Spain v Commission* [1999] ECR I-1251.

The second case saw several companies bring annulment and damages actions against the Commission due to it reducing aid granted to a project within the framework of an EU–Argentina Fisheries Agreement.[31] The companies alleged this was incompatible with the Fisheries Agreement on the grounds, first, that it did not contain a provision entitling the Commission to reduce financial aid and, secondly, that it requires the Commission to consult the Joint Committee set up under the Agreement and to obtain approval from Argentinian authorities before reducing financial aid. The first argument was rejected because although the Agreement contained no such provision, where the EU grants financial aid for the creation of joint enterprises it must also, according to the Court, have the power to reduce that aid if the conditions for its grant have not been observed. The second argument was rejected because there was no ground for inferring from the Agreement's provisions such a requirement.

The third case involved a challenge, on a preliminary reference from a Danish court, to the rule of EU-wide exhaustion of distribution rights in the Information Society Directive which allegedly breached international copyright agreements.[32] This was given short shrift, in line with the submissions of the Council, Commission, and European Parliament: the Court holding that neither of the two relevant World Intellectual Property Organization (WIPO) treaties imposed an obligation to provide for a specific exhaustion rule.[33]

3.2 The Aarhus Convention and EU law standing requirements

Significant doubts have been expressed as to EU compliance with the access to justice provisions of the Aarhus Convention, given in particular the restrictive public participation rights articulated in the EU level implementing Regulation (1367/2006—the 'Aarhus Regulation') combined with

[31] T-44/01, T-119/01 & T-126/01 *Vieira v Commission* [2003] II-1209. The appeal was dismissed without providing any illumination on the EU Agreement issue: C-254/03 P *Vieira v Commission* [2005] ECR I-237.

[32] C-479/04 *Laserdisken* [2006] ECR I-8089.

[33] WIPO Copyright Treaty and Performances and Phonograms Treaty to which the EU and the Member States are parties.

the notoriously stringent EU law standing requirements.[34] The Aarhus Convention was involved in an attempted challenge to certain total allowable catches adopted via a Council Regulation.[35] One ground of challenge was non-compliance with the EU-concluded UN Fish Stocks Agreement. The Council and the Commission raised a standing-based admissibility objection. WWF-UK argued that under the Aarhus Convention and the Aarhus Regulation it was entitled to be informed early in the decision-making procedure and to be involved in the adoption of the contested Regulation such that it was directly and individually concerned for standing purposes. However, the GC ruled that any Aarhus Convention and Aarhus Regulation entitlements were conferred upon WWF-UK as a member of the public and did not differentiate it from all other persons. The GC went on to assert that in any event the Aarhus Regulation was only applicable after the contested Council Regulation was adopted. This was indeed so. However, as WWF-UK rightly emphasized, the Convention bound the EU prior to the entry into force of the Aarhus Regulation and the Council Regulation being challenged. That the GC did not propose a liberalization of the standing criteria is perhaps unsurprising given the response to its previous attempt.[36]

The Aarhus Convention Compliance Committee was soon faced with an environmental organization alleging EU non-compliance with its obligations because of the standing rules.[37] The *WWF-UK* appeal was nevertheless dismissed with no indication that the Aarhus Convention had been raised in the pleas.[38] This led to renewed communications before the

[34] See eg Wenneras (2007: ch 5, and 320 et seq); Pallemaerts (2011).

[35] T-91/07 *WWF-UK v Council* [2008] ECR II-81.

[36] Compare T-177/01 *Jégo-Quéré* [2002] ECR II-2365 with C-50/00 P *Unión de Pequeños Agricultores* [2002] ECR I-6677 and C-263/02 P *Jégo-Quéré* [2004] ECR I-3425.

[37] Communication ACCC/C/2008/32.

[38] C-355/08P *WWF-UK v Council and Commission* [2009] ECR I-73. The GC ruling was followed in T-37/04 *Região autónoma dos Açores v Council* [2008] ECR II-103 where the autonomous region of the Azores, supported by several environmental associations, sought the annulment of a Council fisheries Regulation and invoked the Convention to bypass the strict standing requirements. This was to no avail for the GC held that the action was brought prior to EU approval of Aarhus, which is the date upon which admissibility is assessed. That conclusion certainly makes sense for it would be inappropriate to allow an EU Agreement to have retroactive impact on how standing is interpreted. However, the GC unnecessarily appeared to set itself against a different approach in that it proceeded to assert that there is an EU Regulation in place to facilitate access to the EU judicature and that 'it is not for the Court to substitute itself for the legislature and to accept, on the basis of the Aarhus Convention, the admissibility of an action which does not meet the condition laid down in Article 2[63].' The appeal was dismissed with no

Compliance Committee, with respect to the pending complaint, as to the ECJ stance confirming the incompatibility of EU standing rules with the Aarhus Convention. In April 2011 the report of the Compliance Committee was adopted and it concluded that if the existing standing jurisprudence continued, without adequate administrative review procedures, the EU would fail to comply with Article 9 of the Convention.[39] The recommendations called quite explicitly for the EU Courts to adopt a different approach to the standing jurisprudence in order to ensure compliance with the Convention. There was already an argument to be made that the EU judiciary should liberalize the standing criteria in light of the Aarhus Convention, as it binds all EU institutions under Article 216(2) TFEU.[40] This argument has been bolstered by the Compliance Committee's findings and recommendations. However, if the ECJ were to allow the Aarhus Convention to influence its approach to interpretation of the standing requirements, and thus the meaning of Article 263, this would arguably require overruling the GC judgment in which it was held that consistent interpretation could not be used vis-à-vis provisions of the Treaty.[41] Of course, from an international law perspective even internal law of constitutional rank provides no justification for failure to perform treaty obligations.[42] Whilst concerns with allowing treaty obligations to be employed in a manner that alters the EU's primary law are wholly understandable,[43] an

indication that the pleas concerned the Aarhus Convention: C-444/08 P *Região autónoma dos Açores v Council* [2009] ECR I-200.

[39] ACCC/C/2008/32.

[40] See also Pallemaerts (2011: 311).

[41] T-201/04 *Microsoft* [2007] ECR II-3601, discussed in Chapter IV. In addition in T-18/10 *Inuit Tapiriit Kanatami v Parliament and Council*, Order of 6 September 2011, applicants challenging a Regulation on Trade in Seal Products invoked both the Aarhus Convention and the Convention on Biological Diversity in support of a broad interpretation of Art 263(4) TFEU but for the Court the applicants did not state how the admissibility conditions should be interpreted; their arguments were viewed as very general and having no bearing on the admissibility conditions with the GC taking the opportunity to underscore, by invoking *Kadi* (C-402/05 & C-415/05) and its earlier *Microsoft* ruling, that international conventions may not depart from EU law primary rules.

[42] See Art 27 of the 1969 and 1986 VCLT.

[43] The Treaty itself is subject to an extremely demanding amendment procedure (Art 48 TEU), even via the newly created simplified revision procedure, which requires unanimity at EU level as well as ratification by all the Member States following whatever domestic constitutional hurdles they have in place. EU Agreements, in contrast, can be the product of qualified majority voting in the Council, without requiring European parliamentary approval (albeit this will be rarely so in the post-Lisbon era), and without having to satisfy additional domestic constitutional hurdles (mixed agreements will, however, be subject to additional constitutional hurdles at the Member State level). In short, it had long been a concern, as evinced in the literature on the ex

alternative outcome is arguably warranted with the much-criticized standing requirements that are not dictated by the language in the EU Treaty.[44] The Aarhus Convention and the Compliance Committee report supplies a strong additional reason for reconsidering the existing approach, if only in the limited environmental context to which it applies.[45]

3.3 Espousing maximalist treaty enforcement?

There were important indicators that the maximalist approach to treaty enforcement had the potential to take hold even where EU measures were being challenged. Two cases stood out, both because of the reasoning employed and, crucially, the number of judges hearing the respective cases.

3.3.1 *The Biotech judgment*

In the *Biotech* case, mentioned briefly in Chapter IV, the Netherlands had challenged the Biotech Directive with pleas that it breached WTO Agreements.[46] In addition, it was alleged that it breached the Convention on Biological Diversity (CBD), an international environmental agreement to which the EU is a party. The Council argued that a direct effect hurdle must be surmounted and that this requirement was not satisfied by the CBD. The Court held, however, that the WTO exclusion could not apply to the CBD which, unlike the WTO, is not based on reciprocal and mutually advantageous arrangements. It then famously sought to dissociate

ante and ex post review debate considered in Chapter II, that Agreements could be used as a mechanism that bypasses the rigid amendment procedure. As Chapter I noted, in some legal orders treaties can be accorded a hierarchically superior rank domestically to that of the constitution itself, but in two States where this had been constitutionally provided for, as was the case in Austria and is still the case in the Netherlands, an increased parliamentary threshold for Treaty approval was required.

[44] See on the standing debate, Craig and de Búrca (2011: 491–510).

[45] Of crucial significance to the adequacy vis-à-vis the Aarhus Convention of the administrative review procedures, are several pending internal review decision challenges under the Aarhus Regulation, see T-338/08 *Stichting Natuur en Milieu and Pesticide Action Network Europe v Commission*; T-396/09 *Vereniging Milieudefensie v Commission*. As a result, some issues pertaining to Communication ACCC/C/2008/32 were deferred as *sub judice*.

[46] C-377/98 *Netherlands v Parliament and Council (Biotech)* [2001] ECR I-7079.

direct effect from review vis-à-vis obligations under an EU Agreement by holding:

> Even if, as the Council maintains, the CBD contains provisions which do not have direct effect, in the sense that they do not create rights which individuals can rely on directly before the courts, that fact does not preclude review by the courts of compliance with the obligations incumbent on the [EU] as a party to that agreement. (Para 54)

The ECJ here appeared to position itself as the handmaiden of the international legal order, there to ensure that the EU legislative actors made good on the international commitments which they had voluntarily assumed.[47] Direct effect and the language of individual rights with which it has been so closely associated could not, it seemed, be invoked to preclude review in relation to Treaty commitments. Or, if one prefers, this famous paragraph could simply be read as rejecting the narrow approach to direct effect understood as the capacity of a provision to create judicially enforceable individual rights, but not the broad notion of direct effect which focuses rather on mere justiciability or invocability of the provisions. Direct effect is thus relevant on this reading, but individual rights are not. The artificiality of this distinction has already been alluded to in Chapter I, for direct effect can simply be used as a label affixed to norms permitted to be used as criteria for review whether or not they can be said to confer individual rights, and what is or is not an individual right is hardly an issue free from contestation. In any event, a hurdle of provisions needing to create rights which individuals can rely on directly before the courts was rejected and this could be read as embracing a more receptive approach to review of EU norms in relation to EU Agreements. It is this message that was warmly received by segments of the scholarly community, albeit they rarely expressly engage with the normative implications that follow, the unspoken assumption is simply that greater judicial enforcement is to be commended. For Lenaerts and Corthaut it fitted their attempt to build a general theory of invocability around the primacy principle rather than the elusive doctrine of direct effect,[48] and for Cremona the trend away from regarding direct effect as a condition of judicial review in direct actions was praised.[49]

[47] Surprisingly there was no reference to Art 216(2) TFEU.
[48] (2006). They refer expressly to the *Biotech* ruling at 298.
[49] (2006: 352–3).

The sweeping rejection of the rights hurdle, and potentially direct effect depending perhaps on whether it is construed narrowly or broadly, was followed by the curious proposition that the plea should be understood as being directed not at a direct EU breach of its Treaty obligations, but an obligation imposed on the Member States by the Biotech Directive to breach their international law obligations while it in fact claimed not to affect those obligations. These international law obligations on the Member States come from several sources: the CBD and the WTO are mixed agreements and thus by definition impose international law obligations on the Member States.[50] In effect, however, this meant that as the plea was accepted for the aforementioned reasons we were not in fact told whether the CBD was considered to create rights that individuals could rely on directly. In any case, the Directive emerged unscathed from the review vis-à-vis the CBD.[51]

3.3.2 *The IATA ruling*

Some five years after the *Biotech* ruling, the Grand Chamber handed down a preliminary ruling that prima facie sat comfortably with the bold approach to treaty enforcement long exhibited where domestic action was the subject of challenge. In the *IATA* case, an EU Regulation concerning compensation for passengers in the event of a boarding refusal, cancellation, or long delay of flights (the Air Passenger Rights Regulation: 261/2004), was challenged on the grounds of, inter alia, an alleged incompatibility with the Montreal Convention on the Unification of Certain Rules for International

[50] A Treaty to which the Member States alone were parties (the European Patent Convention) was also at issue.

[51] The allegation was that making biotechnological inventions patentable ran counter to the CBD objective of fair and equitable sharing of benefits arising out of the utilization of genetic resources; the ECJ found that there was no provision requiring that conditions for the grant of a biotech patent should include consideration of the interests of the country from which the genetic resource originates or the existence of measures for transferring technology. As to the possibility that the Directive could represent an obstacle to the international cooperation necessary to achieve CBD objectives, it was emphasized that under the Directive the Member States were to apply it in accordance with their biodiversity obligations, in other words suggesting that the Directive should not be used by the Member States to shirk their international cooperation obligations under the CBD. The reading of the compatibility of the Directive with the CBD obligations does not appear to have generated any adverse commentary, see briefly Spranger (2002: 1154–6).

Carriage by Air.[52] The ECJ was content to conclude in a single sentence that the provisions were among the rules in light of which it reviewed the legality of EU acts 'since, first, neither the nature nor the broad logic of the Convention precludes this and, second, those three articles appear, as regards their content, to be unconditional and sufficiently precise.' One might easily be persuaded that this is so, given that the Convention is concerned essentially with air passengers' rights vis-à-vis air carriers, but that conclusion was not actually preceded by any analysis of the nature or broad logic of the Montreal Convention or of the unconditionality or precision of the provisions at issue. Conceptually, it was thus of clear constitutional significance for it represented an approach to EU Agreements which took as its starting point their capacity to be used as criteria for legality review. In other words, the judgment, like the Advocate General's Opinion, read as if there was a clear presumption of invocability such that no reasoned justification other than passing reference to Article 216(2) TFEU, and the oft-repeated assertion that provisions of EU Agreements are an integral part of EU law, was actually required.[53] Whilst the criteria referred to for the agreement to be used in legality review are those of the *Kupferberg* and *Demirel* two-part direct effect test, even if their express application was absent, the language of direct effect and individual rights was wholly absent.[54] In this sense, the ruling sat comfortably with the *Biotech* judgment and the then emerging emphasis on the primacy-based

[52] C-344/04 *IATA* [2006] ECR I-403. Domestic proceedings between airlines and individuals seeking compensation have led to preliminary rulings in which the Montreal Convention was mentioned in the context of interpreting the Air Passenger Rights Regulation (C-173/07 *Emirates Airlines* [2008] ECR I-5237; C- 549/07 *Wallentin-Hermann v Alitalia* [2008] ECR I-11061; C- 204/08 *Rehder v Air Baltic* [2009] ECR I-6073) or engaged with extensively in the one instance where the domestic court expressly sought an interpretation of the Convention (C-63/09 *Axel Walz v Clickair* [2010] ECR I-4239) but it is two pending cases that have seen national courts directly raise questions pertaining to the validity of the Air Passenger Rights Regulation vis-à-vis the Montreal Convention: C-629/10 *TUI Travel v Civil Aviation Authority* and C-12/11 *McDonagh v Ryanair*.

[53] The question put by the High Court in the UK was not framed in terms of direct effect and individual rights which renders it less surprising that the response did not employ the language of individual rights and direct effect. That said, in a contemporaneously decided preliminary ruling, challenging a domestic measure for incompatibility with an EU Agreement (Euro-Med–Tunisia), where the question was also not framed in terms of individual rights and direct effect, the ECJ conducted a direct effect determination within a section of the judgment expressly so entitled: C-97/05 *Gattoussi*.

[54] One explanation for this may be the fact that here, unlike in *Kupferberg* and *Demirel*, along with many other cases using the individual rights and direct effect language, we were not dealing with challenges to domestic measures but rather to EU measures.

approach to invocability. Indeed, in a co-authored article by Judge Lenaerts, who was a member of the *IATA* Grand Chamber formation, this case was cited in support of the proposition that whether an Agreement confers individual rights is not an issue in legality review of EU acts, the articles simply need to be unconditional and sufficiently precise to the extent that they are apt to serve as a yardstick for review and not in the sense that they confer rights on individuals as is required in cases involving direct effect.[55]

The second stage of the analysis in *IATA* might, however, be read as providing some grounds for hesitation as to the extent of the judicial receptiveness to treaty enforcement actually exhibited. An interpretation of the Convention provisions was put forth that preserved the validity of the Regulation, consistently with the views put forth by the three EU institutions (Council, Commission, and European Parliament) and the sole intervening Member State (the UK). A distinction was drawn between the types of obligations under the Regulation and those falling within the Convention's scope. In doing so, the ECJ proposed a distinction between two types of damage: first, excessive delay causing damage almost identical for every passenger and redress of which may take the form of standardized and immediate assistance or care for everyone (eg refreshments, meals, accommodation, telephone calls); and, secondly, individual damage inherent in the reason for travelling requiring a case-by-case assessment. The Convention provisions were held to govern the latter damages. And it was held not to follow from the Convention that the drafters intended to shield the carriers from other forms of intervention, particularly action by public authorities to redress, in a standardized and immediate manner, the damage that delay causes without having to suffer the inconvenience inherent in bringing judicial damages actions. For the ECJ, the assistance and taking care of passengers envisaged by the Regulation were standardized and immediate compensatory mechanisms unregulated by the Convention and that simply operate at an earlier stage than the Convention system.

The Court's analysis has come in for trenchant criticism from a leading aviation law expert who acted for the airline associations.[56] The distinction between types of damage is alleged to be 'novel and . . . misconceived'. Essentially the argument runs that the first type of damage is not as standardized and immediate as the ECJ would have us believe, for the

55 Lenaerts and Corthaut (2006: 299).

56 Balfour (2007). See also Wegter (2006).

reimbursement obligation under the Regulation, unmentioned by the ECJ and the Advocate General, will vary significantly and 'in many instances individual factors and circumstances will have to be taken into account on a case-by-case basis'.[57] Moreover, the view that the Convention governs the second type of damage is also contested given that there are instances in which courts have held passengers entitled to reimbursement of hotel and transport costs under the delay provisions of the predecessor to the Montreal Convention, which contains essentially identical provisions. Furthermore, no consideration was given to the possibility that if a carrier failed to comply with its obligations under the Regulation for a passenger to then bring a damages action would be in direct tension with the exclusivity provision in the Convention (Art 29).[58] Thus, despite the ECJ having commenced its analysis of the scope of the Convention's provisions by paying lip-service to the Vienna Convention rules on treaty interpretation, it is arguable that the Regulation might not have emerged unscathed had a more textually faithful interpretative exercise been conducted.[59]

3.4 Embracing judicial avoidance techniques

A much anticipated judgment was handed down by the Grand Chamber in June 2008 which arguably provided the first test of how the theoretically generous approach to the review hurdles employed in cases like *IATA* and *Biotech* would play out where there were significant question marks about the compatibility of an EU legislative measure with an EU Agreement.

3.4.1 *The* Intertanko *ruling*

In the *Intertanko* case, several organizations representing substantial proportions of the shipping industry brought a challenge to the recently enacted Ship-Source Pollution Directive before the High Court in the

[57] Balfour (2007: 558).

[58] It provides that damages actions in the carriage of passengers can only be brought under the terms of the Convention. Both Balfour (2007) and Wegter (2006) highlighted two judgments, from the House of Lords and US Supreme Court, which had emphasized the exclusivity of the predecessor Convention. This issue has been raised in a pending Dutch preliminary reference: C-315/11 *Van de Ven & Van de Ven-Janssen v KLM NV*.

[59] Contrast Denza (2008: 876–7) referring to a careful interpretation of the relevant provisions in light of the Vienna Convention rules.

UK.[60] They alleged that the Directive provided a stricter standard of liability—serious negligence—for accidental discharges than was permitted by the International Convention for the Prevention of Pollution from Ships (MARPOL) of which it was accordingly in breach, and that this also amounted to a breach of the right of innocent passage in the UN Convention on the Law of the Sea (UNCLOS). In support of this argument they invoked the powerful and unequivocal voice of the former President of the judicial body established under UNCLOS, the International Tribunal for the Law of the Sea.[61] Unlike MARPOL, to which only the Member States are party, UNCLOS is an EU Agreement. However, MARPOL could nevertheless be relevant for review purposes in one of two ways: first, if the ECJ accepted that the EU had succeeded to the rights and obligations therein, as it had held with respect to the GATT; secondly, because compliance with UNCLOS only permits (Art 211(5)) coastal States in respect of their exclusive economic zones, to adopt vessel pollution laws and regulations conforming to generally accepted international rules and standards, which in this case would be those enunciated by MARPOL.[62]

The submissions before the Court were illuminating, involving as they did all three institutional actors and ten Member States. The Council and one intervening Member State sought outright to preclude review vis-à-vis UNCLOS in the context at hand by contesting jurisdiction over this mixed EU Agreement. Such challenges offer an EU context-specific avenue for avoiding the consequences that otherwise flow from adherence to an automatic incorporation model. This argument was only addressed by the Advocate General and was rightly given short shrift; the reasoning being that there is jurisdiction over UNCLOS where EU rules exist within the areas covered by the Convention provisions, which was clearly so here via the very Directive at issue.

Of greater significance were the views as to review in relation to UNCLOS. The requirements that review not be precluded by the nature or broad logic of an EU Agreement, and that the provisions at issue be unconditional and sufficiently precise, were considered unsatisfied by four Member States,[63] the Council, and the European Parliament. The written observations submitted by the Commission did not address themselves to

[60] C-308/06 *Intertanko* [2008] ECR I-4057.

[61] Mensah (2005).

[62] This is clear from Directive 2005/35/EC itself (see recital 2 and Art 1(1)).

[63] Three of which (France, Italy, and Spain) automatically incorporate treaties.

this issue,[64] though it did argue for the validity of the Directive. As will be suggested further below, given the nature of UNCLOS, and the scope of its provisions, it is difficult but to conclude that the position advanced by the institutions was a call for use of an avoidance technique to avoid the otherwise logical consequences resulting from adherence to the automatic treaty incorporation model. The stance of those Member States arguing unreservedly for annulment of the Directive's provisions was relatively predictable given that two (Greece and Malta) were outvoted on the Directive in the Council, whilst the other (Cyprus) abstained, precisely because of the compatibility concerns. The accidents of litigation are such that States in favour of a particular outcome in one case advance a view that need not be representative of a broader normative vision of the place of EU Agreements in the EU legal order.[65]

The Grand Chamber's ruling outlined a twin-pronged test for review vis-à-vis international rules in preliminary rulings. The first was the requirement from *International Fruit* that the EU be bound by the relevant rules and, the second, that the nature and broad logic of a treaty not preclude review and that its provisions appear unconditional and sufficiently precise. The *IATA* ruling was invoked in support of this second requirement, it constituting a change in formulation from the language first used in *International Fruit* and requiring that the international law provision be capable of conferring rights on EU citizens. MARPOL was unable to surmount the first requirement on the grounds, inter alia, that there had not been a full transfer of Member State powers to the EU.[66]

The analysis of UNCLOS generated the conclusion that its nature and broad logic precluded validity review. The essence of the reasoning was that

[64] The fact that the Advocate General identified four Member States, the Council, and the Parliament as arguing against the possibility of review suggests that the Commission made no such argument.

[65] However, given that the EU Courts have been bold when it comes to EU Agreements invoked by litigants vis-à-vis domestic action, both as to the preliminary question of being a relevant review criterion and the substantive interpretation duly proffered (even where direct effect was rejected as in C-240/09 *LZ VLK*), it is unsurprising that, where those same Member States find themselves outvoted in the Council where serious compatibility concerns with an EU Agreement are apparent, they will attempt to benefit from the ostensibly open channels provided for the invocability of EU Agreements.

[66] It was, nevertheless, held that in view of the customary international law principle of good faith, and Art 4(3) TFEU, it was required to take account of MARPOL in interpreting UNCLOS and secondary law falling within its field of application. For comment on this issue, see Eeckhout (2009: 2051–3).

although it lays down legal regimes governing the territorial sea, international straits, archipelagic waters, the exclusive economic zone, the continental shelf, and the high seas, it does not in principle grant independent rights and freedoms to individuals. Rather, on the Court's understanding, the rights and freedoms, as well as obligations, attach to the flag State. Whilst it was conceded that some UNCLOS provisions appeared to attach rights to ships, it did not follow that those rights were thereby conferred on the individuals linked to those ships. Nor did the Court consider doubt to be cast on its analysis by the fact that Part XI of UNCLOS involved natural and legal persons in the exploration and use of the sea-bed and ocean floor, since the case at issue did not concern such provisions. It was, accordingly, held that UNCLOS did not establish rules intended to apply directly and immediately to individuals and to confer upon them rights or freedoms capable of being relied upon against States.

3.4.2 *Assessing the* Intertanko *ruling*

The most striking aspect of the *Intertanko* ruling was that the language of individual rights reared its head as a mechanism to preclude review. It was, of course, with the establishment of this criterion as the second prong in a two-part test, that the GATT was first rejected as a review criterion for EU law in *International Fruit*. Over 35 years on, despite the emergence of a rich body of jurisprudence—including with respect to EU Agreements—that dissociated their invocability from an individual rights conceptualization, and the individual rights criterion has been resurrected and read into the exploration of whether the nature and broad logic of an EU Agreement precludes review. It is difficult not to recognize the convenience in its resurrection when it is an EU legislative measure being challenged, especially when it is difficult to envisage how, were review to have been conducted, a substantive scope interpretation of the UNCLOS provisions could have left the Directive intact.[67] We might well ask whether the seemingly self-evident answer to the second step of the analysis, the actual review that the judgment itself avoided, is influencing the answer to the first

[67] See, however, the Advocate General's attempt, employing the doctrine of consistent interpretation, and König (2007). Compliance with both UNCLOS and MARPOL was also defended in a book published shortly before the *Intertanko* ruling by a maritime law expert who acted as the Commission's agent, though it is noteworthy that he had also suggested that UNCLOS would satisfy the first step of the direct effect test: Ringbom (2008: 401–27, 123). Contrast the strong doubts expressed as to compliance in Tan (2010).

step as to the capacity of the Agreement itself to form a review criterion for EU law.

It is surprising, then, that one respected commentator asserted that 'The conclusion that UNCLOS . . . sets out rights and duties among states and is not capable of being applied directly by individuals is clearly correct.'[68] It may be axiomatic that UNCLOS sets out rights and duties among States,[69] but it does not follow that it is not capable of being applied directly by individuals, much less that this is clearly a correct conclusion. The ECJ was faced with a specific question pertaining to a specific EU Agreement but the broader outcome is central to the EU's external relations constitution—the criteria for review in relation to EU Agreements. In addressing this question, it opted to resurrect the individual rights criterion, however, it could equally have opted, as one would have expected based on recent case law, to ignore individual rights and to explore whether the nature or broad logic of UNCLOS precluded review. To resort to the argument that the absence of individual rights is a manifestation of the nature or broad logic of an Agreement precluding review, is for the Court to endow itself with a fail-safe mechanism or judicial avoidance technique that could generally be invoked at will to reject EU Agreement-based review of EU measures when persuasive and politically contentious challenges arise, as was the case in *Intertanko*. After all, it will commonly be the case that an EU Agreement can be interpreted as not establishing 'rules intended to apply directly and immediately to individuals and to confer upon them rights or freedoms capable of being relied upon against States'. It is essential to probe further and ask whether this is even the right question to ask. If the ECJ has interpreted the founding constitutional document as attaching the EU to a model of automatic treaty incorporation, then this could be viewed as creating a presumption of enforceability that cannot simply be offset by the proposition that a particular Agreement does not establish rules intended to apply directly and immediately to individuals. For which Agreement is so intended to apply? And how are we to discover this intention? Are we concerned here with the intention simply of the drafters of the Agreement invoked? And, if so, how is this to be weighed against the intentions that some would, and appear to, read into Article 216(2) TFEU?

[68] Denza (2008: 875).

[69] The Advocate General did refer to peaceful use as also being directed precisely at individuals involved in maritime transport and noted that shipping is operated for the most part by private individuals.

Denza proceeded to suggest that the Advocate General, for whom review was possible vis-à-vis UNCLOS, failed 'to distinguish properly between rights... given to ships and enforceable by the flag state and rights capable of being relied on by individuals or enterprises before national courts.'[70] But it was surely because such a formalistic distinction would have been in marked tension with the extant jurisprudence dissociating invocability and review from individual rights conferral, that no such distinction was defended. Indeed, to the contrary, the Advocate General expressly drew attention to the fact that individuals do not derive rights from the legal bases of the treaties but they may question the legality of secondary law by contesting the legal basis thereof.

That the Advocate General found herself wrong-footed by the Grand Chamber ruling is not surprising, considering that the earlier Grand Chamber ruling in *IATA* provided no express support for the re-emergence of the individual rights analysis (though, of course, it involved an Agreement concerned with passenger damages claims against air carriers). Indeed, as previously noted, the well-known contribution by Judge Lenaerts relied on *IATA* in explicitly disavowing any link between individual rights and review of EU acts.[71]

And if we look back to the *EDF* case, which preceded *IATA* by less than 18 months, the language of individual rights did not even rear its head. A direct effect analysis was conducted, as requested by the French court, but it will be recalled that it started with the text of the relevant provisions invoked, a stage which the ECJ did not even embark upon in *Intertanko*,[72] and an assertion of their clarity, precision, and unconditionality. This was then bolstered by reasoning that seemed to amount to the proposition that direct effect could only serve the purpose of the instrument to prevent pollution. Now, UNCLOS is a treaty of astonishing breadth, so it becomes difficult simply to pinpoint a purpose as the ECJ did with the Mediterranean Sea Protocol; however, there is a section of this grand Treaty devoted expressly to, and so entitled, 'innocent passage in the territorial sea'. Could one not then say that recognition of direct effect—or rather review of EU norms vis-à-vis UNCLOS—could only serve the purpose of ensuring innocent passage in the territorial sea? And that the UNCLOS provisions

70 (2008: 875).

71 Lenaerts and Corthaut (2006).

72 Likewise with the GATT/WTO jurisprudence subject to *Nakajima/Fediol* and consistent interpretation.

invoked on the right of passage[73] are clear, precise, and unconditional, and contribute to this purpose? Perhaps this is too narrow a manner in which to construe purpose and does not do the *EDF* reasoning justice. Nonetheless, if we were to transpose the judicial language employed in *Intertanko*, are we now to believe, and would those persuaded by the individual rights reasoning employed in *Intertanko* concede, that the Mediterranean Sea Protocol established 'rules intended to apply directly and immediately to individuals and to confer upon them rights or freedoms capable of being relied upon against States'? The fact that the ECJ required that individuals be allowed to rely on the provisions invoked in *EDF* is a somewhat different matter, because this did not suggest that the Court was addressing whether the Agreement was intended to confer *rights* on individuals. Undoubtedly, it is now possible, with ex post rationalization, to assert that we were dealing with individual rights in *EDF* and accordingly to square it with *Intertanko*. But this would be to resort to word-games. The critics can inevitably be expected to emphasize that whilst *EDF* shares with *Intertanko* an important trait—a multilateral agreement, or at least not a bilateral agreement (the Barcelona Convention and the Protocol are often classified as regional agreements)[74]—it is the important distinction—a challenge to domestic rather than EU action—that might explain, or at least contribute to explaining, the contrasting outcomes.

The Council, however, did emphasize in its submissions that UNCLOS does not confer individual rights and resorted to employing the logic used against review of EU measures vis-à-vis WTO Agreements such as: the absence of reciprocity, that is, other national courts generally avoid interpreting UNCLOS, and that it has a variety of dispute settlement procedures which confer on Contracting States a degree of flexibility. The ECJ, however, was not to be drawn on this issue. And so, in this sense, whilst it might be tempting to view the *Intertanko* ruling as the ECJ applying the principles underlying its WTO case law to other treaties,[75] should be resisted for that reasoning was eminently defensible, grounded as it was in the DSU text and not in the absence of individual rights. Undoubtedly, had the WTO dispute settlement reasoning been employed by analogy, the

[73] Articles 17, 19, and 211(4).

[74] It is identified as a multilateral treaty in the EU treaties database but that only provides for a bilateral/multilateral distinction. Eeckhout's coverage also appears in a section entitled 'multilateral agreements' (2011: 352).

[75] See Bronckers (2008: 886). Cannizzaro (2012: 48–9) and Cremona (2011: 242) both rightly underscore the distinction with the reasoning employed in the WTO context.

criticism would have been severe given the sophisticated nature of the WTO dispute settlement system alongside the express preservation, at least temporarily, of outcomes that do not comply with the substantive provisions of WTO Agreements, both of which would be threatened if EU Courts became, in effect, WTO courts of first instance. UNCLOS does not operate in this fashion and, as the Advocate General emphasized, it does not establish exclusive interpretive competence on the part of other institutions, nor does it provide its Contracting States, in general terms, with flexibility or opportunities to derogate.[76]

Ultimately, it should be conceded that there was nothing inherent in UNCLOS precluding the Court from reviewing the compatibility of EU measures with its provisions. Many WTO provisions may well be sufficiently clear, precise, and unconditional on their own terms to support their capacity to be used for review purposes; however, there we do have important significant countervailing factors concerning the broad nature and logic of the Agreement. The thin reasoning advanced in *Intertanko* is a thoroughly unsatisfactory basis on which to choose not to engage with the specific UNCLOS provisions at issue. Both the reasoning and the outcome sit uneasily, to put it mildly, with the internal logic of the model of EU Agreement enforcement that the ECJ had constructed. It was incoherent given the elaboration, in particular, of its own recent case law, for the ECJ in mid-2008 to invoke formalistic reasoning that sought to paint a picture of an interstate treaty that does not have the protection of individual rights at its core. For, in reality, few treaties—human rights treaties being the obvious exception—do have the protection of individual rights at their very core. Ultimately, it behoves the Court to provide more reasoned and credible justification, as it did in the WTO context, as to why the nature of a particular Agreement is such as in principle to preclude review, particularly given that we have seen time and time again the more maximalist approach to treaty enforcement take hold where domestic action has been challenged.

It has been suggested that had the ECJ abandoned its direct effect test, it would have been accused of judicial activism.[77] Putting to one side the fact that the Court did not actually use the language of direct effect nor did the referring court in its questions,[78] to abandon the direct effect test could be

[76] Advocate General's Opinion at paras 57–8. See also Cannizzaro (2012: 48–9).

[77] Denza (2008: 867).

[78] It is understandable that the review test enunciated has been viewed as essentially the criteria for direct effect (eg Cremona (2011: 242)), but the ECJ is effectively indirectly

viewed as wholly consistent with the severing of individual rights and direct effect from review in the Full Court's *Biotech* judgment. Moreover, even if a direct effect test were used, it is not clear why a usage coterminous with the conferral of independent rights for the individual is relevant given, for example, the absence of any such consideration in the *EDF* ruling, which did reason in the language of direct effect.[79] In any event, even if the direct effect test is to be wedded to individual rights, it does not follow that the conclusions as to UNCLOS are warranted.[80] Individual rights are in the eye of the beholder, as we have long seen with the ECJ's own approach to direct effect over the years, and accordingly it was unsurprising that the Advocate General had no difficulty viewing the UNCLOS provisions as crossing that hurdle if necessary. Indeed, as one commentator suggested with respect to the identification of individuals' rights, it was not easy to distinguish clearly between the collective interests of airline passengers at issue in the *IATA* case and the 'interests and needs of mankind as a whole' which was identified as an objective of UNCLOS in *Intertanko*.[81] The language of judicial activism employed by Denza is also problematic. Accepting review sat more comfortably with the model that the ECJ had constructed; a model in which it has adopted an especially receptive approach to EU Agreements that is arguably unparalleled in other legal orders. One could seek to ground this generosity in the nature of the Agreements at issue combined with the constitutional reception norm, in the form of Article 216(2) TFEU even if the ECJ has itself been remarkably silent on the relevance of this provision. And, ultimately, if a presumption of judicial enforceability had emerged, as recently decided cases such as *Biotech*, *EDF*, and *IATA* suggested, then accepting UNCLOS as a review criterion would hardly merit a judicial activism critique, instead the contrary conclusion, at least when combined with the absence of a persuasive attempt at justification, leads perfectly naturally to criticism for employing a judicial avoidance technique.

incorporating a substantive rights-based requirement into a test that had long retreated from a rights requirement as concerned internal EU law and was clearly retreating from this as concerns external EU law.

[79] That case, of course, involved a challenge to Member State rather than EU action.

[80] See also Eeckhout (2011: 381–3) who supports a rights-based test but was critical of its application. Cremona (2011: 242–3) in contrast queried whether 'the link to individual rights might be more appropriately directed at specific provisions of the agreement rather than its overall "nature and broad logic"...'.

[81] Cremona (2011: 242).

A further striking aspect of the judgment was that the ECJ did not feel compelled to employ or comment on the use of the consistent interpretation principle, given that the Advocate General made this the centrepiece of her analysis.[82] That is, having concluded that review was possible vis-à-vis the relevant UNCLOS provisions, the Advocate General interpreted the Directive in a manner she viewed as UNCLOS-compatible. The intellectual acrobatics performed illustrate that a natural reading of the Directive is unlikely to be consistent with the clear terms of UNCLOS and MARPOL, and the reading provided was arguably *contra legem* despite the Advocate General's insistence to the contrary. To read the terms 'recklessly' and 'serious negligence' in the Directive as requiring in both cases 'recklessness in the knowledge that damage would probably result' flies in the face of legislative intent. The proposed reading suffered from an obvious defect: there are three standards for liability, first, intent; secondly, recklessness; and, thirdly, serious negligence; accordingly to read recklessness narrowly, and then to read serious negligence coterminously, is to leave it with no independent role to play given that any such activity purportedly caught by serious negligence would appear equally to be caught by the definition proposed for recklessness. The interpretation, in other words, was tantamount to reading out one of the standards provided for in the Directive.[83]

There are certain contextual factors that might have contributed to the recalcitrance to review the Ship-Source Pollution Directive vis-à-vis international law in *Intertanko*. The fact previously mentioned, that the Directive was the subject of considerable controversy in the legislative process as attested to by recourse to majority voting for its adoption, is one. But, in addition, the ECJ had only recently upheld the Commission's challenge to the then third pillar framework decision on ship-source pollution on the basis that it should have been adopted under the first pillar in the face

[82] Especially as Art 1 of the Directive expressly states that its purpose is to incorporate international standards for ship-source pollution into EU law, and Art 9 provides that 'Member States shall apply the . . . Directive . . . in accordance with applicable international law'. One reading of the 'muteness' on this issue is that the Court may not have been convinced that it was possible to interpret the Directive in conformity with MARPOL and UNCLOS: see Eeckhout (2009: 2056).

[83] At least outside the territorial sea, for within the territorial sea the Advocate General proposed an unreservedly broader interpretation of serious negligence and, accordingly, precisely the same terms in the Directive would be interpreted one way as far as liability within the territorial sea was concerned, and, through use of the consistent interpretation doctrine, in a different way for liability beyond the territorial sea.

of the Council and 22 Member States arguing the contrary.[84] This led one commentator to suggest that it would seem extremely unlikely that it would have reopened this highly politicized debate on criminalization of ship-source pollution by reviewing the Directive in light of international law.[85] A further factor is that the attempted reliance on UNCLOS was an indirect way of ensuring review in relation to MARPOL, a convention within the IMO framework which is an organization for which the Commission has long (unsuccessfully) sought accession given the extent of EU competence in the maritime field;[86] in effect, to have allowed indirect review in relation to MARPOL would have seen EU legislative output constrained by rules stemming from an organization in which the EU is not a direct participant.[87] Whilst these contextual factors should not be ignored, ultimately the bottom line is that the Grand Chamber has erected a clear barrier to review of EU action vis-à-vis UNCLOS and has done so via the reintroduction of a rights-based hurdle which is likely to have significant ramifications for the capacity of EU Agreements to be used to challenge EU and, indeed, domestic level action. It has been suggested that the *Intertanko* ruling does not appear to exclude a priori other types of action, in particular by the Member States and the EU institutions.[88] This is reminiscent of the post-*International Fruit* debate where commentators felt that the possibility of GATT-based annulment actions by the Member States and institutions remained. They, of course, were proved wrong by the seminal German challenge to the bananas regime (C-280/93). An alternative outcome would have been difficult to sustain and we can certainly expect the same outcome should Member States or the institutions seek to challenge an EU measure for alleged incompatibility with UNCLOS. An alternative outcome would not only invite the criticism that this is to enshrine double standards, but also require the Court to retreat from the symmetry it first created in the famous 1994 *Bananas* ruling accordingly and either revisit the general inability for Member States and EU institutions to challenge the WTO compatibility of EU measures or find a justification for why what is not

[84] C-440/05 *Commission v Council* [2007] ECR I-9097.

[85] Mitsilegas (2010: 405).

[86] The Council has not authorized the Commission to negotiate accession: see Hoffmeister and Kuijper (2006: 26–7).

[87] The Commission and Member States have, however, been criticized for not having 'resorted to the IMO to bring about the desired measures laid down by the Directive' (Tan 2010: 486).

[88] Boelaert-Suominen (2008: 709).

possible in the WTO context should be possible vis-à-vis UNCLOS. It may be, however, that the infringement procedure could, as appears to be the case in the WTO context, still be used.[89] This might be viewed as leaving Article 216(2) TFEU with some role to play but, equally, it would generate accusations of double standards. A related point to note is that one might have expected post-*Intertanko* cases invoking UNCLOS pleas to be summarily rejected with a simple invocation of the *Intertanko* ruling.[90] And yet in a preliminary ruling decided three weeks after *Intertanko*, an attempt to rely on an UNCLOS provision to prevent the application of the EU Waste Framework Directive was rejected by the Grand Chamber without invoking this reasoning.[91] The case involved an attempt by an oil company to have the obligations in two oil pollution conventions to which the EU was not a party read into EU law via UNCLOS. The ECJ reiterated the French argument that this provision was confined 'to establishing a general obligation of cooperation between the parties to the convention'. One suspects that were the reading proposed by the oil company convincing, as it patently was not given the wording of UNCLOS, the *Intertanko* reasoning may well have been repeated.

4. Conclusions

Despite the growth of EU treaty-making activity outside the trade sphere and its well-established jurisprudence on the legal effects of EU

[89] This possibility appears confirmed by the earlier assertion that the Court has jurisdiction to assess Member State compliance with UNCLOS: C-459/03 *Commission v Ireland* [2006] ECR I-4635, para 121. See also Jacobs (2011: 538–9).

[90] Subject, that is, to the capacity of UNCLOS norms to be employed for consistent interpretation purposes, to represent customary international law, and thus be potentially capable of a more potent effect within EU law, or if the case involved Part XI provisions. UNCLOS had in fact been engaged with in earlier judgments. Prior to its entry into force, the Court noted that many of its provisions were considered to express the current state of customary international maritime law and drew on it in interpreting an EU Fisheries Conservation Regulation: C-286/90 *Poulsen and Diva Navigation* [1992] ECR I-6019. In C-410/03 *Commission v Italy* [2005] ECR I-3507, a breach of EU law for non-implementation of a provision of the Seafarers' Enforcement Directive (1999/95/EC) relied partially at least on that provision being a corollary of public international law responsibilities with UNCLOS provisions invoked in support. In C-111/05 *Aktiebolaget NN* [2007] ECR I-2697, the ECJ drew on UNCLOS provisions in interpreting the territorial scope of the Sixth Vat Directive (Directive 77/388/EC).

[91] C-188/07 *Commune de Mesquer v Total* [2008] ECR I-4501.

Agreements, challenges invoking non-trade Agreements have been surprisingly scarce. As Figure V.1 illustrates, the first ruling was not until 1998 and only 15 rulings have followed.[92]

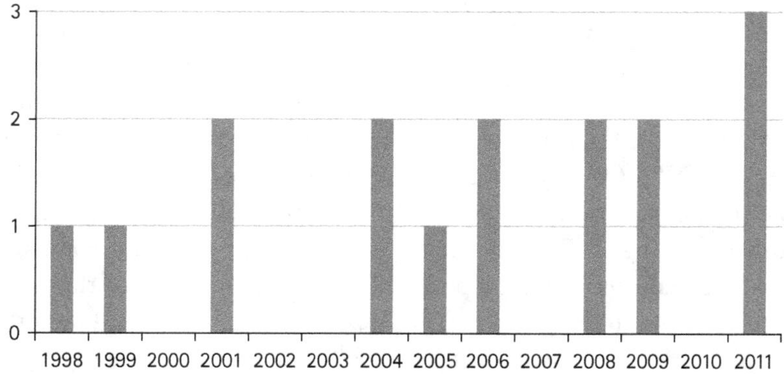

Figure V.1 Challenges invoking non-trade EU Agreements (16 judgments, 1998–2011)

The activity before the EU Courts has clearly been increasing of late and this trend is likely to continue given the growth in treaty-making activity outside the purely trade sphere; and, indeed, pending cases at the time of the cut-off point for the data-set attest to this.[93]

There are several explanatory hypotheses that could be adduced at this stage for this paucity of litigation before the EU Courts. First, it may be that the Member States and the EU are especially diligent with respect to

[92] Cases that led to appeals are included as at the year the appeal was decided. This list consists of C-1/96; C-179/97; C-377/98; C-189/01; C-213/03; C-239/03; C-254/03; T-201/04; C-344/04; C-479/04; C-308/06; C-355/08; C-444/08; C-115/09; C-240/09; T-18/10. The previously mentioned cases referencing the consistent interpretation doctrine are not included (C-284/95 and C-341/95) nor are the Montreal Convention-related disputes between private parties (C-173/07; C-549/07; C-204/08; C-63/09).

[93] Three pending cases directly raised questions pertaining to the Aarhus Convention (C-177/09, C-178/09 & C-179/09 *Le Poumon vert de la Hulpe*; C-128/09, C-129/09, C-130/09, C-131/09, C-134/09 & C-135/09 *Boxus and Roua*; and C-182/10 *Solvay and Others*) and pending Aarhus Convention challenges to EU action include: T-278/11 (challenge to Commission Decision); T-245/11 (challenge to European Chemicals Agency); pending questions pertaining to the validity of the Air Passenger Rights Regulation vis-à-vis the Montreal Convention include: C-629/10 *TUI Travel v Civil Aviation Authority* and C-12/11 *McDonagh v Ryanair*; a challenge to the Aviation Directive (2008/101/EC) based on, inter alia, an Air Transport Agreement with the US and the Kyoto Protocol to the Framework Convention on Climate Change was also before the Court: C-366/10 *Air Transport Association of America v Secretary of State for Energy and Climate Change* (on which see further Chapter VI).

complying with their international (and EU) obligations, such that there is rarely a serious case to be made as to non-compliance. There does not, however, appear to be any existing evidence in support of such a proposition.[94] Secondly, and perhaps more plausibly, in many of the spheres occupied by EU Agreements even if there were a credible claim to be made as to non-compliance with a particular Agreement there is no particular individual party sufficiently affected, and with sufficiently deep pockets, to be willing to pursue litigation. This, of course, will be a common problem where a particular EU Agreement might have as its objective the protection of diffuse and collective interests. A third important factor is that many EU Agreements have been the subject of detailed EU-level, and in due course national, implementing legislation. There is considerable secondary legislation that essentially seeks to implement provisions of EU—and indeed non-EU—Agreements.[95] This is particularly so with respect to EU environmental agreements. The introduction to this book has already noted that aspects of the Aarhus Convention have been implemented via several EU legislative measures resulting in the powerful EU law enforcement tools becoming available to ensure compliance with those EU measures, which has led to a string of infringement rulings against Member States (as well as related preliminary rulings). We can assume that where EU implementing legislation exists there will be less EU litigation directly invoking the EU Agreements as the basis for any challenge. A final factor of relevance is that only one infringement ruling has resulted directly from this category of EU Agreements and, indeed, none were pending at the time the data-set was completed, which is an indicator that policing compliance with such Agreements has perhaps not been a priority for the Commission.[96]

Turning back to the specifics of the 16 cases, Figure V.2 below illustrates that the EU Courts, in contrast to the Trade Agreements jurisprudence explored in Chapter III, have been overwhelmingly called upon to adjudicate in cases in which it has been the compatibility of EU measures, rather than domestic action, that is at issue.[97]

[94] Indeed, simply as concerns the Aarhus Convention we have seen both the EU and the Member States subject to successful complaints before the Compliance Committee. We have also seen courts dealing with EU Agreements without referring questions, for one such example see above at n 9.

[95] See further the introduction to this book.

[96] The Commission continues to be criticized for not monitoring or pursuing infringements of EU environmental agreements: Krmer (2011: 400, 431); Hedemann-Robinson (2012).

[97] A number of cases do not fit smoothly into this twofold categorization. Of the three cases identified expressly invoking the Aarhus Convention (T-91/07 *WWF-UK*, T-37/04 *Região*

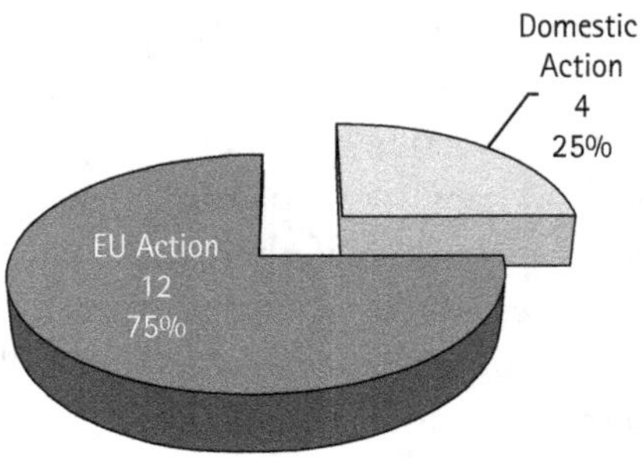

Figure V.2 Challenges to domestic or EU action invoking non-trade EU Agreements (16 judgments)

Three of the cases concerning challenges to national measures were of considerable significance: *EDF* as it was the first occasion in which a non-trade-related agreement, and a non-bilateral one at that, was held directly effective and crucially because the reasoning enunciated in reaching that conclusion evinced a strong attachment to the maximalist enforcement logic characteristic of how EU law proper is treated; *Étang de Berre* partially because it suggested that the Commission was perhaps becoming more diligent in policing Member State compliance with EU Agreements, but more significantly because it saw the adoption of an expansive approach to jurisdiction over mixed agreements which results in the EU enforcement machinery vis-à-vis EU Agreements being accorded an expansive remit. That last dimension has been further bolstered by the even bolder jurisdictional conclusions reached in *LZ VLK* coming as they did in the presence of a declaration of competence and a carefully reasoned contrary conclusion by the Advocate General. In the *LZ VLK* ruling that was followed by a textually irreproachable rejection of the direct effect of Article 9(3) of the

autónoma dos Açores, T-18/10 *Inuit Tapiriit Kanatami*) the challenges were not to EU measures as conventionally understood (in T-91/07 *WWF-UK* the Regulation being challenged was, however, allegedly in breach of a different EU Agreement (the UN Fish Stocks Agreement)) but rather challenges to standing rules in Art 263 TFEU as interpreted by the EU judiciary. One might then view those two cases as essentially attempts to have the consistent interpretation doctrine employed vis-à-vis the standing rules. In C-189/01 *Jippes* reliance was unsuccessfully placed on an EU Agreement to try and generate a general principle of EU law with a view to annulling a provision of EU law. C-115/09 *Trianel*, which involved a challenge to German law, could also be viewed as simply interpretation of the EU implementing measure consistently with the Aarhus Convention obligations. The broader point remains that the challenges involving the non-trade-related EU Agreements have been primarily in relation to EU rather than Member State action.

Aarhus Convention, however, in doing so the ECJ crucially sought to impose a strikingly stringent interpretative obligation on Member State legal orders. Given that it reached this outcome in the context of challenges to domestic action, it would seem only fitting that the EU Courts take seriously the inevitably forthcoming pleas relying on the Aarhus Convention and its Compliance Committee's findings against the EU's standing criteria, in order to relax the standing criteria. The alternative will predictably be accusations of double standards that would be difficult to refute.

Thus far, there has not been a successful challenge to an EU measure relying upon this category of EU Agreements. Undoubtedly, in a number of these cases the alleged incompatibility appeared spurious.[98] Furthermore, the *Biotech* and *IATA* cases could and were invoked as evidence of a receptive approach to review in relation to EU Agreements. In the former because of the willingness to separate direct effect and individual rights from review of EU law vis-à-vis EU Agreements, and in the latter because of an apparently manifest willingness to employ an EU Agreement as a review criterion for EU law. However, the actual review conducted in *IATA* was not free from controversy. And a clear concession that review is possible, even leaving indicia of a receptive approach to EU Agreements (*Biotech* and *IATA*), should never lead one to pay insufficient attention to the actual outcome and the substantive interpretation of the relevant provisions. For limiting oneself to a yes/no tick-box approach to the invocability question, as previous chapters have stressed, can generate a relatively superficial picture. In any event, the real litmus test for the potency of the legal effects of EU Agreements is arguably to be provided on those occasions when the challenge to an EU measure appears most convincing. This is one of the reasons why the judicial response in *Intertanko* was eagerly awaited. And the response where the substantive interpretation would appear to provide little shelter was to resort to closing the gateway to review by resurrecting a conferral of individual rights requirement for review to be permissible.[99] The mantra of EU Agreements as an integral part of EU law

[98] Notably C-479/04; C-1/96; C-189/01; C-179/97; C-254/03 P; C-377/98; C-188/07. The attempted use of the Aarhus Convention in T-37/04 *Região autónoma dos Açores* was also unconvincing.

[99] One wonders if a different outcome to the review or invocability question might have been forthcoming had the first express UNCLOS challenge arisen to a non-legislative measure that did not raise such transparent compliance concerns.

and having primacy over secondary EU legislation can thus be duly recited, as indeed was the case in *Intertanko*, but the air of artificiality in doing so, where this is combined with the wholesale rejection of the Agreement to form a review criterion for EU law,[100] is palpable.

[100] The Court is still likely to have to resolve whether it would accept a customary international law-based challenge to EU action where the customary international law at stake reflects relevant UNCLOS provisions and a challenge relying on the Part XI provisions which the Court emphasized were not at stake in *Intertanko*.

VI

Concluding Assessment

1. Introduction

A core premise of this book has been the need for greater empirical work exploring how courts in constitutional systems adhering to automatic treaty incorporation actually deal with treaties when they are invoked, rather than relying on the untested assumption that the particular phrasing of a constitutional provision that provides the point of entry for treaties into the domestic legal arena and/or seminal judicial assertions on their legal effect and status are necessarily reflected in judicial practice. Having explored the body of case law pertaining to key questions on the constitutional status and legal effects of EU Agreements in the EU legal order, it is now possible to consider further the significance of these findings.[1] The data-set which formed the basis for the analysis conducted in Chapters II–V contained 337 cases,[2] of which nearly all can be grouped into one or more of the following three categories: ex post challenges to the substance or to the

[1] A fuller picture of the judicial application of EU Agreements would necessitate an analysis of how courts across the 27 Member States have responded when EU Agreements have been invoked. Some studies have touched upon certain dimensions of domestic judicial application of EU Agreements: see Xenopoulos (2006) and Bocker and Guild (2002). There is existing evidence of both recalcitrance and boldness on the part of domestic courts. With respect to recalcitrance, the French Conseil d'État offers examples of determining the non-directly effective status of an Agreement and a provision of an Agreement without referring the question to the ECJ, for the first example from the late 1970s see Stein (2000: 292), for the second example from 2006, see Chapter V, n 9. Examples of boldness include the 'pre-emptive strikes' on the Europe Agreements cited in Chapter III, as well as the Dutch and Polish Supreme Court TRIPs judgments cited below at n 15.

[2] A small number of additional cases were noted in the data-set, and were cited in this book, that touched upon EU Agreements, but have not been included as part of the data-set that formed the basis for the Figures used in this book.

procedure for concluding EU Agreements; challenges to domestic action; and challenges to EU action.[3] This concluding chapter is structured around the findings pertaining to the three aforementioned core strands of case law.

2. Ex Post Challenges to EU Agreements: The Triumph of Constitutionalism

Ex post challenges to EU Agreements have, as Figure VI.1 illustrates, generated 19 rulings.

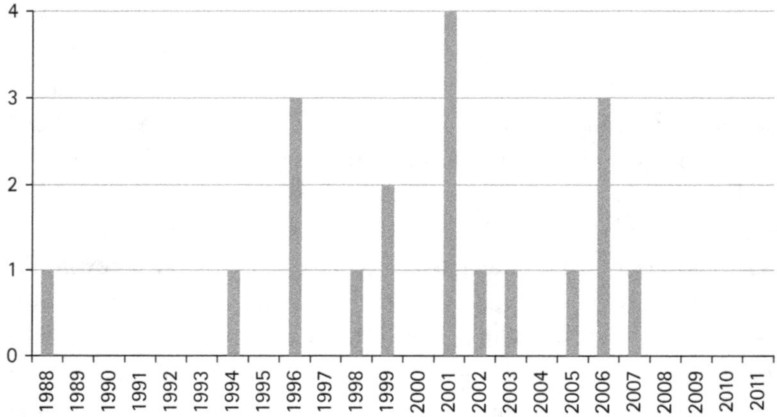

Figure VI.1 Ex post challenges to EU Agreements (19 cases)

These 19 cases, which have mainly been annulment actions,[4] have involved a total of 18 different Agreements.[5] Only annulment actions have ever proved successful (seven of the total 14 annulment actions). And

[3] Those that cannot be so grouped were a number of rulings in Chapter IV where consistent interpretation was either relied upon by litigants successfully, or not, or in any event employed by the Court seemingly to influence the interpretation of EU legislation, but where no express allegation of breach of GATT or WTO Agreements was apparent. These exclusively consistent interpretation-related cases are not touched upon further in this concluding chapter, suffice it to note that this is a potentially significant conduit for current WTO law to wield legal effects in EU law, indeed, at least two such cases were identified where subsidiary EU measures were annulled (T-163/94 & T-165/94 *NTN Corp* and T-256/97 *BEUC*).

[4] Preliminary rulings accounted for two cases (C-347/03 and C-231/04), and damages actions for three cases (T-196/99, C-293/95 P, and T-212/02).

[5] Some cases involved two Agreements (C-211/01 and C-293/95 P) whilst others involved repeat litigation on the same agreement (namely C-300 & 388/99 P, C-301/99 P, and T-196/99; and C-347/03 and C-231/04).

only one of these successful actions resulted from a challenge to the substantive content of an Agreement rather than issues of the appropriate legal basis. The inter-institutional battles over appropriate legal basis appear to be in decline, but they in any event have posed little threat to the internal legal effect of duly concluded EU Agreements given the recourse by the ECJ to maintaining the effects of the annulled decisions and the use of new concluding decisions with retroactive effect.

The catastrophic scenarios that some had envisaged flowing from accepting such review have, thus, clearly not materialized and indeed the case law itself has been rarer than one might have anticipated. Chapter II sought to defend both the need for this form of ex post review, which the EU system is not alone in practising and, crucially, the constitutional appropriateness of depriving EU Agreements, or at least certain of their provisions,[6] of their internal legal effect where they are in tension with important constitutional values reflected in EU primary law, even where this outcome cannot be squared with the limited scenarios in which international law allows States and international organizations to invoke their own law vis-à-vis their treaty commitments. The core of the argument advanced was that treaties should not be considered sacrosanct and especially so in an era where they can be, and are, employed to house constitutionally egregious outcomes. The EU–US PNR Agreements of 2004, 2006, and 2007 illustrate precisely why such review should exist. They were bilateral and wholly executive negotiated Agreements in which the Parliament and fundamental rights were sidelined. Such Agreements should not escape the salutary reach of domestic constitutionalism simply because they can hide behind the formal veneer of legitimacy offered by *pacta sunt servanda* and the Vienna Convention on the Law of Treaties. It is worth noting that two of the most powerful recent contributions against constitutional rights review of legislation are premised on the democratic shortcomings of constitutional review in functioning democratic systems where parliamentarians do have appropriate input into the legislative process.[7] Drawing on that logic only serves to bolster the case for accepting the possibility of ex post constitutional review of treaty law, first, because the direct democratic

[6] See the comment with respect to the Bananas Framework Agreement ruling (C-122/95) in Chapter II, n 146.

[7] Waldron (2006); Bellamy (2007).

(via the legislature) input into the treaty-making process is usually at best negligible[8] and, secondly, because where constitutional review exists vis-à-vis measures with greater input legitimacy (by virtue of being produced via the ordinary legislative process), as in the EU, it is arguably anomalous wholly to immunize other norms simply because they are housed in treaties.[9]

The only judicial justification expressly offered for ex post review was that the exercise of the powers delegated to the EU institutions in international matters could not escape judicial review of the legality of the acts adopted. The ex ante review jurisprudence, however, has employed the notion of an autonomous legal order to preserve the Court's exclusive power to interpret EU law.[10] And it was also employed in the *Kadi* ruling, considered further below, in justifying its unwillingness to allow UN Security Council Resolutions to trump EU primary law and, thus, a context sharing parallels with the ex post review authorities. The autonomy of the EU legal order may well be acquiring negative connotations as a rhetorical device to protect the EU legal order from international law or, for those inclined to use such language, as signalling an inappropriate manifestation of dualism.[11] Nevertheless, as none of the ex post review authorities have ever actually invoked the notion and because the Court is ultimately being faced with a tension that other constitutional systems with ex post review of treaty commitments must resolve, it is suggested that one can frame the tension as that essentially between constitutionalism and *pacta sunt servanda*. And, indeed, the development of the EU's ex post review tools may well offer important insight for constitutional design and practice elsewhere.

[8] Whilst in the EU context, as with many other constitutional systems, the Parliament's approval is now generally required, that hardly compensates for its limited capacity to influence the actual treaty-making process. See, however, on parliamentary preconditions where its assent will be required, Passos (2010).

[9] A constitutional text can provide precisely for this outcome.

[10] See the analysis of judicial usage of this notion by de Witte (2010).

[11] Unfortunately less attention by the critics has been paid to the reference in C-402/05 P & C-415/05 P *Kadi* (para 281) to the EU being based on the rule of law inasmuch as neither its Member States nor the institutions can avoid review of their acts with the basic constitutional charter, in other words traditional concerns of constitutionalist thinking.

3. EU Agreements in Challenges to Domestic Action: Embracing Maximalist Treaty Enforcement

This section first considers some general findings from the case law challenging domestic action, before turning to specific findings pertaining to infringement rulings.

3.1 General findings

The 159 cases involving EU Agreements in challenging domestic action are represented in Figure VI.2.

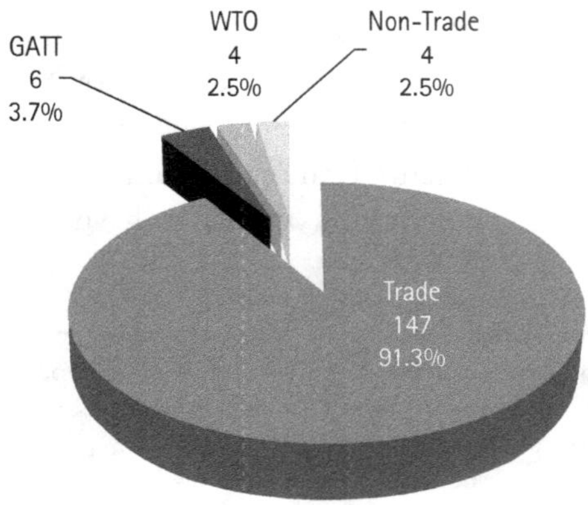

Figure VI.2 EU Agreements in challenges to domestic action[12]

Clearly, the case law has been dominated by the trade-related Agreements jurisprudence which represents over 90 per cent of the case law.[13] The challenges to domestic action case law has clearly witnessed the embrace of a maximalist approach to treaty enforcement, that is, a model exhibiting a powerful commitment to ensuring the greatest possible effect

[12] The total of 161 in Figure VI.2 is explained by the fact that *Chiquita Italia* (C-469/93) and *SIOT* (266/81) have been included under the Trade and GATT categories as they involved challenges involving both types of Agreement.

[13] And rises to 98 per cent if we use the trade label to encapsulate both the Chapter III agreements and the GATT and WTO.

for this additional category of EU law. There have been at least three core indicators of this.[14] First, the ECJ has taken a bold stance to its jurisdiction over mixed agreements. This is of immense significance because this preliminary question needs to be answered in the affirmative for EU law enforcement tools[15] to be available at the behest of litigants (including the Commission) for policing domestic compliance with mixed agreements. This boldness was particularly marked in cases such as *Demirel*, *Sevince*, *Hermès*, *Irish Berne*, *Étang de Berre*, and *LZ VLK*, where cogent Member State and/or Council arguments against jurisdiction were rejected. Indeed, *LZ VLK* was particularly striking for that was a rare case in which the Advocate General too had rejected jurisdiction, and, not unsurprisingly so, given that to do otherwise appears to deprive the EU's declaration of competence of its intended purpose, namely, to allocate responsibility for breach of Article 9(3) (Aarhus), in the absence of EU legislative activity, to Member States and to this extent by implication to deprive the ECJ of jurisdiction over that provision. In short, jurisdiction over mixed agreements has been interpreted generously indeed, as recognized in most of the literature.[16]

Secondly, the direct effect lens has been employed in a bold manner that paralleled the evolving approach applied in 'EU law proper'. The Trade Agreements jurisprudence is the clear manifestation of this: explicitly textually envisaged implementation measures have often not precluded

[14] Further evidence of the bold stance of the ECJ was provided by the unwillingness to allow the non-publication, and absence of an entry into force date, of Association Council Decisions (respectively C-192/89 *Sevince* and C-277/94 *Taflan-Met*, considered in Chapter III) to shield domestic action from review.

[15] As contrasted with domestic law enforcement tools being used in the purely domestic setting. Clearly the result of, eg, C-431/05 *Merck* was that Member State courts could determine the legal consequences that the relevant TRIPs provision would have in their domestic legal orders (whether this will stand post-Lisbon remains to be seen). Indeed, in Poland Art 33 of TRIPs had been held directly effective by the Supreme Administrative Court in 2006, see Wyrozumska (2011: 483–4). The Dutch Supreme Court in 2003 also made its own affirmative direct effect finding of a TRIPs provision (Art 45), see Nollkaemper (2009a: 368). However, if the question of jurisdiction is answered in the affirmative and the invocability as a review criterion question in the negative, this precludes the application of EU (and domestic) enforcement tools to that Agreement. This, however, is subject to two potentially important riders. First, the possibility that infringement proceedings could be brought for non-compliance with such an Agreement and, secondly, the applicability of the EU-consistent interpretation doctrine. An expansive approach to jurisdiction can thus be viewed as a double-edged sword: if the EU Courts then take a restrictive approach to the invocability question it can preclude domestic courts from conducting direct review of domestic action vis-à-vis EU Agreements.

[16] There is an argument for a more expansive approach, extending to provisions falling under Member State competence, that relies on Art 4(3) TFEU: see Neframi (2010: 332–6).

affirmative direct effect findings (eg *Kziber*, *Sevince*, *Surul*, *Simutenkov*) nor in one controversial case did the absence of imperative language preclude the ECJ from opting to read the verb 'may' as if it were indeed imperative (*Gürol*). Furthermore, the direct effect analysis is often conducted without recourse to an individual rights conceptualization, as was evident in, for example, *Anastasiou* and, outside the trade sphere, in *EDF*. In fact, in the Trade Agreements cases concerning goods provisions since *Kupferberg*, the Court has only framed its inquiry in terms of whether a given provision was 'directly effective' when responding to a direct challenge to the direct effect of a provision (*Anastasiou* and *Chiquita Italia*) or when rejecting the direct effect of a provision (*Katsivardas*). For many this approach has much to commend it, as the judicial stance appears premised on a presumption of enforceability. There have certainly been rejections of the capacity of certain provisions to be directly effective. But across the large number of Trade Agreements cases this has been a rare occurrence (*Demirel*, *Taflan-Met*, *Savas*, *Katsivardas*). With regard to the non-trade Agreements jurisprudence the two relevant cases led to, respectively, a rejection of the direct effect of a specific provision (*LZ VLK*) and an acceptance of direct effect (*EDF*). The *EDF* ruling was a significant development because the Trade Agreements jurisprudence has mainly involved bilateral treaties with States with which the EU has certain ties and they often involve provisions that have directly effective EU law counterparts. This is sometimes viewed as an explanation for the bold judicial stance.[17] *EDF*, however, concerned a non-bilateral environmental agreement and thus attested to the judicial stance being by no means confined to Trade Agreements.[18] The negative conclusion on the direct effect of Article 9(3) of the Aarhus Convention in *LZ VLK* was a predictable outcome given its wording,[19] but the ECJ nevertheless enunciated what will likely prove a powerful interpretative obligation on domestic courts nonetheless to seek to ensure their domestic procedural law complies with Article 9(3). The GATT and WTO have been the obvious outliers in this respect in that direct effect was rejected. However, in the GATT era this

[17] See briefly discussion in Jacobs (2011: 537–9), Cremona (2011: 240–4).

[18] The Aarhus Convention Compliance Committee drew attention to EU membership and the *EDF* (C-213/03) and *Étang de Berre* (C-239/03) cases in concluding that it would be likely that some Aarhus provisions would be directly applicable in EU Member States: see ECE/MP.PP/C.1/2006/4/Add.2, 28 July 2006 (Communication ACCC/C/2005/11).

[19] One might view the fact that the ECJ did not trouble itself with the stage of the direct effect test concerning the nature and purpose (or broad logic more recently) of the Agreement as an indicator that this is unlikely to prove a problematic hurdle for the Aarhus Convention.

was combined with an acknowledgement that infringement proceedings could nonetheless be brought, which should remain possible in the WTO era. And, in the WTO era, the obligation to employ the consistent interpretation doctrine vis-à-vis domestic law has, in certain contexts, been emphasized,[20] and the possibility of domestic judicial review in those areas outwith the ECJ's jurisdiction has been preserved. In total the GATT era gave rise to six challenges to domestic action, and the WTO thus far some four cases.[21]

Thirdly, the substantive interpretation of EU Agreements has been particularly bold. This is patently so in the Trade Agreements jurisprudence where we have often seen the transposition of internal EU law readings, most strikingly in *Simutenkov*, where the *Bosman* ruling was transposed to a PCA. This interpretative transposition to the Europe Agreements, much less a PCA, is unlikely to have been anticipated when the *Bosman* ruling was delivered, given that the judgment appeared heavily conditioned by its fundamental freedoms underpinning. Outside the trade and GATT/WTO cases, which leaves little to consider, it was nonetheless noteworthy that in *Étang de Berre*, concerning the Barcelona Convention and Mediterranean Sea Protocol, a narrower substantive interpretation of due diligence advanced by France was rejected in favour of a rigorous obligation strictly to limit pollution.

Perhaps what might prima facie appear striking is the dearth of challenges to domestic action invoking the non-trade-related EU Agreements. A mere four cases have been identified (*EDF*, *Étang de Berre*, *LZ VLK*, *Trianel*), and one of those is in reality about the EU level implementing legislation (*Trianel*) and two others (*EDF*, *Étang de Berre)* arose out of the same factual background. However, the EU actively implements EU Agreements legislatively and this, particularly in the environmental field, results in domestic action being policed using EU law enforcement tools.

[20] See C-53/96 *Hermès*; C-300 & 392/98 *Christian Dior*; C-89/99 *Groeneveld.*

[21] The GATT cases were: 266/81 *SIOT*; 267–9/81 *SPI and SAMI*; 290–1/81 *Singer and Geigy*; 193/85 *Cooperativa Co-Frutta*; C-469/93 *Chiquita Italia*; C-61/94 *IDA*. The WTO cases that can be so construed were C-53/96 *Hermès*; C-300 & 392/98 *Christian Dior*; C-88/99 *Groeneveld*; C-431/05 *Merck*. The first three saw Dutch courts ask questions as to the direct effect and meaning of TRIPs provisions in cases concerning the Dutch Civil Procedure Code and domestic judicial interpretations of TRIPs, whilst in the fourth Portuguese law on the period of patent protection was in tension with TRIPs. *BSB* (C-288/09 & C-289/09) could be viewed as involving challenges to domestic action in the form of UK-issued Binding Tariff Information, but as that was merely with a view to giving effect to EU customs rules, it has been classified instead under challenges to EU action.

A further significant point concerns the institutional dynamics that have been at play in building this especially receptive treaty enforcement model vis-à-vis domestic action for it has frequently been built in the face of dissent from at least some Member States. The Commission, however, has rarely erred on the side of caution. On all three of the aforementioned questions (jurisdiction, direct effect, substantive scope interpretation), it has usually opted for the boldest of readings and the ECJ has usually obliged.[22] Rarely has there been anything resembling a common front on the questions before the Court whereby substantial Member State opposition is advanced in unison with the Commission and Council stance.[23] This is not altogether surprising, given that the vast majority of this case law has concerned bilateral trade agreements and especially Turkey Association Agreement law. This is significant because the cases often stem from those few countries with sizeable numbers of relevant resident workers and their dependants. Accordingly, whilst opposition to a bold line on direct enforceability or a particular substantive interpretation has often been forthcoming, it has tended to be via submissions from few Member States.[24] In effect much of this jurisprudence was built without substantial Member State opposition (in terms of court interventions), which is likely to have impacted on the boldness of the line that the ECJ has usually taken.[25]

Finally, it must also be acknowledged that the bulk of the cases have concerned a small number of agreements and primarily only a few different types of provision, mainly of the non-discrimination and standstill clause variety and often with similarly worded directly effective EU law

[22] The notable exception on which it was unwilling to oblige is with respect to jurisdiction. The Commission has generally called for jurisdiction over all of a mixed agreement where it is an area of shared competence. The ECJ has, however, taken a more expansive approach than the position advanced by the Council and various Member States on those occasions where their submissions have been forthcoming.

[23] See, however, the first batch of cases on the substantive interpretation of the establishment provisions of the Europe Agreements in Chapter III.

[24] C-374/03 *Gürol* offers an example on the direct enforceability question where two Member States made a sound, but unsuccessful, textual argument against direct effect of a Turkey Association Council Decision provision.

[25] As Chapters II and III suggested, on occasion it appeared that once the import of what was at stake dawned on the Member States, they contributed in greater numbers. We witnessed this with *Kupferberg* (104/81), and much later with *Sürül* (C-262/96). In both instances, to have heeded the arguments against direct effect, employed by the large number of intervening Member States, would have led to incoherence across EU Trade Agreement jurisprudence whereby largely identical provisions would have been accorded direct effect in one or more Agreements but not in others.

counterparts. One might argue that this is as ripe a terrain as possible for a receptive judicial stance particularly as the dominant source of litigation has been the persons-related provisions, thus bringing to the fore the rights of non-EU nationals and their family members where we might expect underlying judicial sympathy.

3.2 Specific findings pertaining to infringement rulings

As Figure VI.3 illustrates, of the 159 cases referred to above, 27 (17 per cent) have resulted from infringement proceedings.

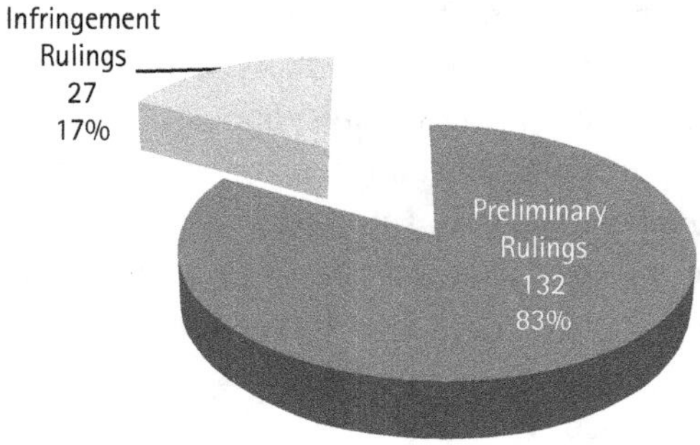

Figure VI.3 Preliminary rulings and infringement rulings

The first of the infringement rulings did not arise until 1988, with 22 of the 26 remaining rulings having come since the turn of the century as illustrated in Figure VI.4.

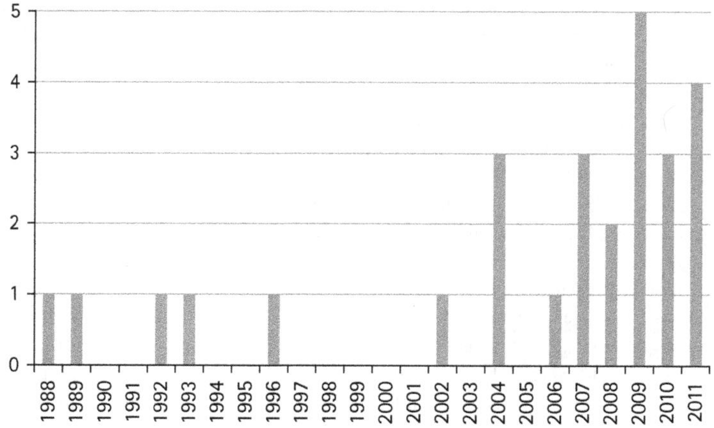

Figure VI.4 Infringement rulings including pleas of breach of EU Agreement (27 rulings)

The figures, however, are deceptive unless probed further. This demonstrates, as Figure VI.5 illustrates, that a large majority of cases (some 70 per cent) have concerned the EEAA.

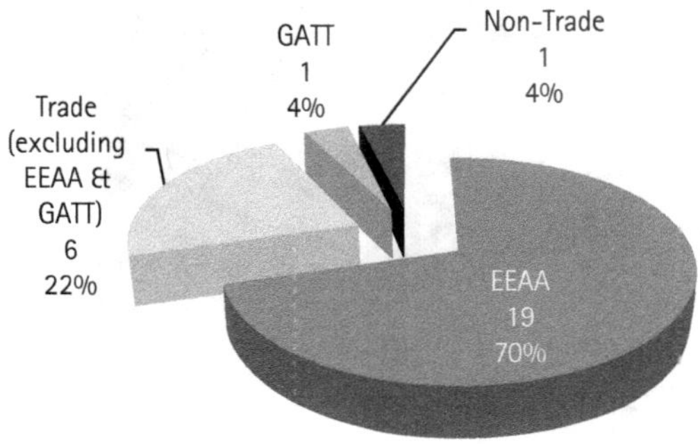

Figure VI.5 EU Agreement infringement rulings by type

In addition, the ECJ has only been required to pronounce on one occasion as to a Member State infringement of a non-trade Agreement; the *Étang de Berre* ruling which, given the generous judicial approach to jurisdiction over mixed agreements exhibited therein, and in cases since (most strikingly in C-240/09 *LZ VLK*), may well herald greater recourse to infringement proceedings in the large and expanding category of Agreements outside the trade sphere.[26] Of these 27 cases, 22 found a breach of an EU Agreement.[27]

A further significant finding is that, as illustrated in Figure VI.6 below, the vast majority of infringement rulings (close to 90 per cent) have concerned what can be referred to as 'incidental' rather than 'pure EU Agreement' infringement rulings.

Only three cases (*Irish Berne*, *Étang de Berre*, *Turkish Residence Permit Charges*) involved pure EU Agreement infringement rulings; that is, the alleged violation involved infringement only of an EU Agreement and not also internal EU law provisions.[28] To put the point most cynically, one could argue that tacking on a plea of an EU Agreement infringement where EU law proper pertaining to the internal market is at issue does not indicate a marked Commission commitment to this type of centralized enforcement of EU Agreements. It is, however, crucial to recognize that infringement

[26] For doubts concerning the environmental field, see Hedemann-Robinson (2012).

[27] The five exceptions were touched in Chapter III (340/87, C-267/09, C-540/07, C-487/08, C-105/08).

[28] Excluding Art 216(2) TFEU itself. See further on this classification, Chapter III.

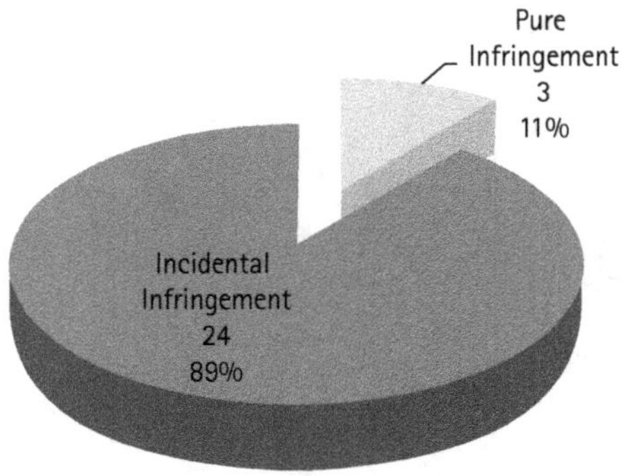

Figure VI.6 EU Agreement infringement rulings (pure infringement/incidental infringement)

rulings are likely to be merely the 'tip of the iceberg' and that, as with 'EU law proper', the threat of litigation will frequently result in Member States complying. The initiation of proceedings gives rise to a very small percentage of rulings. The system is built, and in practice operates, to encourage Member States to come into compliance in the pre-litigation stage.[29] One would accordingly expect the 27 EU Agreement infringement rulings to form a small percentage of the number of occasions in which Member States have sought to come into compliance with Commission readings of their EU Agreement obligations.[30]

There is a fascinating recent example of the powerful compliance-inducing impact of infringement proceedings in the EU Agreement context.[31] In January 2011 the UK received a reasoned opinion giving it two

[29] The latest Commission report (2011) states that 88 per cent of the cases closed did not reach the Court because Member States corrected the legal issues raised by the Commission before it would have been necessary to initiate the next stage in the infringement proceedings. The figures for the two previous years were respectively 96 per cent and 94 per cent.

[30] The annual reports on the application of EU law, first introduced in 1985, provide little indication that this has been so. They do, however, attest to the fact that both the *IDA* (C-61/94) and *Irish Berne* (C-13/00) rulings originated in proceedings against an array of Member States, it being only the two Member States (Germany and Ireland) that did not come into compliance that found themselves brought before the Court.

[31] It has become all the more powerful given the introduction of—and increasing Commission willingness to have recourse to—the penalty payment procedure. Though we have yet to see a penalty payments ruling in the EU Agreements context, this will surely only be a matter of time. The *Irish Berne* case saw the penalty payment procedure initiated but it was discontinued once Ireland came into compliance (C-165/04 *Commission v Ireland*, order of the President of the Second Chamber (02.03.05)). With respect to *Étang de Berre*, France received a formal notice under Art 260 TFEU: see Commission (2005: 52).

months to act in respect of the Race Relations Act 1976 which permitted nationality-based direct and indirect pay discrimination of non-UK seafarers.[32] UK law was considered to infringe EU law as concerned EU nationals,[33] and over a dozen EU Agreements containing the equal treatment clause pertaining to working conditions, remuneration, and dismissal.[34] Within six months, a legislative instrument was passed making such pay discrimination unlawful vis-à-vis EEA nationals and those of States that were parties to the relevant EU Agreements.[35] That this change was forced upon the UK by EU law and the threat of both the penalty payment procedure and individual compensation claims was made abundantly clear during the legislative process.[36] Two additional points are worth noting. First, the Commission was clearly not pursuing pure EU Agreement infringements although one suspects that had the UK legislation been compliant with EU law proper—that is, not discriminated against EU nationals (and for that matter been EEAA-compliant)—infringement proceedings would still have been pursued given the many EU Agreements involved. In any event, whether it was a pure EU Agreement infringement proceeding or not, the outcome for those working or aspiring to work in the relevant sector who are nationals of the many States party to the EU Agreements at stake (including the Cotonou Agreement to which 79 ACP States are party), is that the compliance-inducing enforcement machinery of EU law has generated a favourable outcome. Secondly, the UK has come into compliance with a number of Agreements that have yet to be the subject of ECJ litigation.[37] This raises two possibilities. The first is that direct effect was a foregone conclusion as the equivalent provision in a range of Agreements had long been held directly effective including in relation to the least integrationist of agreements, the Russian Partnership Agreement (*Simutenkov*). The difficulty with this is it raises the issue of the

[32] Where they were hired abroad to work on UK ships, or worked on UK ships outside the UK.

[33] Article 45 TFEU and Art 7 of Regulation No 1612/68.

[34] The EEA Agreement and the Agreements with the ACP States, Morocco, Montenegro, San Marino, Algeria, Andorra, Albania, Croatia, Macedonia, Tunisia, Turkey, Russia, Switzerland.

[35] The Equality Act 2010 (Work on Ships and Hovercraft) Regulations 2011 (SI 2011/1771).

[36] See both the statement of the Parliamentary Under-Secretary of State for Transport before the 12th delegated legislation committee of the House of Commons (11.07.11), and the impact assessment.

[37] The Agreements with Albania, Andorra, Croatia, Macedonia, Montenegro, and San Marino have neither been the subject of litigation nor are they the successors to Agreements that were the subject of litigation before the Court.

value of the first stage of the direct effect determination concerning the nature and purpose of the Agreement.[38] The second is simply that direct effect will not be relevant where EU Agreements are the basis for infringement proceedings.[39]

Infringement proceedings clearly provide a powerful tool for the enforcement of this additional category of EU law, thus giving individuals a further channel for seeking to ensure compliance with EU Agreements.[40] However, the scarcity of non-EEAA-related rulings, combined with the general paucity of rulings, especially of the 'pure infringement' variety, does suggest that, despite the hallowed judicial language of EU Agreements as an integral part of EU law, it is unlikely to have been matched by equally diligent treatment in terms of Commission enforcement strategy. The suggestion advanced long ago by the Director General of the Commission legal service that it dislikes using EU law tools to do non-Member countries' business for them, may well be lingering on.[41]

4. EU Agreements in Challenges to EU Action: The Allure of Judicial Avoidance Techniques

This section is divided into two subsections. The first focusing on general findings pertaining to the case law involving challenges to EU measures, whilst the second focuses primarily on the broader implications of recourse to judicial avoidance techniques for the EU's normative commitment to international law.

[38] A well-placed observer has queried its value: Jacobs (2011: 536–8).

[39] The norm will clearly still need to impose an obligation, however, which would explain why a number of the Agreements with former Russian Federation states which use the language of 'shall endeavor to ensure' (see further Chapter III) were not included in the seafarers infringement proceedings against the UK.

[40] At the end of 2009, 53 per cent of the active cases originated from complaints, in 2010 this figure was at slightly over 40 per cent: see Commission (2011). Commencement of infringement proceedings remains at the Commission's discretion: see Craig and de Búrca (2011: 415–18).

[41] Ehlermann (1986: 139). Resources are inevitably scarce and enforcement priorities will exist, indeed, the Commission now expressly articulates priorities: see Smith (2008).

4.1 General findings

The 134 cases in which EU Agreements were invoked to challenge EU measures are represented in Figure VI.7.

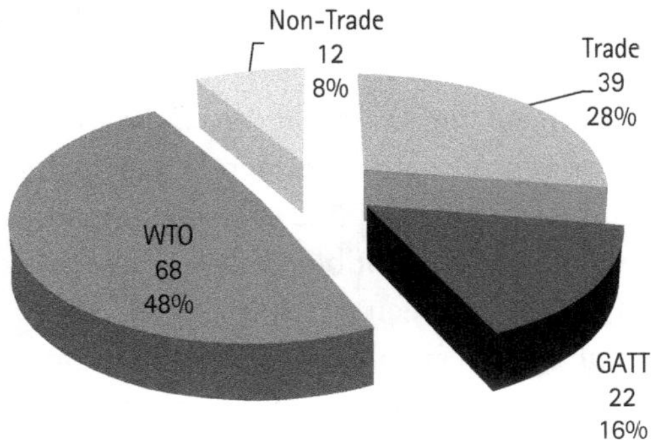

Figure VI.7 EU Agreements in challenges to EU action[44]

The largest category of cases (68 or 48 per cent) have stemmed from the predominantly unsuccessful attempts to review EU action vis-à-vis WTO norms,[42] followed by the Trade Agreements cases considered in Chapter III (28 per cent). The GATT and WTO cases combined generated over 60 per cent of the case law and it is clear that had a more receptive stance been adopted, as contrasted with the principled stance against review, the figures would no doubt have increased substantially. The low number of non-trade-related Agreements challenges, a mere 12 cases (8 per cent of the total), is perhaps the most surprising finding, given the large number of Agreements that could be invoked. Nonetheless, we can expect that with the expansion of EU treaty-making activity into new areas, this will give rise to a growing number of cases challenging EU (and indeed domestic) action where the non-trade EU Agreements are invoked.[43]

[42] The figures are likely to be higher given that some of the 22 cases in the exclusively consistent interpretation category noted in the introduction to this chapter may also have expressly sought review vis-à-vis the WTO even though this is not apparent from the cases themselves.

[43] This is the current trend as Chapter V illustrated. Moreover, accession to the ECHR will rapidly transform the figures as it will quickly become the most relied upon EU Agreement to challenge EU action.

[44] The total of 141 in Figure VI.7 is explained by the fact that seven cases span two categories of Agreement: 9/73 *Schluter*; C-377/98 *Biotech*; T-115/94 *Opel Austria*; C-280/93 *Germany v*

The most significant finding is that in not one of these cases can it be said that a challenge to an EU measure was successful on the basis of the EU Agreement alone. Arguably, we can point to merely two cases (*Petrotub* and *Opel Austria*) in which it is the EU Agreement that leads, albeit via a tortuous route, to the annulment of an EU measure.[45] Thus, in *Opel Austria* the EEAA breach was linked to a violation of the general principles of EU law in order to annul a Council Regulation; whilst in *Petrotub*, in the WTO domain, an even more tortuous route was used to annul an EU Regulation.[46] In addition to those two cases, the *Soysal* judgment was noteworthy for essentially authorizing certain Member States to ignore the express wording of the Visa List Regulation due to its incompatibility with Turkey Association Agreement law. It is not being suggested that we should expect any particular correlation between the number of cases brought and the number of successful actions involving pleas pertaining to an EU Agreement. Clearly, many examples have arisen of pleas pertaining to EU Agreements that ranged from the unconvincing to the spurious and measures have also been annulled without having to address the EU Agreement point.[47] Nevertheless, the findings are surprising given both the extent of the EU's treaty-making activity and the extent of its legislative and administrative law-making in the nearly 40 years that have passed since *Haegeman II* signalled adherence to automatic treaty incorporation.

It is where challenges to EU action are involved that we have seen the EU Courts employing, and the other EU institutions calling for, techniques that seek to avoid the logical consequences of adherence to the automatic treaty incorporation model (namely employing EU Agreements to conduct meaningful review of EU measures). Courts in automatic treaty incorporation systems often, as Chapter I emphasized, exhibit varying degrees of reluctance in adhering to the generous language of their constitutional

Council; C-377/02 *Van Parys*; C-104/97 P *Atlanta*; C-76/00 P *Petrotub*. Two cases also involved challenges to domestic action (C-228/06 *Soysal* and C-251/00 *Ilumitrónica*). Three of the WTO cases are also in the ex post review category (C-149/96 *Portugal v Council (Portuguese Textiles)*, C-347/03 *ERSA*, C-231/04 *Confcooperative*).

[45] This list excludes a number of cases in which consistent interpretation led to annulment of a measure.

[46] As noted at the beginning of this chapter, at least two cases in the exclusively consistent interpretation category can be viewed as manifestations of consistent interpretation leading to annulment of EU measures (T-163/94 & T-165/94 *NTN Corp*; T-256/97 *BEUC*).

[47] See Chapters III and IV. In the WTO context this included examples of what could be viewed as unacknowledged consistent interpretation.

documents, and similarly high-sounding judicial pronouncements. In such systems, with treaties accorded a rank at least equivalent to statute, then the judiciary will be faced not simply with addressing the *vires* of executive action but also that of legislative action. And this will, as with the EU, include later-in-time legislation where a higher rank than primary legislation is accorded to treaties. It is particularly in this context, that of judicial review of legislative action, that courts are especially conscious of their limited democratic mandate. This is even so where they have been expressly accorded such powers of review, for the 'counter-majoritarian difficulty'[48] does not lose its purchase simply because the constituent power may have expressly accepted legislative review powers.[49] Whilst the EU Courts have express powers of legislative review, they are reluctant to engage in legislative review, as contrasted with administrative review, and legislative acts are rarely struck down.[50] This reticence is perhaps even more pronounced where EU Agreements are the yardstick for assessing EU action. In terms of the avoidance techniques to preserve EU action, there are several tools at the disposal of the EU Courts. The first is restrictive standing criteria. In EU law the standing requirements for non-privileged applicants have long been heavily critiqued, and have unsurprisingly been used in some instances to dispense with cases involving EU Agreement challenges.[51] Clearly, the standing criteria will constitute a formidable impediment to review of EU action whether vis-à-vis EU Agreements or any other norms.[52] Indeed, we have seen in Chapter V that the Aarhus Convention Compliance Committee has concluded that in the absence of an alternative interpretation of the EU's standing criteria, the EU will not be in compliance with its Aarhus Convention obligations. If the EU Courts respond by offering a more

[48] A term coined by Bickel (1962).

[49] Ireland is an example of a system where such powers were expressly accorded (see art 34 of the Irish Constitution 1937). In many legal systems constitutional review powers may either not exist or be confined to a specialist constitutional court as is generally the case in the EU's Member States (although they have since been empowered by EU membership such that their ordinary courts—indeed even bodies not recognized as courts domestically—can review legislation for its EU law compliance).

[50] Tridimas and Gari (2010). See also Chalmers (2005).

[51] T-47/95 touched on in Chapter III and C-355/08 touched on in Chapter V, as well as a GATT and a WTO case (respectively 191/88 and T-170/04), touched on in Chapter IV, where surmounting the standing requirements would surely in any event have led to reiteration of extant case law concerning reviewability of EU action vis-à-vis GATT and WTO law.

[52] The argument against the ability of the preliminary ruling procedure to compensate for the stringent standing requirements in annulment actions were famously articulated, albeit to no avail, by AG Jacobs in C-50/00P *UPA v Council* [2002] ECR I-6677.

generous approach to standing in the environmental field with a view to ensuring greater consistency with the Aarhus Convention, this will offer a particularly significant additional illustration of the powerful legal effects to which EU Agreements can give rise.

A second possible tool as a matter of theory is to adopt a narrow approach to jurisdiction where mixed agreements are at issue in order to avoid dealing with contentious challenges to EU action. But there is no evidence of this having taken place, despite at least one significant example of Council promptings to the contrary.[53] Use of such an avoidance technique would, however, impact negatively on the judicial ability to advance the jurisprudence involving challenges to domestic action, for it would make it harder to resist Member State arguments against jurisdiction employed in cases such as *Étang de Berre* and *LZ VLK*.

The other two clear avoidance mechanisms are, first, the invocability of an EU Agreement as a review criterion and, where that hurdle is surmounted, the interpretation of the relevant Agreement that is offered. The only clear indication of the latter potentially being utilized in a manner that shields an EU measure from meaningful review is the *IATA* case.[54] The preliminary question of invocability as a review criterion is an altogether different matter. This question usually, albeit not exclusively, goes under the label of direct effect where preliminary ruling challenges to domestic measures are at issue and has been generously resolved in that context. However, so the argument runs, it has been treated diversely where EU action is at issue. In the past the evidence for this would be provided by the treatment meted out to the GATT and WTO Agreements. After all, the Agreements housed therein are precisely those that will lead to frequent challenges to EU legislative and administrative action. This is in contrast to the primarily bilateral trade-related agreements, considered in Chapter III, which result predominantly in challenges to Member State legislative and

[53] C-308/06 *Intertanko*. There are examples of Member State and even Council attempts, where it is not EU action being challenged, to have a narrower approach to jurisdiction than that for which the Court ultimately opted (cases such as C-53/96 *Hermès*, C-13/00 *Irish Berne*, C-239/03 *Étang de Berre*, C-240/09 *LZ VLK*).

[54] There is, however, further evidence of EU institutions seeking to defend EU measures via questionable interpretations of the provisions (eg the Commission and Council positions advanced in T-115/94 *Opel Austria*, and the Council, Parliament, and Commission pleas in C-308/06 *Intertanko*).

administrative action.[55] Put simply, this, it might well be suggested, is no coincidence. This book has, nonetheless, argued that the tailored treatment accorded to the GATT and WTO is not inconsistent with a generally receptive treaty enforcement model. For that model must be capable of accommodating the particular idiosyncrasies of the Agreements raised. It is for this reason that the approach to the WTO Agreements could be viewed as an unlikely harbinger of change. The WTO Agreements, after all, are characterized by idiosyncrasies that are likely absent in other treaties. In particular, the DSU could be read as pointing away from the normative desirability of the EU Courts converting themselves into WTO courts of first instance.[56] And as this can be grounded in the text of the WTO, it too can be read consistently with the judicially created gateway for EU Agreement enforcement in the EU legal order. The frequent assertions of purely political motivations thus do the judicial reasoning (curtly articulated as it may have been) a disservice.

A further point to note, is that the implications of the EU Courts transforming themselves into WTO courts of first instance was sufficiently alarming as to generate a hitherto unseen response (see, however, Council Decision 2011/265/EU), namely, the Council in its Decision concluding the WTO Agreements putting the EU Courts on notice as to its position on the use of those Agreements as a review criterion. And this was followed by powerful submissions from the institutions and the Member States when the WTO was invoked before the EU Courts.[57] It would be naïve to suppose that this vehement opposition to the EU Courts becoming independent enforcers of WTO law would not carry weight. Whilst this can be framed as the EU Courts bowing to political pressure, the uniform opposition can equally be viewed as testament to the idiosyncratic characteristics of the WTO. Indeed, the dramatic institutional and Member State response was significant in attesting to the need for a strong case to be made to disturb what would otherwise have been the ECJ's default maximalist mode of enforcement.

[55] Though when they are invoked in challenges to EU action the political institutions have been quick to argue that the relevant provisions are not directly effective or do not confer rights (T-244/94 *Stahl*, T-33 & T-34/98 *Petrotub*, C-74/98 *DAT-SCHAUB*).

[56] In a more limited sense they are already WTO courts of first instance by dint of the EU implementing legislation in a number of significant areas such as anti-dumping.

[57] This involved all three of the institutions in two instances (C-377/98 *Biotech* and C-491/01 *British American Tobacco*).

The pronounced opposition to the invocability of the WTO Agreements as a standard of review was also significant because it was difficult to conceive of an existing EU Agreement the text of which might justifiably generate such a robust reaction. And yet the ECJ was faced with a most robust of reactions in *Intertanko*. It was also of particular significance, and in this sense the institutional reaction cannot be considered analogous to that in the WTO line of cases, that the Commission defended the measure by means of a substantive interpretation of UNCLOS norms, rather than by following the Council and Parliament line (and that of four Member States) that sought to immunize the measures from review against UNCLOS norms.[58]

The *Intertanko* ruling is considerably more revealing as to the judicial receptiveness towards EU Agreements than the much-maligned GATT and WTO line of case law. For in the case of the GATT and WTO whilst the reasoning itself could have been expanded, the principled stance against review is eminently defensible. Closing the gateway to review in relation to UNCLOS, however, smacks rather potently of seeking to avoid the consequences of reviewing the specific EU legislative measure at issue. The formalistic reasoning pertaining to individual rights and the interstate nature of UNCLOS that was invoked to reject review sits uneasily with the way this preliminary question had been addressed in other cases challenging EU measures (to say nothing of those challenging domestic action).[59] Ultimately, it is unclear precisely why the broad logic and nature of UNCLOS precluded review vis-à-vis its norms, for the ECJ provided no compelling explanation. It remains unlike the WTO, for a carefully constructed dispute settlement system with forward-looking remedies has not been put in place, the *raison d'être* of which, as far as the EU is concerned, would be circumscribed if EU Courts policed compliance with its norms. In contrast also to the WTO terrain, it seems unlikely that accepting review of

[58] The Parliament's written submissions adopted the Commission line, however, at the hearing it supported the non-review stance (see para 49 of the Advocate General's Opinion).

[59] In C-377/98 *Biotech* and C-344/04 *IATA* the ECJ had only recently appeared to indicate that the preliminary question of 'invocability' would rarely prove an obstacle for EU Agreements. Indeed, there is little better manifestation of this commitment than having the Full Court assert, in riposte to the Council in *Biotech*, that the absence of direct effect, understood in individual rights terms, will not stand in the way of the judiciary policing EU compliance with EU Agreements. That crucial holding is no longer tenable post-*Intertanko*, unless eg the Court were to confine the rejection of a direct effect and individual rights hurdle to cases where privileged applicants are bringing the action, as was the case in *Biotech* itself.

EU measures in relation to UNCLOS would lead the EU Courts to be inundated with pleas of UNCLOS violations.

Where an EU Agreement is rejected as a review criterion for EU action, then this should rule out (following logic first employed with regard to the GATT) the use of that agreement to review domestic action via the preliminary ruling procedure. Use of this technique relative to EU action thus has direct implications for the judicial capacity to develop the bold jurisprudence vis-à-vis domestic action. That certainly does not mean that such Agreements are no longer in any sense part of EU law,[60] for they can remain so for a variety of other purposes, most obviously the consistent interpretation doctrine but more powerfully so to the extent that they can still be employed as the basis for infringement proceedings. That outcome will, however, generate a prima facie powerful double standards critique. One can seek to counter such criticism where persuasive support for the rejection of an Agreement as an EU review criterion exists, as Chapter IV attempted to do with respect to the GATT and WTO. Countering such criticism where the Court itself fails to provide a persuasive rationale for why an Agreement should not form a review criterion for EU action, as with UNCLOS, is a different matter. Ultimately, the EU's treaty enforcement model is such that the ECJ can immunize EU action from review against some Agreements without compelling explanation, whilst retaining the possibility of centralized enforcement of that same Agreement against Member State action.

4.2 Judicial avoidance techniques and the EU's normative commitment to international law

The *Intertanko* ruling raises a key issue that flows from adhering to the automatic treaty incorporation model, namely, how the EU Courts will respond where legislative action is being challenged where treaty-compliance considerations have arguably been insufficiently accommodated in the legislative process. Research has indicated that the EU Courts have exhibited an aversion to legislative review despite the existence of formal

[60] Note amongst others emphasizing the distinction between being part of the legal order and the conditions for review: Rosas (2008), Schütze (2007: 138–140).

powers coterminous with those of constitutional courts.[61] Chalmers makes the valuable observation that:

> legislative review involves second-guessing the measures taken by representative institutions affecting a wide array of actors, and draws courts into legislative politics by requiring them to take politically salient, comprehensive positions about the nature of the polity. If this is a politically challenging task for domestic constitutional courts, the failure of the Union courts to undertake it suggests that it would be political suicide for a supranational judiciary.[62]

The first sentence touches on the controversial tension posed by attachment to the now dominant legislative review model of constitutionalism.[63] Clearly, this is likely to be exacerbated for a supranational judiciary which does not possess a comparable legitimacy reservoir to that of its domestic counterparts, embedded as the latter are in the domestic legal arena with the concomitant legitimacy anchor provided by the domestic political community. Nevertheless, recalcitrance where EU Agreements would form the review yardstick, or indeed immunizing EU measures from review vis-à-vis such norms as appears to be the implication vis-à-vis UNCLOS following *Intertanko*,[64] has weighty ramifications. Chapter II underscored one significant dimension of the EU's attachment to an automatic treaty incorporation model: Member States having lost their independent treaty-making capacity across a whole swathe of activity would now find themselves obliged to follow the centralized judicial interpretation as to the legal effects of the EU's treaty-making output. The implication advanced was that this, if allied to a generous direct effect or invocability test, could produce greater compliance with treaty norms than could be expected if the matter were left as an issue for domestic judicial determination.[65] But if the Member States collectively, acting as a core component of the EU legislature in the form of the Council, are subject to unwilling review of such EU-level legislative (and administrative) output, then this assumption may not hold. Thus, EU law may operate aggressively to thwart domestic (Member State) legislative and administrative preferences that

[61] Chalmers (2005). See also Tridimas and Gari (2010).

[62] (2005: 470).

[63] See generally Hirschl (2004).

[64] Subject to the possible riders noted in Chapter V.

[65] Given, in particular, the judicial avoidance techniques employed in automatic treaty incorporation States and the fact that other Member States have systems of non-automatic treaty incorporation.

are incompatible with EU Agreements. But it may have the opposite effect as far as obstructing the collective preferences of the Member States adopted through the EU legislature.[66]

The significance of the judicial choices that lie ahead should not be underestimated. It is the type of commitment that the EU seeks to evince in relation to international law that has been at stake in the emerging case law, and the real litmus test of this commitment is provided where EU action is challenged. A primarily one-sided attachment to bold treaty enforcement—where domestic and not EU action is challenged—arguably exhibits little by way of commitment to international law per se. The policing of Member States in such contexts can simply be viewed as policing their EU law obligations, under Article 216(2) TFEU, vis-à-vis the EU which in turn is internationally responsible for such compliance.[67] Clearly, it would have significant ramifications for the EU as an international actor if it were not capable of ensuring that the constituent States—even if unlike in the conventional federal system they are independent sovereign entities that are frequently also party to EU Agreements—comply with obligations assumed by the centre.[68] It can, thus, be viewed as instrumentalist from a wholly internal EU law perspective rather than indicative of a normative commitment to international law. In short, then, a considerably more revealing and direct commitment to international law is capable of being manifested by the judicial approach to challenges to EU action rather than domestic action.

From a comparative perspective, the current trajectory of EU Agreement enforcement by the EU Courts is capable of being analogized with that in the US. Research there indicates a marked reluctance to enforce treaties against the centre, that is not present in treaty enforcement relative to the states.[69] *Intertanko* raised the obvious question as to whether a similar trend

[66] As noted, this can feed into challenges vis-à-vis domestic action given that existing case law appears to preclude individuals, as contrasted with the Commission, from invoking as review criteria for domestic action Agreements that cannot be invoked as review criteria for EU action.

[67] Even with mixed agreements where at least some Member States will also be parties and thus internationally bound, there is, depending on the Agreement and provisions at issue, an argument as to whether there would be joint and several liability. Thus one could also read a bold approach in relation to mixed agreements as symptomatic of this purely instrumentalist approach of avoiding liability.

[68] Obligations undertaken alongside at least some Member States where mixed agreements are at issue.

[69] See Wu (2007) with respect to Supreme Court practice. See Sloss (2009c) for more recent empirical analysis.

is emerging. Many would regard such a development with dismay given the tendency to view the US as having in recent times exhibited disdain for international law, and certainly for its judiciary to have exhibited a marked reluctance to police compliance with treaty norms.[70] Most recently and controversially this was in evidence in the Supreme Court's *Medellín* ruling rejecting the self-executing nature of a UN Charter provision.[71]

The US analogy has (ostensibly) gained in purchase as a result of the *Kadi* ruling.[72] In that case, Council Regulations implementing UN Security Council Resolutions under Chapter VII were annulled due to fundamental rights violations. A core controversy to which the judgment gave rise lay in the fact that the UN Charter, to which the EU is not a party, expressly provides that it prevails over other international treaties (Art 103). Despite lip-service being paid to the EU having to respect international law in the exercise of its powers, the judgment comes complete with several references to the autonomy of the EU legal order, including the bold assertion that as such it 'is not to be prejudiced by an international agreement'.[73] The ECJ did, however, underscore the self-evident proposition that its review of the implementing Regulation 'would not entail any challenge to the primacy of that resolution in international law'.[74]

One EU law scholar was quick to draw a tentative parallel with the Supreme Court's *Medellín* ruling rejecting the self-executing nature of a UN Charter provision.[75] It is an analogy which is likely to be frequently invoked,[76] and accordingly several important points are worth making as to the analogy to which *Kadi*, and the seemingly emerging reluctance to review EU action vis-à-vis EU Agreements, give rise. The first point to emphasize is that the ECJ arguably operates under different constraints to that of

[70] Even the US consistent interpretation canon currently appears under threat: see Dubinsky (2011: 648–50). On US treaty enforcement, see further the citations in Chapter I.

[71] *Medellín v Texas*, 128 S Ct 1346 (2008).

[72] C-402/05 P & C-415/05 P *Kadi and Al Barakaat v Council and Commission* [2008] ECR I-6351.

[73] Paragraph 316 (see in addition para 282).

[74] Ibid, para 288.

[75] De Búrca (2010: 2–3, 49).

[76] The judgment led two prominent US scholars who co-authored a controversial monograph entitled *The Limits of International Law* (Goldsmith and Posner (2005)) to pen a comment piece in the *Wall Street Journal* (25.11.08) entitled 'Does Europe Believe in International Law? Based on the record, it has no grounds to criticize the US'. The essence of their argument, which serves to bolster their earlier monograph, is that the EU has a merely rhetorical commitment to international law and like the US will not submit its values to the requirements of international law.

national courts with legislative review powers. The institutional legitimacy of the US Supreme Court (and federal courts in general), though admittedly contested as far as legislative review is concerned, remains the product of over two centuries of development. The ECJ, in contrast, is a young judicial actor that is embedded in the institutional framework of a supranational organization that has long suffered from a legitimacy deficit. But whilst the US Supreme Court does not exhibit an aversion to reviewing the actions of the centre, it is certainly increasingly unwilling to do so where treaty law is at issue. Moreover, despite the primordial status of the UN Charter in the international legal order, it is not actually an EU-concluded Agreement and therefore cannot be brought within Article 216(2) TFEU.[77] In any event, Article 216(2) TFEU is unquestionably less of a textual anchor for review of EU action than its US counterpart—the supremacy clause[78]—the textual history of which appears to indicate that the constituent power was seeking precisely to make treaties directly enforceable vis-à-vis state and federal law.[79] In this sense, the US courts might be viewed as exhibiting less respect for their founding constitutional document than is the case across the Atlantic.

Secondly, we simply have less evidence of judicial reticence in relation to EU Agreements given that for much of its history the EU has had a limited treaty-making capacity and ultimately few challenges to EU measures, outside the GATT/WTO context, of a non-spurious nature have arisen. The WTO analogy is also arguably misplaced.[80] Indeed, it is telling that whilst the judicial enforceability of the GATT and WTO in the EU has generated a veritable avalanche of mostly hostile academic comment, it has in the US, as with most other WTO members, been an issue that is simply not the subject of significant scholarly attention.[81] Furthermore, various channels for the judicial application of WTO law exist which clearly do not

[77] As contrasted with Art 351 TFEU.

[78] In addition art III, sect 2 (US Constitution 1787) provides expressly for a judicial role in relation to treaties.

[79] See generally Vazquez (1992; 1995; 1999; 2008).

[80] European non-compliance with the WTO is touched on by Goldsmith and Posner in their *Wall Street Journal* article (n 76 above).

[81] This absence of scholarly attention is not because elsewhere the GATT and WTO have been warmly received as an additional judicial tool by which to police domestic legislative and administrative practice. The US implementing legislation expressly precluded WTO enforceability against the centre, whilst permitting the centre to enforce the Agreements in relation to the states: Uruguay Round Agreements Act 1994 (S102).

in the same vein in the US.[82] The judicial application/non-application in the EU also operates against a backdrop of greater respect for WTO norms in the legislative process than appears to be the case in the US. Moreover, the EU has a markedly better compliance record with adverse WTO rulings. Research indicates a clear reluctance to amend congressional action found to 'breach' WTO rules.[83] The US approach of, at best, tardy compliance speaks to a more profound hostility to international norms and international tribunals 'interfering' in the US domestic process.[84]

Thirdly, there is the significant issue of the interests and values at stake in the aforementioned ECJ cases that might now be held up as signalling a merely rhetorical commitment to international law. The principled stance against review vis-à-vis the WTO has already been defended on its own terms. Nevertheless, it is worth emphasizing that in the notorious examples of legislative reticence from the EU, most obviously in the *Hormones*, *GMO*, and *Bananas* context, there were noteworthy countervailing factors. Both the *Hormones* and *GMO* controversies evidence a significant malaise with the quality of risk regulation that flows partially from the food scandals that have rocked Europe. In addition, refuge was sought, unsuccessfully, in an emerging principle in international environmental law, the precautionary principle. These were by no means open and shut cases. The *Bananas* controversy is a rather different matter, which now finally appears resolved, but there the EU had also sought waivers and the ECJ itself was eager in *Van Parys* to draw attention to the need to reconcile WTO obligations with those owed to the ACP States. The US practice in relation

[82] See Davies (2007) on consistent interpretation with regard to the WTO in the US. See on the recent judicial retreat from this doctrine, Dubinsky (2011).

[83] See Davey (2006: 12–13).

[84] Admittedly it has been argued that the WTO preserves the 'option to breach' albeit not indefinitely. There is, however, an example of the US being in indefinite non-compliance. The *Irish Music* case involved a section of the US Copyright Act being held incompatible with TRIPs obligations in 2000 (United States—Section 110(5) of the US Copyright Act, WT/DS/160/R). Although for a short period compensation was paid, we appear to be no nearer the US amending its legislation even though more than a decade has passed since the reasonable period of time for compliance elapsed. It is striking that the US over a relatively trivial issue, where no significant countervailing considerations appear to be in play, allows its leadership on TRIPs-related issues, to which it and its domestic industry is profoundly committed, to be called into question. During the US approval of the WTO Agreements the US ambassador emphasized an option to breach on a permanent basis albeit subject to compensation (as noted by Kuijper (1995b: 61)) which, of course, is absent in the *Irish Music* case.

to negative WTO rulings does not appear to reflect any such countervailing considerations.[85]

If we turn to *IATA*, we must recognize that the Air Passenger Rights Regulation sought to enhance consumer protection, an objective that in the manner framed therein is arguably in considerable tension with Montreal Convention obligations. As for *Intertanko*, it concerned a Directive with powerful environmental protection underpinnings adopted as a response to the perceived inadequacies of the international regime for environmental ship-source pollution and the sinking of two tankers in quick succession off the French and Spanish coasts.[86] *Kadi* brought to the fore the long-running critique as to the legitimacy of the Security Council's sanctions regime given the marked absence of due process rights,[87] and the ECJ can thus be viewed as seeking to uphold its commitment to fundamental rights (due process) as represented in the ECHR, to which the EU is not (yet) a party, and as it was constitutionally charged to do by the then Article 6(2) TEU.[88] *Kadi* can even be read as upholding international law in the form of international human rights standards.[89]

If we turn to *Medellín*, there the Supreme Court was unwilling to accord a UN Charter provision—Article 94 requiring compliance with ICJ decisions in cases to which the State is party—the effect of invalidating the specific application of State-level criminal procedures.[90] This resulted in the execution of an individual who had not been accorded his right of consular assistance as provided for under the Consular Relations Convention and in direct contravention of an ICJ ruling. In *Kadi*, by contrast, the ECJ was seeking to uphold due process rights, albeit in tension with UN obligations. In *Medellín* in effect it was the ICJ ruling, the domestic legal enforceability

[85] Countervailing considerations need not be viewed as wholly legally irrelevant in that they do provide the EU with its own internal justification to pursue a waiver or to be willing to be subjected to WTO counter-measures.

[86] This, of course, is not intended as justification for an outcome that appears to immunize EU action from UNCLOS review.

[87] See eg Bianchi (2006) and additional citations therein.

[88] The GC ruling refusing to subject EU action implementing UN Security Council Resolutions to searching fundamental rights review was quickly and rightly criticized: thus Eeckhout (2007: 206) emphasized that fundamental rights review need not be seen as conflicting with the binding force of the UN Charter, as the ECHR standards applicable by EU Courts are comparable to those in other UN instruments.

[89] See also Scheinin (2009).

[90] State-level limitations on successive filing of habeas petitions.

of which was rejected, that sought to protect due process rights.[91] The other obvious distinction is that *Medellín* was concerned with ensuring State-level compliance with treaty obligations. It therefore appeared in tension with US practice where active enforcement vis-à-vis the states was in evidence. Part of the explanation for this is no doubt the difficulty in holding the relevant UN provision self-executing in relation to state law, only then not to do so in relation to federal law.[92] Be that as it may, the outcome was that US states were permitted free rein to flout obligations assumed by the centre.[93]

It is hoped that enough has been done here to justify caution in drawing analogies between the respective judicial approaches in the EU and US. Nonetheless, it cannot be denied that recent judgments have placed the EU's commitment to international law firmly under the spotlight. Rightly or wrongly, the WTO line of case law, *Intertanko* and *Kadi*, have been prominent in fuelling this criticism.[94] As concerned the approach in *Kadi*, de Búrca argued that it was 'at odds with the conventional self-presentation of the EU as an organisation which maintains particular fidelity to international law and institutions.'[95] Crucially, she drew attention to the fact that this general perception is fed by legal, political, and judicial pronouncements of the EU and bolstered by academic and popular commentary.[96] It is this image that the ECJ risks jeopardizing with its emerging case law. The professed fidelity to international law that is at stake should leave the EU institutions with little doubt that the forthcoming judgments pertaining to international law will be scrutinized especially closely by a broad audience. Indeed, those scholars of a realist bent may well be looking for this to further substantiate their preferred paradigm.[97] And certainly it is doubtful that a better fillip exists for the veracity of such

[91] The very different kinds of obligation at issue in *Kadi* and *Medellín* were appropriately noted by de Búrca (2010: 2–3).

[92] The judgment acknowledged that contrary federal law would be subject to the same fate as state law (at 1364).

[93] Subject, it seems, to Congress legislating to the contrary.

[94] See eg Eckes (2012) and Ziegler (2011). An international law scholar has also cast a perceptively critical eye over the respect accorded to international law in the judicial treatment of both treaties concluded prior to the entry into force of the European Community, or prior to a Member State's accession, and those concluded thereafter: Klabbers (2009). See also Lavranos (2010).

[95] (2010: 41).

[96] De Búrca (2010: 47).

[97] Not least Goldsmith and Posner whose recent work has become the standard-bearer.

theorizing than finding an international law recalcitrance from a Court that is founded by treaty—thus itself a product of international law—and that has been so exigent as to the requirements stemming from the Treaty of which it is the authoritative interpreter.

If the EU is to continue to preach the virtues of compliance with international law,[98] then it behoves the EU Courts to uphold the image of the EU as 'a virtuous international actor which maintains a distinctive commitment to international law and institutions'.[99] This type of message was apparent in the Commission and Council submissions in *Kadi*.[100] Both emphasized that review of the EU implementing Regulations 'would cause serious disruption to the international relations of the [EU] and its Member States' and would lead the EU to breach its general duty to observe international law.[101] It might appear that it was the EU's two political institutions, the Council and the Commission, which were acutely attuned to the potential ramifications that an absence of reverence to the UN Charter and Security Council might entail for the EU's carefully cultivated image, but it should be recalled that the case involved a challenge to an EU measure. When the *Intertanko* litigation arose, admittedly arousing a scintilla of the international attention generated by *Kadi*, the Council and the Parliament, resorted to that classic avoidance technique of calling for a rejection of UNCLOS as a review criterion for EU action. The Commission was exhibiting greater concern as to the repercussions that such an avoidance technique would have for the EU's meticulously constructed image of adherence to international law.[102] By defending a questionable substantive compatibility interpretation, the Commission might be viewed as having called for an alternative judicial avoidance technique, however, that stance not only unquestionably poses less of a challenge to the EU's

[98] Upon the execution of Mr Medellín, the EU called on the US to introduce a moratorium on the death penalty and for the federal and state level to take the necessary legislative measures to give effect to ICJ decisions: EU Presidency Declaration 12431/08, Brussels, 11.08.08.

[99] The quotation is drawn from de Búrca (2010: 1).

[100] See especially the Council submissions, recounted in T-315/01 *Kadi v Council and Commission* [2005] ECR II-3649, para 174.

[101] Ibid, paras 162–3, 174.

[102] This was particularly noteworthy given that the then head of the Commission legal service external relations team had suggested that the logic of the *Portuguese Textiles* reasoning, viewed as adjusting the emphatic *Kupferberg* conclusions, should not be confined to the WTO: see Kuijper in Kuijper and Bronckers (2005: 1321).

image but, crucially, would also have left UNCLOS still able to function as a review criterion for both EU and domestic action.[103]

Challenges to EU legislative action raise an ineluctable problem for the EU and its judiciary. For where measures are adopted under the ordinary legislative procedure we can expect a highly politically charged scenario in which all three institutions—and most likely a considerable number of Member States as well—defend their legislative output. If in the EU Agreement context they do so by successfully advancing arguments that immunize EU action from EU Agreement review, the argumentation of the Council and Parliament (and that of four Member States) in *Intertanko*, then the image of the EU they have been at pains to build will suffer with attendant consequences.[104] Political expediency may lead the EU's political institutions to lose sight of these implications in their zeal to protect the product of the frequently arduous supranational legislative process. The ECJ has at its disposal the tools to act as the counterweight to what might be the short-sighted political interests that can occasionally reign; in effect, for the EU's supreme judicial arbiter to make its contribution to ensuring that the EU makes good on the EU's much-vaunted commitment to

[103] As previously noted, UNCLOS review of domestic action should still be possible via infringement proceedings.

[104] Since the cut-off date for the data-set, the Grand Chamber has handed down its judgment in C-366/10 *Air Transport Association of America v Secretary of State for Energy and Climate Change*, 21 December 2011. Here a US Air Transport Association and three US airlines unsuccessfully challenged the Directive (2008/101/EC) bringing airlines into the EU emissions trading scheme on international law grounds, that included both customary international law, a non-EU-concluded Agreement (the Chicago Convention to which all the Member States are parties), and two EU Agreements (the Kyoto Protocol and an Air Transport Agreement with the US). All the institutions and 11 intervening EU Member States, along with two EEA States, argued that the Kyoto Protocol was not of direct application. The Court did not quite expressly reject the capacity of the Kyoto Protocol to be used as a review criterion for EU action, but did expressly conclude that the specific provision invoked, which required the Contracting Parties to pursue limitations or reduction of certain emissions through the International and Civil Aviation Organization, was not unconditional and sufficiently precise. As for the Air Transport Agreement, it appears (see para 88 of the AG Opinion) that only the Commission and France accepted that it could be invoked by natural and legal persons before the Court. The ECJ concluded that it could, indeed, be used to challenge EU acts, persuaded it seems by the fact that it contains specific provisions designed to confer rights directly on airlines and others designed to impose obligations upon them. The Directive, however, emerged unscathed from review vis-à-vis the Air Transport Agreement. It is thus tempting to see this episode as another illustration of the willingness of the institutions and Member States to seek to insulate EU action from EU Agreement review, only here unlike in *Intertanko*, at least concerning one Agreement, the Court followed the Commission (rather than the Council, Parliament, and a number of intervening Member States) in accepting that an Agreement could be used to review EU action.

international law. In this era of a 'Global Community of Courts',[105] engaged in a transnational constitutional dialogue, the stakes are particularly high. The pronouncements of a regional 'constitutional court'[106] for over 500 million individuals, and soon to be more than 27 Member States, are especially significant. Whilst *Kadi* can be read as offering courts encouragement to assert their particular constitutional priorities over international norms,[107] *Intertanko* offers them dubious grounds on which to immunize domestic action from review vis-à-vis binding treaty norms.[108] In sum, by dint of their increasing stature, origins, and a framework within which they operate that propagates a normative commitment to international law, the EU Courts can be viewed as bearing a special onus in contributing to this commitment.

This is certainly not intended as a plea for the EU Courts simply to become uncritical decentralized enforcement mechanisms for all EU treaty-making. This book has offered a defence of both the principled stance against WTO review of EU action and the principled stance in favour of ex post review of EU Agreements including supporting the appropriateness of depriving treaty norms of internal EU law effect. Unsurprisingly, then, it is perfectly possible to find fault with the judicial treatment of international law in particular instances without viewing everything short of slavish enforcement of all treaty norms contemptuously. It is submitted that it is precisely the one-size-fits-all approach that is problematic. For the kind of logic that sees in the few words of a constitutional reception norm such as Article 216(2) TFEU, and related judicial language (such as that first employed in *Haegeman II*), the answer to all the central questions to which treaty law gives rise in the internal sphere is likely to fail to engage in a measured way with the arguments against, for example, WTO review of EU law by EU Courts, with or without a DSB decision in play, or with why depriving an EU Agreement of internal effect can be

[105] Slaughter (2003).

[106] A tentative analogy with a constitutional court was drawn by a former ECJ judge as early as 1964: Catalano (1964: 74–80).

[107] De Búrca (2010: 42) made this point with respect to courts outside the EU. The point applies equally to domestic courts within the EU where, eg, they are engaged with treaties to which Member States alone are party, and potentially provisions of mixed agreements considered outwith the jurisdiction of the EU Courts. In any event, asserting one's own particular constitutional priorities over international law need not always be viewed negatively (note the ex post review of EU Agreements coverage in this book).

[108] *Intertanko* is likely to have implications for how UNCLOS will be treated by other 'municipal courts'.

constitutionally appropriate even if not acceptable when viewed from an international law perspective. Indeed, this is partly why the growing recourse to the monism and dualism language in the EU context, which *Kadi* appears to have fuelled,[109] has become increasingly unhelpful. These labels often appear to be used as shorthand for praise or criticism of particular rulings or strands in the case law,[110] and can detract from the necessary critical engagement precisely because the language is misleadingly value-laden, with dualism often used synonymously with an inappropriate and unwarranted closure to international norms whilst monism signifies the enlightened opposite.[111] As Chapter I has already suggested, we can dispense with this language whilst nonetheless engaging carefully with the difficult questions to which the relationship between international law and domestic (or EU) law gives rise.

So if the one-size-fits-all approach to judicial enforceability is undesirable, it is essential to ask what a more appropriate judicial stance would entail. Given the breadth of treaty law and the variety of extant provisions, it would be foolhardy to even attempt an ex ante answer. What can, however, be said is that complete rejection of a whole Agreement as a review criterion for EU action (and, thus, potentially domestic action), particularly where it is a broad multilateral agreement such as the WTO or UNCLOS, places a heavy onus on the Court to justify such an uncompromising stance. Ultimately, we are entitled to expect a credible attempt at reasoned justification

[109] Though the EU Courts in *Kadi* did not use this language expressly, indeed have made no use of such terminology in any of the cases identified in this book, few have been able to resist using this terminology in referring to the approaches of either or both EU Courts: examples include de Búrca (2010); Murkens (2009); Hilpold (2009); Krenzler and Landwehr (2011); Ziegler (2011); Wouters (2010); Pellet (2009); Van Rossem (2009); Gattini (2009); Tomuschat (2009). Stein and Halberstam (2009: 43) expressly avoided the terminology.

[110] A number of commentators have used the adjective dualist or dualistic in relation to the WTO-related case law (eg Ziegler (2011); Eckes (2012); Klabbers (2009) (referring to prudent dualism in this context); Krenzler and Landwehr (2011); Rodriguez Iglesias (2003: 397); Pescatore (2003) (but see Rosas (2008: 76)); in relation to *Intertanko* see Krenzler and Landwehr (2011)). That language, as Chapter I noted, is also commonly employed in relation to reviewing the act concerning conclusion.

[111] In the *Kadi* context it was the commonly labelled monistic approach of the GC, with commentators usually adding an adjective such as radical (eg Murkens (2009), Pavoni (2009)), that was more heavily criticized (but contrast Tomuschat (2006)). The ECJ approach usually characterized as dualist, with various additional adjectives such as sharply, strongly and robust often affixed, was also criticized (see de Búrca (2010); Gattini (2009); Sauri (2011)). Eeckhout (2011), Eckes (2009), and Murkens (2009), amongst others, have offered cogent defences of the ECJ ruling.

for why a particular Agreement will be deprived of its most potent internal legal effects where we are dealing with a supreme judicial arbiter created by treaty that generally deploys a maximalist approach to treaty enforcement where Member State action is challenged and operates in a system that continuously professes its normative commitment to international law, including via its recently amended constitutional text.[112] Whilst providing carefully reasoned justification for outcomes has often been in short supply in the jurisprudence of the Luxembourg Courts,[113] the WTO jurisprudence at least offered a credible attempt at such justification even if not all are convinced. The curt and formalistic reasoning employed vis-à-vis UNCLOS in *Intertanko*, in contrast, will rightly leave very few persuaded that this burden has been met.

A final point worth developing draws on the interesting suggestion that to reconcile openness towards international law with EU legislative discretion, the Court should more readily accept direct effect but show reluctance to find a breach where general EU legislation is concerned.[114] Generosity on the direct effect or invocability question certainly sits considerably more comfortably with the EU's normative commitment to international law than the unpersuasively reasoned stance adopted in *Intertanko* which clashes precisely with the image that the EU's political institutions seek to cultivate. Moreover, generosity on the invocability question even where EU action is challenged, the opposite of the stance adopted in relation to UNCLOS in *Intertanko*, should leave the relevant Agreement as a possible review criterion for domestic action via the preliminary ruling procedure.[115] Generosity on invocability is thus not just a question of permitting the judicial enforceability of EU Agreements vis-à-vis EU action, but also bolstering its applicability vis-à-vis domestic action.[116]

Whilst many may be comfortable with the idea of generosity on the direct effect or invocability question, supporting judicial reluctance to find a breach is unlikely to be as warmly received. Indeed, it is more likely to be viewed as advocacy of a judicial avoidance tactic that will simply consolidate a twin-track enforcement approach, but one where it is not

[112] Article 3(5) TEU and Art 21 TEU.

[113] See Weiler (2001b) for criticism of the style of judicial decision-making. And most recently Conway (2012).

[114] Advanced by Eeckhout (2009: 2057).

[115] That outcome would only be possible vis-à-vis UNCLOS if the ECJ revisits the stance it first adopted vis-à-vis the GATT or if it overruled the *Intertanko* conclusions on UNCLOS.

[116] Bolstering as infringement proceedings could well still be possible.

the invocability question that manifests the diverging trajectory but rather the substantive interpretation itself. However, it should be underscored that Eeckhout only expressly advocated such reluctance in relation to general legislative measures.[117] And, in a sense, that is the most international law-friendly stance that one could realistically expect from the EU Courts. After all, the statistics show that they operate as particularly reluctant reviewers of general legislative measures and rarely thwart the policy preferences of the EU legislature.[118] Given that this is so, one can hardly expect them to throw caution to the wind when faced with challenges to the compatibility of general policy measures with EU Agreements. Nor would that be appropriate and, indeed, one can go further and justify at least some measure of recalcitrance even where EU administrative action is at stake. For it is right not to expect the authoritative interpreters of the EU norms invoked in challenges to EU measures to deal as boldly with external treaty norms of which they are ultimately not the authoritative interpreters. This is only accentuated with treaty norms housed in multilateral agreements that seek to accommodate as many participants as possible often at the expense of the precision of the norms.

5. Conclusions

Whilst the EU in principle automatically incorporates treaties it concludes into its legal order, it is the EU legal order that will ultimately determine the types of internal legal effect which such Agreements can display and, indeed, can potentially deprive them, through ex post review, of internal legal effects where they clash with EU primary law. Those internal legal effects have been particularly powerfully articulated by the Court where it has been Member State action that has been challenged, but the Full Court's indications that this maximalist stance might also apply where EU action was challenged (*Biotech*) appears to be wavering given the response offered when UNCLOS was relied upon to challenge EU legislation (*Intertanko*).[119] In one sense, this outcome may be consistent with a general trajectory in EU Court litigation which operates to protect EU

[117] Eeckhout (2009: 2057), and specifically advocated the Court stepping in where obligations were clearly disregarded.

[118] See generally Tridimas and Gari (2010) and Chalmers (2005).

[119] See also Mendez (2010a).

action, particularly of the general legislative variety, from intrusive review while imposing precisely the opposite outcome on Member State action. But for a similar logic to prevail where EU Agreements are at stake has additional implications. How the ECJ treats EU legislative and administrative output vis-à-vis EU law proper, primary or otherwise, of which it is the authoritative interpreter, is of limited concern outside the EU. How it treats such output vis-à-vis EU Agreements of which it is not the authoritative interpreter is of much broader concern. The EU, after all, constantly proclaims its commitment to international law and inevitably for it to function as a beacon in this respect it is not enough simply to hope for the EU's legislative and executive actors meticulously to manifest that commitment in their legislative and administrative practice. The treaty-created Courts of the EU will rightly be seen as having an important contributing role to play. A hands-off judicial attitude is likely to have ramifications for the respect accorded to EU Agreements in the EU law-making process. Wholly defensive submissions from the EU institutions are to be expected, but for them to be always heeded by the EU Courts will be damaging to the normative commitment to international law that the EU proclaims. Treaty enforcement recalcitrance from such a high-profile treaty-created judicial actor, in an era of increasing judicial dialogue and borrowing, could also contribute to treaty enforcement recalcitrance elsewhere. The Lisbon Treaty has supplied the EU Courts with a powerful additional anchor with which to hold a more unreserved embrace of treaty enforcement, in the form of the EU's constitutional charter stating: 'the Union . . . shall contribute to . . . the strict observance and the development of international law'.[120]

The EU Courts are unlikely to become anything other than reluctant to allow an EU Agreement to be used as a successful ground of challenge to an EU general legislative measure; but simply by not closing off EU action to review vis-à-vis EU Agreements, absent compelling reasons, it will be making a more positive contribution to the strict observance and development of international law than it signalled with its (admittedly pre-Lisbon) *Intertanko* ruling. Even if a measure of recalcitrance were to remain in play in relation to EU action, it is worth reiterating that the stance relative to domestic action has, thus far, ensured that EU Agreements come equipped with powerful EU enforcement tools that can, and are, regularly invoked at

[120] Article 3(5) TEU.

the behest of individuals and (seemingly rarely but perhaps increasingly) by the Commission. This ensures greater judicial treaty enforcement, and thus compliance with treaty norms, than could have been expected in the EU's absence.[121]

As a final remark, it should be recalled that one of the clear lessons from the European project is that the harder the legal status domestically of treaty-based norms, the more questions will be asked as to the input and output legitimacy of the norms themselves. Equipping norms in EU Agreements with the most powerful of enforcement machinery in relation to both domestic and EU action will therefore inevitably exacerbate existing concerns with the international law-making process.[122]

[121] See also Mendez (2010b). Even in the WTO context with a principled stance against review of EU action vis-à-vis the WTO, the fact that currently 27 Member States are precluded from tracking their own course in the WTO—assuming infringement proceedings can be pursued against Member States purporting to do so—is likely to lead to greater compliance with WTO rules than would have existed in the EU's absence (assuming, of course, that EU administrative and legislative action is generally WTO-compliant).

[122] The international law-making process significantly empowers the executive branch which can accordingly serve to bolster a core tenet of the existing democratic deficit critique of the EU; that is, that it empowers executive actors at the expense of national parliaments. For illuminating engagement with the core tenets of the EU democratic deficit critique, see Follesdal and Hix (2006).

EU Agreements Case Law Data-Set

The data-set of case law involving EU Agreements created for this study was developed using the EUR-Lex search engine tool <http://eur-lex.europa.eu/RECH_jurisprudence.do>. The objective was essentially to gather those cases in which EU Agreements were being invoked in three core ways (or were in any event engaged with by the ECJ in such contexts), to challenge either EU or Member State-level action or where in effect it is either the substance of the Agreement or the procedure by which it was concluded that is being challenged. The searches by procedure were limited to judgments and orders of the European Court of Justice and the General Court and were refined to search for cases in which the words 'agreement' or 'agreements' (searching for a?reement* in the 'search for' box incorporates both categories) or 'convention' or 'conventions' (likewise) or 'European Economic Area' or 'EEA' appear using the full text search option. The cut-off date for these searches was 3 October 2011 and this produces several thousand cases across the different procedures. The key issue then becomes that of sifting the cases to produce the data-set of those considered pertinent to this study. The vast majority of cases arising from these searches were easily dispensed with in having no connection to the subject of this study, for example:

- use of the word agreement or convention in a fashion that has nothing to do with international agreements or conventions, examples include in the competition law sense of the term and in the context of the social partners;
- agreements and conventions to which the EU is not a party,[1] which predictably is dominated by the many cases involving ECHR-related pleas;
- the mere reference to the text of a Regulation or Directive as being of EEA relevance.

There are several categories of cases which contain a direct reference to a EU Agreement but which are also excluded:

- cases where the entry into force of an Agreement has been referred to by the ECJ; EEA examples include: C-396/05; C-28/00; C-389/99; C-277/99; C-412/96; C-389/98; C-290/00; a non-EEA example is C-452/04;

[1] With the exception of GATT 1947, which as noted in the introduction falls within the scope of this study.

- the many additional cases in which there are what appear to be merely descriptive references to EU Agreements: eg 96/75; 86/75; 51/78; 124/84; 165/84; 386/87; 80/89; 328/89; 230/98; 179/00; C-100/05;
- cases on the Trade Mark Directive in which amendments to it by the EEA Agreement are acknowledged by the Court: eg 405/03; 16/03; 143/00; 443/99;
- the numerous cases on the technicalities of EU customs measures in which multilateral EU customs-related agreements are touched on: this includes cases on the International Transport of Goods under Cover of TIR Carnets (eg C-371/99; C-310 & C-406/98; C-161/08; C-488/09; 78/01 and including in infringement proceedings where the plea does not concern breach of that Convention, eg C-377/03; C-105/02; C-312/04); cases on the International Convention on the Harmonized Commodity Description and Coding System which was the foundation of the Community nomenclature in Regulation 2658/87 (C-376/07; C-375/07; C-486/06; C-400/5; C-514/04; C-15/05; C-260/00; C-288/99; C-201/99; C-270/96); cases on the International Convention on the Simplification and Harmonization of Customs Procedures (26/88) At most, some of these cases appear to relate to consistent interpretation of the EU implementing measure vis-à-vis the relevant EU Customs Agreement. Only one was discovered involving a direct plea of breach of the EU Agreement and it has accordingly been included (C-267/94) in the data-set.

Having sifted the cases using 3 October 2011 as the cut-off date, some 337 cases remained which are listed below.[2] The methodology employed for producing this data-set is subject to numerous pitfalls. Sifting through thousands of cases using the find tool for key words such as agreement and convention generates considerable scope for human error in searching through the cases to identify those of relevance. Secondly, any shortcomings with the EurLex search tool will be replicated in the search. Thus any cases that do not appear via the Eur-Lex search even using the case reference number, something that the author has noticed on occasion, will not be accessible via the search tool. A further shortcoming will be the cases that have not been translated into English. Many of those cases will not have been identified in the searches. It is also clear that pleas pertaining to, for example, breaches of EU Agreements can only be identified if they are acknowledged in the text of the judgment or an Advocate General's Opinion. There are no doubt many examples

[2] A number of additional cases where EU Agreement references could be found were discovered and some are cited in a number of footnotes in Chapters II, IV, and V, but have as noted therein, not been included in the charts in those chapters (10/61 *Commission v Italy* [1961] ECR 1; 2–3/62 *Commission v Luxembourg and Belgium* [1962] ECR 445; C-284/95 *Safety Hi-*Tech [1998] ECR I-4301; C- 341/95 *Bettati v Safety Hi-Tech* [1998] ECR I-4355; C-410/03 *Commission v Italy* [2005] ECR I–3507; C-111/05 *Aktiebolaget NN* [2007] ECR I-2697; C-173/07 *Emirates Airlines* [2008] ECR I-5237; C- 549/07 *Wallentin-Hermann v Alitalia* [2008] ECR I-11061; C-204/08 *Rehder v Air Baltic* [2009] ECR I-6073; C-63/09 *Axel Walz v Clickair* [2010] ECR I-4239).

of such pleas during oral proceedings which might not then be recounted in the judgment, not least given that the extent to which judgments actually recount pleas of the parties and interveners has been dramatically reduced over the years. Nevertheless, it is hoped that the 337 cases identified constitute a reasonable attempt at comprehensiveness.

156/85 *Perles Eurotool* [1986] ECR 1595 p 111, 112.
C-183/85 *Itzehoe* [1986] ECR 1873 p. 196.
187/85 *Fediol v Commission* [1988] ECR 4155 p 196.
193/85 *Cooperativa Co-Frutta* [1987] ECR 2085 p 114, 177, 245, 294.
194 & 241/85 *Commission v Greece* [1988] ECR 1037 p 157, 158, 162.
12/86 *Demirel* [1987] ECR 3719 p 67, 68, 105, 113, 116, 117, 118, 125, 149, 151, 154, 165, 167, 172, 239, 251, 268, 292, 293.
114/86 *UK v Commission* [1988] ECR 5289 p 162.
70/87 *Fediol v Commission* [1989] ECR 1781 p 197–199, 200, 203, 204, 205, 206, 211, 218, 219, 221, 225, 226, 230, 233, 237, 245, 247, 248, 275.
165/87 *Commission v Council* [1988] ECR 5545 p 78, 81, 83, 86.
C-175/87 *Matsushita* [1992] ECR I-1409 p 196, 244.
C-178/87 *Minolta v Council* [1992] ECR I-1577 p 177, 245.
C-179/87 *Sharp v Council* [1992] ECR I-1409 p 196.
247/87 *Star Fruit Company SA v Commission* [1989] ECR 291 p 163.
340/87 *Commission v Italy* [1989] ECR 1483 p 157–158, 169, 297.
125/88 *Nijman* [1989] ECR 3533 p 110, 172.
C-188/88 *NMB v Commission* [1992] ECR I-1689 p 199, 245.
C-189/88 *Cartorobica* [1990] ECR I-1269 p 177, 245.
191/88 *Co-Frutta v Commission* [1989] ECR 793p 177, 245, 303.
C-17/89 *Deutsche Olivetti* [1990] ECR I-2301 p. 196.
C-69/89 *Nakajima v Council* [1991] ECR I-2069 p 197–199, 200, 203, 204, 205, 206, 211, 218, 219, 220, 221, 225, 226, 229, 230–238, 245, 247, 248, 275.
C-192/89 *Sevince* [1990] ECR I-3461p 67, 114, 116–119, 120, 121, 124, 125, 130, 131, 153, 154, 172, 239, 292, 293.
C-18/90 *Kziber* [1991] ECR I-199 p 115, 128–132, 134, 151, 152, 153, 156, 293.
C-50/90 *Sunzest v Commission* [1991] ECR I-2917 p 162.
C-105/90 *Goldstar v Council* [1992] ECR I-677 p. 196, 244.
C-163/90 *Legros* [1992] ECR I-4625 p 108, 110, 167.
C-228–34/90, 339/90 & 353/90 *Simba* [1992] ECR I-3713 p 114, 172.
C-65/91 *Commission v Greece* [1992] ECR I-5245 p 157, 158.
C-188/91 *Deutsche Shell AG* [1993] ECR I-363 p 113, 114.
C-207/91 *Eurim-Pharm GmbH* [1993] ECR I-3723 p 111, 155.
C-228/91 *Commission v Italy* [1993] ECR I-2701 p 157–158.
C-237/91 *Kus* [1992] ECR I-6781 p 120–122, 130, 135.
C-292/91 *Weis* [1993] ECR I-2219 p 111, 112.
C-312/91 *Metalsa Srl* [1993] ECR I-3751 108. 109.
C-327/91 *France v Commission* [1994] ECR I-3641 78, 80, 81, 85, 86, 90, 91, 93.
C-12/92 *Huygen* [1993] ECR I-638 p 111, 112.
C-432/92 *Anastasiou* [1994] ECR I-3087 p 111–113, 150, 151, 293.
C-58/93 *Yousfi* [1994] ECR I-1353 p 130.

T-94/00, T-111/00 & T-159/00 *Rica Foods v Commission* [2002] ECR II-4677 (appeal was C-41/03 P *Rica Foods v Commission* [2005] ECR I-6875) p 206.
T-123/00 *Thomae v Commission* [2002] ECR II-5193 p 207, 247.
C-76/00 P *Petrotub v Council* [2003] ECR I-79 (appeal of T-33 & 34/98 *Petrotub and Republica v Council* [1999] ECR II-3837) p 166, 170, 232–234, 236, 237, 247, 248, 302, 305.
T-151/00 *Laboratoire du Bain v Council and Commission* [2005] ECR II-23 p 222.
C-162/00 *Pokrzeptowicz-Meyer* [2002] ECR I-1049 p 135, 136, 137.
C-188/00 *Kurz* [2002] ECR I-10691 p 120, 122, 155.
C-251/00 *Ilumitrónica* [2002] ECR I-10433 p 142, 143, 145, 148, 149, 171, 302.
T-301/00 *Groupe Fremaux SA v Council and Commission* [2005] ECR II-25 p 222.
T-320/00 *CD Cartondruck AG v Council and Commission* [2005] ECR II-27 p 222.
T-383/00 *Beamglow* [2005] ECR II-5459 p 222.
C-422/00 *Capespan* [2003] ECR I-597 p 206.
C-438/00 *Kolpak* [2003] ECR I-4135 p 135, 136, 137–139, 153, 156, 254.
T-19/01 *Chiquita v Commission* [2005] ECR II-315 p 219–220, 221, 231 235.
T-35/01 *Shanghai v Council* [2004] ECR II-3663 p 229, 247.
T-64/01 & T-65/01 *Afrikanische Frucht-Compagnie* [2004] ECR II-521 p 219.
C-76/01 P *Eurocoton v Council* [2003] ECR I-10091 p 229, 247.
T-132/01 *Euroalliages v Commission* [2003] ECR II-2359 p 229, 247.
C-171/01 *Wählergruppe* [2003] ECR I-4301 p 135, 136, 137.
C-189/01 *Jippes* [2001] ECR I-5689 p 261, 282, 284, 285.
C-211/01 *Commission v Council* [2003] ECR I-8913 p 78, 80, 81, 288.
C-213/01 P *T. Port v Commission* [2003] ECR I-2332 (appeal of T-52/99 *T. Port v Commission* [2001] ECR II-981) p 218.
C-281/01 *Commission v Council* [2002] ECR I-2049 p 78, 80, 82.
C-300/01 *Salzmann* [2003] ECR I-4899 p 142.
C-317/01 & 369/01 *Abatay & Sahin* [2003] ECR I-12301 p 124–125, 155, 156.
C-452/01 *Ospelt* [2003] ECR I-9743 p 142, 172.
C-465/01 *Commission v Austria* [2004] ECR I-8291 p 160, 162.
C-491/01 *British American Tobacco* [2002] ECR I-11453 p 206, 305.
C-23/02 *Alami* [2003] ECR I-1399 p 132, 133.
C-49/02 *Heidelberger* [2004] ECR I-6129 p 228, 247.
C-93/02 P *Biret v Council* [2003] ECR I-10497 p 218–219, 224, 233.
C-94/02 P *Biret and Cie v Council* [2003] ECR I-10565 218–219, 224.
T-212/02 *Commune de Champagne v Council and Commission* [2007] ECR II-2017 p 79, 80, 206–207, 288.
C-245/02 *Budvar* [2004] ECR I-1989 p 227–228, 247.
T-274/02 *Ritek v Council* [2006] ECR II-4305 p 234, 247.
C-275/02 *Ayaz* [2004] ECR I-8765 p 120, 121, 123.
C-286/02 *Bellio* [2004] ECR I-3465 p 143, 145.
C-327/02 *Panayotova* [2004] ECR I-11055 p 140, 155.

T-498/04 *Zhejiang Xinan Chemical Industrial Group v Council* [2009] ECR II-1969 p 234, 247.
C-502/04 *Torun* [2006] ECR I-1563 p 120, 123.
C-522/04 *Commission v Belgium* [2007] ECR I-5701 p 160.
C-4/05 *Güzeli* [2006] ECR I-10279 p 120, 135, 136.
C-16/05 *Tum* [2007] ECR I-7415 p 126, 154, 155.
C-97/05 *Gattoussi* [2006] ECR I-11917 p 135, 136, 141, 268.
C-173/05 *Commission v Italy* [2007] ECR I-4917 p 160.
T-221/05 *Huvis v Council* [2008] ECR II-124 p 236–237, 247, 248.
C-246/05 *Häupl* [2007] ECR I-4673 p 228, 247.
T-295/05 *Document Security Systems v ECB* [2007] ECR II-2835 p 207.
C-325/05 *Derin* [2007] ECR I-6495 p 120, 123.
C-335/05 *Řízení* [2007] ECR I-4307 p 228. 247.
C-336/05 *Echouikh* [2006] ECR I-5223 p 132, 133.
C-345/05 *Commission v Portugal* [2006] ECR I-10633 p 160.
C-431/05 *Merck* [2007] ECR I-7001 p 212, 240, 241, 242, 247, 292, 294.
C-447/05 & C-448/05 *Thomson Multimedia* [2007] ECR I-2049 p 228, 247.
T-45/06 *Reliance Industries* [2008] ECR II-2399 p 229, 237–238.
C-56/06 *Euro Tex* [2007] ECR I-4859 p 111, 112.
C-104/06 *Commission v Sweden* [2007] ECR I-671 p 160.
T-119/06 *Usha Martin Ltd v Council and Commission*, Judgment of 9 September 2010, nyr p 234.
C-120/06 P & C-121/06 P *FIAMM v Council and Commission* [2008] ECR I-6513 (appeal of T-69/00 FIAMM [2005] ECR II-5393 and T-135/01 *Fedon & Figli* [2005] ECR II-29) p 222–223, 224, 226, 231, 233, 235, 243,
C-143/06 *Ludwigs-Apotheke* [2007] ECR I-9623 p 110–111, 172.
T-143/06 *MTZ Polyfilms v Council* [2009] ECR II-4133 p 234, 247.
C-228/06 *Soysal* [2009] ECR I-1031 p 126, 143, 147, 148, 155, 171, 172, 302.
C-238/06 P *Develey v OHIM* [2007] ECR I-9375 p 206.
C-242/06 *Sahin* [2009] ECR I-8465 125.
C-248/06 *Commission v Spain* [2008] ECR I-47 p 160.
C-255/06 P *Yedaş Tarim v Council and Commission* [2007] ECR I-94 (appeal of T-367/03 P *Yedaş Tarim v Council and Commission* [2006] ECR II-873) p 164–165, 170.
C-265/06 *Commission v Portugal* [2008] ECR I-2245 p 160.
C-275/06 *Promusicae* [2008] ECR I-271 p 228, 247.
C-276/06 *El Youssfi* [2007] ECR I-2851 p 132, 133.
C-294/06 *Payir* [2008] ECR I-203 p 120, 121, 124, 155.
C-308/06 *Intertanko* [2008] ECR I-4057 p 130, 270–286, 304, 306–310, 313–321.
C-325/06 P *Galileo* [2007] ECR I-44 (appeal of T-279/03 *Galileo v Commission* [2006] ECR II-1291) p 227–228.
C-310/06 *FTS International* [2007] ECR I-6749 p 230, 247.
C-349/06 *Polat* [2007] ECR I-8167 p 120, 121, 123.

C-372/06 *Asda Stores* [2007] ECR I-11223 p 143, 146.
T-407/06 & T-408/06 *Zhejiang Aokang Shoes v Council* [2010] ECR II-747 p 234.
T-409/06 *Sun Sang Kong Yuen Shoes Factory v Council* [2010] ECR II-807 p 229, 247.
C-92/07 *Commission v Netherlands (Turkish Residence Permit Charges)* [2010] ECR I-3683 p 160, 162, 297.
C-157/07 *Krankenheim* [2008] ECR I-8061 p 141–142, 151.
C-188/07 *Commune de Mesquer v Total* [2008] ECR I-4501 p 281, 285.
C-204/07 P *CAS v Commission* [2008] ECR I-6135 (appeal of T-23/03 *CAS v Commission* [2007] ECR II-289) p 164, 168, 169.
C-337/07 *Altun* [2008] ECR I-10323 120.
C-406/07 *Commission v Greece* [2009] ECR I-62 160–161.
C-453/07 *Er* [2008] ECR I-7299 p 120.
C-484/07 *Pehlivan*, 16 June 2011 p 120, 121.
C-485/07 *Akdas*, 26 May 2011 p 132, 133.
C-521/07 *Commission v Netherlands* [2008] ECR I-4873 p 161–162.
C-540/07 *Commission v Italy* [2009] ECR I-10983 p 161, 169, 297.
C-562/07 *Commission v Spain* [2009] ECR I-9553 p. 160–161.
C-13/08 *Stamm* [2008] ECR I-11087 p 141, 151.
C-105/08 *Commission v Portugal* [2010] ECR I-5331 p 161, 169, 297.
C-152/08 *Kahveci* [2008] ECR I-6291 p 135, 136, 139, 153.
C-153/08 *Commission v Spain* [2009] ECR I-9735 p 161.
C-214/08 P *Guigard v Commission* [2009] ECR I-91 p 163.
T-237/08 *Abadía v OHIM* [2010] ECR II-1583 p 228, 247.
C-260/08 *HEKO* [2009] ECR I-11571 p 228, 247.
C-303/08 *Bozkurt* [2010] ECR I-13445 p 120, 121.
C-351/08 *Grimme* [2009] ECR I-1077 p 135, 141, 151.
C-355/08 P *WWF-UK v Council and Commission* [2009] ECR I-73 (appeal of T-91/07 *WWF-UK v Council* [2008] ECR II-81) p 263, 282, 283–284, 303.
T-367/08 *Abouchar v Commission* [2009] ECR II-128 p 162.
C-373/08 *Hoesch Metals and Alloys* [2010] ECR I-951 p 228, 247.
C-386/08 *Brita* [2010] ECR I-1289 p 63, 67, 111, 112.
C-428/08 *Monsanto v CefetrA* [2010] ECR I-6765 p 228, 247.
C-444/08 P *Região autónoma dos Açores v Council* [2009] ECR I-200 (appeal of T-37/04 *Região autónoma dos Açores v Council* [2008] ECR II-103) p 263–264, 282, 283–284, 285.
C-462/08 *Bekleyen* [2010] ECR I-563 p 120, 121, 124.
C-487/08 *Commission v Spain* [2010] ECR I-4843 p 161, 169, 267.
C-541/08 *Fokus Invest AG* [2010] ECR I-1025 p 142, 149.
T-584/08 *Cantiere v Commission* [2011] ECR II-63 p 222.
C-14/09 *Genc* [2010] ECR I-931 p 120, 121, 123.
C-20/09 *Commission v Portugal*, Judgment of 7 April 2011 p 160, 161.

C-39/09 P *SPM v Council and Commission* [2010] ECR I-38 (appeal of T-128/05 *SPM v Council & Commission* [2008] ECR II-260) p 163–164.
C-70/09 *Hengartner* [2010] ECR I-7233 p 142, 149, 172.
C-72/09 *Rimbaud* [2010] ECR I-10659 p 130, 142, 149.
T-292/09 *Mugraby v Council and Commission*, Judgment of 6 September 2011 nyr p 165.
C-102/09 *Camar* [2010] ECR I-4045 p 108, 110, 115, 150, 151.
C-115/09 *Bund für Umwelt und Naturschutz Deutschland (Trianel)*, Judgment of 12 May 2011 p. 256, 257, 282, 284, 294.
C-155/09 *Commission v Greece* [2011] ECR I-65 p 160–161.
C-160/09 *Katsivardas* [2010] ECR I-4591 p 63, 67, 70, 115, 150, 151, 154, 293.
T-210/09 *Formenti Soleco v Commission*, Judgment of 19 May 2011 p 162–163.
C-240/09 *Lesoochranárske zoskupenie VLK v Ministerstvo životného prostredia Slovenskej republic (LZ VLK)*, 8 March 2011 nyr p 253–256, 258, 259, 272, 282, 284, 285, 292, 293, 294, 297, 304.
C-267/09 *Commission v Portugal*, Judgment of 5 May 2011 p 161, 169, 267.
C-288/09 & C-289/09 *BSB and Pace*, 14 April 2011 p 228, 230, 294.
C-300/09 & 301/09 *Toprak and Oguz* [2010] ECR I-12845 p 125–126, 156.
C-393/09 *Bezpečnostní softwarová asociace v Ministerstvo kultury* [2010] ECR I-13971
C-10/10 *Commission v Austria*, 16 June 2011 p 228, 247.
T-18/10 *Inuit Tapiriit Kanatami v Parliament and Council*, 6 September 2011 p 234, 264, 282, 283, 284.
C-101/10 *Pavlov*, 7 July 2011 p 135, 136, 151.
C-186/10 *Tural Oguz*, 21 July 2011 p 126.
C-187/10 *Unal*, 29 September 2011 p 120, 121.
C-387/10 *Commission v Austria*, 29 September 2011 p 160–161.

BIBLIOGRAPHY

A

Adam, S., *La procédure d'avis devant la Cour de justice de l'Union européenne*, Brussels, Bruylant, 2011.

Alkema, E.A., 'Netherlands' in D. Shelton (ed), 2011, p 407.

Allott, P., 'Preliminary Rulings—Another Infant Disease' (2000) 25 *European Law Review* 538.

Allott, P., 'The Emerging Universal Legal System' (2001) 3 *Forum du droit international* 12.

Alston, P., 'Resisting the Merger and Acquisition of Human Rights by Trade Law: A Reply to Petersmann' (2002) 13 *European Journal of International Law* 815.

Amerasinghe, C.F., *Local Remedies in International Law*, 2nd edn, Cambridge, CUP, 2004.

Anderson, M. and Galizzi, P., *International Environmental Law in National Courts*, London, BIICL, 2002.

Anderson, W., 'Implementing MEAs in the Caribbean' (2002) 10 *Review of European Community and International Environmental Law* 227.

Antoniadis, A., 'The European Union and WTO Law: A Nexus of Reactive, Coactive and Proactive Approaches' (2007) 6 *World Trade Review* 45.

Anzilotti, D., *Il diritto Internazionale nei giudizi interni*, Bologna, Zanichelli, 1905.

Anzilotti, D., *Cours de droit international*, Paris, Sirey, 1929.

Arangio-Ruiz, G., 'Dualism Revisited: International Law and Interindividual Law' (2003) 86 *Rivista di Diritto Internazionale* 909.

Arangio-Ruiz, G., 'International Law and Interindividual Law' in J. Nijman and A. Nollkaemper (eds), 2007, p 15.

Arnull, A., *The European Union and its Court of Justice*, 2nd edn, Oxford, OUP, 2006.

Aust, A., *Modern Treaty Law and Practice*, 2nd edn, Cambridge, CUP, 2007.

Aust, A., 'United Kingdom' in Sloss (ed), 2009a, p 476.

Azoulai, L., 'The Acquis of the European Union and International Organisations' (2005) 11 *European Law Journal* 196.

B

Balfour, J., 'Further Comment on Case C-344/04, *The Queen ex parte International Air Transport Association, European Low Fares Airline Association v. Department for Transport*, Judgment of the Court (Grand Chamber) of 10 January 2006' (2007) 44 *Common Market Law Review* 555.

Beaulac, S. and Currie, J., 'Canada' in D. Shelton (ed), 2011, p 116.

Bebr, G., *Judicial Control of the European Communities*, London, Stevens & Sons, 1962.

Bebr, G., *Development of Judicial Control in the European Communities*, The Hague, Martinus Nijhoff, 1981.

Bebr, G., 'Agreements Concluded by the Community and their Possible Direct Effect: From *International Fruit Company* to *Kupferberg*' (1983) 20 *Common Market Law Review* 35.

Beemelmans, H. and Treviranus, H., 'Federal Republic of Germany' in D. Hollis et al (eds), 2005, p 317.

Bellamy, R., *Political Constitutionalism*, Cambridge, CUP, 2007.

Bello, J.H., 'The WTO Dispute Settlement Understanding: Less is More' (1996) 90 *American Journal of International Law* 416.

Belohlavek, A., 'The Czech Republic' in D. Shelton (ed), 2011, p 195.

Benvenisti, E., 'Judicial Misgivings regarding the Application of International Norms: An Analysis of Attitudes of National Courts' (1993) 4 *European Journal of International Law* 159.

Benvenisti, E., 'Reclaiming Democracy: The Strategic Uses of Foreign and International Law by National Courts' (2008) 102 *American Journal of International Law* 241.

Benvenisti, E. and Downs, G., 'National Courts, Domestic Democracy, and the Evolution of International Law' (2009) 20 *European Journal of International Law* 59.

Berman, F., 'International Treaties and British Statutes' (2005) 26 *Statute Law Review* 1.

Bermejo Garcia, R. et al, 'Spain' in P.M. Eisemann (ed), 1996, p 183.

Bernhardt, R., 'Judgments of International Human Rights Courts and their Effects in the International Legal Order of States' in *Studi di diritto internazionale in onore di Gaetano Arangio-Ruiz*, Naples, Editoriale Scientifica, 2004, p 433.

Betlem, G. and Nollkaemper, A., 'Giving Effect to Public International Law and European Community Law before Domestic Courts: A Comparative Analysis of the Practice of Consistent Interpretation' (2003) 14 *European Journal of International Law* 569.

Beyerlin, U., Stoll, P., and Wolfrum, R. (eds), *Ensuring Compliance with Multilateral Environmental Agreements*, Leiden, Martinus Nijhoff, 2006.

Bhuiyan, S., *National Law in WTO Law*, Cambridge, CUP, 2007.

Bianchi, A., 'Assessing the Effectiveness of the UN Security Council's Anti-Terrorism Measures: The Quest for Legitimacy and Cohesion' (2006) 17 *European Journal of International Law* 881.

Bickel, A., *The Least Dangerous Branch*, Indianapolis, Bobbs-Merrill, 1962.

Biering, P., 'The Application of EU Law in Denmark: 1986 to 2000' (2000) 37 *Common Market Law Review* 925.

Biever, R. et al, 'Luxembourg' in P.M. Eisemann (ed), 1996, p 407.

Blackburn, R. and Polakiewicz, J., *Fundamental Rights in Europe: The European Convention on Human Rights and its Member States, 1950–2000*, Oxford, OUP, 2001.

Bocker, A. and Guild, E., *Implementation of the European Agreements in France, Germany, the Netherlands and the UK*, London, Platinum, 2002.

Boelaert-Suominen, S., 'The European Community, the European Court of Justice and the Law of the Sea' (2008) 23 *International Journal of Marine and Coastal Law* 643.

Boulouis, J., 'La jurisprudence de la Cour de justice des Communautés européennes relative aux relations extérieures des Communautés' (1978) 160 *Recueil des Cours* 335.

Boulouis, J., 'Le droit des Communautés européennes dans ses rapports avec le droit international général' (1992) 235 *Recueil des Cours* 9.

Bourgeois, J., 'The Effects of International Agreement in European Community Law: Are the Dice Cast?' (1984) 82 *Michigan Law Review* 1250.

Bourgeois, J., 'The European Court of Justice and the WTO: Problems and Challenges' in J. Weiler (ed), 2000, p 71.

Bourgeois, J. and Lynskey, O., 'The Extent to Which the EC Legislature Takes Account of WTO Obligations: Jousting Lessons from the European Parliament' in A. Dashwood and M. Maresceau (eds), *Law and Practice of EU External Relations*, Cambridge, CUP, 2008, p 202.

Boyle, A. and Chinkin, C., *The Making of International Law*, Oxford, OUP, 2007.

Bribosia, H., 'Report on Belgium' in A.M. Slaughter et al (eds), 1998, p 1.

Brolmann, C. and Vierdag, E., 'Netherlands' in P.M. Eisemann (ed), 1996, p 443.

Bronckers, M., 'La jurisprudence des juridictions communautaires relatives à l'OMC demande réparation: plaidoyer pour les droits des États membres' (2001) 37 *Cahiers de droit européen* 3.

Bronckers, M., 'From "Direct Effect" to "Muted Dialogue": Recent Developments in the European Courts' Case Law on the WTO and Beyond' (2008) 11 *Journal of International Economic Law* 885.

Brouwer, J., 'The Netherlands' in D. Hollis et al (eds), 2005, p 483.

Brown-Weiss, E. and Jacobson, H., 'Strengthening National Compliance with International Environmental Agreements' in I. Serageldin and J. Martin-Brown (eds), *Partnerships for Global Ecosystem Management*, Washington, World Bank, 1998, p 145.

Brownlie, I., *Principles of Public International Law*, 7th edn, Oxford, OUP, 2008.

Buergenthal, T., 'Self-Executing and Non-Self-Executing Treaties in National and International Law' (1992) 235 *Recueil des Cours* 303.

Burgess, M., *Comparative Federalism: Theory and Practice*, London, Routledge, 2006.

Burgorgue-Larsen, L. and Úbeda de Torres, A., *The Inter-American Court of Human Rights: Case Law and Commentary*, Oxford, OUP, 2011.

Butler, W., 'Russian Federation' in Sloss (ed), 2009a, p 410.

C

Cameron, I., 'Swedish Parliamentary Participation in the Making and Implementation of Treaties' (2005) 74 *Nordic Journal of International Law* 429.

Candela Soriano, M., 'The Reception Process in Spain and Italy' in H. Keller and A. Stone Sweet (eds), 2008, p 393.

Cannizzaro, E., 'The Effect of the ECHR on the Italian Legal Order: Direct Effect and Supremacy' (2010) 19 *Italian Yearbook of International Law* 173.

Cannizzaro, E., *Corso di diritto internazionale*, Milan, Giuffrè, 2011.

Cannizzaro, E., 'The Neo-Monism of the European Legal Order' in Cannizzaro et al (eds), 2012, p 35.

Cannizzaro, E., Palchetti, P., and Wessel, R.A. (eds), *International Law as Law of the European Union*, Leiden, Martinus Nijhoff, 2012.

Carmody, C., 'Remedies and Conformity under the WTO Agreement' (2002) 5 *Journal of International Economic Law* 307.

Casolari, F., *L'incorporazione del diritto internazionale nell'ordinamento dell'Unione Europea*, Milan, Giuffrè, 2008.

Cass, D., *The Constitutionalization of the World Trade Organization*, Oxford, OUP, 2005.

Cassese, A., *International Law*, 2nd edn, Oxford, OUP, 2005.

Cassese, A.,'Modern Constitutions and International Law' (1985) 192 *Recueil des Cours* 335.

Castillo de la Torre, F., *El Control Judicial de Los Acuerdos Internacionales de la Comunidad Europea*, Madrid, Dykinson, 2001.

Catalano, N., *Manuel de droit des communautés européennes*, Paris, Dalloz et Sirey, 1964.

Cataldi, G. and Iovane, M., 'International Law in Italian Courts 1999–2009' (2010) 19 *Italian Yearbook of International Law* 3.

Cebada Romero, A., *La Organización Mundial del Comercio y la Unión Europea*, Madrid, Editorial La Ley, 2002.

Chalmers, D., 'Judicial Authority and the Constitutional Treaty' (2005) 3 *International Journal of Constitutional Law* 448.

Chalmers, D., Davies, G., and Monti, M. (eds), *European Union Law*, 2nd edn, Cambridge, CUP, 2010.

Charpentier, J., 'Le contrôle par la Cour de justice de la conformité au Traité des accords en vigueur conclus par la Communauté' (1997) 409 *Revue du Marché Commun et de l'Union européenne* 413.

Claes, M., *The National Courts' Mandate in the European Constitution*, Oxford, Hart, 2006.

Claes, M. and de Witte, B., 'Belgium' in Slaughter et al (eds), 1998.

Colares, J.F., 'The Limits of WTO Adjudication: Is Compliance the Problem?' (2011) 14 *Journal of International Economic Law* 403.

Collins, D., 'Efficient Breach, Reliance, and Contract Remedies at the WTO' (2009) 43 *Journal of World Trade* 225.

Combacau, J. and Sur, S., *Droit international public*, 9th edn, Paris, Montchrestien, 2010.

Commission, 23rd Annual Report on Monitoring the Application of Community Law (2005) SEC/2006/0999.

Commission, 28th Annual Report on Monitoring the Application of EU Law (COM(2011) 588 final).

Conant, L., *Justice Contained: Law and Politics in the European Union*, New York, Cornell University Press, 2002.

Condorelli, L., *Il giudice italiano e I trattati internazionali*, Padua, CEDAM, 1974.

Conforti, B., *International Law and the Role of Domestic Legal Systems*, Dordrecht, Martinus Nijhoff, 1993.

Conforti, B., 'Notes on the Relationship Between International Law and National Law' (2001) 3 *Forum du droit international* 18.

Conforti, B. and Francioni, F. (eds), *Enforcing International Human Rights in Domestic Courts*, The Hague, Kluwer, 1997.

Conseil d'État, *Rapport Public 2006—Sécurité juridique et complexité du droit*, Etudes et documents du Conseil d'État, no 57, Paris, La documentation Française, 2006.

Constantinesco, V. and Simon, D., 'Quelques problèmes des relations extérieures des Communautés européennes' (1975) 11 *Revue Trimestrielle de Droit Européen* 432.

Conway, G., *The Limits of Legal Reasoning and the European Court of Justice*, Cambridge, CUP, 2012.

Copithorne, M., 'Canada' in D. Hollis et al (eds), 2005, p 91.

Corbett, R., Jacobs, F., and Shackleton, M., *The European Parliament*, 8th edn, London, John Harper, 2011.

Cottier, T., 'Dispute Settlement in the World Trade Organization: Characteristics and Structural Implications for the European Union' (1998) 35 *Common Market Law Review* 325.

Cottier, T. and Schefer, K., 'The Relationship between World Trade Organization Law, National and Regional Law' (1998) 1 *Journal of International Economic Law* 83.

Council of the European Communities, *EEC–Turkey Association Agreement and Protocols and other Basic Texts*, Brussels, 1992.

Craig, P., 'Once Upon a Time in the West: Direct Effect and the Federalization of EEC Law' (1992) 12 *Oxford Journal of Legal Studies* 453.

Craig, P., 'Britain in the European Union' in J. Jowell and D. Oliver (eds), *The Changing Constitution*, 7th edn, Oxford, OUP, 2011.

Craig, P. and de Búrca, G., *EU Law: Text, Cases, and Materials*, 5th edn, Oxford, OUP, 2011.

Crawford, J., 'The International Law Standard in the Statutes of Australia and the United Kingdom' (1979) 73 *American Journal of International Law* 628.

Cremona, M., 'Citizens of Third Countries: Movement and Employment of Migrant Workers within the European Union' (1995) 2 *Legal Issues of European Integration* 87.

Cremona, M., 'EC External Commercial Policy after Amsterdam: Authority and Interpretation within Interconnected Legal Orders' in Weiler (ed), 2000, p 5.

Cremona, M., 'External Relations of the EU and the Member States: Competence, Mixed Agreements, International Responsibility, and Effects of International Law' in X. Xenopoulos (ed), External Relations of the EU and the Member State (FIDE 2006 National Reports), Nicosia, Theopress, 2006, p 319.

Cremona, M., 'Defending the Community Interest: The Duties of Cooperation and Compliance' in M. Cremona and B. de Witte (eds), *EU Foreign Relations Law*, Oxford, Hart, 2008.

Cremona, M., 'External Relations and External Competence of the European Union: The Emergence of an Integrated Policy' in P. Craig and G. de Búrca (eds), *The Evolution of EU Law*, 2nd edn, Oxford, OUP, 2011, p 217.

D

Daillier, P. and Pellet, A., *Droit international public*, 2nd edn, Paris, LGDJ, 1980.

Daillier, P., Forteau, M., and Pellet, A., *Droit International Public*, 8th edn, Paris, LGDJ, 2009.

Dalton, R., 'United States' in D. Hollis et al (eds), 2005, p 765.

Dam, K., *The GATT: Law and International Economic Organization*, Chicago, University of Chicago Press, 1970.

Dani, M., 'Remedying European Legal Pluralism: The *FIAMM* and *Fedon* Litigation and the Judicial Protection of International Trade Bystanders' (2010) 21 *European Journal of International Law* 303.

Danilenko, G., 'Implementation of International Law in CIS States' (1999) 10 *European Journal of International Law* 51.

Dashwood, A., 'Preliminary Rulings on the Interpretation of Mixed Agreements' in D. O'Keeffe and A. Bavaso (eds), *Liber Amicorum in Honour of Lord Slynn*, The Hague, Kluwer, 2000.

Dashwood, A. et al, *Wyatt & Dashwood's European Union Law*, 6th edn, Oxford, Hart, 2011.

Davey, W., 'The WTO Dispute Settlement System: the First Ten Years' (2005) 8 *Journal of International Economic Law* 17.

Davey, W., 'The WTO Looking Forwards' (2006) 9 *Journal of International Economic Law* 3.

Davies, A., 'Connecting or Compartmentalizing the WTO and United States Legal Systems? The Role of the *Charming Betsy* Canon' (2007) 10 *Journal of International Economic Law* 117.

De Búrca, G. and Scott, J. (eds), *The EU and the WTO*, Oxford, Hart, 2001.

De Búrca, G. and Scott, J., 'The Impact of the WTO on EU Decision-Making' in G. de Búrca and J. Scott (eds), 2001, p 1.

De Búrca, G., 'The European Court of Justice and the International Legal Order after Kadi' (2010) 51 *Harvard International Law Journal* 1.

De Búrca, G., 'The ECJ and the International Legal Order: A Re-Evaluation' in G. de Búrca and J.H.H. Weiler, *The Worlds of European Constitutionalism*, Cambridge, CUP, 2012.

Decaux, E., 'France' in D. Shelton (ed), 2011, p 207.

De Hert, P. and Gutwirth, S., 'Data Protection in the Case Law of Strasbourg and Luxemburg: Constitutionalisation in Action' in S. Gutwirth et al (eds), *Reinventing Data Protection?*, Dordrecht, Springer, 2009, p 3.

Denza, E., 'A Note on *Intertanko*' (2008) 33 *European Law Review* 870.

Denza, E., 'The Relationship Between International and National Law' in M. Evans (ed), *International Law*, 3rd edn, Oxford, OUP, 2010, p 411.

Desmedt, A., 'European Court of Justice on the Effect of WTO Agreements in the EC Legal Order' (2000) 27 *Legal Issues of Economic Integration* 93.

De Walsche, A., 'Le contrôle juridictionnel des accords internationaux' in J. V. Louis and M. Dony (eds), *Relations extérieures*, 2nd edn, Brussels, Editions de l'Université de Bruxelles, 2005.

De Wet, E., 'The Reception Process in the Netherlands and Belgium' in H. Keller and A. Stone Sweet (eds), 2008, p 229.

De Wet, E., 'South Africa' in D. Shelton (ed), 2011, p 567.

De Witte, B., 'European Union Law: How Autonomous is its Legal Order?' (2010) 65 *Zeitschrift für öffentliches Recht* 141.

De Witte, B., 'Direct Effect, Primacy and the Nature of the Legal Order' in P. Craig and G. de Búrca (eds), *The Evolution of EU Law*, 2nd edn, Oxford, OUP, 2011, p 217.

Díez-Hochleitner, J., *La posición del Derecho Internacional en el Ordenamiento Comunitario*, Madrid, McGraw-Hill, 1998.

Dillon, S., *International Trade and Economic Law and the European Union*, Oxford, Hart, 2002.

Djajic, S., 'Serbia' in D. Shelton (ed), 2011, p 526.

Dominicé, C. and Voeffray, F., 'Suisse/Switzerland' in P.M. Eisemann (ed), 1996, p 529.

Dougan, M., *National Remedies Before the Court of Justice*, Oxford, Hart, 2005.

Dougan, M., 'When Worlds Collide! Competing Visions of the Relationship Between Direct Effect and Supremacy' (2007) 44 *Common Market Law Review* 931.

Drzemczewski, A., *European Human Rights Convention in Domestic Law*, Oxford, Clarendon Press, 1983.

Dubinsky P., 'United States' in D. Shelton (ed), 2011, p 631.

Dugard, J., 'South Africa' in D. Sloss (ed), 2009a, p 448.

Dupuy, P.-M. and Kerbrat, Y., *Droit international public*, 10th edn, Paris, Dalloz, 2010.

E

Ebbesson, J., 'Access to Justice at the National Level: Impact of the Aarhus Convention and European Union Law' in M. Pallemaerts (ed), 2011.

Eckes, C., *EU Counter-Terrorist Policies and Fundamental Rights*, Oxford, OUP, 2009.

Eckes, C., 'International Law as Law of the EU: the Role of the ECJ' in Cannizzaro et al (eds), 2012, p 353.

Eeckhout, P., 'The Domestic Legal Status of the WTO Agreement: Interconnecting Legal Systems' (1997) 34 *Common Market Law Review* 11.

Eeckhout, P., 'Case C-61/94, *Commission* v. *Germany*' (1998) 35 *Common Market Law Review* 557.

Eeckhout, P., 'Judicial Enforcement of the WTO Law in the European Union: Some Further Reflections' (2002) 5 *Journal of International Economic Law* 91.

Eeckhout, P., *External Relations of the European Union*, Oxford, OUP, 2004.

Eeckhout, P., 'Does Europe's Constitution Stop at the Water's Edge? Law and Policy in the EU's External Relations', Walter Van Gerven Lectures (2005).

Eeckhout, P., 'Community Terrorism Listings, Fundamental Rights, and UN Security Council Resolutions' (2007) 3 *European Constitutional Law Review* 183.

Eeckhout, P., 'Case C-308/06, *The Queen on the application of Intertanko and Others* v. *Secretary of State for Transport*' (2009) 46 *Common Market Law Review* 2041.

Eeckhout, P., *EU External Relations Law*, 2nd edn, Oxford, OUP, 2011.

Ehlermann, C.D., 'Application of GATT Rules in the European Community' in M. Hilf et al (eds), 1986, p 127.

Ehlermann, C.D., 'On the Direct Effect of the WTO Agreements' in T. Einhorn (ed), *Spontaneous Order, Organization and the Law: Roads to a European Civil Society*, The Hague, TMC Asser Press, 2003, p 413.

Eisele, K. and van der Mei, A.P., 'Portability of Social Benefits and Reverse Discrimination of EU Citizens vis-à-vis Turkish Nationals: Comment on *Akdas*' (2012) 37 *European Law Review* 204.

Eisemann P.M. (ed), *The Integration of International and European Community Law into the National Legal Order*, The Hague, Kluwer, 1996.

Eisemann, P. and Rivier, R., 'France' in D. Hollis et al (eds), 2005, p 253.

Espersen, O., 'Denmark and the European Convention on Human Rights' (1970) 18 *American Journal of Comparative Law* 293.

Everling, U., 'The Law in the External Economic Relations of the European Community' in M. Hilf et al (eds), 1986, p 153.

Everling, U., 'Will Europe Slip on Bananas? The *Bananas* Judgment of the Court of Justice and National Courts' (1996) 33 *Common Market Law Review* 401.

F

Ferdinandusse, W.N., *Direct Application of International Criminal Law in National Courts*, The Hague, TMC Asser Press, 2006.

Ferreres Comella, V., *Constitutional Courts and Democratic Values—A European Perspective*, New Haven, Yale University Press, 2009.

Fleuren, J., 'The Application of Public International Law by Dutch Courts' (2010) 57 *Netherlands International Law Review* 245.

Flory, T., *Le G.A.T.T: droit international et commerce mondial*, Paris, LGDJ, 1968.

Follesdal, A. and Hix, S., 'Why There is a Democratic Deficit in the EU: A Response to Majone and Moravcsik' (2006) 44 *Journal of Common Market Studies* 533.

Folz, H.P., 'Germany' in D. Shelton (ed), 2011, p 240.

Footer, M.E., 'Some Theoretical and Legal Perspectives on WTO Compliance' (2007) 38 *Netherlands Yearbook of International Law* 61.

Fox, H. et al, 'United Kingdom' in Eisemann (ed), 1996, p 495.

Francioni, F., 'The Jurisprudence of International Human Rights Enforcement: Reflections on the Italian Experience' in B. Conforti and F. Francioni (eds), 1997.

Franck, T. and Thiruvengadam, A.K., 'International Law and Constitution-Making' (2003) 2 *Chinese Journal of International Law* 467.

Friedmann, W., *The Changing Structure of International Law*, London, Stevens & Sons, 1964.

Frowein J., 'Federal Republic of Germany' in F. Jacobs and S. Roberts (eds), 1987, p 63.

Frowein, J., 'International Law in Municipal Courts' (1997) 91 *ASIL Proceedings* 290.

Frowein J., and Hahn, M.J., 'The Participation of Parliament in the Treaty Process in the Federal Republic of Germany' (1992) 67 *Chicago-Kent Law Review* 361.

Frowein, J. and Oellers-Frahm, K., 'L'application des traités dans l'ordre juridique communautaire' in P.M. Eisemann (ed), 1996a, p 11.

Frowein, J. and Oellers-Frahm, K., 'Allemagne/Germany' in P.M. Eisemann (ed), 1996b, p 69.

Fukunaga, Y., 'Securing Compliance through the WTO Dispute Settlement System: Implementation of DSB Recommendations' (2006) 9 *Journal of International Economic Law* 383.

G

Gaja, G., 'Italy' in F. Jacobs and S. Roberts (eds), 1987, p 87.

Gaja, G., 'Il preambolo di una decisione del Consiglio preclude al GATT 1994 gli effetti diretti nell'ordinamento comunitario?' (1995) 78 *Rivista di Diritto Internazionale* 407.

Gaja, G., 'Trends in Judicial Activism and Judicial Self-Restraint Relating to Community Agreements' in E. Cannizzaro (ed), *The European Union as an Actor in International Relations*, The Hague, Kluwer, 2002, p 117.

Galmot, Y. and Bonichot, J.-C., 'La Cour de justice des Communautés européennes et la transposition des directives en droit national' (1988) 4 *Revue Française de Droit Administratif* 1.

Garlicki, L., Masternak-Kubiak, M., and Wojtowicz, K., 'Poland' in D. Sloss (ed), 2009a, p 370.

Gattinara, G., 'The Relevance of WTO Dispute Settlement Decisions in the US Legal Order' (2009) 36 *Legal Issues of Economic Integration* 285.

Gattini, A., 'Joined Cases C-402/05 P & 415/05 P, *Abdullah Kadi, Al Barakaat International Foundation* v. *Council and Commission*' (2009) 46 *Common Market Law Review* 213.

Germer, P., 'Denmark' in Blackburn and Polakiewicz (eds), 2001.

Gilsdorf, P., 'Les organes institués par des accords communautaires: effets juridiques de leurs décisions' (1992) 357 *Revue du Marché Commun* 328.

Goldsmith, J. and Posner, R., *The Limits of International Law*, Oxford, OUP, 2005.

Gomula, J., 'Responsibility and the World Trade Organization' in J. Crawford, A. Pellet, and S. Olleson (eds), *The Law of International Responsibility*, Oxford, OUP, 2010.

Gonzalez Campos, J. et al, *Curso de Derecho Internacional Público*, 3rd edn, Madrid, Thomson Civitas, 2005.

Griller, S., 'Judicial Enforceability of WTO Law in the European Union: Annotation to Case C-149/96, Portugal v. Council' (2000) 3 *Journal of International Economic Law* 441.

Gross Espiell, H., 'L'application du droit international dans le droit interne en Amérique latine' in *Studi di diritto internazionale in onore di Gaetano Arangio-Ruiz*, Naples, Editoriale Scientifica, 2003, Vol 1, 529.

Groux J. and Manin, P., *The European Communities in the International Order*, Luxembourg, Office for Official Publications of the European Communities, 1985.

Gulmann, C., 'Denmark' in F. Jacobs and S. Roberts (eds), 1987, p 29.

Guzman, A., 'The Design of International Agreements' (2005) 16 *European Journal of International Law* 579.

H

Hae Bong, S., 'Japan' in D. Shelton (ed), 2011, p 360.

Hahn, M. and Schuster, G., 'Le droit des états membres de se prévaloir en justice d'un accord liant la Communauté. L'invocabilité du GATT dans l'affaire République fédérale d'Allemagne contre Conseil de l'Union européenne' (1995) 99 *Revue Générale de Droit International Public* 367.

Hailbronner, K. and Polakiewicz, J., 'Non-EC Nationals in the European Community: The Need for a Coordinated Approach' (1992) 3 *Duke Journal of Comparative & International Law* 49.

Handl-Petz, E., 'Austria' in Shelton (ed), 2011, p 55.

Hanqin, X. and Qian, J., 'International Treaties in the Chinese Domestic Legal System' (2009) 8 *Chinese Journal of International Law* 299.

Harhoff, F., 'Danemark/Denmark' in P.M. Eisemann (ed), 1996, p 151.

Hartley, T., 'International Agreements and the Community Legal System: Some Recent Developments' (1983) 8 *European Law Review* 383.

Hartley, T., *The Foundations of European Community Law*, 5th edn, Oxford, OUP, 2003.

Hathaway, O., 'Do Human Rights Treaties Make a Difference?' (2002) 111 *Yale Law Journal* 1935.

Hathaway, O., McElroy, S., and Solow, S., 'International Law at Home: Enforcing Treaties in US Courts' (2012) 37 *Yale Journal of International Law* 51.

Hedemann-Robinson, M., 'An Overview of Recent Legal Developments at Community Level in Relation to Third Country Nationals Resident within the European Union, with Particular Reference to the Case Law of the European Court of Justice' (2001) 38 *Common Market Law Review* 525.

Hedemann-Robinson, M., 'EU Enforcement of International Environmental Agreements: The Role of the European Commission' (2012) 21 *European Energy and Environmental Law Review* 2.

Heliskoski, J., 'Jurisdiction of the European Court of Justice to Give Preliminary Rulings on the Interpretation of Mixed Agreements' (2000) 69 *Nordic Journal of International Law* 395.

Heliskoski, J., *Mixed Agreements as a Technique for Organizing the International Relations of the European Community and its Member States*, The Hague, Kluwer, 2001.

Henkin, L., *How Nations Behave: Law and Foreign Policy*, 2nd edn, New York, Columbia University Press, 1979.

Henkin, L., 'Treaties in a Constitutional Democracy' (1989) 10 *Michigan Journal of International Law* 406.

Henkin, L., *International Law: Politics and Values*, Dordrecht, Martinus Nijhoff, 1995.

Hermann, C., 'Case C-351/04, *IKEA Wholesale Ltd v. Commissioners of Customs & Excise*' (2008) 45 *Common Market Law Review* 1507.

Herzog, R. and Gerken, L., 'Stop the European Court of Justice', Freiburg, Centre for European Policy, 2008.

Heun, W., *The Constitution of Germany*, Oxford, Hart, 2011.

Heyns, C. and Viljoen, F., 'The Impact of the United Nations Human Rights Treaties on the Domestic Level' (2001) 23 *Human Rights Quarterly* 483.

Higgins, R., *Problems & Process: International Law and How We Use It*, Oxford, Clarendon Press, 1995.

Higgins, R., 'The Role of Domestic Courts in the Enforcement of International Human Rights: The United Kingdom' in B. Conforti and F. Francioni (eds), 1997, p 37.

Hilf, M., 'The Application of GATT within the Member States of the European Community, with Special Reference to the Federal Republic of Germany' in M. Hilf et al (eds), 1986.

Hilf, M. and Petersmann, E.-U., *National Constitutions and International Economic Law*, Deventer, Kluwer, 1993.

Hillion, C., 'Case C-162/00 *Land Nordrhein-Westfalen v. Beata Pokrzeptowicz-Meyer*, with Annotation' (2003) 40 *Common Market Law Review* 465.

Hillion, C., 'Case C-265/03, *Igor Simutenkovv. Ministerio de Educación y Cultura, Real Federación Española de Fútbol*' (2008) 45 *Common Market Law Review* 815.

Hillion, C. and Koutrakos, P. (eds), *Mixed Agreements Revisited*, Oxford, Hart, 2010.

Hillion, C. and Wessel, R., 'Restraining External Competences of EU Member States under CFSP' in M. Cremona and B. de Witte (eds), *EU Foreign Relations Law*, Oxford, Hart, 2008, p 79.

Hilpold, P., 'EU Law and UN Law in Conflict: The Kadi Case' (2009) 13 *Max Planck Yearbook of United Nations Law* 141.

Hirschl, R., *Towards Juristocracy*, Cambridge, Harvard University Press, 2004.

Hoffmeister, F., 'The Contribution of EU Practice to International Law' in M. Cremona (ed), *Developments in EU External Relations Law*, Oxford, OUP, 2008, p 37.

Hoffmeister, F., 'Curse or Blessing? Mixed Agreements in the Recent Practice of the European Union and its Member States' in C. Hillion and P. Koutrakos (eds), 2010, p 249.

Hoffmeister, F. and Kuijper, P. J., 'The Status of the European Union at the United Nations: Institutional Ambiguities and Political Realities' in Wouters et al (eds), *The United Nations and the European Union*, The Hague, TMC Asser Press, 2006.

Hogan, G., 'The European Convention of Human Rights Act 2003' (2006) 12 *European Public Law* 331.

Holdgaard, R., 'Case C-431/05, *Merck Genéricos Produtos Farmacêuticos Lda v. Merck & Co. Inc and Merck Sharp & Dohme Lda*' (2008b) 45 *Common Market Law Review* 1233.

Holdgaard, R., *External Relations Law of the European Community: Legal Reasoning and Legal Discourses*, Alphen a/d Rijn, Wolters Kluwer, 2008a.

Hollis, D., 'A Comparative Approach to Treaty Law and Practice' in Hollis et al (eds), 2005, p 1.

Hollis, D., Blakeslee, M., and Ederington, L.B., *National Treaty Law and Practice*, Leiden, Martinus Nijhoff, 2005.

Holloway, K., *Modern Trends in Treaty Law: Constitutional Law, Reservations and the Three Modes of Legislation*, London, Stevens, 1967.

Hoogenboom, A., 'Moving Forward by Standing Still? First Admission of Turkish Workers: Comment on *Commission v Netherlands (Administrative Fees)*' (2010) 35 *European Law Review* 707.

Hopkins, J., 'New Zealand' in D. Shelton (ed), 2011, p 429.

House of Lords, External Competence of the European Communities, Session 1984–85, 16th Report (European Communities Select Committee), London, HMSO, 1985.

Hudec, R., 'The GATT Legal System: A Diplomat's Jurisprudence' (1970) 4 *Journal of World Trade Law* 615.

Hudec, R., 'GATT or GABB? The Future Design of the General Agreement on Tariffs and Trade' (1971) 80 *Yale Law Journal* 1299.

Hudec, R., *The GATT Legal System and World Trade Diplomacy*, New York, Praeger, 1975.

Hudec, R., *Developing Countries in the GATT Legal System*, Aldershot, Gower/Trade Policy Research Center, London Thames Essay, 1987.

Hudec, R., *Enforcing International Trade Law*, Salem, Butterworths, 1993.

Hunt, M., *Using Human Rights Law in English Courts*, Oxford, Hart, 1997.

I

Iwasawa, Y., 'The Doctrine of Self-Executing Treaties in the United States: A Critical Analysis' (1986) 26 *Virginia Journal of International Law* 627.

Iwasawa, Y., *International Law, Human Rights, and Japanese Law*, Oxford, Clarendon Press, 1998.

J

Jackson, J.H., *World Trade and the Law of GATT*, Indianapolis, Bobbs-Merrill, 1969.

Jackson, J.H., 'Status of Treaties in Domestic Legal Systems: A Policy Analysis' (1992) 86 *American Journal of International Law* 310.

Jackson, J.H., *The World Trading System*, Cambridge MA, MIT Press, 1989.

Jackson, J.H., *The World Trading System*, 2nd edn, Cambridge MA, MIT Press, 1997.

Jackson, J.H., 'The WTO Dispute Settlement Understanding—Misunderstandings on the Nature of the Legal Obligation' (1997) 91 *American Journal of International Law* 60.

Jackson, J.H., *The World Trade Organization: Constitution and Jurisprudence*, London, Chatham House Papers, The Royal Institute of International Affairs, 1998.

Jackson, J.H., 'International Law Status of WTO DS Reports: Obligation to Comply or Option to "Buy-Out"?' (2004) 98 *American Journal of International Law* 109.

Jacobs, F.G., 'The Internal Legal Effects of the EU's International Agreements and the Protection of Individual Rights' in A. Arnull et al (eds), *A Constitutional Order of States*, Oxford, Hart, 2011, p 529.

Jacobs, F.G. and Roberts, S., *The Effect of Treaties in Domestic Law*, London, Sweet & Maxwell, 1987.

Jacot-Guillarmod, O., *Droit communautaire et droit international public*, Geneva, Georg et Cie, 1979.

Jans, J.H., 'Who is the Referee? Access to Justice in a Globalised Legal Order' (2011a) 1 *Review of European Administrative Law* 85.

Jans, J.H., 'European Environmental Law Before Dutch Courts: Observations on Direct Effect and Consistent Interpretation', SSRN, 2011b, available at <http://dx.doi.org/10.2139/ssrn.1970270>.

Jayawickrama, N., 'India' in D. Sloss (ed), 2009a, p 243.

Jendrośka, J., 'Public Participation in Environmental Decision Making' in M. Pallemaerts (ed), 2011.

Jenisch, U., 'The European Union as an Actor in the Law of the Sea. The Emergence of Regionalism in Maritime Safety, Transportation and Ports' (2006) 48 *German Yearbook of International Law* 223.

Jennings, R., 'The Judiciary, International and National, and the Development of International Law' (1996) 45 *International and Comparative Law Quarterly* 1.

Jennings, R. and Watts, A., *Oppenheim's International Law*, 9th edn, London, Longman, 1992.

Jiménez de Aréchaga, E., 'Self-Executing Provisions of International Law' in K. Hailbronner et al (eds), *Staat und Völkerrechstordnung (Festchrift für Karl Doehring)*, Berlin, Springer, 1989, p 409.

Joliet, R., *Le droit institutionnel des Communautés européenes*, Liège, Université de Liège, 1983.

K

Kaddous, C., 'L'arrêt France c. Commission de 1994 (accord concurrence) et le contrôle de la "légalité des accords externes en vertu de l'art. 173 CE' (1996) *Cahiers de Droit Européen* 613.

Kaddous, C., *Le droit des relations extérieures dans la jurisprudence de la Cour de Justice des Communautés européennes*, Brussels, Bruylant, 1998.

Kälin, W., 'Implementing Treaties in Domestic Law: From "Pacta sunt servanda" to "Anything Goes"?' in V. Gowlland-Debbas (ed), *Multilateral Treaty-Making*, The Hague, Kluwer, 2000, p 95.

Kapteyn, P.J.G., 'The "Domestic" Law Effect of Rules of International Law Within the European Community System of Law and the Question of the Self-Executing Character of GATT Rules' (1974) 1 *The International Lawyer* 74.

Kapteyn, P.J.G., 'Quelques réflexions sur le contrôle de la constitutionnalité des accords conclus par la Communauté avec des pays tiers' in G.C. Rodríguez Iglesias et al (eds), *Mélanges en hommage à Fernand Schockweiler*, Baden-Baden, Nomos, 1999, p 275.

Kapteyn, P.J.G., 'Quelques réflexions sur les effets des accords internationaux liant la Communauté dans l'ordre juridique communautaire' in M. Pérez González et al (eds), *Hacia un nuevo orden internacional y Europeo*, Madrid, Tecnos, 1993, p 1014.

Karapuu, H. and Rosas, A., 'Economic, Social and Cultural Rights in Finland' in A. Rosas (ed), *International Human Rights Norms in Domestic Law*, Helsinki, Finnish Lawyers' Publishing Co, 1990, p 201.

Karayagit, M., 'Vive la Clause de Standstill: The Issue of First Admission of Turkish Nationals into the Territory of a Member State Within the Context of Economic Freedoms' (2011) 13 *European Journal of Migration and Law* 411.

Keller, H. and Stone Sweet, A. (eds), *A Europe of Rights. The Impact of the ECHR on National Legal Systems*, Oxford, OUP, 2008.

Kelly, J.M., *The Irish Constitution*, G. Hogan and G. White (eds), 4th edn, Dublin, Butterworths, 2003.

Kelsen, H., 'Les rapports de système entre le droit interne et le droit international public' (1926) 14 *Recueil des Cours* 227.

Kelsen, H., *General Theory of Law and State*, New York, Russell and Russell, 1961.

Kinsch, P., 'Luxembourg' in D. Shelton (ed), 2011, p 385.

Klabbers, J., 'International Law in Community Law: The Law and Politics of Direct Effect' (2002) 21 *Yearbook of European Law* 263.

Klabbers, J., *Treaty Conflict and the European Union*, Cambridge, CUP, 2009.

Knop, K., 'Here and There: International Law in Domestic Courts' (2000) 32 *New York University Journal of International Law And Politics* 501.

Koh, H., 'Why Do Nations Obey International Law?' (1997) 106 *Yale Law Journal* 2599.

Konig, D., 'The EU Directive on Ship-Source Pollution and on the Introduction of Penalties for Infringements: Development or Breach of International Law?' in T.M. Ndiaye and R. Wolfrum (eds), *Law of the Sea, Environmental Law and Settlement of Disputes*, Leiden, Martinus Nijhoff, 2007, p 767.

Korff, D. and Brown, I., *Opinion on the Compatibility of ACTA with the ECHR and the EU Charter of Fundamental Rights* (2011), available at <http://act-on-acta.eu/Opinion_on_the_compatibility_of_ACTA_with_the_ECHR_and_the_EU_Charter_ of_Fundamental_Rights>.

Koutrakos, P., 'The Interpretation of Mixed Agreements under the Preliminary Reference Procedure' (2002) 7 *European Foreign Affairs Review* 25.

Koutrakos, P., *EU International Relations Law*, Oxford, Hart, 2006.

Koutrakos, P., 'Interpretation of Mixed Agreements' in C. Hillion and P. Koutrakos (eds), 2010, p 116.

Kovar, R., 'Les accords liant les communautés européennes et l'ordre juridique communautaire: à propos d'une jurisprudence récente de la Cour de justice' (1974) 17 *Revue du Marché Commun et de l'Union européenne* 345.

Kovar, R., 'La Compétence consultative de la Cour de justice et la procédure de conclusion des accords internationaux par la Communauté économique européenne' in D. Bardonnet et al (eds), *Mélanges offerts à Paul Reuter—Le droit international: unité et diversité*, Paris, Pedone, 1981, p 357.

Krämer, L., *EC Environmental Law*, 4th edn, London, Sweet & Maxwell, 2000.

Krämer, L., *EU Environmental Law*, 7th edn, London, Sweet & Maxwell, 2011.

Krawczyk, D., 'The Slovak Brown Bear Case: The ECJ Hunts for Jurisdiction and Environmental Plaintiffs Gain the Trophy' (2012) 14 *Environmental Law Review* 53.

Krenzler, H.G. and Landwehr, L., '"A New Legal Order of International Law": On the Relationship between Public International Law and European Union Law after *Kadi*' in U. Fastenrath et al (eds), *From Bilateralism to Community Interest*, Oxford, OUP, 2011.

Kretzmer, D., 'Israel' in D. Sloss (ed), 2009a, p 273.

Krisch, N., *The Pluralist Structure of Postnational Law*, Oxford, OUP, 2010.

Kuijper, P.J., 'The Conclusion and Implementation of the Uruguay Round Results by the European Community' (1995a) 6 *European Journal of International Law* 222.

Kuijper, P.J., 'The New WTO Dispute Settlement System: The Impact on the European Community' (1995b) 29 *Journal of World Trade* 49.

Kuijper, P.J., 'The Court and the Tribunal of the EC and the Vienna Convention on the Law of Treaties 1969' (1998) 25 *Legal Issues of European Integration* 1.

Kuijper, P.J., 'From Initiating Proceedings to Ensuring Implementation: The Links with the Community Legal Order' in G. Sacerdoti, A. Yanovich, and J. Bohanes (eds), *The WTO at Ten*, Cambridge, CUP, 2006, p 266.

Kuijper, P.J., 'International Responsibility for EU Mixed Agreements' in C. Hillion and P. Koutrakos (eds), 2010, p 208.

Kuijper, P.J. and Bronckers, M., 'WTO Law in the European Court of Justice' (2005) 42 *Common Market Law Review* 1313.

Kuijper, P.J. and Paasivirta, E., 'Further Exploring International Responsibility: The European Community and the ILC's Project on Responsibility of International Organizations' (2004) 1 *International Organizations Law Review* 111.

Kuilwijk, K., *The European Court of Justice and the GATT Dilemma*, Beuningen, Nexed Editions, 1996.

Kumm, M., 'International Law in National Courts: The International Rule of Law and the Limits of the Internationalist Model' (2003) 44 *Virginia Journal of International Law* 19.

Kumm, M., 'The Legitimacy of International Law: A Constitutionalist Framework of Analysis' (2004) 15 *European Journal of International Law* 907.

Kumm, M., 'Constitutional Law Encounters International Law: Terms of Engagement' in S. Choudhry (ed), *The Migration of Constitutional Ideas*, Cambridge, CUP, 2006, p 256.

Kumm, M., 'The Cosmopolitan Turn in Constitutionalism: On the Relationship Between Constitutionalism In and Beyond the State' in J. Dunoff and J. Trachtman (eds), *Ruling the World*, Cambridge, CUP, 2009, p 258.

L

Lauterpacht, H., 'The Grotian Tradition in International Law' (1946) 23 *British Yearbook of International Law* 1.

Lauterpacht, H., *The Development of International Law by the International Court*, London, Stevens, 1958.

Lavranos, N., *Legal Interaction between Decisions of International Organizations and European Law*, Groningen, Europa, 2004.

Lavranos, N., 'The *Chiquita* and *Van Parys* Judgments: an Exception to the Rule of Law' (2005) 32 *Legal Issues of Economic Integration* 449.

Lavranos, N., 'Protecting European Law from International Law' (2010) 15 *European Foreign Affairs Review* 265.

Leary, V., *International Labour Conventions and National Law*, The Hague, Martinus Nijhoff, 1982.

Leben, C., 'Hans Kelsen and the Advancement of International Law' (1998) 9 *European Journal of International Law* 287.

Leebron, D., 'Implementation of the Uruguay Round Results in the United States' in J.H. Jackson and A. Sykes (eds), *Implementing the Uruguay Round*, Oxford, OUP, 1997.

Lenaerts, K. and Corthaut, T., 'Of Birds and Hedges: The Role of Primacy in Invoking Norms of EU Law' (2006) 31 *European Law Review* 287.

Lenaerts, K. and de Smijter, E., 'The European Union as an Actor under International Law' (2000) 19 *Yearbook of European Law* 95.

Lenaerts, K. and Van Nuffel, P., *European Union Law*, 3rd edn, London, Sweet & Maxwell, 2011.

Lenaerts, K. et al, *Procedural Law of the European Union*, 2nd edn, London, Sweet & Maxwell, 2006.

Leray, E. and Potteau, A., 'Réflexions sur la cohérence du système de contrôle de la légalité des accords internationaux conclus par la Communauté européenne' (1998) 34 *Revue Trimestrielle de Droit Européen* 535.

Lester, S. and Mercurio, B., *World Trade Law*, Oxford, Hart, 2008.

Levinson, S., *Our Undemocratic Constitution*, New York, OUP, 2006.

Li, J. and Guo, S., 'China' in D. Shelton (ed), 2011, p 158.

Lillich, R., 'Invoking International Human Rights Law in Domestic Courts' (1985) 54 *University of Cincinnati Law Review* 367.

Louis, J.V., 'Mise en œuvre des obligations internationales de la Communauté et de ses états membres' (1977) 13 *Revue Belge de Droit International* 122.

Louis, J.V. and Brückner, P., *Le Droit de la Communauté Économique Européenne: Relations extérieures*, Brussels, Editions de l'Université de Bruxelles, 1980, Vol 12.

M

Macleod, I., Hendry, L., and Hyett, S., *The External Relations of the European Communities*, Oxford, OUP, 1996.

Maluwa, T., *International Law in Post-Colonial Africa*, The Hague, Kluwer, 1999.

Mancini, G., 'The Making of a Constitution for Europe' (1989) 26 *Common Market Law Review* 595.

Manin, P., 'L'Article 228 paragraphe 2 du traite CEE' in *Études de droit des Communautés européennes: mélanges offerts à Pierre-Henri Teitgen*, Paris, Pedone, 1984, p 289.

Maresceau, M., 'The Effect of Community Agreements in the UK' (1979) 28 *International and Comparative Law Quarterly* 241.

Maresceau, M., 'Bilateral Agreements Concluded by the European Community' (2006) 309 *Recueil des Cours* 125.

Martin, D., 'Comments on *Nazli* (Case C-340/97 of 10 February 2000)' (2000) 2 *European Journal of Migration and Law* 431.

Martin, D., 'The Privileged Treatment of Turkish Nationals' in E. Guild and P. Minderhoud (eds), *The First Decade of EU Migration and Asylum Law*, Leiden, Martinus Nijhoff, 2012, p 75.

Martin, D. and Guild, E., *Free Movement of Persons in the European Union*, London, Butterworths, 1996.

McCorquodale, R., 'The Individual and the International Legal System' in M. Evans (ed), *International Law*, 3rd edn, Oxford, OUP, 2010, p 284.

McGoldrick, D., *International Relations of the European Union*, London, Longman, 1997.

McNair, A.D., *The Law of Treaties*, Oxford, Clarendon Press, 1961.

Meesen, K., 'The Application of Rules of Public International Law within Community Law' (1976) 13 *Common Market Law Review* 485.

Megret, J., 'Conclusions, formes et effets des accords internationaux passés par la CEE' (1965) *Revue du Marché Commun* 25.

Mehdi, R., 'The French Supreme Courts and EU Law: Between a Historical Compromise and an Accepted Loyalty' (2011) 48 *Common Market Law Review* 439.

Mendez, M., 'The Impact of WTO Rulings in the Community Legal Order' (2004) 29 *European Law Review* 517.

Mendez, M., 'Passenger Name Record Agreement' (2007) 3 *European Constitutional Law Review* 127.

Mendez, M., 'The Legal Effect of Community Agreements: Maximalist Treaty Enforcement and Judicial Avoidance Techniques' (2010a) 21 *European Journal of International Law* 83.

Mendez, M., 'The Enforcement of EU Agreements: Bolstering the Effectiveness of Treaty Law?' (2010b) 47 *Common Market Law Review* 1719.

Mengozzi, P., 'The Marrakesh DSU and its Implications on the International and European Level' in J. Bourgeois et al (eds), *The Uruguay Round Results: A European Lawyer's Perspective*, Brussels, European Interuniversity Press, 1995, p 115.

Mensah, T., 'Sovereign Rights in Legislation of Member States under UNCLOS and MARPOL', Eighth Cadwallader Memorial Lecture, London, London Shipping Law Centre, 2005.

Miguel Díaz, L., 'Mexico' in D. Hollis et al (eds), 2005, p 439.

Mitsilegas, V., 'The European Union and the Globalisation of Criminal Law' (2010) 12 *Cambridge Yearbook of European Legal Studies* 337.

Monjal, P.-Y., 'La Cour de justice et les accords externes conclus par la Communauté européenne: une intégration contrôlée dans l'ordre juridique communautaire' in *Mélanges en hommage à Guy Isaac 50 ans de droit communautaire*, Toulouse, Presses de l'Université des Sciences sociales, 2004, Vol 1, p 409.

Morgenstern, F., 'Judicial Practice and the Supremacy of International Law' (1950) 27 *British Yearbook of International Law* 42.

Mosler, H., 'L'application du droit international public par les tribunaux nationaux' (1957) 91 *Recueil des Cours* 619.

Moura Ramos, R.M., 'Portugal' in P.M. Eisemann (ed), 1996, p 461.

Murkens, J.E., 'Countering Anti-Constitutional Argument: The Reasons for the European Court of Justice's Decision in *Kadi* and *Al Barakaat*' (2009) 11 *Cambridge Yearbook of European Legal Studies* 15.

Murphy, S., 'Does International Law Obligate States to Open Their National Courts to Persons for the Invocation of Treaty Norms that Protect or Benefit Persons' in D. Sloss (ed), 2009a, p 61.

N

Neframi, E., *Les accords mixtes de la Communauté européenne*, Brussels, Bruylant, 2007.
Neframi, E., 'The Duty of Loyalty: Rethinking its Scope through its Application in the Field of EU External Relations' (2010) 47 *Common Market Law Review* 323.
Neframi, E., 'Mixed Agreements as a Source of European Union Law' in Cannizzaro et al (eds), 2012, p 325.
Neill, P., 'The European Court of Justice: A Case Study in Judicial Activism' London, European Policy Forum, 1995.
Neuwahl, N., 'Social Security under the EEC–Morocco Cooperation Agreement' (1991) 16 *European Law Review* 326.
Nijman, J. and Nollkaemper, A., *New Perspectives on the Divide between International and National Law*, Oxford, OUP, 2007.
Nollkaemper, A., 'The Netherlands' in D. Sloss (ed), 2009a, p 326.
Nollkaemper, A., *National Courts and the International Rule of Law*, Oxford, OUP, 2011.
Nolte, G., 'Case 12/86, *Meryem Demirel* v. *Stadt SchwäbischGmünd*' (1988) 25 *Common Market Law Review* 403.
Nußberger, A., 'The Reception Process in Russia and Ukraine' in H. Keller and A. Stone Sweet (eds), 2008, p 603.

O

O'Connell, M.E., 'Enforcement and the Success of International Environmental Law' (1995) 3 *Indiana Journal of Global Legal Studies* 47.
O'Leary, S., 'Employment and Residence for Turkish Workers and their Families: Analogies with the Case-Law of the Court of Justice on Article 48 EC' in *Scritti in onore di Giuseppe Federico Mancini*, Milan, Giuffrè, 1998.
Orrego Vicuna, F. and Orrego Bauza, F., 'Chile' in D. Hollis et al (eds), 2005, p 123.

P

Pallemaerts, M. (ed), *The Aarhus Convention at Ten*, Groningen, Europa, 2011.
Pallemaerts, M., 'Access to Environmental Justice at EU Level—Has the Aarhus Regulation Improved the Situation?' in M. Pallemaerts (ed), 2011, p 271.
Palmeter, D. and Mavroidis, P., *Dispute Settlement in the World Trade Organization*, 2nd edn, Cambridge, CUP, 2004.
Papier, H.-J., 'Execution and Effects of the Judgments of the European Court of Human Rights in the German Judicial System' (2006) 27 *Human Rights Law Journal* 1.

Passos, R., 'Mixed Agreements from the Perspective of the European Parliament' in C. Hillion and P. Koutrakos (eds), 2010, p 269.

Paulus, A., 'The Emergence of the International Community and the Divide Between International and Domestic Law' in J. Nijman and A. Nollkaemper (eds), 2007, p 216.

Paulus, A., 'Germany' in D. Sloss (ed), 2009a, p 209.

Paust, J., 'Self-Executing Treaties' (1988) 82 *American Journal of International Law* 760.

Paust, J., 'International Law as Law of the United States' (2002) 2 *Chinese Journal of International Law* 615.

Paust, J., *International Law as Law of the United States*, 2nd edn, Durham, Carolina Academic Press, 2003.

Pauwelyn, J., 'Enforcement and Countermeasures in the WTO: Rules are Rules—Towards a More Collective Approach' (2000) 94 *American Journal of International Law* 621.

Pauwelyn, J., 'A Typology of Multilateral Treaty Obligations: Are WTO Obligations Bilateral or Collective in Nature?' (2003a) 14 *European Journal of International Law* 907.

Pauwelyn, J., *Conflict of Norms in Public International Law*, Cambridge, CUP, 2003b.

Pauwelyn, J., 'The Transformation of World Trade' (2005) 104 *Michigan Law Review* 1.

Pauwelyn, J., *Optimal Protection of International Law: Navigating Between European Absolutism and American Voluntarism*, Cambridge, CUP, 2008.

Pavoni, R., 'Freedom to Choose the Legal Means for Implementing UN Security Council Resolutions and the ECJ *Kadi* Judgment' (2009) 28 *Yearbook of European Law* 626.

Peers, S., 'Towards Equality: Actual and Potential Rights of Third-Country Nationals in the European Union' (1996a) 33 *Common Market Law Review* 7.

Peers, S., 'Case C-434/93, *Ahmet Bozkurt* v. *Staatssecretaris van Justitie*, Judgment of 6 June, 1995' (1996b) 33 *Common Market Law Review* 93.

Peers, S., 'Social Security Equality for Turkish Nationals' (1999a) 24 *European Law Review* 627.

Peers, S., 'Banana Split: WTO Law and Preferential Agreements in the EC Legal Order' (1999b) 4 *European Foreign Affairs Review* 195.

Peers, S., 'The EC–Switzerland Agreement on Free Movement of Persons: Overview and Analysis' (2000) 2 *European Journal Migration and Law* 127.

Peers, S., 'Fundamental Right or Political Whim?: WTO Law and the European Court of Justice' in G. de Búrca and J. Scott (eds), 2001a, p 111.

Peers, S., 'WTO Dispute Settlement and Community Law' (2001b) 26 *European Law Review* 605.

Peers, S., 'EC Immigration Law and EC Association Agreements: Fragmentation or Integration?' (2009) 34 *European Law Review* 628.

Peers, S., *EU Justice and Home Affairs Law*, Oxford, OUP, 2011.

Pellet, A., 'Constitutionnalisation du droit des Nations unies ou triomphe du dualisme?' (2009) 529 *Revue du Marché Commun et de l'Union Européenne* 415.

Pernice, I., '*Costa v ENEL* and *Simmenthal*: Primacy of European Law' in M. Maduro and L. Azoulai (eds), *The Past and Future of EU Law*, Oxford, Hart, 2010.

Pescatore, P., 'Les relations extérieures des communautés européennes: contribution à la doctrine de la personnalité des organisations internationales' (1961) 103 *Recueil des Cours* 1.

Pescatore, P., *Conclusion et effet des traités internationaux selon le droit constitutionnel, les usages et la jurisprudence du Grand-Duché de Luxembourg*, Luxembourg, Office des Imprimés de l'État, 1964.

Pescatore, P., *L'ordre juridique des communautés européennes: étude des sources du droit communautaire*, 2nd edn, Liège, Presses Universitaires de Liège, 1973.

Pescatore, P., 'The Doctrine of "Direct Effect": An Infant Disease of Community Law' (1983) 8 *European Law Review* 155.

Pescatore, P., 'L'application judiciaire des traités' in *Études de droit des communautés européennes: mélanges offerts à Pierre-Henri Teitgen*, Paris, Pedone, 1984.

Pescatore, P., 'Introduction' in Hilf et al (eds), 1986, p XV.

Pescatore, P., 'Treaty-Making by the European Communities' in Jacobs and Roberts (eds), 1987, p 171.

Pescatore, P., 'Monisme, dualisme et "effet utile" dans la jurisprudence de la Cour de justice de la Communauté européenne' in N. Colneric et al (eds), *Une communauté de droit*, Berlin, BWV, 2003.

Peters, A., 'The Position of International Law within the European Community Legal Order' (1997) 40 *German Yearbook of International Law* 9.

Peters, A., 'The Globalization of State Constitutions' in J. Nijman and A. Nollkaemper (eds), 2007, p 251.

Petersmann, E.U., 'Application of GATT by the Court of Justice of the European Communities' (1983) 20 *Common Market Law Review* 397.

Petersmann, E.U., 'International and European Foreign Trade Law: GATT Dispute Settlement Proceedings Against the EEC' (1985) 22 *Common Market Law Review* 441.

Petersmann, E.U., 'The EEC as a GATT Member—Legal Conflicts between GATT Law and European Community Law' in M. Hilf et al (eds), 1986, p 23.

Petersmann, E.U., 'Grey Area Measures and the Rule of Law' (1988) 22 *Journal of World Trade Law* 22.

Petersmann, E.U., 'The Uruguay Round Negotiations 1986–1991' in E.U. Petersmann and M. Hilf (eds), *The New GATT Round of Multilateral Trade Negotiations*, Deventer, Kluwer, 1991.

Petersmann, E.U., 'Proposals for a New Constitution for the European Union: Building-Blocks for a Constitutional Theory and Constitutional Law of the EU' (1995) 32 *Common Market Law Review* 1123.

Petersmann, E.U., 'From "Negative" to "Positive" Integration in the WTO: Time for "Mainstreaming Human Rights" into WTO Law?' (2000a) 37 *Common Market Law Review* 1363.

Petersmann, E.U., 'The WTO Constitution and Human Rights' (2000b) 3 *Journal of International Economic Law* 19.

Petersmann, E.U., 'European and International Constitutional Law: Time for Promoting Cosmopolitan Democracy in the WTO' in G. de Búrca and J. Scott (eds), 2001, p 81.

Petersmann, E.U., 'Time for a United Nations "Global Compact" for Integrating Human Rights into the Law of Worldwide Organizations: Lessons from European Integration' (2002) 13 *European Journal of International Law* 621.

Petersmann, E.U., 'Multilevel Judicial Trade Governance without Justice: On the Role of Domestic Courts in the WTO Legal and Dispute Settlement System' in M. Janow et al (eds), *WTO: Governance, Dispute Settlement and Developing Countries*, New York, Juris, 2007.

Petersmann, E.U., 'Can the EU's Disregard for "Strict Observance of International Law" (Article 3 TEU) be Constitutionally Justified?' in I. Govaere, R. Quick, and M. Bronckers (eds), *Trade and Competition Law in the EU and Beyond*, Cheltenham, Edward Elgar, 2011.

Phelan, W., 'Can Ireland Legislate Contrary to European Community Law?' (2008) 33 *European Law Review* 530.

Polakiewicz, J., 'The Legal Status of the Convention in Domestic Law' in R. Blackburn and J. Polakiewicz (eds), 2001.

Prechal, S., 'Does Direct Effect Still Matter?' (2000) 37 *Common Market Law Review* 1047.

Prechal, S., 'Direct Effect Reconsidered, Redefined and Rejected' in J. Prinssen and A. Schrauwen (eds), *Direct Effect: Rethinking a Classic of EC Legal Doctrine*, Groningen, Europa, 2002.

Prechal, S., *Directives in EC Law*, 2nd edn, Oxford, OUP, 2005.

Prechal, S., 'Direct Effect, Indirect Effect, Supremacy and the Evolving Constitution of the European Union' in C. Barnard (ed), *The Fundamentals of EU Law Revisited*, Oxford, OUP, 2007, p 35.

R

Rapport de la Délégation française sur le Traité et la Convention signés à Paris, le 18 avril 1951: Traité instituant la Communauté Européenne du charbon et de l'acier. Convention relative aux dispositions transitoires, Paris, Imprimerie Nationale, 1952, p 353.

Raustiala, K., 'Form and Substance in International Agreements' (2005) 99 *American Journal of International Law* 581.

Reiff, T.M. and Forestal, M., 'Revenge of the Push-Me, Pull-You: The Implementation Process under the WTO Dispute Settlement Understanding' (1998) 32 *International Law* 755.

Reuter, P., 'La Cour de Justice des Communautés européennes et le droit international' in *Recueil d'études de droit international en hommage à Paul Guggenheim*, Geneva, Tribune, 1968, p 665.

Rideau, J., 'Les accords internationaux dans la jurisprudence de la Cour de justice des Communautés Européennes' (1990) 94 *Revue Générale de Droit International Public* 289.

Rideau, J. and Rainaud, J.M., 'Chronique de Jurisprudence, Cour de Justice des Communautés Européennes' (1974) 71 *Revue du marché commun* 28.

Rideau, J., 'Droit international et droit communautaire' (1973) *Cahiers* de *droit européen* 461.

Riesenfeld, S., 'The Doctrine of Self-Executing Treaties and Community Law: A Pioneer Decision of the Court of Justice of the European Communities' (1973) 67 *American Journal of International Law* 504.

Riesenfeld, S., 'The Doctrine of Self-Executing Treaties and US v. Postal: Win at Any Price!' (1980) 74 *American Journal of International Law* 892.

Ringbom, H., *The EU Maritime Safety Policy and International Law*, Leiden, Martinus Nijhoff, 2008.

Rodriguez Iglesias, G.C., 'Quelques réflexions sur la singularité des rapports du droit communautaire avec d'autres ordres juridiques' in G. Vandersanden (ed), *Mélanges offerts à Jean-Victor Louis*, Brussels, Editions de Université de Bruxelles, 2003, Vol I, p 389.

Rosas, A., 'Case C-149/96, *Portugal* v. *Council*' (2000a) 37 *Common Market Law Review* 797.

Rosas, A., 'The European Union and Mixed Agreements' in A. Dashwood and C. Hillion (eds), *The General Law of EC External Relations*, London, Sweet & Maxwell, 2000b, p 203.

Rosas, A., 'Finland' in R. Blackburn and J. Polakiewicz (eds), 2001.

Rosas, A., 'The European Court of Justice and Public International Law' in J. Wouters, A. Nollkaemper, and E. De Wet (eds), *The Europeanisation of International Law*, The Hague, TMC Asser Press, 2008.

Rosas, A., 'The Future of Mixity' in C. Hillion and P. Koutrakos (eds), 2010, p 367.

Roscini, M., 'Great Expectations: The Implementation of the Rome Statute in Italy' (2007) 5 *Journal of International Criminal Justice* 493.

Rothwell, D., 'Australia' in D. Sloss (ed), 2009a, p 120.

Rouconas, E., 'Greece' in P.M. Eisemann (ed), 1996, p 287.

Ruda, J.M., 'Relación jerárquica entre los ordenamientos jurídicos internacional e interno: reexamen de los problemas teoricos' in *International Law in an Evolving World*, Montevideo, Fundación de cultura Universitaria, 1994, Vol 1, p 115.

Rudden, B. and Phelan, D., *Basic Community Cases*, 2nd edn, Oxford, OUP, 1997.

S

Sacerdoti, G., 'Application of GATT by Domestic Courts: European and Italian Case-Law' (1976) 2 *Italian Yearbook of International Law* 246.

Sampson, G., 'Safeguards' in J.M. Finger and A. Olechowski (eds), *The Uruguay Round: A Handbook on the Multilateral Trade Negotiations*, Washington DC, World Bank, 1987, p 143.

Sauri, A., 'The Relationship Between Community Law and International Law after *Kadi*: Did the ECJ Slam the Door on Effective Multilateralism?' in M. Happold (ed), *International Law in a Multipolar World*, Abingdon, Routledge, 2011, p 303.

Scelle, G., 'Règles générales du droit de la paix' (1933) 46 *Recueil des Cours* 327.

Scheinin, M., 'Incorporation and Implementation of Human Rights in Finland' in M. Scheinin (ed), *International Human Rights Norms in the Nordic and Baltic Countries*, The Hague, Martinus Nijhoff, 1996, p 257.

Scheinin, M., 'Is the ECJ Ruling in *Kadi* Incompatible with International Law?' (2009) 28 *Yearbook of European Law* 637.

Schermers, H., 'Community Law and International Law' (1975) 12 *Common Market Law Review* 77.

Schermers, H., *Judicial Protection in the European Communities*, 2nd edn, Deventer, Kluwer, 1979.

Schermers, H., 'Strengthening GATT' (1983) 20 *Common Market Law Review* 393.

Schermers, H., 'Netherlands' in F. Jacobs and S. Roberts (eds), 1987, p 109.

Schermers, H. and Waelbroeck, D., *Judicial Protection in the European Communities*, 5th edn, Deventer, Kluwer, 1992.

Schmid, C., 'A Theoretical Reconstruction of WTO Constitutionalism and its Implications on the Relationship with the EU', EUI Working Paper Law, No 5/2001.

Schütze, R., 'The Morphology of Legislative Power in the European Federal Division of Powers' (2007) 25 *Yearbook of European Law* 91.

Schwartz, W. and Sykes, A., 'The Economic Structure of Renegotiation and Dispute Settlement in the World Trade Organization' (2002) 31 *Journal of Legal Studies* 179.

Scott, J., 'European Regulation of GMOs: Thinking About "Judicial Review" in the WTO' (2004) Jean Monnet Working Paper 04/04.

Scott, R. and Stephan, P., *The Limits of Leviathan: Contract Theory and the Enforcement of International Law*, New York, CUP, 2006.

Scovazzi, T., 'The Application by Italian Courts of Human Rights Treaty Law' in B. Conforti and F. Francioni (eds), 1997, p 59.

Seibert-Fohr, A., 'Domestic Implementation of the International Covenant on Civil and Political Rights Pursuant to its Article 2 para. 2' (2001) 5 *Max Planck Yearbook of United Nations Law* 399.

Seidl-Hohenveldern, I., 'Transformation or Adoption of International Law into Municipal Law' (1963) 12 *International and Comparative Law Quarterly* 88.

Shany, Y., 'Should the Implementation of International Rules by Domestic Courts be Bolstered?' in A. Cassese (ed), *Realizing Utopia: The Future of International Law*, Oxford, OUP, 2012, p 200.

Sharpston, E., 'Different But (Almost) Equal: The Development of Free Movement Rights Under EU Association, Co-operation and Accession Agreements' in M. Hoskins and W. Robinson (eds), *A True European*, Oxford, Hart, 2003.

Shaw, M., *International Law*, 6th edn, Cambridge, CUP, 2008.

Shelton, D. (ed), *International Law and Domestic Legal Systems*, Oxford, OUP, 2011.

Shelton, D. and Kiss, A., *Judicial Handbook on Environmental Law*, Geneva, UNEP, 2005.

Simma, B., 'The Contribution of Alfred Verdross to the Theory of International Law' (1995) 6 *European Journal of International Law* 33.

Simma, B. et al, 'The Role of German Courts in the Enforcement of International Human Rights' in B. Conforti and F. Francioni (eds), 1997.

Simon, D., *Le système juridique communautaire*, 3rd edn, Paris, PUF, 2001.

Sinclair, I. et al, 'United Kingdom' in D. Hollis et al (eds), 2005, p 727.

Slaughter, A.-M., 'A Global Community of Courts' (2003) 44 *Harvard International Law Journal* 191.

Slaughter, A.-M. and White, W., 'The Future of International Law is Domestic (or, the European Way)' in J. Nijman and A. Nollkaemper (eds), 2007, p 110.

Slaughter, A.-M. et al (eds), *The European Courts & National Courts*, Oxford, Hart, 1998.

Sloss, D., 'Non-Self-Executing Treaties: Exposing a Constitutional Fallacy' (2002) 36 *University of California Davis Law Review* 1.

Sloss, D. (ed), *The Role of Domestic Courts in Treaty Enforcement: A Comparative Study*, Cambridge, CUP, 2009a.

Sloss, D., 'Treaty Enforcement in Domestic Courts a Comparative Analysis' (2009b) in Sloss (ed), 2009a, p 1.

Sloss, D., 'United States' (2009c) in D. Sloss (ed), 2009a, p 504.

Sloss, D., 'Executing *Foster v. Neilson*: The Two-Step Approach to Analyzing Self-Executing Treaties' (2012a) 53 *Harvard International Law Journal* 135.

Sloss, D., 'Legislating Human Rights: the Case for Federal Legislation to Facilitate Domestic Judicial Application of International Human Rights Treaties' (2012b) 35 *Fordham International Law Journal* 445.

Smith, M., 'Enforcement, Monitoring, Verification, Outsourcing: The Decline and Decline of the Infringement Process' (2008) 33 *European Law Review* 777.

Snyder, F., 'The Gatekeepers: The European Courts and WTO Law' (2003) 40 *Common Market Law Review* 313.

Spielmann, D., 'Luxembourg' in R. Blackburn and J. Polakiewicz (eds), 2001.

Spiermann, O., 'The Other Side of the Story: An Unpopular Essay on the Making of the European Community Legal Order' (1999) 10 *European Journal of International Law* 763.

Spranger, T., 'Case C-377/98, *Kingdom of the Netherlands* v. *European Parliament and Council of the European Union*' (2002) 39 *Common Market Law Review* 1147.

Starke, J., 'Monism and Dualism in the Theory of International Law' (1936) XVII *British Yearbook of International Law* 66.

Stein, E., 'Assimilation of National Laws as a Function of European Integration' (1964) 58 *American Journal of International Law* 1.

Stein, E., 'Toward Supremacy of Treaty-Constitution by Judicial Fiat: On the Margin of the Costa Case' (1965) 63 *Michigan Law Review* 491.

Stein, E., 'Lawyers, Judges, and the Making of a Transnational Constitution' (1981) 75 *American Journal of International Law* 1.

Stein, E., 'International Law in Internal Law: Toward Internationalization of Central-Eastern European Constitutions?' (1994) 88 *American Journal of International Law* 427.

Stein, E., *Thoughts from a Bridge*, Ann Arbor, University of Michigan Press, 2000.

Stein, E. and Halberstam, D., 'The United Nations, the European Union, and the King of Sweden: Economic Sanctions and Individual Rights in a Plural World Order' (2009) 46 *Common Market Law Review* 13.

Steiner, H. et al, *International Human Rights in Context*, 3rd edn, Oxford, OUP, 2007.

Swiss Federal Council, *Le relation entre droit international et droit interne*, 5 March 2011.

Sykes, A., 'Protectionism as Safeguard' (1991) 58 *University of Chicago Law Review* 255.

Sykes, A., 'The Remedy for Breach of Obligations Under the WTO Dispute Settlement Understanding: Damages or Specific Performance?' in M. Bronckers and R. Quick (eds), *New Directions in International Economic Law*, The Hague, Kluwer, 2000.

Symmons, C., 'Irlande/Ireland' in P.M. Eisemann (ed), 1996, p 317.

T

Tagaras, H., 'L'effet direct des accords internationaux de la Communauté' (1984) *Cahiers de droit européen* 15.

Tan, A.K.-J., 'The EU Ship-Source Pollution Directive and Coastal State Jurisdiction over Ships' (2010) 3 *Lloyd's Maritime and Commercial Law Quarterly* 469.

Tancredi, A., 'On the Absence of Direct Effect of the WTO Dispute Settlement Body's Decisions in the EU Legal Order' in E. Cannizzaro et al (eds), 2012, p 249.

Tezcan-Idriz, N., 'Free Movement of Persons between Turkey and the EU: To Move or Not to Move? The Response of the Judiciary' (2009) 46 *Common Market Law Review* 1621.

Thakore, K., 'India' in D. Hollis et al (eds), 2005, p 349.

Thies, A., 'Case C-93/02, *Biret International SA* v. *Council*' (2004) 41 *Common Market Law Review* 1661.

Thies, A., 'Cases T-69/00, *FIAMM and FIAMM Technologies*, T-151/00, *Le Laboratoire du Bain*,T-301/00, *Fremaux*, T-320/00, *CD Cartondruck AG*, T-383/00, *Beamglow Ltd* and T-135/01, *Giorgio Fedon & Figli S.p.A., Fedon S.r.l. and Fedon America USA Inc*' (2006) 43 *Common Market Law Review* 1145.

Thies, A., 'The Impact of General Principles of EC Law on its Liability Regime Towards Retaliation Victims after *FIAMM*' (2009) 34 *European Law Review* 889.

Thomas, C. et al, 'The Use of International Labour Law in Domestic Courts: Theory, Recent Jurisprudence, and Practical Implications' in J.-C. Javillier and B. Gernigon (eds), *Les norms internationales du travail: un patrimoine pour l'avenir*, Geneva, ILO, 2004, p 249.

Thym, D., 'Foreign Affairs' in A. von Bogdandy and J. Bast (eds), *Principles of European Constitutional Law*, Oxford, Hart, 2009, p 309.

Tikhomirov, A., 'Russia' in D. Shelton (ed), 2011, p 517.

Timmermans, C., 'The EU and Public International Law' (1999) 4 *European Foreign Affairs Review* 181.

Tomkins, A., 'Introduction: On Being Sceptical About Human Rights' in T. Campbell et al (eds), *Sceptical: Essays on Human Rights*, Oxford, OUP, 2001, p 1.

Tomuschat, C., 'International Law Ensuring the Survival of Mankind on the Eve of a New Century: General Course on Public International Law' (1999) 281 *Recueil des Cours* 9.

Tomuschat, C., 'Case T-306/01, *Ahmed Ali Yusuf and Al Barakaat International Foundation* v. *Council and Commission*; Case T-315/01, *Yassin Abdullah Kadi* v. *Council and Commission*' (2006) 43 *Common Market Law Review* 537.

Tomuschat, C., *Human Rights: Between Idealism and Realism*, 2nd edn, Oxford, OUP, 2008.

Tomuschat, C., 'The *Kadi* Case: What Relationship is There Between the Universal Legal Order under the Auspices of the United Nations and the EU Legal Order?' (2009) 28 *Yearbook of European Law* 654.

Trachtman, J., 'The WTO Cathedral' (2007) 43 *Stanford Journal of International Law* 127.

Trachtman, J. and Moremen, P., 'Whose Right is it Anyway? Private Parties in EC–U.S. Dispute Settlement at the WTO' (2003) 44 *Harvard International Law Journal* 221.

Trebilcock, M. and Howse, R., *The Regulation of International Trade*, 2nd edn, London, Routledge, 1999.

Trebilcock, M. and Howse, R., *The Regulation of International Trade*, 3rd edn, London, Routledge, 2005.

Treves, T., *Diritto Internazionale*, Milan, Giuffrè, 2005.

Treves, T. and Frigessi di Rattalma, M., 'Italie' in P.M. Eisemann (ed), 1996, p 365.

Tridimas, T., 'Constitutional Review of Member State Action: The Virtues and Vices of an Incomplete Jurisdiction' (2011) 9 *International Journal of Constitutional Law* 737.

Tridimas, T. and Gari, G., 'Winners and Losers in Luxembourg: A Statistical Analysis of Judicial Review Before the European Court of Justice and the Court of First Instance (2001–2005)' (2010) 35 *European Law Review* 131.

Triepel, H., *Völkerrecht und Landesrecht*, Leipzig, Hirschfeld, 1899.

Triepel, H., 'Les rapports entre le droit interne et le droit international' (1923) 1 *Recueil des Cours* 77.

Tumlir, J., 'A Revised Safeguard Clause for GATT' (1973) 7 *Journal of World Trade Law* 404.

Tumlir, J., *Protectionism: Trade Policy in Democratic Societies*, Washington DC, American Enterprise Institute, 1985.

U

Uerpmann-Wittzack, R., 'Implementation of United Nations Human Rights Law by German Courts' (2003a) 46 *German Yearbook of International Law* 87.

Uerpmann-Wittzack, R., 'International Law as an Element of European Constitutional Law' (2003b), Jean-Monnet Working Paper 9/03.

Uerpmann-Wittzack, R., 'The Constitutional Role of International Law' in A. von Bogdandy and J. Bast (eds), *Principles of European Constitutional Law*, Oxford, Hart, 2009, p. 131.

Ulfstein, G. et al, *Making Treaties Work: Human Rights, Environment and Arms Control*, Cambridge, CUP, 2007.

UNEP, *Manual on Compliance with and Enforcement of Multilateral Environmental Agreements*, 2006, available at <http://www.unep.org/dec/MEA_Manual.html>.

V

Van Alstine, M., 'The Role of Domestic Courts in Treaty Enforcement: Summary and Conclusions' in D. Sloss (ed), 2009a, p 555.

Van Den Bogaert, S., 'And Another Uppercut from the European Court of Justice to Nationality Requirements in Sports Regulations' (2004) 29 *European Law Review* 267.

Van Den Bossche, P., *The Law and Policy of the World Trade Organization*, 2nd edn, Cambridge, CUP, 2008.

Van Den Broek, N., 'Legal Persuasion, Political Realism, and Legitimacy: The European Court's Recent Treatment of the Effect of WTO Agreements in the EC Legal Order' (2001) 4 *Journal of International Economic Law* 411.

Van der Mei, A.P., 'The *Bozkurt*-Interpretation Rule and the Legal Status of Family Members of Turkish Workers under Decision 1/80 of the EEC–Turkey Association Council' (2009) 11 *European Journal of Migration and Law* 367.

Van Dijk, P. and Tahzib, B., 'Parliamentary Participation in the Treaty-Making Process of the Netherlands' (1992) 67 *Chicago-Kent Law Review* 413.

Van Ert, G., 'Canada' in D. Sloss (ed), 2009a, p 166.

Van Panhuys, H.F., 'The Netherlands Constitution and International Law' (1953) 47 *American Journal of International Law* 537.

Van Rossem, J.W., 'Interaction Between EU Law and International Law in the Light of *Intertanko* and *Kadi*: The Dilemma of Norms Binding the Member States but not the Community' (2009) 40 *Netherlands Yearbook of International Law* 183.

Vandaele, A. and Claes, E., 'L'effet direct des traités internationaux. Une analyse en droit positif et une théorie du droit axée sur les droits' (2001) 34 *Revue Belge de Droit International* 411.

Vauchez, A., 'The Transnational Politics of Judicialization. *Van Gend en Loos* and the Making of EU Polity' (2010) 16 *European Law Journal* 1.
Vazquez, C., 'Treaty-Based Rights and the Remedies of Individuals' (1992) 92 *Columbia Law Review* 1082.
Vazquez, C., 'The Four Doctrines of Self-Executing Treaties' (1995) 89 *American Journal of International Law* 695.
Vazquez, C., 'Laughing at Treaties' (1999) 99 *Columbia Law Review* 2154.
Vazquez, C., 'Treaties as Law of the Land: The Supremacy Clause and the Judicial Enforcement of Treaties' (2008) 122 *Harvard Law Review* 599.
Velu, J., *Les effets directs des instruments internationaux en matière de droits de l'homme*, Brussels, Bruylant, 1981.
Verhoeven, J., 'La notion d'applicabilité directe du droit international' (1980) 15 *Revue Belge de Droit International* 243.
Verhoeven, J., 'Belgique' in P.M. Eisemann (ed), 1996, p 115.
Verhoeven, J., *Droit international public*, Brussels, Larcier, 2000.
Verschueren, H., 'The *Surul* Judgment: Equal Treatment for Turkish Workers in Matters of Social Security' (1999) 1 *European Journal of Migration and Law* 371.
Victor, D., Raustiala, K., and Skolnikoff, E.B. (eds), *The Implementation and Effectiveness of International Environmental Commitments*, Cambridge MA, MIT Press, 1998.
Von Bogdandy, A., 'Pluralism, Direct Effect, and the Ultimate Say: On the Relationship Between International and Domestic Constitutional Law' (2008) 6 *International Journal of Constitutional Law* 397.

W

Waelbroeck, M., *Traités internationaux et juridictions internes*, Paris, Pedone, 1969.
Waelbroeck, M., 'Effect of GATT Within the Legal Order of the EEC' (1974) 6 *Journal of World Trade Law* 614.
Waelbroeck, M., 'Enforceability of the EEC–EFTA Free Trade Agreements: A Reply' (1978) 3 *European Law Review* 27.
Waelbroeck, M., 'Les effets internes des accords internationaux conclus par la Communauté Economique Européenne' in *Le Droit des peuples à disposer d'eux-mêmes. Mélanges Ch. Chaumont*, Paris, Pedone, 1984, p 579.
Waelbroeck, M. and Waelbroeck, D., 'Article 173' in J.V. Louis et al (eds), *Commentaire Mégret: Le droit de la Communauté Économique Européenne*, Brussels, Éditions de l'Université de Bruxelles, 1993, Vol 10, p 98.
Wainwright, R., 'Techniques of Drafting European Community Legislation: Problems of Interpretation' (1996) 17 *Statute Law Review* 7.
Waldron, J., 'The Core of the Case Against Judicial Review' (2006) 115 *Yale Law Journal* 1346.
Waters, M., 'Creeping Monism: The Judicial Trend Toward Interpretive Incorporation of Human Rights Treaties' (2007) 107 *Columbia Law Review* 628.

Wathelet, M., 'The Case Law of the European Court of Justice and Nationals of Non-European Community Member States' (1996) 20 *Fordham International Law Journal* 603.
Wegter, J., 'The ECJ Decision of 10 January 2006 on the Validity of Regulation 261/2004: Ignoring the Exclusivity of the Montreal Convention' (2006) XXXI *Air and Space Law* 133.
Weiler, J.H.H., 'The Community System: The Dual Character of Supranationalism' (1981) 1 *Yearbook of European Law* 268.
Weiler, J.H.H., 'The Transformation of Europe' (1991) 100 *Yale Law Journal* 2403.
Weiler, J.H.H., 'The Reformation of European Constitutionalism' (1997) 35 *Journal of Common Market Studies* 97.
Weiler, J.H.H. (ed), *The EU, the WTO, and the NAFTA*, Oxford, OUP, 2000.
Weiler, J.H.H., 'The Rule of Lawyers and the Ethos of Diplomats: Reflections on the Internal and External Legitimacy of WTO Dispute Settlement' (2001a) 35 *Journal of World Trade* 191.
Weiler, J.H.H., 'Epilogue: The Judicial Après Nice' in G. de Búrca and J.H.H. Weiler (eds), *The European Court of Justice*, Oxford, OUP, 2001b.
Weiler, J.H.H., 'The Geology of International Law—Governance, Democracy and Legitimacy' (2004) 64 *Zeitschrift für ausländisches öffentliches Recht und Völkerrecht* 547.
Weiler, J.H.H. and Trachtman, J.P., 'European Constitutionalism and its Discontents' (1997) 17 *Northwestern Journal of International Law & Business* 354.
Wenneras, P., *The Enforcement of EC Environmental Law*, Oxford, OUP, 2007.
Wheatley, S., *The Democratic Legitimacy of International Law*, Oxford, Hart, 2010.
Wildhaber, L., *Treaty-Making power and Constitution*, Basel, Helbing & Lichtenhahn, 1971.
Wildhaber, L. et al in D. Hollis et al (eds), 2005, p 627.
Wildhaber, L., 'The European Convention on Human Rights and International Law' (2007) 56 *International and Comparative Law Quarterly* 217.
Wilson, B., 'Compliance by WTO Members with Adverse WTO Dispute Settlement Rulings: The Record to Date' (2007) 10 *Journal of International Economic Law* 397.
Winter, J., 'Direct Applicability and Direct Effect: Two Distinct and Different Concepts in Community Law' (1972) 9 *Common Market Law Review* 425.
Wolfrum, R., 'Legitimacy of International Law from a Legal Perspective: Some Introductory Considerations' in R. Wolfrum and V. Röben (eds), 2008, p 1.
Wolfrum, R. and Röben, V. (eds), *Legitimacy in International Law*, Berlin, Springer, 2008.
Wouters, J., 'The Tormented Relationship Between International Law and EU Law' in P. Bekker et al (eds), *Making Transnational Law Work in the Global Economy: Essays in Honour of Detlev Vagts*, Cambridge, CUP, 2010, p 198.
Wu, T., 'Treaties' Domains' (2007) 93 *Virginia Law Review* 571.
Wyatt, D., 'New Legal Order, or Old?' (1982) 7 *European Law Review* 147.
Wyrozumska, A., 'Poland' in D. Shelton (ed), 2011, p 468.

X

Xenopoulos, X.L. (ed), *External Relations of the EU and the Member State* (FIDE 2006 National Reports), Nicosia, Theopress, 2006.

Y

Yokaris, A., 'Greece' in Shelton (ed), 2011, p 249.

Yoo, J., 'Globalism and the Constitution: Treaties, Non-Self-Execution, and the Original Understanding' (1999a) 99 *Columbia Law Review* 1955.

Yoo, J., 'Treaties and Public Lawmaking: A Textual and Structural Defense of Non-Self-Execution' (1999b) 99 *Columbia Law Review* 2218.

Z

Ziegler, K., 'International Law and EU Law: Between Asymmetric Constitutionalisation and Fragmentation' in A. Orakhelashvili (ed), *Research Handbook on the Theory of International Law*, Cheltenham, Edward Elgar, 2011.

Zimmermann, R., 'Germany' in R. Blackburn and J. Polakiewicz (eds), 2001.

Zonnekeyn, G., 'The Status of WTO Law in the Community Legal Order: Some Comments in the Light of the *Portuguese Textiles* Case' (2000) 25 *European Law Review* 293.

INDEX

The manufacturer's authorised representative in the EU for product safety is Oxford University Press España S.A. of el Parque Empresarial San Fernando de Henares, Avenida de Castilla, 2 – 28830 Madrid (www.oup.es/en or product.safety@oup.com). OUP España S.A. also acts as importer into Spain of products made by the manufacturer.

www.ingramcontent.com/pod-product-compliance
Lightning Source LLC
LaVergne TN
LVHW011905200926
848484LV00002B/540

9780199606610